Finally, the decisive moment had arrived. The German dog-sniffing operations had failed and the first undetected mine was set to go off around two P.M.

An enemy train approached from Koroston moving at about fifty kilometers per hour. All the cars were passenger cars: that meant officers!

Now!

A powerful explosion blew snow, gravel, sand, rails, and ties in all directions. The locomotive crashed down the embankment, dragging the coaches behind it. There was a grinding of shattered iron, splintering wood, and crackling flames as Germans began leaping from the cars that had not yet fallen over.

"Everything's in order. Shall we go, Comrade Colonel?" Kal'nitskiy asked.

"Okay, Comrade Engineer Major, let's go," I replied.

We heard firing for a long while afterward as the Germans carried on a desperate battle with the empty forest. . . .

OVER
THE ABYSS

My Life in Soviet Special Operations

Colonel I. G. Starinov

Translated by Robert Suggs

IVY BOOKS • NEW YORK

Ivy Books
Published by Ballantine Books
Translation and compilation copyright © 1995 by Robert Suggs
Maps copyright © 1995 by Bob Rosenburgh

Library of Congress Catalog Card Number: 95-94026

ISBN 0-8041-0952-4

Manufactured in the United States of America

First Edition: April 1995

10 9 8 7 6 5 4 3 2 1

Table of Contents

Foreword

Col. Il'ya Grigoryevich Starinov has compared crossing enemy lines to walking on a bridge over an abyss—one false step and it's all over. In fact, Starinov's entire active service career was spent over an abyss: his lifetime spans the entire history of the rise and fall of the Soviet state, including all of the most shameful episodes of that dark history, episodes in which he himself was often in danger. His extended combat service in the civil war, the Spanish civil war, the "Winter War" against Finland, and in World War II was mainly in hazardous operations behind enemy lines. Throughout most of his military career, he specialized in the manufacture and use of mines and explosives, a specialty that is not generally associated with excessive longevity. Finally, although a distinguished soldier, he was frequently in mortal danger from the organs of Soviet state security, i.e., the OGPU and NKVD. During the internal Soviet political convulsions of the twenties and thirties, his military specialties, professional experience, and his associations were more than enough justification for suspicion, and he narrowly escaped arrest and execution on several occasions.

Starinov is a rare survivor, a firsthand witness, of a still poorly known period of Soviet history. His memoirs present a vivid, if understated, chronicle of life under one of the most despotic regimes of human history: the Stalin era. His personal story abounds with colorful characters, deftly portrayed, ranging from earthy peasants and private soldiers to some of the leading members of the Soviet bestiary with whom he dealt, including Voroshilov, Mekhlis, Malenkov, Khrushchev, and Stalin himself. There are also more than a few touching portraits of friends and associates who fell in the continuing genocide that many in the West viewed as a normal feature of Soviet internal political processes.

The man who emerges from these pages is a complex individual, a dedicated professional who, although completely absorbed in the technical details of his specialty, nevertheless formed strong and lasting friendships with superiors and subordinates alike. He was a man who clearly felt the full range of human emotions quite strongly, yet always kept them in control. At a time when abandonment of all principle seemed to be the only means of escaping death, he clung to his principles, and survived. Yet, although he has suffered much from the regimes which he served, those same principles still prevent him from discussing many aspects of his unusual career and violating security concerns which have long been an integral part of his life.

Starinov is a quintessential special operations man, independent, self-reliant, and action oriented. He expresses the strong disdain that the special operator normally manifests for military bureaucracies and military bureaucrats. Despite this, he seems to have instinctively found ways to manipulate the stifling Soviet military bureaucracy when it was in the interests of his nation to do so. This often involved confronting some of the most dangerous men of his day on very sensitive issues, a task from which he did not shrink.

Starinov's personal views of the great dramas of history in which he participated are of interest to the military historian and the Soviet analyst as well as to the general reader. Several sections of his memoirs have special interest, however, for those who seek to improve their perspective on Soviet international activities in the twenties and thirties. Starinov's memoirs contribute substantially to the early history of Soviet special operations forces or *spetsnaz*. Until the late 1980s, many analysts refused to believe that such forces existed, and some "native Russian speakers" even denied that the term itself was a valid Russian military term. Starinov refers to special units in the twenties, was actively involved in training "partisan" and "diversionary"[1] (sabotage) units in the late twenties and early thirties, at least partially for foreign operations, and served in a unit that bore the explicit title of *spetsnaz* in Spain in 1936, conducting penetrations behind enemy lines and guerrilla operations in the enemy rear. Further on this topic, the memoirs describe, in greater detail than ever before, the significant Soviet effort to train partisans and saboteurs, not only for use on Soviet soil in the event of an invasion, but for employment in western Europe. The individuals trained for these activities in the early thirties included leading European Communists, such as Thorez and Togliatti. The extent and nature of Soviet special operations to the Republican forces in the Spanish civil war is also described more fully than before. Finally, Starinov's description of the disorganized, faltering, and often leaderless offi-

---

1. The Soviet *Military Encyclopedic Dictionary* (Moscow, Military Press, 1983) defines "diversion" as: "the actions of individuals or groups (squads, units or partisan detachments) in the enemy rear to put military production and other facilities out of commission, interfere with the command and control, cut communications lines, and destroy military personnel and equipment." In the following pages, the term "sabotage" will be used to translate *diversiya* and "saboteur" will be used to translate *diversantnik* (an individual who carries out diversion).

cial Soviet partisan movement of World War II provides a refreshing antidote to the flood of Soviet propaganda on that subject and reveals yet another instance in which an utterly cynical leadership sacrificed hundreds of thousands of its people for Stalin's personal aggrandizement.

The memoirs that follow represent an edited compilation of five manuscripts: Starinov's two published books: *Miny zhdut svoego chasa*, (Mines await their time), Moscow, 1964; and *Proyti nezrimym*, (Pass unseen), Moscow, 1988; and two of his unpublished manuscripts, *A moglo byt' inache*, (And it might have been otherwise), Moscow, 1989, and *Stalin i voina v tylu vermakhta: a moglo bit' inache* (Stalin and the war in the *Wehrmacht* rear: it might have been otherwise), Moscow 1991, and a fascinating manuscript entitled *Nasha soyuznitsa-noch'* (Night is our ally) written between 1963 and 1983 by Anna Kornilovna Starinova, his first wife, who was his interpreter and combat companion in Spain. The published works have provided the main chronological framework for Starinov's biography, while the unpublished works, which have a professional military-historical flavor, have provided much of the unique material that distinguishes these memoirs. A historian rarely has the opportunity to examine a man's military performance through the eyes of his wife, and a comparison of the Starinov and Starinova memoirs provides some fascinating perspectives on Colonel Starinov's operational skills as well as Starinova's important personal role.

The translator wishes to express his thanks to Mr. Owen Lock, vice president, Ballantine/Del Rey Books, and to Dr. John J. Dziak, Office of the Secretary of Defense, for their support; to 1st Lt. Matt Suggs, U.S. Army Engineers, for technical advice on demolitions, and to Mrs. Carol Pendas Whitten for her assistance on Spanish surnames.

RCS
Alexandria, Virginia
July 1992

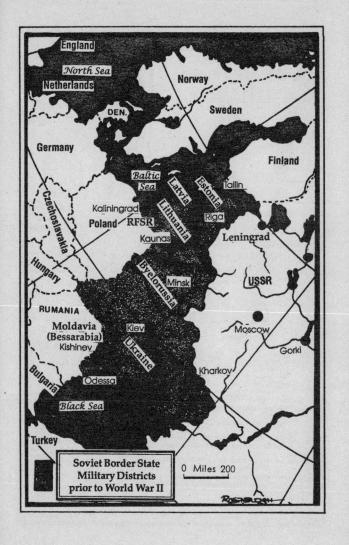

Soviet Border State
Military Districts
prior to World War II

0 Miles 200

The Soviet Union and Eastern Europe 1945 - 1948

Miles
0   100   200

FINLAND

Vyborg

Tallin (Reval)

ESTONIA

Riga

LATVIA

Baltic Sea

LITHUANIA

Konigsberg

Vilna

East Prussia

Minsk

Steffin

Berlin

GERMANY

Warsaw

POLAND

Bonn

Dresden

Prague

Silesia

Cracow

Galicia

Lvov

USSR

FRANCE

CZECHOSLOVAKIA

Munich

Vienna

SWITZ.

AUSTRIA

Budapest

HUNGARY

RUMANIA

Trieste

Bucharest

Belgrade

Adriatic Sea

ITALY

YUGOSLAVIA

Sofia

BULGARIA

ALBANIA

Tirana

GREECE

Aegean Sea

The "Iron Curtain" in 1948.

Pre-war German frontier.

1939-1940: Annexed by the Soviet Union
1945: Re-incorporated into the Soviet Union.

1945: Annexed by the Soviet Union from Germany and Czechoslovakia.

1945-1948: Communist governments come to power in nations liberated by the Soviet Union.

Soviet occupation zone.

British, French, and American occupation zones.

Partisans in the Russian Civil War

Introduction

Matthew Arnold's chilling image of ignorant armies, clashing by night on a darkling plain, has been quite appropriately applied to the conflict that we now know as the Russian civil war.[1] The "ignorant armies" were numerous, including Reds, the various shades of Whites (in 1918, there were some thirty-nine different anticommunist governments coexisting in Russia), as well as regular troops of the Allies and the Central Powers, Cossacks, miscellaneous bandit gangs, and one of the most motley collections of guerrilla groups ever to take the field in modern war. The "darkling plain," littered with seven million corpses (six million of them peasant noncombatants), extended over five thousand miles, from the outskirts of Warsaw to Vladivostok, and from Murmansk on the shores of the frozen Barents Sea to the Caucasus in the south. More than most of the conflicts of this century, the Russian civil war is a vast, dim landscape of mindless inhumanity, worthy of the palette of some cosmic Heironymus Bosch. It is a landscape suffused with that insidious obscurant of all military operations, aptly designated by Clausewitz as the "fog of war," a fog so thick that, even from this remote standpoint in time, confusion is perhaps the salient characteristic of this conflict.

Partisan War

The history of this conflict contains much of value for the historian, the social scientist, and even for the contemporary policy maker (e.g., some may well see disturbing analogies between the Russia of 1917–1920 and the "postcoup" Russia of today with its seeming inability to adapt to a free-market economy and democratic forms of government, and its numerous ethnic hot spots). Completely aside from the fact that the future Red Army colonel, Il'ya Grigoryevich Starinov, received his baptism of fire in the Russian civil war, it is important, in introducing this memoir, to briefly consider the role played by guerrilla or partisan warfare in that conflict. The partisans of the civil war were of every political

---

1. See E. M. Halliday's excellent description of Allied intervention forces, *Ignorant Armies*. New York, Award Books, 1964.

stripe, including none at all. They fought for the Reds, for the Whites, for anarchy, for Ukrainian independence, for fun, for a drink, a warm body, a roof for the night; or to defend their homes and families from any outsiders. They changed sides sometimes, with disastrous consequences, but they had a profound influence on the course of campaigns and the overall course of the war. Soviet experiences in partisan operations gathered in the civil war significantly influenced subsequent military thinking and internal politics in the USSR; therefore, a sketch of partisan operations in the Russian civil war will better prepare the reader for many of the otherwise puzzling developments described by Starinov in the following pages. Starinov spent his whole military career in special operations and partisan work: Soviet experience in this conflict powerfully shaped his career and almost terminated it prematurely on a few occasions. His career faithfully reflects the tortuous evolution of Soviet doctrine in partisan and special operations. The following pages will outline some of the major partisan activities in selected campaigns of the Russian civil war. These operations will be discussed in their political and military contexts to show the various factors which gave rise to partisan resistance, the ways in which the partisans were employed, and their net effect. No attempt has been made to devote equal coverage to all fronts or theaters of this struggle; the areas selected for coverage are those in which partisan warfare played an especially important role: the Baltic states, Belorussia, the Ukraine, the southeast, Central Asia, and Siberia.[2] No attention has been given to the otherwise important operations on the Northern Front where the Allied expeditionary forces confronted the Bolsheviks in what seems to have been predominantly conventional, positional warfare, and discussion of partisan operations in Siberia have been limited to that conducted by Red partisan groups against Kolchak.

Belorussia, the Ukraine and the Baltic States

The first use of partisans came very close upon the heels of the October Revolution. In 1917, German and Austrian forces were occupying Poland and parts of Belorussia and the Ukraine. Although Lenin's government signed an armistice with the Central Powers in December, these forces continued to advance deeper into Russia while peace negotiations continued. As the Germans advanced, the Central Staff of Partisan Detachments of the operational department of the fledgling Red Army staff was inserting

2. In preparing this summary, I have relied heavily on Prof. W. Bruce Lincoln's *Red Victory: A History of the Russian Civil War* (New York; Touchstone. 1989), and Prof. Robert Conquest's *Harvest of Sorrow: Soviet Collectivization and the Terror Famine*. (London; Hutchinson. 1986).

and controlling partisan units in the rear of the Central Powers forces. In addition to recruitment and training, and gathering weapons and supplies, these partisans were operationally active. According to Col. Stanislas Vaupshasov, who participated in these early operations (and later led NKVD partisans in World War II, winning the coveted Hero of the Soviet Union award),[3] they attacked small enemy garrisons and facilities, supply dumps, and communications lines.

In March 1918, hostilities between Russia and Germany were terminated by the treaty of Brest-Litovsk, which imposed very strict terms upon Russia, stripping it of Poland, Belorussia, and the Ukraine, and the Baltic states. At the same time, Romania made a separate peace with Germany, acquiring Bessarabia and thereby stripping away one more jewel from the empire's crown. Lenin viewed the terms of Brest-Litovsk as a necessary evil, providing a bit of breathing space for himself and the troubled government that he had just imposed on Russia. The Germans also wanted Russia out of the war so that German troops could be released from the Eastern Front and redeployed to the west. Lenin had no intention of permanently relinquishing the territory lost at Brest-Litovsk, however, and partisans certainly figured prominently in his plans to maintain a Soviet presence in these lands and to finally reclaim them. An underground network of clandestine Party cells had long since been established throughout Europe, including all the lost territories. According to Starinov, partisan operations in Belorussia, the Baltic states, and the Ukraine continued after the Brest-Litovsk treaty. These operations were still controlled by the same section of the Red Army staff operations department as before, although the name of that section had now been changed, for security reasons, to the Special Intelligence Section of the operations department. It was directed by S. I. Aralov, first chief of the GRU, or Main Intelligence Directorate—the military intelligence arm of the Soviet intelligence services. Lenin was counting on the clandestine network of Party cells and partisan forces to foment successful Red revolutions throughout Europe—particularly in Germany and Poland, thus restoring the situation to his favor. The treaty of Brest-Litovsk was therefore seen as only a temporary tactical setback, and the real work of spreading the underground Party organization, training and equipping partisans, acquiring weapons, setting up clandestine supply dumps, gathering intelligence, and penetrat-

3. Vaupshasov, S. A. *Na trevozhnykh perekrestkakh.* (At dangerous crossroads). Moscow, Politizdat. 1988.

4   I. G. Starinov

ing foreign intelligence, military, and police organizations continued in the territories.

By spring 1918, both Finland and the Ukraine had declared their independence from Russia. The declarations were recognized by Germany, which established a puppet government in the Ukraine under Ukrainian general Pavlo Skoropadsky. Part of the price of recognition of Ukrainian independence by the Central Powers was the obligation imposed on the Ukraine to provide food and other supplies to the Central Powers. The brutal measures involved in gathering this material from peasants on the brink of starvation stimulated the creation of numerous effective Ukrainian peasant partisan groups, which managed to inflict nineteen thousand casualties on the Central Powers's troops during the summer and fall of 1918 alone.

Following the surrender of the Central Powers in November 1918, the German-backed Ukrainian puppet government collapsed. The power vacuum thus created was immediately filled by several partisan groups, including those under S. V. Petlyura, a Ukrainian nationalist, who squared off against the highly irregular force led by the flamboyant peasant anarchist, Nestor Makhno. Makhno's force varied in size, but on occasion reached a level of thirty thousand. Petlyura's efforts failed, and he fled to Galicia where he ultimately received military support from the Poles, who entered the Ukraine after the German surrender, hoping to restore the Polish-Russian border to the line fixed in 1722. Red forces moved into the Ukraine from the other direction, stubbornly persisting in trying to regain what they regarded as their lands, confronting the Polish forces which had supplanted the Germans. At this time, Soviet partisans, including Vaupshasov, were operating in the Polish rear area, coordinating their operations with those of the frontline Red regulars. One of the more capable Red leaders, Nikifor Grigoryev, a former tsarist officer, invaded the Ukraine for the Reds in 1919, but switched sides with his own Cossack entourage to fight against the Reds who he—and other Ukrainian leaders—believed to be supporting some vague Communist-Jewish plot for domination of the Ukraine. Traditional age-old religious bigotry was thus introduced as yet another reason for men to die. As a result, the noncombatant Jewish population of the Ukraine suffered enormous casualties—perhaps as much as 10 percent in the savage *pogromy* of 1919. (Grigoryev paid in full for his crimes, however: he was assassinated by the wily Makhno.) In this bewilderingly multisided affair, control of the Ukraine changed hands nine times between 1918 and 1920. Makhno, who had fought the Central Powers and the Reds, was pleased to take on any and all comers and wound up fighting against the White Army under General Denikin, which invaded the eastern Ukraine in 1919 on their offensive northward. The anarchist's forces were extremely effective in destroying Denikin's rear area, contributing significantly to Denikin's defeat in late 1919–early 1920. During Denikin's offensive, due to the highly fluid nature of operations and the lack of any extensive fixed defensive lines, many units of both Red and White troops were cut off at various times in enemy-held areas and had to exist off the land until they either rejoined their main forces or were destroyed. Starinov survived a few such experiences himself and refers to his adaptation to operations in enemy territory.

Southeast Russia

The October Revolution was followed in November 1917 by the formation of the Russian Volunteer (White) Army at Novocherkasssk in the northern Caucasus. This force, supported by a large contingent of Don Cossacks, aimed at replacing the new Red government with a legal government and scored an impressive initial victory over Red Guards at Rostov in December 1917. By early 1919, the same White Army, now much stronger, better trained, and commanded by Gen. A. I. Denikin, set off on offensive toward Moscow. This drive would carry it north past Orel and east to Tsaritsyn (formerly Stalingrad, now Volgograd). Although Denikin's military forces were greatly improved, he was still seen by many as desiring to restore the old regime and did not enjoy great support. In August, while advancing toward Orel, Denikin's Don Cossacks under General Mamontov broke through Red lines and went on a forty-day spree doing what Cossacks seemed to do best—looting, raping, killing, and generally alienating potential White supporters. By September 1919, Denikin had major rear area security problems in the form of peasant and tribal partisans operating along his supply lines, including the numerous, capable forces of the ubiquitous Nestor Makhno. Denikin, nevertheless, managed to push north of Orel by October. Faced by Budenny's elite First Cavalry Army and bereft of rear area security, Denikin's offensive collapsed. He retreated to the Caucasus, from whence he evacuated his force to the Crimea, turning over command to Baron Petr Wrangel in April 1920. Wrangel, an outstanding military professional, massed his forces, supplies, and weapons in the northern Crimea, and then threw them into action against the Reds in April 1920 at the same time that the Poles attacked the Soviet Union in an attempt to regain territory that they also believed was theirs (see below: Russo-Polish War). Wrangel struck north into the southern Ukraine and southeast toward the Kuban, hoping to link up with anti-Soviet partisan formations there, but his effort was frustrated by Red Army forces directed by Trotsky. The Soviets, routed by Polish forces in August 1920, went to the peace table with the Poles in order to be able to devote full attention to this threat from the south. Faced by strong Red forces—assisted again by Makhno's anarchists!—Wrangel was driven back into the Crimea and, in November 1920, forced to evacuate his troops from there, effectively terminating the civil war.

Central Asia

After Brest-Litovsk, Georgia, Armenia and Azerbaijan declared their independence. Georgia came within the German sphere of influence, and Turkey—a traditional enemy of Russia—took Azerbaijan, which had already swallowed Armenia. Western Allied intervention included landings by British and French troops in several Black Sea ports in the summer of 1918 and operations by British forces and intelligence assets in Turkistan in the summer of 1918. The military operations in this volatile area seem to have combined with the forces of traditional nationalism, Islamic fundamentalism, and the animosities that the subject peoples and nations of Central Asia felt toward their Russian overlords. This mixture ignited anti-Soviet partisan warfare all along the borders of Turkey, Iran, Afghanistan, and China. Although official Soviet sources state that the main partisan forces—the *basmachi*—were defeated in 1922, these same sources also admit that anti-*basmachi* partisan fighting in these areas continued until *1933*.

Siberia

In Siberia, regular White forces formed in 1917–18 around the various competing local governments, which established themselves there. These forces were of decidedly mixed quality, and after some initial successes, achieved very little against the Reds. Throughout most of 1918, by far the most effective forces operating in Siberia were those of the remarkable Czech Legion, a thirty-five-thousand–man force composed of veterans of a Russian-Czech battalion in the tsarist army, reinforced by large numbers of Czech prisoners and deserters from Austro-Hungarian forces. In May 1918, the Legion had been on its way to Vladivostok to embark for the European Front. When ordered by Red forces to surrender their arms, the Czechs attacked and overran Red outposts along the Trans-Siberian Railroad, gaining control of a good portion of that line. Advancing west and south with White forces during the spring and summer of 1918, the Czechs dramatically weakened Soviet power throughout Siberia and even came close to liberating the tsar and his family at Ekaterinburg.

On 18 November 1918, Russian admiral Aleksandr Kolchak assumed command of all White armed forces in Russia, in the Siberian town of Omsk. Although strongly supported by the British, Kolchak's military dictatorship was absolutely unacceptable to the intensely democratic Czechs who soon withdrew from combat and filtered out of Russia. Without the expert assistance of the Czech Legion, Kolchak was forced to rely heavily on the independent groups such as the Cossacks of the ataman Semenov ("a robber, a murderer and a dissolute scoundrel," according to U.S. general Robert Graves) and Kalmykhov ("a fully qualified war criminal" according to Baron Budberg, an official in the Kolchak regime). These Cossacks operated with such gratuitous brutality—at a time when what we would currently call "brutality" was standard operating procedure—that the Reds found Siberia to be fertile soil for establishing a widespread, effective Communist underground, linking hundreds of villages and raising numerous partisan groups. Red Siberian partisans, such as the Forest Commune in the Transbaikal region and the fifteen thousand-man Peasant Army of western Siberia, wreaked havoc on Kolchak's supply lines. Although Kolchak had done well in 1918 and early 1919, Red regulars commanded by Frunze, Chapayev, and Tukhachevskiy counterattacked in the summer of 1919 and systematically wasted his White troops. With his supply lines swarming with angry partisans, his crumbling frontline troops faced with elite Red Army formations, and his own administration crippled by corruption, Kolchak fled for his life—only to be captured by some Czechs at Irkutsk. Turned over to local Mensheviks, he was in turn passed to the Bolsheviks who shot him. Kolchak's death did not end the struggle in Siberia, however, because anti-Soviet partisan operations continued in Siberia until *late 1922*. These were conducted by the Cossacks of Semenov and Kalmykhov and remnants of the Siberian Whites, supported by a large force of Japanese regulars who remained in the area after the withdrawal of other Allied expeditionary troops.

The Russo-Polish War

In early 1920, prior to the Polish attack on the USSR, Soviet military and OGPU personnel, among them Vaupshasov, were sent behind Polish lines to set up partisan or "revolutionary" groups, to use the jargon of the time. It appears that the timing of these assignments was not accidental but was chosen based on good intelligence that revealed Polish plans for attack. These groups went into operation across Belorussia and the Ukraine prior to the Polish invasion, carrying out arson, attacking police units, police stations, hunter-killer groups, and small garrisons, and defending pro-Soviet settlers from Polish police and military. Large-scale military training of partisan forces was under way. The police force, the church, and the Jewish community were successfully infiltrated for intelligence gathering. After the initial Polish thrust lost its momentum, Red troops began to drive Polish forces back across Russia. It seemed that the time had come for the Communist parties of Belorussia and Lithuania to rise. In fact, a Polish government in exile had been established at Bialystok, including the triumvirate of Feliks Dzerzhinskiy, chief of the Cheka, Julian Marchlewski, and Felix Kon. The Soviets miscalculated on a number of points, however, including underestimating the military capability of the Poles and overestimating the strength of the Communist revolutionary sentiment in the Polish population.

Driven back to Warsaw by Tukhachevskiy's Red troops, the Poles launched a brilliant counterattack in August 1920, inflicting a stunning series of defeats on the forces of the "Red Napoleon," both on Polish soil and in Belorussia. The Polish and Belorussian parties failed to raise the people in rebellion, and Dzerzhinskiy's Polish government in exile had to flee back to Soviet soil. Threatened by the Poles in the north and Wrangel's advances in the south, Lenin was induced to sue for peace, to end the two-front conflict and be able to concentrate his forces on defeating Wrangel. In the aftermath of this defeat, partisans led by Vaupshasov and other Soviet military and intelligence personnel in Belorussia and Lithuania had to go to ground. Units broke up, stored their weapons, and tried to maintain some contact among members. Although he left Belorussia in November 1920, Vaupshasov was back on Polish territory by December, conducting agitation and propaganda work, setting up illegal organizations, and training partisans for the next attempt against Poland.

By the Treaty of Riga (18 March 1921), the Soviets ostensibly yielded the western Ukraine and Belorussia to Polish control and left Polish troops occupying eastern Lithuania, including the capitol, Vilno. Once more, however, Lenin had no intention of abandoning this territory to the uncertainty of self-determination or foreign influence. Again, intensive efforts were launched to use Red Army and OGPU men to strengthen and spread the underground Party, and organize, train, and equip partisan formations to fight the Poles. Vaupshasov, for example, remained "in the forest" of Belorussia, working with partisans of the Disna and Vileyka areas until May 1921. He then moved to the Oshmyansk district and began operations in the fall of 1921, occasionally skirmishing with Polish police or troops, attacking trains, railroad stations, and small garrisons, carrying out assassinations, and executing spies. These operations continued, despite increasingly severe Polish countermeasures, until *1925*, when it finally became apparent to the Soviet leaders that the people of Poland, western Belorussia, and the Ukraine and Lithuania were not ready to support a Red revolution, and the partisan operations were suspended. This was understandably a difficult decision for Vaupshasov to explain away to partisans who had been fighting for seven years or more. Many of the veterans of this warfare fled to the USSR, where they became involved in the accelerated Soviet preparations for partisan warfare of the twenties and early thirties in which Starinov took part.

War Communism, the Peasant War, and Kronshtadt

In 1920, in the Soviet controlled eastern Ukraine, over 150 anti-Soviet partisan groups were in operation. These forces included the still-powerful anarchists led by Nestor Makhno. Life was extremely difficult, at best, for the military participants in the Russian civil war, but few military men experienced the prolonged suffering inflicted on the civilian population, forced under Lenin's "war communism" program to provide food to the Red Army, as well as being exposed to pillage by any other belligerent group that happened by. It has been said that war communism was not a military measure at all but a part of an attempt to create a new social order by destroying the peasantry, which had become as much a problem for the Reds as it had been for the tsars. As early as 1918, the "peasant war" had begun, with armed groups resisting Red Army food collection detachments across the length and breadth of Russia, e.g., in Karelia, the Ukraine, Belorussia, southwest Russia, Siberia, the Caucasus, and Central Asia. These peasant groups were often more than just small local groups with a couple of rifles and some pitchforks. One of the most famous of these was the "Greens" of the poverty stricken Tambov Province in the "black earth" area, led by Aleksandr Antonov. Antonov's group began attacking food collection detachments in their region in 1918 but moved into open revolt against all Red authority in 1920. Antonov's force, numbering *forty thousand* at its peak, then found itself pitted against crack troops led by the versatile and ruthless Tukhachevskiy, and Cheka detachments led by V. A. Antonov-Ovseyenko, whose thugs decimated the civilian population. In a struggle marked by routine acts of revolting depravity on both sides (nailing live Bolshevik sympathizers to trees was one of Antonov's favorite methods of punishment), most of Antonov's forces were wiped out by the summer of 1921, but it was not until a year later that the Reds were able to kill Antonov and stamp out the last vestiges of his Greens. In addition to the Tambov peasants, a group of fifty-five thousand to sixty thousand men were operating against the Reds in Siberia, and another group of twenty thousand (armed with cannon!) were operating in the Ukraine. In some areas of the Ukraine, these anti-Soviet operations continued until 1928. Even after 1928, there was considerable anti-Soviet and anti-Russian unrest in the Ukraine and Belorussia, enabling the Germans in 1941 to enlist significant numbers of Soviet citizens in their cause. Some of the present-day violence in the Ukraine, Belorussia, and the former Soviet republics may be nothing more than a continuation of the tradition of resistance established at this early period of Soviet history.

The ill feelings generated by war communism and the measures associated with it were not confined to the peasants alone, however, but spread to the cities and to the military as well. And while the negotiations at Riga were moving to their conclusions, the Soviet regime suffered one more severe shock: on 7 March 1921 the Red sailors of the Kronshtadt naval base rose up in armed rebellion against the Soviet government. The sailors, always considered as the vanguard of the revolution, were accustomed to expressing their feelings directly. They were not speaking for themselves alone, but for a significant proportion of the workers and peasants of the new nation who were disillusioned with the progress of the revolution and the hardship that it had brought. Although their rebellion was put down with the usual extreme measures, the sailors managed to inflict heavy casualties on the attacking army forces under command of Tukhachevskiy, and their short-lived resistance must have once again raised in the minds of the new Soviet leaders the great threat of popular uprisings against the Red regime—a regime that supposedly represented the will of the people. It is significant that after Kronshtadt, the Soviet Navy was considered politically unreliable until well after World War II, and still ranked last in terms of precedence among Soviet armed forces in 1985 when the lengthy tour of the "Soviet Mahan," Fleet Admiral of the Soviet Union Sergey Gorshkov, finally came to an end.

Conclusions

An objective assessment of Soviet partisan and antipartisan operations in the Russian civil war must have convinced Soviet military leaders of the strong advantages of this form of warfare against both internal and external foes. First, partisan warfare was politically (i.e., ideologically) correct. Based on an underground apparatus, run on sound principles of subversive organization and operations, partisans could be interpreted as a legitimate expression of popular disagreement with whoever happened to govern the real estate in question. This form of warfare was also (erroneously) depicted as a uniquely Russian tradition, linked to such glorious victories as the defeat of Napoleon in 1812, thus giving it greater national appeal.

On a more practical note, such forces were relatively cheap: they generally supported themselves, and (at least until the latter days of World War II) did not have to be supplied with standard equipment or manned according to approved tables of manpower. They also did not have to be paid. Most partisans did not have to be transported to the theater of operations: they were already in place, and they knew the terrain better than the enemy in many cases. Although partisans required some professional military guidance, the need was at a minimum, and they multiplied the effectiveness of every professional military man sent to advise, train, or lead them. Well-trained partisans were actually strategic forces, able to operate along enemy supply and communications lines with far more precision and effectiveness than other strategic forces and weapons of the day. Since the Russian highway system was very poorly developed at the time of the civil war, the majority of east-west movement of freight and military personnel took place by rail, a relatively untutored muzhik with a couple of kilos of dynamite could successfully put out of action an important stretch of railroad (and perhaps a military unit or two along with it), thus causing major problems at the front (incidentally, this vulnerability of railroad lines to partisan action is probably one of the reasons for the militarization of the railroads in the Soviet system and for the creation of a separate railroad security department under the Cheka, OGPU, and subsequent security organs of the USSR). Partisan operations, supporting those of regular troops, enabled the Soviets, for the first time, to launch attacks along the entire depth of an enemy's troop dispositions with the destructive effects seen so clearly in Tukhachevskiy's campaign against Wrangel and Makhno's campaign against Denikin. Tukhachevskiy's further development of this concept of attack in depth led to the creation of parachute infantry and airmobile units, which were certainly innovative for that time, and their employment in maneuvers and combat operations against *basmachi* guerrillas in the thirties. Unfortunately, Tukhachevskiy was purged, and all of his developments became suspect until after Stalin's death. The attack in depth was later reinstated as a major tenet of Soviet military doctrine, remained so until the coup of 1991, and probably continues to be just as important today.

Partisans also held forth the promise of being able to defeat the further foreign invasions that Mikhail Frunze, the leading Soviet military theorist, saw as highly probable in the aftermath of the civil war. The defensive concept adopted was to lure the numerous potential invaders past hidden partisan formations, deep into Soviet territory, after which the partisans were to rise in the enemy rear, cut them off from their supply sources, and help to crush them against strongpoints where strong Red Army units were deployed. This was the concept behind the 1924 crash effort, described below, to prepare the rail lines and railroad facilities in the Ukraine for destruction in the event of an invasion, and the later effort to establish secret partisan supply dumps between the border and the first line of fortified areas. Starinov played an important role in both of these efforts as an assistant to the unfortunate Yakir.

Partisans also enjoyed other advantages: they were completely expendable, deniable (particularly if they were unsuccessful!), and with a little care and ingenuity, could be employed in operations to extend one's national borders or to bring down or alter the complexion of inhospitable or unstable governments, as Vaupshasov's efforts in Belorussia and the Ukraine from 1919 to 1925 were designed to do. Prior to World War II, the Soviet government's main use of partisans was in the Spanish civil war, in which both Starinov and Vaupshasov took part. After World War II, however, under the umbrella of growing Soviet long-range nuclear capabilities, Soviet-trained partisans—often accompanied by Soviet advisers—were an important feature of the "just" Khrushchevian "wars of national liberation" in many areas of the world.

All of these attractive advantages of partisan warfare were counterbalanced, however, by some significant drawbacks that were certainly visible in the early twenties. Perhaps the most serious of these, to the eyes of the Soviet political leadership, was the frequently demonstrated unreliability of partisan forces. To this day, successful partisans and special operators in general are the kinds of people who generally worry good ideologues: the best of this breed are extremely creative, unconventional mavericks who scoff at discipline and control; loners; people with private political or philosophical agendas (often detected too late!), and occasionally borderline or actual crazies. The latter category is best exem-

plified by Baron Roman Ungern-Sternberg, a subordinate of ataman Semenov, who was described by his own staff medical officer as "a pervert and a megalomaniac affected with a thirst for
human blood." Even a cursory examination of the richly variegated panoply of partisan units involved in the civil war certainly
provided ample evidence to Lenin—and Stalin—that even "good"
(Red) partisans might suddenly change sides and become an embarrassment or even a threat to their former sponsors, or even that
"bad" partisans might suddenly want to become "good" (i.e., return to the Red fold)—a perplexing problem of a different nature.
Tight control of partisan forces appeared to be necessary, but that
was hard to ensure, given the nature of the personnel, the primitive means of transportation and communication of the day, the
enormous distances involved, and the irregular nature of partisan
warfare itself. *Tighter* control could be achieved, however, through
improved training and better political training and security vetting
of partisan cadres, and this was done during the twenties and thirties in the USSR, but apparently not to the satisfaction of the leadership, which condemned about 90 percent of the trainees to death
in the purges.

In addition to the problem of partisan unreliability, the Bolsheviks also clearly saw that their enemies—both internal and
external—were also quite capable of mounting partisan operations. The Soviet leaders became aware that successful partisan
operations did not need to be based on some revolutionary political ideology but simply on the cultural traditions of resistance to
central authority, or pure "natural" ethnic hatred. There was certainly plenty of both those commodities lying around at the end of
the civil war, and even more so, several years later, after the ar-
tificially induced famine in the Ukraine. Enemies of the Soviet
state just might be able to set up very effective partisan operations
in the Soviet's own rear area, particularly if the Soviet's own people were dissatisfied. It seems that Stalin, whose personal policies
caused so much dissatisfaction, saw a distinct possibility that the
Soviet state—i.e., Stalin himself—was vulnerable to partisan
forces organized by any one of many disgruntled potential adversaries: e.g., military leaders, ethnic groups or nationalities, peasants, etc.

On the one hand, ideology demanded popular struggle, and partisan warfare—a quintessentially popular form of that struggle—
was cheap and effective and had even greater future potential. On
the other hand, popular struggle could not be safely left up to the
populace, which had shown surprising indications of disagreement
with the "will of the people" as expressed by the Party, and the

promising partisan weapon could turn on its user. The full recognition of this two-edged nature of partisan warfare seems to have left the Soviet leadership with mixed emotions about partisans.

Extended personal experience in partisan and antipartisan operations in the civil war seems to have made a positive impression on Soviet military leaders such as Frunze, Tukhachevskiy, and Yakir. This experience influenced subsequent Soviet military thought, leading to significant military developments, which, although costly, might have produced a very different outcome of World War II. To the great personal misfortune of many of these same military leaders, partisan warfare experience seems to have made an even more profound, but opposite, impression on the mind of I. V. Stalin, in ways that his military leaders unfortunately could not easily foresee—probably due to their lack of insight into the phenomena of psychopathology. Although fully aware of what might be achieved by partisans, Stalin appears to have been terrified at the thought that armed popular partisan forces—no matter how well trained and ideologically "stiffened"—might turn against him. Stalin's actions regarding partisan organization and operations seem to indicate that he had actually begun to believe the trumped-up charges of conspiracy and treason that he allowed his henchman, Yezhov, to level against Tukhachevskiy, Yakir, and other partisan warfare planners in the purges. A born conspirator, his morbid fears of conspiracies against himself prevented him from fully exploiting Russia's potential for partisan warfare, even when the German Army stood at the gates of Moscow. Starinov's remarkably detached chronicle of the frustrating, convoluted twists and turns of the official Party line regarding partisan warfare, and the tragic, criminal loss of life and waste of resources resulting from this continuing vacillation at "the top," becomes comprehensible only if one bears in mind that these bewildering gyrations in policy simply reflected the intense suspicion, fear, and ignorance with which Stalin—the man who knew *everything*—viewed his fellow countrymen and the rest of the world. These dark emotions were most accurately reflected in the actions of the huge Soviet political-military bureaucracy, which quickly learned that disagreement was a capital offense. A few dared to act on their own responsibilities in building partisan capabilities, thus openly supporting points of view which were at odds with the official line. To them goes the credit for the successes achieved by partisans in World War II. Starinov's chronicle is all the more remarkable as the testimony of one of those few who dared to disagree with Number One and managed to survive.

If It Weren't For Luck

The new Communist government of Russia was by no means acceptable to all the Russian people. There was strong resistance to the October Revolution in the Ukraine, southern Russia, Siberia, and the Far East. The Russian civil war began in the south in December 1917 when the Don Cossacks revolted and a volunteer anti-Soviet or White army was raised. This army came to be commanded by General A. I. Denikin in April 1918. Other White armies independently attacked the Communists from the west and the east, and Allied expeditionary forces landed in the north at Murmansk and Arkhangel, and in the west at Vladivostok. Denikin's Whites drove the Communist forces from the eastern Ukraine, the Don, and northern Caucasus, as well as Armenia, Georgia, and Azerbaijan, and launched an offensive on Moscow in late spring and summer of 1919, driving Red forces back to the northeast. The incident that Starinov chooses to open his memoirs took place during that bitterly contested withdrawal, in a seesaw battle around the city of Korocha in the central black earth region of Russia, probably in early August 1919.

It was a hot summer's day in 1919. On the hilly plain, south of the city of Korocha, black plumes of exploding artillery shells rose here and there. Machine guns stuttered hurriedly.

Lying on the ground, I looked to the left, toward the company flank, and saw soldiers rising and rushing forward. Now it was our platoon's turn! Bracing myself with my left hand, I sprang up and dashed ahead with my buddies. Sweat flooded my eyes; my hands were locked around the rifle.

"A-a-a-a-a!" A shout went up across the field.

Bullets screamed through the air. The man next to me fell, as though he ran into an invisible obstacle or wall. Hit the dirt! In an instant, I was pressing myself deep into the warm dusty grass—no bugs with shiny wings could ever crawl any deeper among the stalks than I did! Catch your breath and wait, so that after a minute, having cheated death, you could once more throw yourself against exploding shells and machine guns.

Our unit, the 20th Infantry Regiment, was attacking elite units of Denikin's Markov Division. A week before, the Markov Division whipped us, but now those aristocratic officers were in tough straits. Blazing away, filled with hatred, we surged forward again and again, in spite of the furious enemy fire.

"Break through! No hanging back! Let's get it over with!"

We tumbled into firing positions evacuated by the enemy.

"Take up defensive positions! Take up defensive positions!" the order came down the chain of command. Only then did I feel the pain in my leg. Bending over, I saw a bloodstain spreading on my wrap-leggings. Below the knee, my leg burned like fire: a piece of shrapnel was embedded in the shin.

They relieved us at evening. Limping, I dragged myself along, following the other soldiers, to houses on the outskirts of Korocha, where, on the floor of one of the huts, we slept side by side until morning. But I slept miserably; something seemed to be burrowing and twitching in the wounded leg. At dawn, it was difficult to pull up my trousers, and I saw that the shin was swollen and inflamed. I tried to stand up. Not likely! I almost crashed to the floor from the pain. My head was spinning, and multicolored spots swam before my eyes.

"Oh, great! What's wrong with you?" inquired the worried squad leader. "You've got to go to the field hospital." They carried me to the field hospital. In the car of the military medical train, the stench of iodoform, infected wounds, and clotted blood mingled with the moans and delirious ravings of the wounded.

We barely crawled from station to station. Near Yel'ts, we almost fell into the clutches of Mamontov's Cossacks, who had broken through the front. Demanding weapons, all those capable of moving gathered on the platforms at the ends of the train cars, or pushed their way to the windows and berated the doctors and medical corpsmen. Luckily, the train slipped through the danger area. Another day and we were in Tula. In Tula, I thought, there's a good hospital; there they'll help me!

But the faces of the doctors examining the leg were gloomy and inscrutable. They exchanged glances, threw around some Latin terms, and then one, with a merciless show of feigned affection, patted me on the shoulder.

"We've got to amputate, dear fellow. Above the knee. Do you give permission?"

Amputation! Cutting off my leg? At nineteen years of age, I won't be able to walk like other people? I'll be a cripple, hopping around on crutches like a bird, stumping around on the pavement?

Never! "Is it against the rules to cure me, Doctor?" I asked in despair.

The surgeon shrugged. "Blood poisoning is setting in—you'll die."

I lay in the ward, flat on my face, depressed and worn-out. How could this happen? A tiny piece of shrapnel—a mere scratch—and all of a sudden they want to hack my leg off? Do I really have to give them permission?

"Okay, show it to me!"

Beside the cot stood Ivan Sergeyevich, an elderly medical orderly.

Throwing back the heavy gray blanket, he carefully examined my right leg, which was swollen like a log.

Now, I thought, he's going to chew me out and call me uncivilized because I wouldn't listen to the doctor.

"Good thing you didn't give permission to amputate," said Ivan Sergeyevich. "This isn't really gangrene! We'll heal you!"

I couldn't believe my ears! Ivan Sergeyevich had already called a nurse to bring new bandages.

"To reduce the fever, I'm going to wrap up your leg with plantain leaves, soldier," Ivan Sergeyevich said in a consoling voice. "Even though science doesn't accept this peasant grandma's remedy, it really works. Don't get worked up!"

And Ivan Sergeyevich healed me in his own way, changing the dressings frequently with compresses made from plantain. It actually seemed that there was nothing else more advanced available in the hospital! The young surgeon on his rounds expressed his doubts, but did not scold the medic, relying on his greater experience. Everything turned out miraculously. My temperature began to fall, and the burning sensation in my shin gradually abated.

"You'll be the best dancer in your village!" Ivan Sergeyevich said with satisfaction.

I was even more happy than the medic, and I didn't want to correct him about that village crack; I was born in a village, but I grew up along the railroad. My father was a railroad trackwalker on the section Zavidovo-Red'kino, between Moscow and Petrograd. But let Ivan Sergeyevich think what he wanted to! The main thing was that the leg was whole! I would fight again: I'd be as good as ever. And I would not fall behind in the attack!

At night in the slumbering ward, listening to the distant locomotive whistles, I saw my entire young life pass before me. The whistles reminded me of the cabin where our large family of seven lived from hand to mouth, going from bad to worse. On the sixteen rubles that my father earned per month, is it really possible to feed such a crowd? Everyone worked in our house. We younger children helped Mother with the gardening and herded the cow; the older children worked seasonally cutting peat. And there were also trips to the Shosha River, which looped through the meadows behind the cabin, and walks in the woods on specific missions: catching fish, gathering mushrooms and berries, stripping bark. To return with empty hands was considered shameful.

I loved Mother very much but always felt a special respect for Father, which began in early childhood. For hours, I sat as though bewitched on the embankment, looking at the trains flying past our cabin. It appeared that there was no force on earth that could restrain their furious rush. However, we children knew: the trains were subordinated to Father. If he went out on the roadbed with his red flag or light, the brakes of the most indomitable express train began to screech submissively.

Once on a snowy night, I was awakened by the sound of detonations. It turned out that Father had seen a separated rail. Not relying on the engineer to notice his red signal light, he put dynamite caps on the rail, and the train stopped. That event so struck my youthful imagination that for a long time, Father seemed to me to be a man of fantastic power.

In adolescence, however, I came to understand something different: my father, myself, my brothers, and thousands of other such simple people were driven back into the backyard of life, doomed to exhausting labor, to ignorance.

I was lucky: my youth coincided with the purifying revolutionary storm. In October 1917, together with my factory pals, Misha Yagodkin and Kolya Medvedev, I joined a military group organized by the city Soviet of Workers and Soldiers Deputies. Our group was assigned to delay counterrevolutionary troops sent to Petrograd by railroad.

The group was commanded by an artilleryman fresh from the front, the son-in-law of railroad switchman Vasiliy Gregor'yevich Loshkarev. On the basis of friendship, I wound up in this group together with Ivan, Loshkarev's son, an extremely strong but modest working-class fellow.

The group was small and unarmed, but we were, nevertheless, able to delay several troop trains, blocking the tracks with logs, and putting signal semaphores out of operation.

I considered myself a lucky fellow when I eventually found myself in the operational forces of the Red Army and was issued a weapon.

Even the grim baptism of fire did not cool my ardor. It so happened that in one of the first fights, my regiment sustained heavy casualties, and my company was cut to pieces. Because one former tsarist officer turned traitor, I wound up in prison along with several other Red Army men.

Along with Androsov, the experienced old soldier who commanded my section, I escaped from prison and rejoined my home unit, the 20th Infantry Regiment. There was more fighting, and we were encircled again, this time in the city of Korocha, which was occupied by the enemy. After five days, we crossed the Korochka River and rejoined our own forces without sustaining any losses. Even then, during our wanderings behind lines of Denikin's forces, I had already firmly mastered two truths: the first is that you can survive for a long time, even in the enemy's rear area, if you don't let go of your weapon, and the second is that when you're behind enemy lines, night is your best friend.

I lay on my cot smiling, but my heavily bandaged neighbor, Sapper Petr Pchelkin, who was nicknamed Bumblebee by the other wounded, because of his stoutness, sluggishness, and his last name, looked at me askance. Bumblebee was an ultraphlegmatic personality, a man of very few words who, nonetheless, possessed a very sharp tongue. Bumblebee had broken his left hand, and the cast had not yet been taken off, but this lucky guy could still walk.

"Now our infantry is going to be way ahead of all the generals," Pchelkin said, pensively and seriously, looking me in the eye. "Immediately!"

"Why?" I rose to the bait.

"Well, aren't they going to discharge you from the hospital soon and send you back to the ranks? You're strong!"

"Well, maybe so. On the other hand, the sappers aren't going to be happy to see you again. It's not enough that they have to carry everything around with them—they've still got your dead weight hanging on their necks!"

"You shut up about us sappers, hero," Pchelkin calmly responded. "What the hell do you know about sapper work?"

"What is there to know? You burrow in the earth . . ."

"In the earth . . . you ignoramus! Engineer troops build the bridges for you, break up enemy obstacles for you, and when people like you get your tails kicked, we cover your withdrawal. We're the ones who blow bridges and wreck roads so that you guys can get yourselves organized again! Yeah, and furthermore, we send the Whites to heaven with our explosions! Better you should shut up!"

Bumblebee was really buzzing, but he was defending his service branch, about which I actually knew very little, not himself.

Once at night, noting that my neighbor wasn't sleeping, I asked him: "Listen, Pete, don't get angry. Tell me more—do you really thinks it's true when they say that sappers attack first and are the last to leave? Tell me the truth!"

Pchelkin turned away on the cot, but no matter how much Bumblebee tried to keep silent, it was impossible to lie side by side with your friends in a hospital ward for the better part of three weeks and not talk about one's army life. So he ended up telling me about demolitions men slipping into the rear areas of the Whites in order to cut rail lines and bridges, about pontoon-bridge units who carried out river crossings under fire, about detachments who, during periods of positional warfare, carried out reconnaissance behind enemy lines.

Bumblebee may not have told his tales in a very coherent fashion, but there was something in the rough words of the former peasant that was most exciting.

Now, looking back, I understand—Pvt. Petr Pchelkin was a poet of his difficult trade; in his soul lived the grim romanticism of a totally dedicated military professional.

And then, a fellow from my hometown appeared in the ward: it was Arkhip Tsarkov, the best dancer in Voynovo, a happy-go-lucky guy and a comedian. He also turned out to be a sapper, and decided unconditionally that regardless of what happened, nothing was going to separate us.

"You were destined to be a sapper at birth!" Arkhip said. "Your father toiled his whole life on the railroad, and you yourself grew up near the railroad. He was a sapper, and you're a sapper!"

The exciting tales of Bumblebee, the fervent conviction of Arkhip, and my natural disinclination to separate from friends—all these things played their roles.

My friends were discharged from the hospital. I also asked for a discharge. At that time, units of the 9th Infantry Division were recruiting sappers. Even though my wound was not yet healed, I refused to go on leave. Tsarkov, Pchelkin, and I enlisted in the 27th Independent Sapper Company of the 9th. And thus began my service in the engineer troops of the Red Army—service which would determine all my remaining life.

Unexpected Changes

Almost two years passed. We were on the offensive. First Taganrog, then Azov, Temryuk, the expedition after Wrangel. Combat with changing fortunes. The decisive storming of the Crimea.

Violent winds blew across the Arabatsky railroad semaphore point. On the left was the Azov Sea; on the right, the Gniloye Sea. There was neither shelter nor fuel. We had marched 120 kilometers, making campfires from aquatic plants and bits of wood thrown up on the riverbanks. We had to carefully count every swallow of water. And then, close with the enemy ... But everyone knows what happened to Wrangel and his men.

In the Crimea, they threw us into Kerch to clean out the last remnants of the White bands who were hiding in the catacombs, and from Kerch we crossed the frozen strait to the Kuban in the cool of January and then from the Kuban to Makhachkala, and from there into Georgia via Baku.

We changed sectors of the front; the weather changed; the surrounding population changed, but one thing didn't change: my parent division, my parent company.

I was never sorry that I chose to serve with my friends in the engineer troops. It was difficult, grim, and bitter work, but whatever might happen, we pushed on ahead. We ran!

In early spring 1921, our 9th Infantry Division came out to the Black Sea—to Batumi. The Red Army had saved Georgia.

In June 1921, we were still at Batumi. A force reduction was going on in the army, and I was given a choice: demobilization or study at a military school. I didn't hesitate; I couldn't imagine life outside the army. When enemies threatened society, what could be more important than service to the motherland with weapon in hand?

I requested a school assignment, received a recommendation, and an evaluation report, and soon set out for Moscow, to the Main Directorate of Military Training Institutions (the GUVUZ—*Glavnoe upravlenie voennouchenykh zavedeniy*).

For youngsters, a trip of thousands of kilometers seems like a stroll around the neighborhood. So, taking advantage of the fact

that I had been given permission to visit my father in the village.
I said good-bye to the Kuban and to my old friends at the front.

I hung around, and time flew by unnoticed. Suddenly, it was
time to get moving.

But how? In those days, to get to Moscow by road was extremely difficult.

I decided that my best alternative was to go through Krasnodar,
and arrived there on a beautiful summer day, sitting on the buffer
between two jammed passenger cars. In those days, overcrowded
trains were brought into "accordance with the norms" for passenger loading by agents of the railroad CheKa (Translator's note: the
CheKa was the original Soviet secret police organization, founded
by F. E. Dzerzhinskiy) who removed me from my "sleeping car"
berth.

"You, Comrade, are way off course. Your documents specify a
different travel route. Check in with the commandant. We'll sort
things out."

At headquarters, there was a crowd of more than twenty military service men. Many of them, like me, had had their travel documents confiscated.

I sat and waited. I could just imagine what they were going to
do with me. Then, all at once, I heard that Voroshilov, the commander of the Northern Caucasus Military District, was arriving
in his train! Rather than taking the time to rationally consider the
whole thing, I took off down the road as fast as my legs could
carry me.

I had never met Voroshilov, but I had heard a lot about him, especially when they attached our 9th Infantry Division to the 1st
Cavalry Division during the civil war. For this reason, I decided
that Voroshilov would take me at my word—he'd stand up for
me. I didn't even allow myself to think that I wouldn't be permitted to see him. After all, hadn't we fought together against
Denikin?

And they actually let me in to see him.

The military district commander heard my confused story right
through to the end. He examined the recommendations, which I
had kept. Laughing, he took out a notepad and then and there
wrote a note to the CheKa headquarters, saying that they should
release me. That very day, I left Krasnodar.

After I'd visited my relatives, I finally set out for the capital.
Later, I had the occasion to read much about Moscow in the year
1921. It's hard to say what kinds of epithets have *not* been heaped
upon that city by our adversaries. She's been called dark, shame-
less, and uncivilized . . .

Moscow was certainly dingy. Some of the boulevards were like flea markets during the day and like wastelands at night. Instead of stores, there were "distributors" everywhere, but what they distributed, and when, was not at all certain. Only a few kerosene lamps were burning in the city. Chekists were rooting out bandits. In the squares, homeless orphan children wandered about in rags. On the Sukharevka, a bit of bartering was going on, but now and then, you heard the cry; "Stop thief!"

For some Muscovites, those evicted from their cozy existences in multiroom apartments and single-family homes, such pictures surely represented the threshold of an even more frightening fate. But the city made a completely different impression on me and my comrades. The brightest of hopes lived in our hearts, and at that time, nothing around us seemed gloomy at all. Early in the morning we saw the people hurrying off to the factories and institutions, overloading the trolleys ...

We not only believed, but we *knew*: present hardships were only temporary phenomena. As a guarantee of that, there stood the Kremlin wall, behind which Vladimir Ilyich Lenin was at work.

Of course, before entering the offices of the Main Directorate of Military Educational Institutions, we stood in Red Square listening to the sounds of the carillon, which had only recently begun playing the "Internationale."

The discussion in the Main Directorate turned out to be brief. They collected our orders, recommendations, and evaluations; gave out rations; and after a week, sent us off to Odessa to take examinations in the military engineering school.

We arrived at the school just in time for entrance exams. Those who wanted to study were by no means few in number, but I wasn't worried. In the higher preparatory school, I was considered one of the leading students, even though I had been unable to finish. In school, there had been only one problem: I never liked to learn the laws of God by heart, but now, thanks be to God, there were no laws of God! I did very well on the Russian language exam. Why should I fear any of the remaining subjects? So I went fearlessly ahead, *and failed splendidly on geometry*!

The return trip to Moscow dragged out unhappily. What would happen now? How could I look the leadership of the Main Directorate in the eye? Unfortunately, I had to look them in the eye.

"So that's the way it is, Comrade," they said to me. "You failed, right? Now what the devil are we going to do with you?"

How do you answer a question like that?

I mumbled almost inaudibly:

"I request to be allowed to remain in the engineer troops . . . I'm used to it . . . I'll take the exam again . . ."

The officer who was interviewing me, shaking his head, got more deeply involved in reading my papers, as if he might be able to find in them some indication of how to proceed in my case. And he did read something or other! The signs of concern in his face softened.

"Listen! Why don't you go to the school for military railroad technicians? Since childhood, one might say, you've really been a railroad man!"

My father's profession continued to determine my fate.

"But I'm a sapper . . ."

"We can only send you to the railroad technician's school," the officer said, gathering up my paperwork. "If you want to study, I recommend that you not refuse. We have a great need for railroad technicians."

Railroads . . . What a sorry spectacle to behold at the age of twenty! There was not enough coal, and not enough locomotives or cars. The tracks had been damaged during the war, and bandits continued to damage them. On the road from Odessa to Moscow, I'd had to hang around for several hours because of a wreck caused by some bandit group or other. On the other hand, it was understandable that the army needed people in transportation. And my new profession would not differ all that much from that of a sapper. No, not much . . .

The railroad technicians school was located in Voronezh.

Having learned about academics through bitter experience, I sat down with Kiselev's algebra and geometry, repeated the entire course, and passed the entrance exams with an "outstanding." In September, we were enrolled as cadets.

"I congratulate you, Comrades," said the chief of the 4th Voronezh Military Railroad School to the cadets who were drawn up on the parade ground. "Starting tomorrow—to work!"

The first task was cutting firewood.

Fuel was in short supply everywhere in the country. And Voronezh was not an exception. Our school was a brick building with virtually no glass in the windows, so the window openings were covered with boards, dry leaves and sawdust stuffed between them. Without firewood, we probably would have died like flies in the winter. The winter nights were long, but to the exhausted cadets, they seemed all too short.

Rations were running low, but we volunteered a portion of our food to the starving people of the Volga provinces. Then, things got worse with the lighting in the school. But our company still went off to training with a song. We were young, filled with energy, and we had outstanding teachers, mainly engineers from the Southwestern Railroad Directorate. So what if we were underfed and exhausted from lack of sleep? We'd survive! The young Soviet state needed our specialities. We were needed! So why not sing?

In those years, there was an epidemic of enthusiasm for communes, and so communes arose, even in the Voronezh railroad technicians school. Members of the communes trained together and shared everything that they had. My commune included: myself, Fedor Pankratov, and Aleksandr Azbukin, both of whom were intelligent and energetic fellows. We set ourselves a goal: to pass the graduation exam in January 1922, after the second semester of the first course and the first semester of the second course: that is, we'd finish a two-year school in one year. Some instructors doubted the wisdom of such an undertaking, but others supported us.

There were no rest days. With incredible effort, we caught up with the second course, and then made one more resolution: we'd pass the school with "outstanding" grades. And we did, in fact, receive the highest evaluations in all subjects. All three of us were presented with engraved watches on the day of our graduation.

Not long before transitioning to the second course, I was accepted as a candidate member of the Communist Party, since I was a frontline veteran and distinguished student. You can imagine my happiness and pride.

In fall, 1922, the Military Railroad Technicians School ended. Our commune received orders for Kiev to the 4th Korosten' Red Banner Railroad Regiment.

I had been a private soldier, then a cadet, and now I was an officer: how was my officer career going to turn out? How many times during my thirty-plus years of army service have I received new replacements! How many young officers have I met on the threshold of their army life! If it turned out that I trained those men pretty well, then a lot of credit for my performance belongs not to me but to those superb officers who met me in the 4th Korosten' Red Banner.

How can one forget battalion commanders who had been active participants in the fight against tsarism, brave lieutenant colonels, and that old Bolshevik Zhilinsky? How can one forget company commander Aleksandr Yevdokimovich Kryukov, a veteran of World War I and the civil war?

Aleksandr Yevdokimovich received me and my comrades almost like family members. He concerned himself about our quar-

ters and our uniforms. And what was most important, he did not
assert his seniority to anyone. The company CO was demanding
but very trustworthy, and this won us over.

We three members of the Voronezh commune had no command
experience, so we sometimes made mistakes while training Red
Army enlisted men. Aleksandr Yevdokimovich noted each mistake, but never corrected us in front of the troops. Only after the
training was over would he point out our negligence, and then
only in the most tactful fashion. We were thankful for that!
Kryukov didn't begrudge time spent on the instruction of young
officers. In addition, he quickly learned each man's interests and
capabilities. When he noticed that demolitions was really in my
blood, he immediately tried to get me assigned as chief of the
demolitions team. A year later, Aleksandr Yevdokimovich suffered a great tragedy: his wife died. He remained friendly and
even-tempered. Even his enormous grief could not render him in-
sensitive to the problems of others, however small they might be
by comparison.

Two years passed: our company did not sit on its collective
duff. We improved and repaired roads, protected bridges and culverts from destruction by flash floods, and built new railroad
branch lines. And we studied incessantly. As well, large numbers
of live bombs and artillery shells were being found near cities and
villages. My demolitions team carefully excavated them and carried them off to unpopulated areas to destroy them.

I took full advantage of each piece of unexploded munitions to
study the construction of the fuses. I conducted the first experi-
ments in melting the explosive material out of the bombs and
shells, and managed to convince myself that this was a safe procedure. It was useful as well because we had a great need for
TNT, especially in the spring when it was necessary to break up
ice jams that threatened railroad bridges.

At that time, I first thought about constructing a portable mine
for destroying enemy trains. Anything might happen in the future.
Our mines had to be simple, convenient, and safe; and the fuses
had to work faultlessly. In the civil war, we had already become
acquainted with the construction of a cumbersome, complex,
delayed-action antitrain mine. The 9th Engineer Battalion had several mines of this type, but we set only one of them, in the
Bataysk-Rostov sector. For the rest of the war, we lugged around
the remaining mines with us in our baggage train for no purpose
at all. The Red Army really didn't need such awkward devices!

I began to regularly read the military journals and study mines
and explosives, eagerly supplementing the knowledge and experi-

ence that I had gained in the war and in school. My colleagues gnawed at the hard rock of science with equal persistence. The entire Worker's and Peasant's Red Army was studying.

Life soon began to improve throughout the country. Agriculture, wrecked by two successive wars, began a successful recovery. The new year, 1924, saw the triumph of Bolshevik policies. Then, suddenly, a great sadness descended upon the Party and the people. A cold January day brought news that Vladimir Il'yich Lenin was no more!

The whistles and sirens of all trains and factories wailed inconsolably.

People stopped, stupefied, on the streets, wherever grief overtook them. The whole nation was in mourning. I stood among my men, unable to move, holding my helmet in my hands. No one spoke. We were not ashamed of our tears. What would happen to the Party, to the nation, to the people? we wondered.

And as if in answer to that question, came the Leninist appeal to the Party: Do you desire that Lenin's deeds shall not perish, that they will remain alive, and that the ideas of Leninism will transform the whole world? *Then stand in the ranks of the Communists.* Serve the Party with everything you have; give to it all your capabilities! Even if your talents are not great, there are millions like you, and together, the combined forces of your wills and your capabilities will be invincible.

I had already been accepted as a candidate member of the Revolutionary Communist party (Bolshevik), and so, at the same time as thousands of others in those days, I submitted my application for full membership in the Communist party.

Nearly seventy years have passed, but I have not forgotten the emotions experienced in those minutes when I stood for evaluation before the stern eyes of the Communists of the regiment. I will remember them to my dying day.

Secret Mission

"Il'ya! To the commissar, immediately!"

"D'you know why he wants me?"

My regimental pal, the commander of the neighboring company, Petr Pavlovich Monakhov, shrugged his shoulders, and I took a deep breath. Regimental Commissar Nikolai Georgiyevich Desatkin knew that I was not a very good public speaker, and he was trying to get me accustomed to giving reports in the auditorium. Now it looked like he was going to assign me another report! What the hell! I'd do it and get it over with. Pity the poor audience!

"Permission to enter, Comrade Commissar?"

Desatkin stood up to greet me, extended his hand, and waved me to a chair. He did not speak, just looked me in the eye.

No, this was definitely not just another report—this was something different!

"No one must know about our conversation," he warned. "We have received an order from the military district staff to select an experienced demolitions officer for a special mission. The regimental commander and I are recommending you."

An hour after my conversation with Desatkin, I was locking up my suitcase.

"Going far, Il'ya?"

"Just to the district. Some more courses of some kind . . ."

It was a good thing that one of the locks was giving me trouble so I was unable to look Petr Monakhov in the eye. Even though he was my friend, I couldn't tell him about my assignment. That's how it is in the service.

I departed alone for the railroad station. The wooden planking of the platform glistened in the rain. The gloomy September sky hung right above my head. There was a chill wind. Sooner or later the train would arrive . . . The excuse I had given Petr about taking a course was not very well thought out. Only the year before last, in 1924, I had gone for requalification in Leningrad. But then, a word is not like a sparrow—once it flies away, you'll never catch it again. And what was awaiting me on that special, secret mission, anyway?

In the duty car of the train, everything was explained. I was assigned to a commission under the chairmanship of Ye. K. Afonko, to work under the direct supervision of the commander of the Ukrainian Military District, Comrade Yakir. The work involved the strengthening of the border areas. We were to study the railroad sections on the borders of Poland and Romania and prepare them in advance for destruction in the event of an enemy surprise attack. I was the only demolitions officer on the commission and was expected to make suggestions for the laying out of minefields.

All this was quite flattering, but very embarrassing. After all, I was just a company commander, and only a company commander, and that for just a year, less one week. Could I handle the job?

I regained self-control: I *had* to handle the work. The work situation actually facilitated my doing so. The chairman was an uncommonly well-organized individual, with a shaven head and a powerful physique. Even on the road, Ye. K. Afonko did not forget his daily exercises.

The commission covered the border. We examined railroad bridges, large culverts, depots, pumping stations, water towers, high embankments, and deep hollows. From morning until late night, in all kinds of weather, we walked along the ties on the wet ballast. We estimated, we measured, and then we went back to the lounge car and began careful calculations and graphic layout work.

We had to present our findings to Iona Emanuilovich Yakir himself. Some saw him as preoccupied and gloomy, but in his presence, I never felt shy or awkward. Yakir was always very attentive to people, and he could not bear for someone to bother his subordinates. It was for these reasons that the men in his military district not only loved him but actually worshiped him.

Yakir's advice was always strictly professional. His knowledge of the situation was outstanding. It was as if the district commander had been along with you for the entire length of the border.

At our first meeting, Yakir drew our attention to the necessity for exhaustive planning of barrier operations,[1] and demanded that we take into consideration all forces and means available on the spot.

"Teach people not to rely on orders alone. Teach them to act rationally and decisively depending on the situation. Orders, as you might know, are sometimes given from afar; they can be delayed, and in war delays can lead to casualties. . . ." On 22 June 1941, I remembered these words of Iona Emmanuilovich Yakir with sorrow. (Translator's note: I. E. Yakir was executed in the purges of 1937.)

The pungent smell of locomotive smoke had long since firmly impregnated our clothing. Wet greatcoats did not dry out over-

---

1. Barrier operations involve the creation of systems of artificial barriers across an enemy's line of advance. Barrier operations include the systematic application of, e.g., demolitions and mines to render key railroads, highways, terrain, and facilities unusable, the construction of other artificial obstacles such as antitank traps, "dragon's teeth," barbed-wire emplacements, etc., to hamper movement across country, the modification of natural terrain to impede movement, and the destruction of ground cover to expose enemy forces. Such barriers may not only be used to slow down the enemy's advance but also to channel enemy movement into areas where he is at a distinct disadvantage in defending himself, e.g., areas lacking in natural cover or with poor soil trafficability.

night. A month went by, and our car continued to wander about. One day in October, we crept into the station at Mozyr'. It had been freezing since morning, and the wind whipped at our faces. It would be unpleasant climbing on the supports and girders of the bridge that arched over the Pripyat River. But if we didn't do it, no one would, so better not procrastinate! I was escorted by the chief of the militarized railroad guard; a young fellow, a bit on the chubby side. He flaunted himself in a military manner, incessantly straightening the holster of his Nagant revolver and generally trying to show that his guards were not country bumpkins.

I checked out the girders. Then, it was time to check the deep mine shaft. (Translators note: shafts, niches, or chambers were special structural features, built as integral parts of many Soviet bridges and other types of installations. They were designed to receive demolition charges in the event of war.) We could have requested sketches of the bridge and established the dimensions of the shaft from the sketches, but I had made it a rule to personally inspect each installation with my own eyes.

The chief of the guard remained on the bridge, and I shined an electric light down into the shaft, looked around, and *froze on the spot*. In the shaft was a charge of dynamite, covered with a thick greasy coating . . .

"Close the bridge to traffic!" I shouted to the chief of the guards.

That guy actually turned white. His thick lower lip drooped helplessly, but I wasn't really concerned about the chief of the bridge guard. I rushed to tell the members of the commission of the alarming discovery.

Jellied dynamite or gelignite, covered with a greasy coating, is extremely dangerous. It is extraordinarily sensitive to mechanical shocks; for example, an insignificant shock or even a little friction is sufficient to produce an explosion. Our instructions required that we destroy the material without attempting to move it.

The commission was most concerned, and while I examined the other mine shafts, a report was winging its way to the district staff and to the People's Commissariat for Communications. Movement on the road was stopped—but for how long? Obviously for a while, since I found more dynamite charges with nitroglycerin seeping out of them in other supporting structural members. It was just a matter of luck that the bridge had not gone sky high before this!

The flabby chief of the militarized guard forgot his military bearing, and was fussing about, trying to explain everything by virtue of the fact that he had only been there a short time. Seizing the moment, he asked me: "Surely the charges are old, aren't they? Really old?"

The poor bastard was really not to blame. The charges were old as hell, and I told him so, but in a most severe tone. A man who cannot control himself is a very unpleasant spectacle. To the chief of the guard my tone was irrelevant, however. The only thing he wanted to hear was that he had nothing to do with it. An uncertain smile spread across the fellow's fat face. (Translator's note: The charges could have been emplaced on the bridge by any one of the many military forces that fought across this terrain in World War I, the civil war, and the Russo-Polish war!)

"What has to be done?" Afonko asked me. "Bear in mind that you cannot delay the bridge traffic for a long time."

"Well, Yevseviy Karpovich, no matter what, bridge traffic is impossible right now. I request permission to call a demolitions team. Preferably the team from my regiment."

Nobody argued about my request. A call to the team went off immediately. And I tried to stay off to the side in order to avoid questions: *you see, I didn't know how to proceed, either.* None of the mine-clearing methods appeared to be appropriate in this case. If we started to remove the dynamite, who could say that we would not destroy the troops and blow the bridge? I certainly couldn't! In exercises, I had confirmed that dynamite with a greasy covering is especially sensitive to mechanical shocks. You simply had to blow the stuff up. But how? Together with the bridge?

I couldn't eat or drink. In any case, there wasn't time to touch anything all day long. Exhausted and gloomy, I arrived at our duty train. I couldn't clean my greasy hands so I asked for hot water.

The hot, soapy water washed off the greasy spots of black oil. And suddenly, like an electric shock, it struck me! We would pour black oil into the mine shaft to dissolve the greasy covering, then soak up the oil with sawdust, and then wash off the dynamite with warm alkaline water!

When my troops arrived, I explained to them what the difficulties were, and we went to work. Black oil, dry sawdust, and hot water worked perfectly. Soon I was able to report: "The bridge will be cleared of mines shortly!"

I spent many days on that bridge and caught a severe chill, but it was impossible to leave. And so I hung on, as long as the danger had not passed. But it wasn't possible to rest even then; while we had been busy on the bridge, I had neglected paperwork, and so I had to make up for what I'd overlooked . . .

In spite of the unforeseen delay, the special commission completed its work on time and won the thanks of the district commander.

At the end of November 1926, I returned to my regiment. "Well, how were the courses?" Petr Monakhov asked with a wink.

"Typical. They just repeated stuff we've already had." He didn't say a word, just embraced me and slapped me on the back.

The travels of the special commission to inspect the border were only the beginning of an enormous effort in which even more important people and units were to be included. We were assigned to do everything possible to ensure that an enemy would be unable to take advantage of our roads in an invasion.

Toward the end of 1929, preparations were completed for the creating of barriers on all major railroads and highways along on our borders. In the Ukrainian Military District, more than sixty demolitions teams totaling fourteen hundred men had been trained. Numerous explosive storage dumps had been built, and reserve supplies of explosives had been accumulated. On bridges, more than 160 special shafts, wells, niches, and chambers for demolition charges had been repaired. More than sixteen hundred complex explosive charges had been prepared and placed in storage, and tens of thousands of blasting caps, which could be put to use virtually instantaneously.

I don't know exactly how it was done, but I do know that such preparations were also carried out in other border military districts. For this purpose, a special instruction (the "Red Book") was printed, and a regulation (the "Green Book"). The instruction described in detail how to inflict damage on rail lines, bridges, and other installations on a railroad. This book played a major role in perfecting our mining and demolitions work. The Green Book—the regulations—clearly set forth the variations in destruction and damage to be inflicted on railroad lines, depending on how long one wanted to put them out of action. All necessary calculations were provided to determine the manpower and material necessary to provide complete or partial destruction of targets. Reserves of mines and explosives were deployed near guarded installations, enough for complete destruction of roads in an area from sixty to one hundred kilometers from the border.

In addition to the mine barriers, other barriers were created. All of these systems were coordinated with a system of strongpoints or districts. Now, in a comparatively short time, and with the use of a relatively small number of forces, we could prevent an enemy from moving on our roads for a long time. Then, we got another important mission: we were to come up with a way of rendering the roads unserviceable in areas captured by the enemy, but doing this so as to enable our forces to rapidly restore traffic on those roads when we reoccupied the areas. The leadership of the engineer troops and the military communications of the Red Army clearly thought that this could be achieved by cleverly combining evacuation and destruction by application of command-detonated mines and delayed-action mines (MZD—*mina zamedlennogo deystviya*). According to this thinking, the latter were to play a major role.

A few words about the MZDs: in 1928–1929, the Red Army already had a series of instantaneous and delayed-action antitrain mines. With some of these you were supposed to be able to destroy any train that you were ordered to, and even take out a specific car on a train. These mines all had one essential drawback, however, they worked only when installed under railroad ties or directly under the rails. In addition, they were not sealed well enough.

But steady progress was being made in the areas of mines and demolitions. In particular, methods were perfected for laying series of charges and increasing the reliability of simultaneous detonation of those charges on major targets in any kind of weather. It was hoped that in the near future, we would receive sufficient quantities of high quality mines of the most diverse construction, including antitrain mines that could be installed without contact with rails and ties.

Unfortunately, we never got them! In the years of Stalinist arbitrariness, the mines that the army needed not only never got into production but the plans for such mines died, *along with the engineers who designed them*! Certainly no one could imagine that such things were to happen, and in the fall of 1929, preparing for maneuvers, we were filled with confidence in the future.

During Starinov's work with the commission, Stalin was waging a protracted, Byzantine struggle within the Party to gain total control over the Soviet government by playing off "Left" and "Right" opposition groups against each other, expelling and arresting his opponents, and promoting his own followers to positions of power in the Party bureaucracy. Starinov reported to his new duty station as Stalin was about to take a new and important step in his rise to power: the crushing of the peasantry and the subjugation of the Ukraine by means of the forced collectivization of agriculture. Starinov's new assignment, unknown to him, was also to place him under direct threat of liquidation some eight years later when Stalin decided to assert his control over the Soviet military.

On the Partisan Trail

The things which I will describe in this chapter—the training of partisan cadres in the twenties and early thirties, and the development of special partisan equipment—may surprise and puzzle my readers.

Studying the possibility of an attack on the Soviet nation by imperialist aggressors, the Central Committee of the Party charged the People's Commissariat for Defense and Naval Affairs with the task of taking steps, well in advance of any aggression, to raise the nation's defensive capabilities. The training of partisan cadres and the development of special partisan equipment began in 1922, a few years before our work was getting under way on the construction of barriers on the communications net. A bit later, the construction of heavily fortified areas also began. Partisan training was to continue until 1935.

Much of the intellect, effort, and organizational talent of our outstanding military leaders went into the training of partisan cadres and the construction of secret partisan bases.[1] In the fall of 1929, I was brought in to teach mines and demolitions to saboteurs and subversives in a "special" school at the training establishment of the railroad transport section of the OGPU (Translator's note: OGPU = *ob'edinennoe gosudarstvennoe politicheskoe upravlenie*, or Unified State Political Directorate, the forerunner of the NKVD and KGB) of the Southwest Railroad in Kiev. I also taught at another special school run by the Ukrainian OGPU in Kiev, and at OGPU schools in Kharkov, and Kupyansk. In January 1930, I was placed at the disposal of the chief of Directorate IV of the Red Army staff, i.e. the Main Intelligence Directorate (GRU) and assigned to duty in a department of the staff of the Ukrainian Military District in Kiev, which was responsible for partisan warfare training. I taught in another special school in Kiev and in special courses in Odessa, both run by that staff section. Finally, from 1933 to 1934, I taught in the special school in

1. For example, M. Y. Frunze, I. E. Yakir, I. P. Uborevich, Y. K. Blyukher, and Ya. K. Berzin. All except Frunze—who died in 1925—were executed in the purges of 1937–1938, at least partially because of their success in establishing the very partisan and sabotage capabilities that Stalin had initially ordered but later came to view as threatening to his personal security. There is some doubt, however, as to the actual cause of Frunze's death (see note 3).

Moscow commanded by Karol Swierczewski[2] (see Appendix A for a list of commanding officers of schools at which Starinov taught). Having worked in the district staff department until 1933, then having held the post of chief of the border troops intelligence points of the 4th Department of the Ukrainian Military District staff (during which time I sent many reconnaissance men across the border into Poland), and finally having worked in the intelligence directorate (GRU) of the Red Army staff, I certainly had occasion to participate in partisan warfare training along the lines laid down by the People's Commissariat.

In January 1930, when I was called to Khar'kov to the staff of the Ukraine Military District, I was met by the chief of the staff intelligence department, Division Commander Avgust Ivanovich Baar.[3] He was a tall, rather awkward fellow of a type generally known as big boned. I knew that he was a Latvian, but he resembled nothing more than a woodcutter from the deep taiga who had spent his life among the silent hollows and hills and the evergreens. The hand he extended to me was also a woodcutter's hand: big, hard, as if made coarse by ax handles. He spoke in a thick voice, an obviously restrained basso, in abrupt and ragged phrases. I decided that the man before me was a sullen and reserved man, but I paid careful attention. He gave seemingly set, one-word answers to my questions. Our visit was clearly not going well. Suddenly, Baar got down to business and informed me that I was going to be teaching partisans. "This is a more difficult and complex job than teaching young Red Army recruits. Comrade Yakir will describe it all to you in the greatest detail. Let's go see him."

Comrade Yakir, the district commander, was organizing some papers. He looked up and smiled. Baar presented me. "It's much easier to talk with old friends," said Yakir. He described with considerable passion the methods of instruction to be employed and the goals of the partisan preparations, which included:

a) developing, improving, and ensuring the security of operational plans for initial operations of partisan forces;

2. Karol Swierczewski, a veteran of the Russian civil war, directed the key Moscow school for foreign Communist partisans in which Starinov served. He later served as "General Walter" in Spain. He rose to the Red Army rank of general in World War II, he commanded the 2nd Polish Army in the battles for Berlin and Prague. He was killed in 1947, ostensibly by Ukrainian nationalists. Some CIS sources believe that he was killed by NKVD counterintelligence agents, acting under orders from Stalin and Beria, who had decided to liquidate any Polish military officers whose loyalty to the USSR was uncertain. Swierczewski—a native Pole—was seen as possibly too pro-Polish, and had to be removed.

3. At this time the Red Army did not use personal ranks, e.g., major, colonel etc., but used positional ranks, i.e., ranks reflecting the command responsibility of the bearer, e.g., battalion commander, division commander, etc.

b) moral indoctrination of both troops and civilian population; particularly in the border regions;

c) training and organizing special partisan sabotage groups and detachments, capable of operating on unknown territory, including outside the borders of the Soviet Union on the territory of aggressors;

d) training of deep-cover underground sabotage groups and their insertion into cities and along railroad lines, and the creation of secret partisan bases with hidden supply dumps, to the west of the line of fortified regions in Soviet border areas;

e) training, or more accurately, retraining, officers and political officers of the Red Army and border troops who already had experience in partisan warfare in the civil war years;

f) providing assistance in training of partisan cadres to nations struggling for independence; and

g) improvement of equipment and methods for conducting partisan warfare.

"Clear?"

"Perfectly clear, Comrade Commander."

"Very good! But—there's one big 'but' here: Comrade Baar has obviously warned you that you're going to teach experienced and distinguished people. Very experienced! You must teach them in such a way that they don't get bored. It's not necessary to review the ABCs with them. Give them more new material—as much new material as possible! And remember this—right now, in the tactics of partisan warfare, they're better than you. So don't hurt anyone's feelings, and at the same time take the opportunity to learn for yourself everything that you may need. Clear?"

"Clear, Comrade Commander."

"You have been entrusted with an important party matter, Comrade Starinov," Yakir said without smiling. "You are obliged to handle it well."

After a bit more discussion, Yakir stood up from behind his desk: "I wish you the best of luck! And remember, no one must know about your work, except," and he winked, "myself."

The Schools

The special covert partisan schools were not large, with the exception of the school in Moscow where K. Swierczewski was chief. These schools were always rather unusual. They not only trained partisans but they prepared material for prepositioning in secret caches in the event of war. For training the students, we enlisted the services of the most well-trained officers of the partisan units of the civil war and specialists from military units as well. The schools had sufficient training equipment, and there was no problem in conducting exercises in training areas. For training in "safe houses," we had sets of portable visual aids in suitcases. In the special partisan schools run by the OGPU, between five and twelve partisans were trained at one time; while in the other schools thirty to thirty-five students were trained simultaneously. In Swierczewski's school in Moscow, however, about forty students were trained simultaneously in each of three separate training installations.

The Students

Partisan units, able to operate in unfamiliar territory including that of the enemy, were recruited from physically fit males ranging in age up to forty years, and females from eighteen to twenty-five years of age. These groups included: emigrants from the western regions of the Ukraine and Belorussia, occupied by the Polish "lords" after the Russo-Polish war of 1920 and the Treaty of Riga; emigrants from Bessarabia, occupied by the Romanians in 1918 after the Treaty of Brest-Litovsk; and veterans of partisan operations in the civil war. The majority of the personnel were Party members or members of Komsomol (Young Communists) who were recommended by Party organs, and military personnel recommended by political officers of the Red Army. Underground sabotage groups were recruited from trusted people from the ranks of the Party and Komsomol as well as from non-Party members.

The composition of sabotage groups designated for underground partisan operations in the event of enemy occupation of cities and major railroad junctions was most diverse. These groups included both young women and elderly males. All the males were unfit for military service because of physical incapacities or by virtue of age. The trained underground saboteurs were intentionally recruited from different areas of the USSR so that they would not know anyone except those who were in their own groups. They were all given pseudonyms for the purpose of maintaining cover.

Exceptional credit in training partisan cadres for operations in other countries must go to the Moscow school commanded by K. Swierczewski. In addition to training command personnel for partisan forces in foreign nations, that school also trained famous workers of the Communist movement in partisan warfare, including such figures as: Wilhelm Pieck, Palmiro Togliatti, Maurice Thorez, Aleksandr Zavadski, and Mate Zalka. (Translator's note: Pieck, Togliatti, and Thorez were postwar Communist party leaders in East Germany, Italy, and France respectively. Zavadski was a pro-Soviet Polish military leader; Mate Zalka is one of the cover names used by the Hungarian Communist Bela Frankl, who as commander of the 12th International Brigade—under the cover name of Lukacz—was killed in action in Spain in 1937.) The Swierczewski school principally trained commanders of sabotage groups, partisan detachments, and large units; chiefs of staff; partisan army commanders; and national-level leaders of partisan forces in other countries. In the programs of instruction, we took into consideration the knowledge and experience of the students as well as the situations in which they would have to operate. It's one thing to prepare cadres for nations where the people have no experience in partisan warfare, but quite another thing to train cadres for nations where the people are already carrying on partisan warfare.

For example, in training Chinese partisans, we took into account the developed structure of the partisan forces and their experience. Moreover, we studied their experience and drew general conclusions from it. The Chinese comrades didn't need to study questions of deep cover work, organization of partisan forces, or ambush and raid tactics. They already knew all of these things. For Chinese partisans at the beginning of the thirties, however, particular significance came to be attached to questions of strategy of partisan war and the planning of large-scale operations of partisan forces, the coordination of partisan forces with regular forces, the creation of strongholds, and the selection of objectives and the methods of operating against them.

Workers in the Communist movement and high-level partisan command personnel who studied at the Swierczewski school made in-depth studies of questions of the strategy of partisan warfare. Lectures on these questions were presented by well-known military leaders who possessed experience in the conduct of partisan war, such as Ya. K. Berzin, and V. K. Blyukher.

These were not typical lectures, but discussions in which the audience was small and always played an active role.

Qualifications and Selection
In those covert schools where future partisan maneuver detachments were being trained, the students usually had a sufficiently high level of combined-arms training that they had received, either in Red Army service or in civilian premilitary service. Further, many of them had either one or even two civilian specialties, which were useful in partisan warfare, e.g., electricians, chemists, drivers, and even radio operators.

Premilitary basic and specialist training was conducted in

Osoaviakhim (Translator's note: Osoaviakhim = *Obshchestvo sodeystviya oborone i aviatsionno-khimicheskomu stroitelstvu* SSSR, Society for the Assistance to the Defense, Aviation, and Chemical Industry of the USSR, the national premilitary and paramilitary organization of that period) courses, in which individuals selected by the Party and Komsomol courses studied marksmanship, map reading, automobile driving, swimming, etc. At the same time, political and physical training was conducted, and student personnel were intensively observed to determine their suitability for partisan operations. Usually, preliminary training in Osoaviakhim circles lasted between one to one and a half years if the student had no prior service in the Red Army. Those who had served in the Red Army were also trained in Osoaviakhim technical courses in the skills necessary for partisan warfare, but in nonsecret specialties as radio technicians, electricians, and drivers.

Training

Those who finished the Osoaviakhim schools and displayed suitability for partisan warfare were enrolled in the secret schools.

Training of partisan cadres (i.e., special training) was conducted by specialty groups, i.e., saboteurs, intelligence agents, snipers, and radio operators. The personnel of partisan groups were generally recruited in the course of preliminary training. In selecting candidates for partisan work, much attention was given to moral-political qualities, physical condition, endurance, discipline, and initiative. Sabotage candidates were preferably recruited from people who were knowledgeable in the fields of electrical equipment and chemistry. Intelligence agents were selected from those who had good vision and hearing and knew map reading and photography; snipers were selected from among outstanding marksmen; radiomen from radio amateurs, and armorers from machinists, etc.

In the secret schools, the trainees mastered partisan tactics and equipment and the tactics of sabotage, and improved their knowledge of map reading. The specialists—mine experts, snipers, intelligence men—improved their mastery of their respective specialities. The mine experts learned to make explosives, detonators, many fuses, and detonator switches and mines on their own, while the radiomen could not only use their radio sets but learned to repair them. Some were even able to build them out of spare parts, which we were able to buy in stores.

In training partisan cadres, great attention was devoted to political training of partisans as bearers of the ideas of socialism. This included inculcating the skills of exposing the lies of enemy propaganda, of conducting political work among partisans, the population, and enemy troops, and even how to gain the cooperation of the local population. Attention was also given to questions of demoralizing enemy troops and their administrative apparatus.

Specialists in topographic mapping, including surveyors, were also trained, as well as document specialists who were capable of counterfeiting and preparing passports, passes, certificates, etc. Further attention was given to physical and medical training of partisans, hardening them for operations in various kinds of terrain and weather.

At that time in our nation, the experience of partisan warfare was set forth in the classical works of Marxism-Leninism, in the works of a series of Soviet military leaders, and most of all in the works of M. V. Frunze.[4] We also made use of many works by nineteenth-century tsarist Russian military authorities and printed our own manuals and handbooks. Even fiction was used (see Appendix B, for a list of sources and publications used in training).

By order of I. E. Yakir, various specialists were assembled into partisan detachments. In addition to perfecting their knowledge of their own specialities, they were intensively cross-trained in related military specialties. For example, each mine expert was also a parachutist, a radio operator, and a master of camouflage and deception. Yakir was concerned with forming strong, combat-ready partisan detachments and brigades. He demanded that these detachments be formed in such a way that they included partisans who were experienced in operating behind enemy lines, as well as young cadre officers.

In training sabotage groups, which would be based and operate in cities, special attention was given to questions of security and secret communications. The personnel of partisan raiding formations were trained in long-range patrols, and in utilizing all forms of transport available in the enemy rear. Partisans who were designated for operations deep in the enemy rear had to undergo airborne training, including night jumps. Depending on the composition and the assigned mission (i.e., whether individuals, partisan groups, or underground saboteur groups were being trained), special partisan training varied in length between three months and one year.

Training of sabotage groups and "singletons" (individual operators) required three to six months, depending on the missions as-

4. Mikhail Vasilyevich Frunze, (1885–1925), an extremely talented factory worker with no previous military experience, who rose rapidly through the ranks to command major Red Army formations against Wrangel and Kolchak during the civil war, and replaced Trotksy as commissar for military and naval affairs. He was a prolific writer on military matters. Frunze died from complications following an overdose of chloroform during surgery that Stalin insisted he undergo. Frunze's death made way for Voroshilov, a close associate of Stalin.

signed to them. Basic subjects were: political training, means and methods of sabotage, tactics of partisan warfare, communications, marksmanship, some physical training, and map reading.

Officer and political cadres and specialists designated for deployment in partisan units in the event of enemy aggression were trained by Red Army intelligence personnel according to the following schema: basic general military and technical training, then special training and training in assembling the nucleus of a partisan unit from among the local populace.

In addition to training in the special schools, short conferences were also held for partisan units. These were held under the cover of meetings for "firemen," "hunters," "fishermen," etc. In these short-term conferences, many military officers and political officers passed refresher training. These were mainly former partisans of the civil war and personnel of the partisan units trained before 1930.

After completing training, the non-Party members returned to their previous employment as if returning from routine business travel, while the Party member and Komsomols were posted to new work locations, where they concealed their Party and Komsomol memberships, maintaining complete secrecy, and held themselves in readiness to fulfill their missions in the event of an enemy occupation of their territory. These were extraordinarily dedicated people who understood that in the event of an enemy occupation, they could only successfully execute their missions if they could mislead the enemy into trusting them completely. As a result, when war came, there were many well-trained groups that were able to operate with great effectiveness, as did the group led by Hero of the Soviet Union[5] K. S. Zaslonov, which used "coal" mines (Translator's note: possibly so called because they were made to resemble chunks of coal lying along the tracks) to inflict great losses on the enemy without suffering a single casualty.

Equipment

The military district commander set us the task of improving established methods of partisan warfare and finding new possibilities, seeking ways to increase the maneuverability of partisan groups, and of providing them with logistic support. In accordance with a personal directive of Yakir, I organized a shop-lab where we developed prototype mines suited for partisan warfare. These

5. The title "Hero of the Soviet Union" was the highest military honor bestowed by the USSR. It was established in 1934. Recipients of this award receive the Order of Lenin, the highest decoration awarded by the USSR, and a second decoration: the "Gold Star," which is worn, above all other decorations, on the left breast of both military and civilian dress.

included antitrain and antivehicle mines, the "coal" mines that were so successfully used in World War II, and other types of field-expedient mines, which the partisans could make in the enemy rear areas. In this lab, the ideas were born for some well-known automatic mines, including the so-called wheel switch (Translator's note: these switches were designed to be activated by train wheels passing over them, closing a firing circuit, which detonated the mine placed down the track in front of the train) later christened the *rapida* in the Spanish civil war. We also found ways to destroy autos and trains with mines which were controlled by wire and by string. However, antitrain and antiauto mines of types which could only be produced in factories were never released into general production, even though they had passed tests on proving grounds and with troop units. This was because in 1934, with the murder of S. M. Kirov, the entire official view of sabotage equipment changed markedly, and even the word *saboteur* (i.e., *diversantnik*) gradually fell into disuse as a term to designate Soviet sabotage groups and partisan-saboteurs.

Along with the mines, explosives, and detonators, which were the basic weapons of the majority of the deep-cover underground groups, special attention was also given to radio equipment. Even at the beginning of the thirties, radio communications between the "Great Land" (Translator's note: the term used to designate Soviet-held territory) and the partisans was a basic problem in the organization of partisan warfare. To remedy this problem, we established communications centers, created large reserve stocks of signal lights, set up carrier-pigeon communications, and developed methods of signaling to aircraft.

An unusual amount of attention was given to the logistics support of partisan forces. Various methods of delivering supplies from the air were tested, both with and without parachute. In the latter case, tests were run on dropping supplies into swamps or water.

This new cause attracted and consumed me. At first, I taught the future partisans only mining and demolitions, but I was studying more and more. I got into the history of partisan warfare, the tactics of partisan struggle, and the refinements and wisdom of intelligence. In short, while teaching, I managed to receive better training than was available in any academy at that time, including plenty of opportunity for practical application.

In the Woods at Olevsk

Rain poured out of overcast skies, into darkness and gloom. Alighting from the duty train car onto the slippery, rain-soaked roadbed, Yakir raised his head and looked at the lowering sky. Not a break in the overcast anywhere! The commander shrugged his shoulders, took out his handkerchief, and wiped his forehead. I didn't think we'd be doing anything that day, but Yakir, putting away his handkerchief, motioned us to follow him. His high, dry boots slipped, spattering mud. A muddy country road led away from the station. Yakir didn't slow his pace.

We entered a little woods. It was getting toward evening, and in the torrent of raindrops, the underbrush was growing darker and darker. The commander suddenly stopped and listened. We also stopped and listened. Through the sounds of the rain on the leaves, the champing of horses' hooves and the squeaks of donkeys pulling carts reached our ears.

When the lead cart approached us, the commander jumped up into it. "Sit in the following carts," he ordered quietly.

We traveled a good distance into the dark woods and then stopped unexpectedly.

"Let's pitch the tent here," Yakir's voice rang out of the darkness. Pitching a tent is a pretty routine, simple thing. A linen tent was erected within a small clearing. Inside, someone turned on a flashlight.

"Hey, are you people really covert operators?" Yakir shouted with annoyance. "That light is visible for hundreds of meters. Put it out! And fast!"

All told, ten men huddled in the tent, ready to participate in the caching of a covert partisan base west of Korosten', near Olevsk.

The idea of creating such bases, where weapons, explosives, and ammunition would be prepositioned in the event of an enemy invasion was put forward by Mikhail Vasil'yevich Frunze, who considered that the preparation for partisan warfare was one of the most important tasks of the Red Army general staff. Yakir devoted a great deal of attention to the realization of this idea. He took the lead in organizing numerous partisan bases along our western border during 1931–1933, simultaneous with the construction of the fortified areas farther to the east.

When we left the tent, the rain was pouring down even harder. Night had already fallen on the woods, and the darkness was so thick, it was as if you were actually blind.

Not far from that area, combined arms exercises used to take place, and the countryside was dug up with rifle pits and communications trenches. We used one of the firing pits for caching the weapons and ammunition, and worked in shifts. To conceal the cache from prying eyes, we cut a deep niche into the wall of the firing pit, right under the roots of a birch tree. Yakir also took off his tunic and armed himself with a sapper's spade.

"Get dressed, Iona Emmanuilovich. You shouldn't be doing this," said the adjutant, V. A. Zakharchenko. He moved toward Yakir, holding out Yakir's tunic.

"What is it I shouldn't be doing?" Yakir began to respond in a combative fashion, but then he suddenly bent over in a fit of coughing. His face went purple.

"You'll catch your death of cold, Comrade Commander," we said, supporting the adjutant. We didn't realize that Yakir had tuberculosis.

Iona Emmanuilovich paused until his coughing fit passed, waved his hands, and reached out for his tunic. But he never left the work area, and hung around the firing pit until we filled and tamped down the niche.

It was already getting light when we finished everything and carefully removed all traces of our having been there. No stranger would guess that under the roots of the big birch, under a pile of rotting firewood, there was a cache of weapons for a big partisan detachment and a supply of explosives sufficient to wreck tens of trains and blow up hundreds of enemy vehicles.

Toward morning, the weather cleared, the sun broke through, and it warmed up. Then we could breathe again in the Olevsk forest! And our return was a merry one.

After this, however, there were other towns and villages, other woods, other birches, and other forest ravines . . .

From the late twenties to the early thirties, stocks of supplies and equipment for partisans were prepositioned in the area between the border and the line of strongpoints that had been built some distance east of the border. It was assumed that if an enemy approached the fortified line, well-trained partisan forces would appear in the enemy's rear. The partisans would use stocks of equipment and supplies that had been hidden in the caches. The enemy could not detect these caches, but the partisans had access to them.

Preliminary tests were made on methods of preserving the equipment and supplies in the caches. We cached mainly weapons of foreign manufacture, and the ammunition for them, explosives and fuses, and in numerous cases, canned goods. The caching of stocks of weapons and equipment in the Ukraine was done by command personnel of partisan units under the leadership of instructors and special groups of the reconnaissance department of the staff of the Ukraine Military District, the OGPU, and the DTO/OGPU of the Southwestern Railroad. (Translator's note: DTO = *dorozhno-transportnyy odeli*, or railroad transport section.)

The weapons and explosives safely hidden in the earth awaited their time. But before that time could come, the secret partisan bases were destroyed not only with Stalin's full knowledge but by his direct order.

Workdays and Holidays

The roar of the transport plane's motors was deafening; the fuselage shook and vibrated; the plane was climbing. There, somewhere below, beneath the thick floor of the plane, was the Leningrad area, remote and submerged in darkness of a fall, 1932, night.[1]

As was always the case before a jump, my heart was pounding. It seemed to be expanding, trying to burst out of my chest. The doctor had categorically forbidden me to parachute jump, but I didn't pay any attention to that. It was impossible for me, the chief of the school, not to jump. How would I be able to instruct the partisans on their equipment if I couldn't see my students at work? This jump was unusual, however, because it was a night

1. At this point, Soviet developments in the application of parachute technology for landing military or partisan personnel behind enemy lines was already quite advanced, as is evidenced by this account of a partisan night drop. A few years later, the Soviets were employing units of up to division size in maneuvers. In 1935, Germany began full-scale development of parachute troops. Many other nations of Europe—e.g., Czechoslovakia, France—briefly considered the potential of such forces but never actually fielded any parachute units. There had been interest in parachute troops in the U.S. and British military, (e.g., on the part of Col. Billy Mitchell), since as far back as World War I, but neither the United States or Great Britain took action to develop such forces until June 1940, when a parachute school was formed in Britain, and a parachute infantry test platoon was formed in the United States. In 1940, night drops, even by small units such as that described here, were still in the future for Allied paratroopers.

jump. Could it be that this was the reason my heart was actin
up? A sensible, rational thought sneaked into my mind: I'm ne
feeling well; wouldn't it be better to get myself treated and t
abort the jump?

Nothing is more dangerous than giving in to such self-servin
rationalizations. In any case, I'd already trained myself not to sur
render to such weakness, and when the pilot raised his hand an
turned around, giving the signal that it was time to jump, I sprang
up as though nothing could hold me back. The hatch was opened
The troops didn't take their eyes off my figure, poised above th
black, bottomless opening . . .

"Go!"

Cold! Darkness! Wild acceleration! I pulled the rip cord. I
seemed as though the chute would never open. This was just m
senses deceiving me; in jumping, fractions of seconds stretch int
seconds, and seconds into minutes. I felt a jolt—the chute had fi
nally opened! Everything was going well. My heart was alread
beating normally, and as usual, for some reason, I wanted to sing
The earth was still invisible, that was true. But if I was to thin
sensibly, just the way I did on earth, it seemed that I wasn't reall
falling! Maybe I'd hit in a river or float down into a forest.

I tried to guess the distance to the ground. I braced my legs an
got ready to collapse the chute, but despite my preparations, i
was impossible to precisely calculate the moment of impact.
landed heavily. It was a good thing that I'd hit in a meadow. I go
up, automatically slipped out of my harness, and looked around
nearby, there was the vague shadow of a wood, and from the lef
came a whiff of dampness—probably a pond. Overhead, our plane
roared around among the stars. Up there, my students were
awaiting the signal from the ground, my signal that everything
was all right, that I had hit the drop zone.

I turned on the signal light.

The sound of the plane, which seemed to be moving off to one
side, grew louder and louder; then it was right over my head. Tha
meant that my comrades had already jumped.

I awaited them, happy that we were off to a good start. Ove
the last few days, it had been necessary to get them really moti
vated. After all, we weren't going to the Leningrad Military Dis
trict as guests; we were on maneuvers. We were coming to
demonstrate our experience in cutting the supply lines of the "en
emy." We couldn't afford to wind up with egg on our faces, eve
though it was our first night jump!

No one was interested in the number of jumps we had made
All they wanted from us were successful operations—not excuse

because of unusual conditions. In fact, it wasn't necessary to rely on excuses: everything went off as planned. Of course, some of the troops had bad luck: on landing, they had difficulties collapsing their chutes and suffered pulled muscles, dislocations, and other injuries. But not one dropped out of the war games. The injured were bandaged up and kept going.

In 1932, there had already been secret training exercises involving partisan units, for example, the Bronnitsky maneuvers near Moscow, where K. Ye. Voroshilov (people's commissar for army and naval affairs, i.e., the approximate equivalent of the U.S. secretary of defense) was present. That exercise involved partisan parachutists under the command of S. A. Vaupshasov as well as a division of special troops and personnel from the border guard school, academies, and schools of the Moscow Military District.

The fall 1932 maneuvers in the Leningrad Military District, in which we were participating, however, were the largest combined-arms maneuvers involving trained partisan cadres. Five hundred partisans of the Leningrad, Belorussian, and Ukrainian Military Districts took part in them, dropping by parachute into the enemy rear area. In the maneuver area, the partisans were armed with training grenades and Japanese carbines, and the saboteurs were armed with various kinds of training mines. Everyone wore civilian clothes, with red stripes on their caps, and they had raincoats and rucksacks.

The partisans were to capture army staffs and disrupt enemy communications. You can be sure that I didn't let the opportunity pass by to get permission to set up train "wrecks" by means of detonator switches and explosives.

The section of road set aside for our operations was heavily guarded, and the enemy successfully frustrated our attacks on railroad stations and major bridges, but they could not guarantee the security of movement of trains: on a ten-kilometer stretch of railroad, the partisans managed to plant ten mines. Nine of them worked effectively beneath trains that were sent over the track as part of the maneuvers. But there was some confusion concerning the tenth and we were unable to remove it before the resumption of normal passenger service on the line, and it went off with a roar under a suburban commuter train. When he heard the explosion and saw the flash under the train wheels, the engineer decided that it was a normal railroad dynamite signal cap warning him of hazards on the road, and he slammed on the brakes. The passengers poured out onto the roadbed. No one knew what was happening.

I erred seriously in not reporting this incident. The echoes of

the dynamite cap nevertheless reached all the way up to one of
the highly placed chiefs in Moscow. Unfortunately, he had only
recently been down to my school in Kiev and had praised my
mine and demolition equipment. Of course, he immediately knew
the identity of the guilty party in the suburban train's unscheduled
stop. He was extremely angry, and categorically ordered my removal from the maneuvers.

I suspected that his anger was aroused not so much because of
the ill-starred mine as because of my group's lack of success in
capturing "enemy" staffs. At that time, great significance was being accorded to the capture of a staff, but the partisans had repeat-
edly failed in their attempts.

So there I was, walking along a forest road, unhappily pondering
the events that had occurred. Behind me, I heard the squeaking of
a cart and the snorting of horses. Stepping to the side of the road
I turned. It looked like it was one of our people. Yeah, it was a partisan in a cart. He had seriously injured his leg and had received
permission to go to the field medical station.

"Hop in, I'll give you a lift," the partisan said.

I jumped up and sat down in front, letting my legs dangle.

The road came out of the woods, snaked away along their edge,
then stretched out across broad fields to a village lying on a distant hill. Suddenly, I noticed something. "Whoa!" I ordered the
driver. "Whoa!"

"What's your problem?"

"Look! Wires! Field communications lines!"

"Yeah, so what?"

"The wires lead to the village!"

The partisan shook his head in agreement, but he still didn't understand what I was getting at.

"They took me out of the war games, but you're still 'alive,' so
to speak, right?" I said to him, smiling. "Now you're going to
cause a little excitement in the village. By all indications, the enemy staff is right there!"

My companion looked at the village, then at me, and he gave
in. "Okay, here goes! Let's give it a try! That's why we're partisans. But you tell me what I should do . . ."

When I noticed a checkpoint on the road ahead of us, we
turned off onto a side road, unhurriedly moving far off to one side
of the village. We hid in the trees, and at nightfall, we approached
the village on foot.

Guards were wandering around the perimeter and up and down
the streets, but nobody was checking documents there in the vil-

lage, and simply by noting the presence of guards, we established where the most important departments of the staff were located.

We set up our mines, taking advantage of the darkness. In three areas, we set concealed ignition charges with primers, and in five additional places, we set very small charges without primers, but containing a special compound that produced very bright flashes.

When we had finished the work, we hid.

The ignition charges started going off after midnight. The first detonation produced panic in the village. The startled guards started to round up not only the local inhabitants but also soldiers who had obviously forgotten the password in their haste.

The second detonation occurred almost simultaneously with the arrival of an armored car in the village. The driver backed the vehicle up, slipped into a ditch flooded by recent rains, and simply stayed in the car. Almost all the staff personnel ran out to patrol the village streets, which didn't make any sense at all.

The third charge went off. The enemy patrols rushed to the area where the detonation had occurred. And there, one after the other, the remaining charges went off with dazzling brilliance. The elusiveness of the partisans only heightened the panic.

In the morning, my direct superior arrived in the village, having heard from secondhand sources about the attack on the staff by a "strong sabotage unit." My boss was puzzled because he knew there was no such unit in the area.

I came out of hiding and set off to report to my commander.

"What in hell are you doing here?" he demanded angrily.

I had to divulge my secret. Initially, the commander listened to me with a gloomy countenance. Suddenly his face began to relax a bit; he smiled, and then he banged his palms on the table.

"So, comrades, now do you see the kind of saboteurs we have?"

And right there on the spot, he restored the military rights that had been taken away from me in the aftermath of the unfortunate passenger train incident and gave me permission to once more participate in the maneuvers.

This little incident showed how successfully a small group of partisans could operate. The command decided to employ them on a broad basis right up to the end of the maneuver, and our people proved that they were capable of carrying out the most difficult missions.

Nineteen thirty-two was a memorable year for me because of my many successes.

Airborne training was especially complicated for partisan maneuver units. At that time, there weren't enough troop-carrying aircraft such as appeared later during World War II, and for this reason, many partisans learned to ride on, and jump from, the *wings* of the aircraft.

We worked out three methods for night jumps: jumping onto a secured drop zone, jumping on a beacon dropped from an aircraft, and jumping on a visible directional arrow. These aided the precision of landings and the speed of assembly of the parachutists on the drop zone.

Experience taught us to engage in careful preliminary map reconnaissance of the suggested drop zone. We familiarized ourselves not only with the area immediately adjacent to the drop zone but with other areas which were more remote. For safety's sake, we always designated both primary and secondary assembly points. At that time, we also were able to work out necessary methods of delivering equipment without parachutes, in specially built but rather simple containers. A new way was developed for destroying trains on bridges. We constructed a mine which was actually picked up by the train from the roadbed near the bridge. The train itself would activate the mine, and the explosion would occur after a precisely calculated time had elapsed when the train was passing over a bridge.

The combat training of the partisans was going full tilt, and their artistry was improving. But the bravery and grit of our comrades surpassed that of people such as even Yakir and Baar themselves. During the summer, Yulka, one of the girls, jumped from an aircraft and didn't pop her chute in time. When she landed, she injured her leg so badly that she couldn't stand up. Despite the injury, she *crawled* to the assembly point and arrived there on time. Yulka was eighteen years old, a slender, graceful kid, training to become a partisan parachutist. But in that frail female body beat a fearless heart. After the tragic death of one of our parachutists, when others had lost their nerve, Yulka was the first to offer to jump from the next aircraft.

In those days, Rita, another female partisan, accompanied me in every field exercise. Tenacious, self-confident, always trying to do everything as well as possible, it seemed she didn't know the meaning of fatigue. When she came back from an exercise, she organized games and led singing. We loved to listen to her. Then one day near Kupyansk, when we were setting a mine on a well-guarded stretch of railroad, the blasting cap in the training mine that Rita held in her hands unexpectedly exploded, driving tiny fragments into her face and eyes, blinding her. She was bloodied, but silent. Without a sound, she accompanied me to school, where she was bandaged up, and then I accompanied her on the first train to the hospital in Khar'kov. On the operating table, Rita didn't make a sound. "What strength of character!" the ophthalmologist who was operating on her said. "How old is she?"

"Nineteen, Professor," I blurted out, without taking my eyes from the drawn face of the young girl. Every day until her recovery, I called on Rita, looked after her, and finally told her things that I had never said to any girl before.

Rita's vision was completely restored. We were so happy. It seemed to us that nothing could ever separate us. Nothing ever ...

Mission Accomplished?

By 1933, everything had been done to ensure that in the case of enemy aggression, we could unleash partisan warfare according to a previously developed plan not only on territory occupied by the enemy but in Bessarabia and in the western regions of the Ukraine, then part of eastern Poland. In all three of the USSR's border military districts (Leningrad, Belorussian, Ukrainian), a total of about nine thousand people had been trained to conduct partisan warfare in the enemy rear, including the Baltic states, mostly lost to the Germans in 1918, the areas of eastern Lithuania, western Belorussia, and the western Ukraine, which had been captured by the Poles in 1920, and even on the probable enemy's own territory if favorable political and environmental conditions existed for such warfare.

(Translator's note: it is assumed that the principal "probable enemy" referred to is Poland, although Romania is also definitely considered an enemy as well—see below.)

According to the famous Soviet partisan S. A. Vaupshasov, in Belorussia, six detachments had been raised, each with a strength of between three hundred and five hundred (in Minsk, Borisov, Slutsk, Bobruisk, Mozyr', and Polotsk). For each of these detachments, there was a trained staff, consisting of the detachment leader, his deputy, the deputy for political training, the chief of staff, the chief of intelligence, and a logistics assistant to the chief of staff. In the Belorussian woods, dumps of supplies and weapons had been created for each partisan detachment. Buried deep in the earth in carefully packed, pitch-covered boxes, were explosives and Bickford cord (Translators note: this is an early, more unstable, version of today's detonator cord), cartridges, grenades, 50,000 rifles, and 150 submachine guns. The sizes of the dumps were clearly not calculated on the initial numbers of partisan detachments, but on their anticipated rapid growth in the event of enemy occupation. Similar preparations were made in the Ukraine and in the Leningrad Military District. Large partisan detachments were not created in the Ukraine, but a significant number of smaller, highly maneuverable detachments and sabotage groups were trained and formed. Furthermore, in the Ukraine, more than eighty partisan organizational and sabotage groups, totaling over six hundred people, were formed. These consisted mainly of experienced and well-trained Soviet partisans and immigrants from Romania and Poland. On the territories of these nations, mainly in the formerly Soviet western districts of Moldavia and the Ukraine, drop zones had been designated, and we had people in place who would be able to help our parachutists. According to our plan, the majority of the groups trained to operate outside the borders of the USSR were to be dropped on the first nights after commencement of hostilities. The total quantity of cached supplies in the Ukraine and in the Bessarabian swamps amounted to hundreds of tons. In some areas, more supplies were stored for partisans in 1930–1933 than the partisans in those areas actually received during all of World War II. Foremost among these were the areas of Olevsk, Slavuta, Belokorovichi, Ovruch, and Korosten'. In addition to this, along the rail lines and in cities west of the line of the fortified areas, a network of highly trained and well-supplied sabotage groups was created. Further, many officers and political officers of the Red Army had been cross-trained in organization and tactics of partisan war in our special schools.

In addition, there was the enormous work that we had done with the commission in the last half of the twenties, preparing the railroads in the border regions so that barriers could be erected on them. As early as 1930, in the border regions of the Southwestern railroad (to depths of 180 to 200 kilometers from the border), everything was ready so that in case of a withdrawal of our troops, the enemy could not make any use of the railroad lines that he captured. For this purpose, by 1 January 1930, more than sixty demolitions teams, totaling fourteen hundred men, were raised and trained from personnel of the bridge guards and border troops. These units were to supplement the demolition teams of the two railroad regiments which were already deployed in Kiev. Further,

120 mine tubes, niches, and chambers for installing explosives on bridges were checked out and repaired. To ensure that ground communications lines would be cut in the event of a surprise attack, supply dumps were established in the places where the bridge guard demolitions teams were deployed, around the large bridges and railroad hubs. In these dumps, charges and fuses were kept in readiness. We even intended to use radio-controlled mines.

In field exercises, particularly those held in the Leningrad Military District in 1932, partisan detachments successfully conducted a series of ambushes, but—with the exception of my own sabotage action—attacks on staffs were unsuccessful since the guards were generally so vigilant that they detected the partisans on their approaches to the objectives. However, small sabotage groups were able to operate with outstanding effect on enemy communications routes. Even on heavily guarded stretches of railroad, the partisans contrived to set up so-called nuisance mines, which took less than thirty seconds to set up. On poorly guarded stretches of the road, the partisans were successful in applying the training version of the nonremovable antitrain mine.

On field exercises, regular troops were engaged in securing the rear area, but if overrun by the enemy, they switched to carrying out partisan activity in the enemy's rear. These exercises convincingly demonstrated that as a result of strong, surprise operations of partisan forces, it was possible to put enemy communications lines out of commission for long periods, and even to cut off his frontline troops from their sources of supply. In this activity, well-trained partisan formations, cleverly using various types of mines, remained absolutely invulnerable.

While large partisan detachments were generally observed on the approach to an objective, small sabotage groups were able to penetrate into settled areas where staff sections were deployed, and create confusion by use of training mines. All groups remained undetected in such activity.

If all these preparations for partisan warfare had been kept in place until the beginning of World War II, then, when Germany launched its surprise attack on the USSR, the enemy troops would have been without any ammunition, fuel, or lubricants by the time they got as far as Minsk and Kiev. It would have been impossible for the occupation forces to use the rail lines that they had taken, and at the same time, a fierce partisan war would have been unleashed in the enemy rear. The partisans would have been able to destroy the enemy automotive transport equipment.

You can imagine the kind of catastrophic situation in which the enemy frontline troops would have found themselves, with paralyzed lines of communication and a disorganized rear area. But this never happened!

It must be emphasized that the work of preparing for partisan war in the event of enemy aggression in 1929–1933 took place under most difficult conditions, connected with the forced collectivization of agriculture and the ensuing famine.

While I was working for the intelligence directorate (GRU) of the Red Army staff, I saw how much attention was devoted to the preparations for partisan war by the Central Committee of the Party and by the secretaries of the Party regional committees. It was said that Stalin also devoted great attention to these preparations. But as I now understand, the further course of preparations for partisan war were influenced by the circumstance that the active participants in all the plans and measures in this area were found to be "enemies of the people," and executed prior to World War II. For example, V. K. Blyukher frequently gave lectures at the Swierczewski school. I. E. Yakir, I. P. Uborevich, V. N. Primakov, and Ya. K. Berzin—all enemies of the people—were deeply involved in all questions of preparations for partisan war and gave particular close attention to the creation and improvement of special equipment needed for partisan war.

It all started on 27 December 1929 when Stalin, at a conference of agriculturalists, "initiated the transition to a policy of broad collectivization of agriculture and the liquidation, on this basis, of the kulaks as a class," as stated in his biography (Translators note: kulak, literally "fist," is a derogatory term used for landowner, implying brute force, tightfisted acquisitiveness, etc.). Stalin's address formed the basis for the Central Committee decree of 5 January 1930, entitled: "Concerning the tempo of collectivization and measures to assist in organization of collective farms."

Forced collectivization, liquidation of the so-called kulaks, and the actual genocide of the most productive peasantry, was "the first commandment." In accordance with this commandment, the collective farmer's delivery of grain and the other foodstuffs that they had grown was not conducted *after* the fall field work, but *during* the course of the harvest. In a situation of severely limited draft equipment (at that time there were no autos in villages and very few even in cities—hence the driver training provided by Osoaviakhim mentioned earlier), the need to deliver the harvest to storage points made it impossible to actually gather in all of the harvest on time, and part of it spoiled in the field. The hasty, stoppage-plagued delivery of the grain to the storage points led in turn to a delay in autumn sowing. Despite the reduced grain harvest, the plans for storage were not only fulfilled, but overfulfilled, with the result that only miserly amounts of grain were left to be distributed to the collective farm workers for each workday. As a result, a famine began, striking the most productive regions, some of which had never even suffered from drought.

We do not have exact figures of the number of so-called kulaks who died, kulaks who never really exploited anyone, but more than one million died in exile in the north, and in uninhabitable regions of Siberia. Even more died of hunger. In Kazakhstan alone, 2.5 million died, in the Ukraine about 5 million, and others were dying from famine in the Volga regions and even in the northern Caucasus. Stalin's forced collectivization led to the deaths of millions of peasants, principally those who could farm most effectively. This sharply reduced the nation's readiness for war, and accelerating the process of industrialization could not compensate for the losses. You can imagine the mood of the soldiers of the Red Army whose parents were either "dekulakized" or died from hunger. This had an especially pernicious effect on the preparations that had been made for partisan warfare.

Even our trained partisan cadres were dekulakized, particularly those who had been designated as future underground partisans. As early as 1930, there had been arrests of some immigrants, originally from the formerly Soviet western regions of the Ukraine who were returning from our school to their residences in the USSR. The western Ukraine was, at that time, occupied by the Poles, and the immigrants had been trained by us to conduct partisan warfare in their home regions in the event of an attack on our nation.

In many cases, we learned of such misfortunes in advance and did everything possible to help the innocent suffering people. Some exiled partisans even were able to escape from the transport trains heading into exile, and returned to us. Party regional committees and personnel of the OGPU in border regions, particularly the Moldavian and Ukrainian SSRs, took measures to rescue the dispossessed and starving partisan cadres from the arrests and deportations being carried out by other branches of the OGPU. These cadres were removed from population centers and settled in sugar factories or wood processing plants where they would not starve. Several future partisan detachment commanders were even designated directors of forest industry collectives and sugar factories. In some cases, the partisans were also given food. But the famine in the Ukraine, resulting from Stalinist policies, led to a sharp reduction in the number of the bases forming the foundation for conducting partisan warfare, and this adversely affected the tempo of the deployment of the partisan movement during World War II. In the purges of the late thirties, however, the arrests of the high-ranking so-called enemies of the people turned out to be fatal for many of the partisans who had survived this round of purges. They were declared to be *accomplices* of enemies of the people and were most often shot.

In an attempt to save themselves from famine, some peasants buried grain in hidden caches. Official food-gathering detachments were searching for these caches. It was therefore necessary for us to carefully select the sites for our own weapons and supply caches, and camouflage them so that they would not be discovered. Such discoveries would have led to the most serious consequences.

The results of the great efforts carried on in our country to prepare for partisan war in the case of enemy aggression, and damaged by arbitrary Stalinist policies at the beginning of the thirties, were ultimately liquidated in the purges of 1937–1938, but they did not vanish completely. The specialists who had been trained during that period provided significant help in raising the effectiveness of the Chinese partisans against the Japanese occupation forces and in initiating and carrying on partisan warfare in the rear areas of the German and Italian interventionists and rebels in the Spanish national revolutionary war in 1936–1939.

The trained cadre who survived the famines, the arrests, and the purges of the later thirties—*only about ninety personnel (1 percent of the nine thousand trained)*—were the first chiefs of partisan schools during World War II, and more than ten men became commanders or commissars of famous partisan units and formations, among which were: Heroes of the Soviet Union S. A. Vaupshasov, S. V. Rudnev, N. A. Prokopyuk, K. Orlovskiy, and others.

To the Academy

In April 1933, the plenum of the Central Committee passed a resolution to purge Party ranks. Over eight hundred thousand Party members were purged during the course of the year by a special Purge Commission, which included the relatively unknown N. I. Yezhov, who was later to become the architect of the Great Terror. The increasingly ominous internal situation is well reflected in Starinov's personal experiences at this point.

In April 1933, Rita saw me off to Moscow: I had been transferred to the Main Intelligence Directorate of the central staff of the People's Commissariat for Defense—i.e., the GRU.

"I'll get established and then you can join me," I said, standing on the platform. "Promise me?"

Tightly holding my hand, Rita remained silent.

"What's wrong? Why don't you answer me?"

Rita squeezed my hand: "Don't get upset . . . everything will be all right . . ."

I felt much relieved. "Write often."

"Yes."

"I'll be waiting for your letters!"

"Yes."

Long after the station platform had disappeared from sight, I remained on the platform at the end of the car. An unaccountable feeling of concern came over me. Rita had looked at me too intently, had been too monosyllabic in her answers.

It's nothing, I thought, everything will get settled, everything will be straightened out.

And I was *so* wrong.

My new work got off to a disappointing start. Collecting papers, composing answers to inquiries, spending long hours in boring clerical work—this really wasn't for me. Nothing pleased me, and maybe there were reasons for that. But, I was promoted to military engineer third rank; I was assigned a good room near the center of the city, and my pay was increased.

It seemed as if my teaching at the school (where they were still training partisans) had been just a brief interlude. In the capital, however, I became convinced that preparations for future partisan warfare were not being expanded, but gradually being closed down.

Attempts to speak with my GRU department chief, M. Sakhnovskaya, on this subject produced no result. Sakhnovskaya held me in check, observing that the main thing was no longer the training of partisan cadres (there were already enough of them!), but in the practical consolidation of the work that had already been done.

Lots of unresolved practical questions had, in fact, accumulated, but our directorate wasn't responsible for resolving them.

The future legendary hero of Republican Spain, Karol Swierczewski (known under the cover name General Walter, and familiar to readers of Ernest Hemingway as General Golz of *For Whom the Bell Tolls*) was reassuring: "Up there at The Top," he said, "the leaders know best." I also believed in this. But it was becoming more and more difficult to reconcile this belief with my growing internal protest, and I became depressed. Friends from the 4th Korosten' Red Banner Regiment whom I met in Moscow strongly advised me to enter the academy.

I took their advice. I myself was beginning to feel that my knowledge was inadequate in many areas. It was true that I had previously made two attempts to enter the Military Transport Academy, and had been twice rejected on the grounds of my heart condition, but now it began to seem as if I had simply not displayed the required tenacity and energy in pursuing those attempts.

After acquainting myself with the programs of the departments of particular specialties, where my friends were studying, I convinced myself that I could very well enter the second course directly without taking the first course. And I took the chance—the chance of a humiliating failure if I couldn't handle the course work.

I had just been put on the roster in the department of Mirra Sakhnovskaya. She was an experienced, energetic, and courageous woman, among the first to be decorated with the Order of the Red Star. Later, I learned that she paid more dearly than I did for inadequacies in our work. All her professional proposals were rejected somewhere up above . . . I reported to her my intentions of entering the academy. Sakhnovskaya accepted them, wrote me an evaluation report, and wished me luck in my training.

The rest depended on the chief of our directorate, Ya. K. Berzin.[1] He certainly would be able to assist me in overcoming the obstacles in the road to the Military Transport Academy. Yan Berzin is hardly mentioned by kids today because he was slandered and destroyed, and his deeds condemned to oblivion during the years of Stalin's cult of personality. In my youth, however, Soviet boys and girls read and heard a lot about the selflessness, resourcefulness, and fearlessness of this eminent revolutionary.

In the spring of 1906, a group of militant workers attacked a store to expropriate money for the Party. Such operations were frequently conducted in the Latvian region, and V. I. Lenin made positive reference to them in his writings.

On this occasion, however, the operation failed. The police began to pursue the perpetrators. To lose his pursuers, young Peteris Kjuzis (Ya. K. Berzin's real name) swam the Ogra River with a pistol in his teeth. The police wounded the brave youngster and captured him. The trial took place in Revel. At the time of the attack on the store, Kjuzis was not yet seventeen years old, which saved him from the firing squad, but not from prison. Coming out of confinement in 1909, Peteris Kjuzis departed for Riga and resumed active underground work, but soon the youngster was detained again. He was one of the authors of antigovernment leaflets and participated in their distribution. The prisoner was exiled to the Kirensk District of the Irkutsk region of Siberia.

The war began, and Kjuzis got some documents in the name of "Yan Karlovich Berzin" and escaped from exile to his native Riga. A member of the Bolshevik party from 1905, Berzin took part in the armed defense of the Soviet state after the October Revolution, and after the civil war, he directed one of the directorates of the Red Army staff.

Fame notwithstanding, Yan Berzin remained a simple, sincere man. Setting out to solicit his help, I felt neither timidity nor concern.

The recommendations I got from Yan Karlovich enabled me to overturn the findings of the medical board. The chief of the Military Transport Academy, S. A. Pugachev, wrote a note on my application to enroll me in the academy.

Semen Andreyevich Pugachev was also universally esteemed in the army. The Order of the Red Star, and the Orders of the Bu-

1. Yan Karlovich Berzin (Peteris Kjuzis) became a member of the Communist party in 1905, took part in the revolutions of 1905 and February and October 1917. He joined the Red Army in 1919, and during the civil war served as chief of the political directorate of a division and chief of the Special Section (military counterintelligence) of an army. Beginning in 1921, he served in the intelligence directorate (IGU) of the Red Army, and from 1924 to 1935, and again in 1937, he was chief of that directorate. He was senior Soviet military adviser in Spain during 1936–1937. After his return from Spain, he was arrested in 1937 as an enemy of the people and executed in 1938.

khara and Orezm Republics glistened on his chest. Even during the civil war, I had often heard of S. A. Pugachev. A well-educated former general staff officer of the tsarist army, he had actively participated in the armed defense of the achievements of the October revolution. In 1934, on the recommendation of G. K. Orzhonikidze and S. M. Kirov, the Central Committee of the Communist party accepted him into the Party.

Pugachev himself appended a note of approval on my application, but the senior clerk of the student company refused to enter my name on the enrollment list because, he claimed, the enrollment limit had already been reached! So I had to wait around for two weeks to get a meeting with E. F. Appoga, the chief of military transportation for the Red Army.

"You see how simple it all is," the senior clerk said with a smile when he accepted my properly completed paperwork.

I preferred to hold my tongue.

One last obstacle had to be overcome: I wanted to enter directly into the second course. Pugachev attempted to talk me out of this venture, but help arrived in the person of Dmitriyev, chief of the railroad faculty of the academy, who, behind his back, was affectionately known as Kuzmich to the students.

"Look, Starinov has slipped by this way for so many years [1922 to 1933]. He's got so much time in service that it would be a shame to delay further. Let him try!" he said, delicately contradicting the chief of the academy, and looking down at his magnificent moustache.

And Pugachev agreed.

It seemed as if everything was going well, and my life was gradually getting into a groove so I decided that it was time to call Rita, and so I wrote to Kiev. Time passed, but no answer came. I sent one telegram, then another. Finally, a postcard arrived. It was in Rita's handwriting, but the content was incomprehensible. It was as if the card was not intended for me, and even the signature was unusual.

I wasn't going to be kept in the dark about this. I put in a request and got permission to go on leave. On the way, I bought a paper and tried reading, to take my mind off my concerns. But the papers of that period couldn't begin to calm your nerves. There was alarming news from Germany, where they were burying democracy and culture—violence against authors and scholars; Jew baiting; torture in Gestapo prisons; the nightmare of the concentration camps; burning books on the streets of Leipzig; the growth of the *Wehrmacht*; Hitler's delirious ravings about the need to put an end to Communism . . .

Yes, the newspapers made me even more concerned, but even more strongly, in spite of everything else, I wanted simple human happiness, the nearness of a loved one.

Straight from the train, I set out for the address shown on the postcard. It was a plain house on a quiet street, with a dingy stairwell, with broken stairs, and a door covered in dark oilcloth.

At my knock, a strange woman opened the door. I identified myself.

The woman hesitated, running her hands through her hair.

At first there was no response, but then she sighed . . .

"She's no longer here."

"What do you mean 'no longer here'? Where the hell is she?"

The woman lifted her face; she was sympathetic and embarrassed: "I don't know, believe me, She simply went away."

I excused myself and left. The door with the dark oilcloth covering slammed shut. I left behind the stairway with the broken stairs, in the plain house, on the plain street . . . until the spring of 1944.

A New Assignment

Two years of intensive study followed, and then May 1935 was on the doorstep. Spring was early and gentle: the snow disappeared at the beginning of April, and the forests were already decked with new leaves. On the corners, like mushrooms after a rain, the soft-drink vendors popped up, and the variegated stalls of the ice-cream vendors, who had disappeared somewhere or other during the winter, appeared once more. Couples in love tarried in doorways and entrances almost until dawn.

On the eve of the May Day celebration, the capital was spruced up. Banners hung across the streets, and buildings sprouted flags. The nation added up the results of the First of May competitions. The radio and the press reported on the triumphs of the Magnitka and Kuzbass miners, about the overfulfillment of the production plans in terms of tons of coal, iron, steel, and petroleum, and about the successes of the collective farms. Moscow was happy.

And we, the graduates of the military academies were also happy, possibly more happy than others, because we'd received a higher military education.

Early on May 1, we stood motionless in neat ranks on Red Square, listening to the melodious chimes of the carillon.

On the reviewing stand on Lenin's Tomb, the leaders of the Party and the government came out. The parade commander, A. I. Kork, mounted on his bay, met the people's commissar for defense, K. Ye. Voroshilov, mounted on his jumping horse.

An enormous *"Ura!"* rang out. And in perfect step, we filed past the tomb.

And on 4 May, we were invited to the Kremlin. After the parade, holding our collective breath, we academy graduates listened to Stalin's address. It was the first time that I had seen him so close, and the more I looked at him, the less that little man with the bushy moustache and the low forehead resembled the Stalin that we were used to seeing in photos and signs.

Stalin talked about those things which concerned everyone, about people and cadres. And how convincingly he spoke! There I heard for the first time the statement: "Cadres decide everything." For my entire life, it was engraved in my memory how important it was to concern oneself about people and to take care of them.

Even now I see the carefree happy face of the chief of our academy, Pugachev, and Vani Kir'yanov, a former locomotive engineer and academy graduate, who was sitting beside me.

Before three years had gone by, those two were arrested and shot as a result of groundless accusations, a fate which befell not only them but probably the majority of those who were present at the reception and enthusiastically listened to Stalin.

I finished the academy with outstanding grades and was awarded an engraved watch. Along with the other top students, I was recommended for an assignment on the staff of the People's Commissariat for Transport Communications (*Narodniy kommissariat putei soobshcheniya* = NKPS). The graduates of our academy eagerly went to the NKPS—they were offered high positions there. But I refused: by then I'd served about sixteen years in the Red Army and didn't wish to be separated from it.

Soon, I was called to the military communications department of the Red Army and told that I had been assigned to the post of deputy military commandant of the Leningrad to Moscow railroad sector, the directorate of which was located in the station of the Leningrad-Moscow railroad line. My facial expression obviously spoke more clearly than words about how I received these news. A friend, learning of my new assignment, frowned and thought it necessary to give me a lecture: "They have accorded you a great honor ... quite aside from the fact that you are to support the work of our directorate from the military point of view . . ." In his voice there appeared unexpectedly a solemn note, it seemed almost as if it were a note of genuine pathos, ". . . to you has fallen the honor of meeting and escorting senior military officers!"

I understood that you couldn't get a better assignment, and I kept quiet. What I didn't know was that I would have died in that job had I remained there until the purges of the summer of 1937 because I worked in the sector headquarters under Yakir and Berzin, and had escorted Tukhachevskiy and Primakov, all of whom were destined to be "repressed" as enemies of the people, and anyone even remotely associated with them shared their fates.

The Leningrad commander's office was located in a busy area. Party and government leaders, key figures of the People's Commissariat for Defense, the general staff, and military district commanders frequently arrived in Leningrad. Our duty consisted in meeting them and escorting them from Leningrad to Moscow, making sure that no railroad equipment problems would mar their journey.

I frequently had the occasion to escort Blyukher, Tukhachevskiy, Voroshilov, and Shaposhnikov, who was then the commander of the Leningrad Military District. We were often invited to tea or to dinner with Shaposhnikov and Tukhachevskiy.

One of those dinners with Tukhachevskiy sticks in my memory. At that time, Fascist Italy was attacking Ethiopia. The Italian command made extensive use of containers for delivering the huge quantities of cargo required, and containers were the subject of our dinner conversation. The marshal showed foreign journals in which there were many photos of on-loading and off-loading cargo containers. I was particularly shocked by the photos of the dead Ethiopians and captured Ethiopian prisoners.

When everyone else had departed, I began a discussion with the marshal on the need to be prepared for partisan warfare.

Tukhachevskiy had been standing thoughtfully at the window. He turned and listened attentively to me, then took one of the journals and found a map of the military action in Ethiopia. On the map, partisan operational areas were shown by shading. The marshal didn't respond quickly, but glanced from the maps to the text of the summary. "Look what they say here!" he finally said. "At the beginning of the war, the Ethiopian army numbered about 450,000, with 47 cannon and 7 aircraft. And the aggressor, with 340,000 troops, had about 350 cannon, about 200 tanks, and 270 aircraft. During the course of the war, the numbers of Italian troops and equipment increased, but those of the Ethiopians diminished, and their stores of weapons and ammunition were not replenished. The Ethiopians were forced to go over to partisan warfare, and sustained enormous losses. With us, Comrade Railroad Engineer, it's a totally different situation. We have completely modern tanks, in sufficient quantity, and powerful artillery. And even when our aircraft are just flying in review, they arouse fear in the enemy. Furthermore, our border—from Lake Ladoga right to the Black Sea—is covered by strong fortified areas."

On the table before Tukhachevsky was a pamphlet. After looking at it, he continued: "All this has given Comrade Stalin the basis for saying, at the seventeenth Party Congress, that anyone who tries to attack our country will be dealt a crushing blow. And now, two years, later, we are even stronger . . ."

Mikhail Nikolayevich smiled about something; possibly he was thinking of his own speech at the seventeenth Congress.

"Comrade Marshal of the Soviet Union, may I have your permission to speak? If war is initiated against the Soviet Union, it will have to be conducted not only on the fronts but in the enemy rear. And it's there that you may need officer cadres and entire units capable of conducting partisan warfare. It will definitely be necessary to train them for it and to support them with radio communications and other special equipment."

The marshal made no response. He clearly didn't want to talk about partisan warfare and returned to the subject of containers.

"How do you like the Italians' metal containers, Comrade Military Engineer?"

"Not at all."

"Why?"

"Maybe they're great for transporting freight," I said with embarrassment, "but it's easier for the Ethiopian partisans to destroy the wooden containers."

The marshal was once more silent. The pause became strained, so I again risked addressing Tukhachevskiy.

"If, for example, the Ethiopian partisans use a large quantity of mines against the interventionist vehicles and tanks, then they can force the enemy to divert much of his forces to protecting his lines of communications, and weaken the Italian strike force. Mines are really very easy to make. You could even use a matchbox for a detonator switch."

"How interesting! How do you make a detonator switch out of a matchbox?"

I was pleased by his interest, and right there on the spot I assembled a detonator switch from a common matchbox.

"Clever," said Tukhachevskiy with approval. "The only problem is that the Ethiopians have neither electric batteries, nor electric blasting caps, and very limited explosives. This really isn't suitable for them. They need something, but it must be from the most simple kinds of equipment."

"May I show you a simple device to destroy an automobile tire?"

From crumbs of black bread, I quickly made a model of a device for puncturing a tire.

"Now, that's another story. That might work for them . . ."

"Really, Comrade Marshal, wouldn't such toys be suitable for our troops in the enemy rear?"

Tukhachevskiy again avoided a response. Then he sighed, and with a strange intensity, he said, "I'm involved with other questions . . . and it's really very late. Good night."

The train approached Malaya Vishera. At the stop, I quickly checked the running gear of the cars, and returned to my compartment. Very disturbing thoughts had arisen during my talk with Tukhachevskiy, the deputy people's commissar for defense.

Could it be that my conceptions of the importance of partisan warfare were hopelessly outmoded?[1]

A Friend in Need is a Friend Indeed

In the fall of 1935, trouble suddenly descended upon me. A verification of Party documents was being conducted.[1] I was called to the political department of the special troops of the Moscow garrison. The chief of the political department, after suggesting that I sit down, studied my Party card for a long time.

I had known the chief of the political department for a long time, but he seemed to have changed somehow.

"So . . . you're *really* Starinov?" he finally broke the silence.

"Yes, I am definitely Starinov, and I hope that my Party card is in order."

"Save your questions. Better that you just answer me: didn't you agree with the resolution of the opposition?"

1. As Starinov has pointed out above, the term *saboteur* (*diversantnik*) and the general topic of sabotage and partisan warfare had become politically incorrect after the murder of Kirov in 1934.
1. These verification proceedings were related to Stalin's prolonged campaign to rid himself of political opposition, a campaign which culminated in the purges of 1937–38. An integral part of this campaign was an effort to identify "enemies of the Party and working class," initiated by a secret Party decree of 19 May 1935, which kicked off widespread denunciations in Party·circles.

"No!"

He reflected a minute and then asked: "You were imprisoned by the Whites?"

"Yes, I was. This is set forth in my personnel file, and in my autobiography.[2] I escaped the first night in prison and returned to my own Twentieth Infantry Regiment!"

"That's what you say, and that's what you've written! But who really knows how you were captured and how you were released? Where's the proof that you escaped?"

"There are documents in the archives . . . and my buddies are still alive!"

"Documents . . . buddies . . ."

The chief of the political department once again sank into deep thought, and after a little while reemerged in the kind and sincere guise in which I had previously known him. Then he once more examined my Party card—which he had not released from his hand—and asked:

"Could it be that you're not Starinov, but Starikov?"

"In our village there were four Starinov households, but not one Starikov," I responded, restraining myself with difficulty.

My interlocutor averted his eyes. Pursing his lips, he was silent, obviously coming to some sort of a decision, and then he declared:

"All your words must be verified and proved. Collect your references—but for now, your Party card stays with us."

I must have looked totally confused because the chief of the political department rattled off some quick advice:

"Don't lose your head . . . Collect the necessary documents. We'll make an inquiry to the archives . . ."

His expression displayed no animosity. He seemed to me to be somewhat embarrassed himself.

I don't remember how I got back to the commandant's office. The face of that kindest of all bosses, Boris Ivanovich Filippov, grew long when he learned what had happened.

"How could this be, my dear boy?"

I couldn't discuss the details. I was deeply depressed because it had occurred to me that Boris Ivanovich, with all his good intentions, wouldn't do anything to help. I knew how careful he was. And there stood the political department . . . They suspected me of deliberate alteration of my family name, deception of the Party, of treason almost . . .

"Here's what we'll do, dear boy. Let's go to my place. Yes.

2. Starinov is referring to a detailed autobiography, completed as part of reliability evaluations used in, e.g., Party applications or security clearance processes.

And we'll go fishing. This evening we'll return from fishing," I heard the agitated voice of Boris Ivanovich. "We'll request leave for you, send you off to wherever you need to go, and you'll return with the necessary papers. Don't be upset; let's go fishing!"

I appreciated the friendly sympathy, but I turned down the invitation, went home, and threw myself on my bed.

The telephone rang. It seemed that Boris Ivanovich had already been able to visit the directorate of railroads and the staff of the military district." "Everything's in order, dear boy! You've been given leave. Go for your documents. And don't be worried. Everything will work out all right!"

And that evening I departed, to collect the documents to prove that I was indeed Starinov, that I had actually escaped from prison, and that I had honestly fought for Soviet power.

First, I went to the academy.

"What the hell!" exclaimed Dmitriyev, the chief of the faculty, when he had heard my story. "You just wait a minute . . ."

He got a piece of paper and wrote out a certification in his own hand.

"Everything will be settled, Ilya Grigor'yevich," he said. "You yourself have heard Comrade Stalin. You recall that he appealed to us to protect and value the cadres. This is simply some kind of misunderstanding, and possibly even slander."

Then I had to head for my home village.

I got off the train at Orel with a large rucksack. Knowing that you couldn't buy much in the village stores, I had provided myself with sugar, herring, and white bread.

In 1935, busses didn't go from Orel into the villages, and so I had to walk along the roadside. The Volkhov road was long and muddy after the rains. The chill fall winds were blowing. It was a sad prospect. But along came a line of carts—would they give me a lift, or not? On the first cart sat a peasant. There was something surprisingly familiar in the thin, unshaven face with its inimitable sly smile. If you took off the patched homespun coat and trousers, and the bast sandals, and then dressed him in a Red Army tunic with boots and puttees . . .

"Alesha!" I cried, "Alesha, is that you?"

An older, graying Alesha, my comrade in arms from the 20th Infantry Regiment, did not jump down, but slid right off the cart. We embraced each other affectionately, tore ourselves apart, and then embraced once more.

"How many years has it been, Grigor'yevich?" Alesha mumbled. "Not more than ten, is it? What winds blew you to us?"

Other cart drivers ran up. Someone slapped me on the shoulder. I looked around—and my eyes couldn't believe what I saw standing before me, extending his work-hardened hands, was Arkhip Denisovich Tsarkov; the same Arkhip whose deft touch had led me to become a sapper, way back when.

"Arkhip!"

"Ilyushka!"

"I don't recognize you, Arkhip . . ."

"And you've changed, too. See, you're traveling with the big shots now."

"Rank doesn't mean anything! I'm just so happy to see you guys, my own people . . ."

"It's not right to hang around there on the road," one of the carters commented sensibly. "Let's drive on. You can gab all you want at home!"

The cart train began to move. Sitting on the cart alongside Arkhip Tsarkov and Aleksey Bakayev, I told them what had brought me to the village. Both my friends were surprised and angry.

"You mean they didn't believe you? That's great! You fought right through to the end! They sent you to school because you were a good fighter! What the hell is going on?"

Then Arkhip Tsarkov said angrily, "What bonehead didn't believe that you are really Starinov? It's easy to see that he's never been in our village. There are only five families all together: the Bakayevs, Trunkovs, Klimovs, Starinovs, and us, the Tsarkovs! If your chief doesn't know the people from Orel, then he's goofing off! Don't you doubt it for a minute! All of us will do what's right, we'll confirm your identity. Furthermore, there are other friends still living in nearby villages!"

I stayed with Arkhip Tsarkov: his family was smaller than the Bakayevs, and his cottage was more spacious. I sat down at the table. The lady of the house served up potatoes from a cast-iron pot. I pulled out my herring and bread . . .

Later, I lay down to sleep, but I was freezing: Arkhip didn't have much kerosene for his heater. On the following day, Tsarkov and I set out for the neighboring village to search out friends who remembered me well. We found more than a few, and I collected a whole stack of references. To get the references notarized, we went to the city of Bol'kov, where everything went off without a hitch. My joy would have been complete if I hadn't noticed the neglected huts, the fields and kitchen gardens overgrown with weeds, and the dark windows.

"Heard rumors about this? If nobody plays the accordion, then the whores don't sing," said Arkhip at one point. "The youngsters try to go off to the city, and the people who stay behind get sent off to exile. Crap! If only they conducted collectivization the way they told us they would in the political indoctrination sessions! If only the collective farms looked differently, and we were able to tend to the cattle! I suppose that the biggest difficulties are already past. This year, for example, we sowed more, and the work went more happily. The Party is setting things right in the collective farms! We'll live again!"

Just as when we served in the sapper company, Arkhip was once more clean-shaven, smartly dressed, and feared neither God nor the devil.

He accompanied me to Orel.

"So, Arkhip! Do you think you're going to live again?"

"We'll live!" He shouted emphatically from the station platform. "Good luck to you!"

Boris Ivanovich Fillipov greeted me happily. He examined the mountain of statements that I brought, and endorsed my expensive efforts.

"Paperwork—that's what counts now, my dear boy!"

I carried the statements to the political department. They told me that they would check them all, and in the meantime, advised me to wait. I waited a long time. I was temporarily barred from working with secret documents, and not sent on VIP escort duty.

Throughout this process, Boris Ivanovich suffered no less than I, but he firmly believed in a favorable outcome. "The main thing, dear boy, is that your paperwork is in order!" And he immediately invited me, now for tea, now for a fishing trip.

At last the call came from the political department of the special troops of the Moscow garrison. The chief of the political department greeted me: "Well, everything checks out" he said. "Now no one will have a reason to worry about you. I know it wasn't easy for you to get all this stuff, but . . ." When the formalities were all finished, the department chief handed me a new Party card, and firmly clasping my hand, looked at me with embarrassment, in an almost friendly manner. His embarrassment was difficult for me to take.

And then the office, the corridor, and the stairway were behind me. On the street I felt in my left breast pocket. I had my Party card! I sped off to the commander's office.

"Boris Ivanovich!"

He understood it all without hearing a word. He made me sit down, rubbing his hands with glee. "This is really something, dear boy! God sees the truth!" And with a happy grin, he suddenly knit his brows: "Comrade Starinov, prepare to escort Army Commander First Rank Shaposhnikov. Today!"

Obviously pleased with the effect which he had produced, Fillipov winked and laughed. "It's a good life, despite all that, dear boy! What did I tell you?"

Road to the Pyrenees

The summer of 1936 brought warm cloudless days, bright nights, and alarming news from the wire services: in Spain, where the Popular Front had won the election in February, Fascist generals were openly opposing the legal government.

No one doubted for a minute that Franco and his followers were going to be "muzzled." The rebels, having tricked a portion of the army, would not take a stand against the people anywhere. But Fascist Germany and Italy came to the rebels' assistance. Hitler and Mussolini sent the rebels aircraft, tanks, and regular units.

All over our country, spontaneous meetings bubbled up, and demonstrations of solidarity with Republican Spain were held.

The Soviet people decided to provide our struggling Spanish brothers not only with moral support but with material assistance. Equipment was collected, and worker contributions quickly rose into the millions.

Spain became the front line of the fight for democracy. Weapons in their hands, German and Italian antifascists, Englishmen and Americans, Czechs, Poles, and Hungarians, all went to Spain to fight fascism. Leningrad youngsters even began to greet each other with the gesture of the Popular Front—the raised fist. And I was no longer comfortable in the quiet office of the military commandant.

Spain could really get along without me, but I dreamed of it, all the same. It seemed to me that my partisan training and some of the other military specialties that I had mastered could be of assistance to the Republican Army. I also knew that volunteers from our country were going to Spain! So, after long reflection, I wrote a memo to Voroshilov, the people's commissar for defense, requesting that I be sent to Spain, giving a detailed account of the plans that I had worked out for training Republican troops to operate in the enemy rear. The memo went off quickly to its destination. I was called in for several interviews. Beyond interrogating me on the source of my knowledge that volunteers were being sent from the USSR to Spain, however, the matter never went further.

Then, one day in the railroad station, I happened to meet the former chief of the railroad faculty of the Military Transport Academy of the Red Army, M. V. Obyden. Almost from the first minute of our conversation, we were talking about Spain. Mikhail Vasil'yevich was a veteran of World War I and the civil war, and an old Party member who knew me well from the academy. Naturally, I told him about my desire to go beyond the Pyrenees.

"I'll have to think about it," Obyden responded with hesitation.

"What do you mean, 'Think about it'?"

"Maybe you already know . . . this really has to be held in confidence between the two of us! . . . I have some involvement with sending volunteers."

I couldn't believe my ears. I didn't pull myself together right away.

"Mikhail Vasil'yevich!"

"Hold on, hold on! I can't promise you anything! I'll inform the leadership of your desires, and it'll all be decided up above."

"Mikhail Vasil'yevich!"

"Okay, I'll give it a try."

Obyden left for Moscow, and three days later, a telegram arrived: "Deputy Railway Sector Military Commandant Starinov ordered to report immediately to Moscow."

"So you got what you wanted after all. You want me to believe that meeting with Obyden was really accidental?" Boris Ivanovich said, helplessly raising his hands. "Well, no matter; well done! I'm envious! I wish you success, Ilya Grigor'yevich!"

"Thanks! Don't hold a grudge against me. I hope that I won't stay too long," and I shook Filippov's hand. "Wait for me!"

"We'll have to wait, impatiently, at home. But you'll come back after the victory."

My military training satisfied the comrades in Moscow who were sending off volunteers to Spain. But what could be done about the language problem? "Maybe, I can study . . ." I said shyly to the tall young brigade commander (i.e. brigadier general), Gai Lazarevich Tumanyan.

"You won't be able to. We're going to try to find an interpreter for you."

"That would be great! Just one thing, though, he's got to know the specifics of demolitions."

"We'll look . . ."

They looked, and they found an interpreter, all right, but—she was *female*.

I was simply dumbstruck when I saw the tall, beautiful girl in the office of G. L. Tumanyan. "Comrade Starinov, meet your interpreter. She's also a volunteer," he said solemnly. The girl shook her closely cropped red hair, and extended a cool, delicate hand.

"Anna Obrucheva," she said in a deep contralto, accenting the *o* in the manner of the northerners.

I looked at Tumanyan in confusion and smiled uncertainly at Obrucheva, avoiding the glance of her big blue eyes.

Obrucheva had been born Anna Kornilovna, far to the north, in the little village of Dorogorsk, on the banks of the Mezen' River. In her youth, Anna had worked for farmers and reindeer herders, but after the revolution had quickly become involved with Party work in the field of antireligious propaganda and Communist women's organizations. She was accepted as a Party candidate in 1926, and spent three years working as a district women's organizer, after which she entered the Latin American Department of the historical-economic faculty of the Eastern Yenukidze Institute of Foreign Languages at Leningrad, majoring in Spanish, but studying English, too. After graduation, she was assigned as a translator at the International Leninist School of the Comintern, where Spanish speakers were being trained in subversion. Somewhere along the way, she had been married and had a daughter who would be cared for by a sister while she was in Spain. In addition to her language capabilities, she had been trained in marksmanship in the premilitary courses that she got at the institute, and had learned first aid working with the Russian Society of the Red Cross, all of which would help her in serving as interpreter for a partisan leader!

At evening of the same day, Anna Obrucheva and I stood on the platform of Belorussian station, alongside the Moscow-Stolbce train, which was preparing to depart. Anna was traveling under her own name. I was no longer a Red Army military engineer third class, but carried the papers of a Russian civilian named Aleksandr Porokhniak! The comrades who saw us off behaved like tactful, concerned relatives. One thing was annoying: they urged us a bit too forcefully not to worry about our families, and they hinted that whatever might happen, they wouldn't forget our relatives. These protestations of concern didn't bother me at all—I was a bachelor. But Anna Obrucheva was leaving an eight-year-old daughter behind in Moscow! And she still behaved like a youngster!

Starinov and Obrucheva crossed the Polish border at Stolbce, southwest of Minsk, probably in early October 1936. Although Starinov and Anna were both concerned that Polish counterintelligence might be aware of him and his role in running partisans and intelligence agents into Poland, they crossed the border without incident. Passing through Warsaw, Vienna, and Switzerland on their rail journey, they stopped briefly in Paris for liaison with the Soviet embassy and to purchase equipment for use in Spain. In Paris they joined another Soviet volunteer, Pavel Iosifovich Lipin, who was an armor adviser.[1] In early November, Starinov, Obrucheva, and Lipin crossed the Spanish border at Port Bou, in the extreme northeast corner of Spain, and proceeded directly to Barcelona. There, Starinov was disgusted by what he felt was the frivolous attitude which the population displayed toward the war. Their stay in Barcelona was short, however.

The government of Republican Spain was located in Valencia, along with the representatives of the military authority to which I was to report. So, with the first morning train to Valencia, Anna, Pavel, and I set off once more on our way. At last, we'd arrive at the destination, bring our protracted "tourist" itinerary to a close, and get to work! But trains in those days weren't as fast as they are today: to cross the 350 kilometers separating Barcelona from Valencia took a whole day. The train arrived at the platform in the evening. Volunteers met us, so there was no need to search out our contacts. They sent us off to the hotel immediately.

In Valencia, the hot breath of war was evident. The vehicles and carts of refugees, crammed with simple belongings, most forcibly reminded us of that. Then the sirens howled, warning of the approach of enemy aircraft. Wailing women just intensified the turmoil. Many people didn't budge an inch, however, and just gazed dejectedly at the sky, unable to resist the enemy with anything more than gloomy contempt, from which were born courage and steadfastness.

That evening, the Fascist bombers hit Valencia. Next morning, however, the newspaper vendors were shouting about the victory of the Republican troops, and flowers were being sold on the crowded squares. Republican Spain joyously welcomed the latest news: a routine rebel frontal attack on Madrid had been beaten back with great enemy casualties. The Fascists once more failed

---

1. Pavel Lipin went on to fight in the Winter War against the Finns and in World War II. Severely wounded in the campaigns along the Volga, he finished the war training tankers.

to get through! It appeared that things in Spain were not at all as bad as described in the bourgeois newspapers.

But the danger didn't pass, after all. The government of Largo Caballero didn't do everything possible to ensure victory. The anarchists on the Republican side were committing outrages, and the international situation remained difficult. Nevertheless, the most important thing in those days was the defeat of the rebels at Madrid. The success of the Spanish capital's defenders revived flagging spirits and gave a reason to hope for a change in the course of events.

In Valencia, I had no difficulty in finding the Soviet volunteers who had arrived before us. One of the first whom I saw was my old boss, Yan Karlovich Berzin. According to a pact with the Spanish Republican government, the USSR, in fulfillment of its international duty, sent a group of military advisers commanded by Berzin.

To meet a Soviet citizen outside the USSR was always a joy, and a meeting with someone for whom you held unlimited esteem and love was a twofold joy. The Old Man, as we affectionately called him (although he was only forty years old), recognized me immediately, and despite his enormous workload, spent a few minutes with me.

"You want to go to Madrid? It won't work out! The situation there is changing. I'm leaving you here. We've got to start with small things. Furthermore, the Fascists took heavy losses at Madrid, and their morale was shattered. The defense of Madrid is improving every day, and the steadfastness of the defenders is growing. For the Fascists, the city is becoming impregnable."

Berzin's prognosis turned out to be correct. The Fascists didn't take Madrid until the end of the war, almost two years later. But on other sectors of the front, the situation was far from bright.

"For you, the most important thing to remember is this: *here, there are no such things as continuous front lines*," said Yan Karlovich with a tired smile. Berzin didn't develop this thought, but I understood him perfectly: getting behind enemy lines would be relatively easy.

Like other Soviet advisers, Berzin was concerned about the condition of the Republican Army. It had no clear structure, and no unified command. The army was composed of separate detachments, subordinated to various parties and committees. In his conversation with me, Yan Karlovich didn't hesitate to express his alarm.

"What's my mission?"

"We need demolitions instructors. You will instruct people in the application of mines and demolitions. Sometimes it may also be necessary to work in other specialties, which you acquired in the academy."

There was a knock on the door. A tall, blonde fellow and a striking brunette woman came in.

"What luck!" Berzin said, smiling at the couple. "Get acquainted! This is Starinov, and these are also Soviet volunteers: Artur Karlovich Sprogis[2], and his interpreter, Regina Citron." On the spot, Berzin asked me to show Sprogis the construction of various fuses and switches that might be made from materials that were easily available.

Our discussion was interrupted by a telephone call. Listening to the invisible caller, Berzin became noticeably downcast. I hadn't seen Yan Karlovich in about three years. When we met, I had immediately noticed that he seemed to have aged. Now he was obviously becoming nervous. The call somehow didn't sit well with him; it actually seemed to grieve him. In the past, my boss had never lost his self-control. It was clear that the phone call must have brought some really bad news. Replacing the receiver, Yan Karlovich excused himself, saying that he could no longer continue the conversation.

"We'll see a lot of each other!" he said, putting on the same relaxed smile as before.

"And now Comrade Starinov, you will be taken to General Ivon, and you'll discuss everything with him."

We made arrangements with Sprogis to meet in the hotel, and I was sent off to the mysterious General Ivon.[3]

In response to my knock, the French words: *"Entrez, entrez!"* rang out from within the office. Obrucheva and I entered, and a heavyset fellow with blondish hair arose from behind the table. I began to introduce myself through my interpreter.

"You're from the 'big village'?" he asked me in Russian (at that time, the term "big village" was occasionally used to refer to Moscow). "Then we can dispense with the interpreter."

The general appeared to be really operationally oriented. He did everything necessary for me to start work, including giving us another set of identities: I became "Rudolf Wolf," a Pole with a German surname, while Anna became "Louisa Curting," an

2. A. K. Sprogis was a veteran of the civil war. Prior to serving in Spain, he had served in an NKVD border guard unit on the western border. After 3 years of outstanding service in Spain, he became a leading figure in Soviet partisan, special forces, and intelligence operations in World War II.

3. The true identity of "General Ivon" is uncertain: he may have been Aleksandr Orlov, NKVD chief in Spain. It is also possible that "Ivon" was Naum Eitington, Orlov's deputy for *spetsnaz* activity in Spain.

Englishwoman. Henceforth, we were known to our Spanish comrades as "Rudolfo" and "Luisa."

On the same day, I was assigned to work with a group of comrades composed of older family men. They very much desired to go behind enemy lines, but they reckoned they'd be thrown in there secretly for special deep-cover underground work. Not one of them supposed that you could methodically go behind Fascist lines and, after finishing your mission, return to base.

This view of operations didn't overjoy my students, and it was pretty clear that we wouldn't get far with the old codgers. Where in hell could they go on sorties behind enemy lines? They could hardly even move at a fast walk without gasping for breath.

The staff took a rather cool view of our group. They didn't give me any equipment, and we had to buy tools and parts from our own money. Further, we had no vehicles to carry equipment and personnel to operational or training areas. I had to make all the explosive devices at night in our quarters. Then, we had to travel to the sites, where the students were located, on public transportation—street cars!—carrying detonator switches, fuses, explosives, and model mines in handbags and small suitcases, which Anna/Luisa carried. Just a jolt or a sudden stop of the trolley could have been enough to set off some of the blasting caps and the explosives that she was carrying. Further, since we were working under deep cover, most of the Republican Army did not know of our existence. If we were stopped and searched, they'd find the explosives, and then even our papers wouldn't be enough to save us. Anna also had difficulty translating the technical terms. We got a Spanish regulation on mines and explosives, but it didn't have many of the terms that I was accustomed to using, and Anna wasn't familiar with the terms either, and often got words and concepts confused. Things got especially sticky when we were using mines with live blasting caps. Anna worked night and day, trying to keep up with my teaching, which was based on the knowledge that I had in my head. We had no Russian handbooks or other manuals that she could work with. Finally, a course was organized at Valencia for military interpreters under the direction of O. N. Fillipova, but Anna was involved elsewhere and unable to take it.

These difficulties led me to return to General Ivon, who listened attentively as I energetically argued that we had to advise the Republican Army command to give the most careful attention to staffing and material support for the demolitions group. "Mines aren't for defense—they're specifically offensive weapons!" I tried to persuade the general. "Where does an artillery round fall?

It's always uncertain. A reliable mine, placed in the required spot, however, will go off without a hitch, and the effect of the explosion is much greater than that of an artillery round. You can't destroy a battalion with one artillery round, but a mine that derails a troop train, destroys not only a battalion but its equipment as well. Can we really afford to disregard such weapons?"

General Ivon agreed with me.

"Let's organize courses for training combat-proven soldiers to operate in the Fascist rear," I suggested. "This is nothing new for me. We can set up a shop to supply our special devices, and might even be able to raise a special battalion for operations along enemy lines of communications."

"Your suggestion is useful," the general responded, "but unfortunately the Republican Army has only just been born, and the birth was difficult. You're going to have to work with homemade equipment. You'll have to prove the potential of your demolitions men."

However, soon after that conversation, we were invited to the Valencia Provincial Committee of the Communist party of Spain to meet Comrade Uribe, who informed us of an impending meeting with Jose Dias, the general secretary of the Communist party of Spain, and Dolores Ibarrury.

Dias met with us on the following day. The building of the Central Committee was guarded because remnants of a fifth column were still operating in the city, and the anarchists were committing atrocities. But we were allowed to enter without any special formalities.

Dias was a young man with a thin, intelligent face, strong hands, and rapid movements. He asked me to set forth the main point of my plans. He listened attentively, and nodded his head in approval. After a few moments the door opened and a woman dressed in black entered. I immediately recognized the legendary Pasionaria and stood up, breaking off the presentation of my plans in midsentence.

Dolores Ibarrury smiled, extended her hand to me, and embraced Anna. Then she sat down alongside Jose Dias, and they talked animatedly between themselves. How I envied Anna her Spanish.

Finally, Jose Dias spoke through the interpreter: "In the next few days you'll receive everything we can possibly give, but a lot of difficulties lie ahead. They will not be easy to overcome in our present situation."

Actually, everything was arranged very quickly. We got beautiful accommodations for training demolitions men: a spacious private residence in the suburbs of Valencia. They sent us the necessary equipment. But the most important thing was that the first group of twelve young soldiers arrived, led by thirty-eight-year-old Capt. Domingo Ungria. He didn't simply walk in: he *drove* up to the school building. The twelve men of Domingo's group had five autos and trucks! "Think this'll be enough for a start?" he asked.

And this was how the future special purpose brigade (Translator's note: Starinov's term is: *brigad spetsialnogo naznacheniya* = "brigade of special designation," or more colloquially, special forces or *spetsnaz* brigade) got its start.

A Sortie Behind Enemy Lines

"*Salud, camarada tecnico! Salud, camarada* Luisa!" The tall, fiery-haired chauffeur, Rubio, was dressed in his spanking new uniform, which harmonized surprisingly well with the Hispano-Suiza car glittering in the sunlight. Waiting until we were seated, he released the brakes and took off, slewing the car around beside the hotel entrance. But once he got out on the road, he had to slow down. Valencia was jammed with columns of refugees and vehicles of military units and evacuated government agencies.

A Spanish chauffeur who is forced to drive slowly is a martyr. Suffering etched Rubio's face, but he suffered in silence, as becomes a man. Eventually the Hispano-Suiza rolled up to the house in Beniameta, a suburb of Valencia, where our school was located.

The first who came flying out to meet us was Antonio, the little eight-year-old son of Capt. Domingo Ungria.

"Now get right back here, you little rascal!" yelled the captain's wife, a stout, good-natured woman. Previously she had had but one concern: to watch out so that her son didn't fall off horses or get beneath their hooves (Domingo was a cavalry officer by profession). But from the time that her husband came to command demolitions men, she found dynamite charges and primers in her boy's pockets. By comparison, the boy's training on the Andalusian racehorses seemed to the mother a harmless pastime.

"Don't bother the kid! He just has dummy mines and fuses that have already been used!" Domingo said, as he came out of the main entrance of the house and greeted us with the traditional raised-fist Republican salute.

Domingo was thin with black hair, and in some ways resembled an Uzbek. He was very active for his thirty-eight years, and he actually seemed to be a bit mentally unbalanced. What made him seem unbalanced, however, was just his innate expansiveness, nothing more.

According to his comrades' tales, Domingo was very brave, and I believed them, since combat veterans showed definite respect for the captain. At first, Domingo was slow to master the technical aspects of mines and demolitions work, and he asked a lot of questions about tactics. He preferred to leave the technical matters to others at the beginning, but gradually, I got him to the point where even he was able to mine bridges and roads, and he finally became a master of this "science."

The soldiers were assembling for training. Two brothers appeared separately—Antonio and Pedro. The eldest, Antonio, was twenty-one; the younger, Pedro, was only eighteen. Antonio had married shortly before. His wife was a beauty, and whenever there was a free minute, he was off with her in their room, from which could be heard laughter and the sounds of love.

The younger brother derisively shrugged his shoulders; he considered his elder brother to be a bit irresponsible.

As always, thirty-year-old, handsome Juan was sharply turned out. In the recent past, he had run a small garage. Juan brought three vehicles as a gift to the republic. The only thing that he could not sacrifice to the republic were his evenings, which were devoted to the ladies, with whom he enjoyed great success.

Behind Juan came the young soldier named Pepe who looked rather poorly by comparison. Pepe never censured Juan about his exploits; he simply looked him up and down with a condescending smile. There were no weaknesses in Pepe, unless you considered his pedantic manner, which would drive some people to distraction. In our business, however, to be a pedant is by no means a vice.

Finally, all the troops had arrived in formation, and I began to teach, relying more on demonstration than on talking. I taught them how to manufacture and place mines. How attentively my students listened to the interpreter! And what marvelous students! Each understood that the present calm on the fronts was only temporary. They were dying to get back into combat, but in the meantime they used every minute to learn how to make and employ, what was for them, a peaceful people, totally novel equipment.

If only some of the Republican leaders had been as conscious of the situation! Then they wouldn't have rested on the laurels of their temporary victory at Madrid as did Largo Caballero,[1] for example, who had nothing at all to do with that success, by the way. Madrid was saved by Spanish soldiers, and soldiers of the International brigades, led by Communists. But even then, some people in Valencia were trying to take credit from the Communists, accusing them of all sorts of possible and impossible errors.

Political intrigues aroused anger against those who initiated them, and anger just leads to more anger. We, however, were soldiers above all. We believed in victory, and we were preparing for it.

From the most remote times, saboteurs have been condemned as dark and violent men, with neither conscience nor honor. There's no argument that the dregs of humanity graduating from the intelligence schools of the bourgeois nations are animals of that type. *But in armies fighting for popular causes, demolitions men become the best, most dedicated, and most humane fighters.*

In order to be convinced of that, all you had to do was to look at Captain Ungria's son.

As I've already said, almost all the Spaniards that we trained believed at the outset that they would be employed in underground work in areas occupied by the Fascists, and they were well suited to that type of work.

But how would we set up the delivery of weapons, ammunition, and explosives to the underground workers without transport aircraft? Further, with the complete lack of radio communications, the operational control of such groups was greatly hampered. Finally, it was not easy to maintain deep cover and to become "acclimatized" in rebel-held territory; that took a long time.

For precisely these reasons, I felt that in the increasingly complicated situation we had to create small, well-equipped groups of demolitions men who would periodically cross the front lines and return after accomplishing their missions. But my suggestions were not supported up the chain of command, nor even among my students. Everybody felt it was easier and simpler to organize sabotage behind enemy lines if people were settled there for long periods of time with false documents. This was the reason that the

---

1. Largo Caballero, Francisco. (1869–1946), was one of the right-wing leaders of the Spanish Socialist Party and the large labor organization known as the General Workers Union. He was minister of labor in the first Republican government. In 1936 he joined the Popular Front. In September 1936, he became prime minister. In his role as head of the government and minister of war, he sabotaged the measures for building new armed forces and for strengthening discipline in the rear areas. In May 1937, he was forced to retire, and after Spain fell to the Fascists, he emigrated to France. When the Nazis occupied France, he was arrested and sent off to a concentration camp near Berlin. In the spring of 1944, the Soviet Army freed Largo Caballero. He settled in Paris, where he died in 1946.

first people at the school were selected from among those who were unfit for military service.

Finally, by order of the Communist party of Spain, I transferred my "old boys" to instructors' positions, and Captain Ungria's group began to prepare for sortie operations behind enemy lines. At first, Domingo was very skeptical about the plan for crossing the front lines, but I hoped that he'd change his mind once he got better acquainted with the matter. Anna got involved in training Domingo's men in marksmanship—in which she set a very high standard—and in first aid where she won the admiration of the Spanish doctor and medical orderlies detailed to train our men.

Soon, we were ordered to participate in the Teruel operation. The Republican Army command was absolutely correct in considering that the rebel occupation of Teruel and the formation of the so-called Teruel salient posed a great danger to them.

From Teruel to Valencia, where the Republican government was located, was a little more than one hundred kilometers as the crow flies. If the rebels and the German and Italian interventionists were able to develop a successful offensive, they would break through to the sea, cut off Catalonia from the rest of Spain, and get behind the defenders of Madrid. The liquidation of this Teruel salient would permit the Republican troops to secure Valencia, shorten the front lines, and limit the enemy's advantageous bridgehead.

The rebels occupied settlements distributed along railroad and automobile road between Valencia and Calamocha. From the north of Teruel, the Republican units held tightly to the highway at Montalban and Perales and, farther to the south, almost to Teruel. Continuous front lines were nonexistent. Intelligence data were comforting: according to latest reports, the enemy had not deployed strong forces in the Teruel salient and was not anticipating a decisive Republican attack.

Among the troops training for the Teruel operation, the most combat-ready formation was the 13th International Brigade. In the event of heavy fighting, it was impossible to count on any unusual steadfastness on the part of the anarchist columns. Even less was it possible to rely on the detachments of the POUM, a Trotskyite organization whose detachments were later disarmed.[2] They never actually fought, but just took every opportunity to arm themselves

2. POUM = Partido Obrero de Unificacion Marxista. Contrary to Starinov's description, the POUM was not Trotskyite, but was a small, but well-armed, independent anti-Stalinist Marxist splinter group, allied with the anarcho-syndicalists of Buenaventura Durruti. A number of such groups were operating in Spain at the time.

at the expense of the Republicans, and in the end, to attack the republic itself.

In the second half of December 1936, together with Captain Ungria's group of eighteen men, I went out to the village of Alfambra. Along with us in the car, we loaded dynamite, TNT, simple ampule mines, and wheel switches. Our dynamite possessed extremely unpleasant characteristics: it unfailingly exploded the first time it was struck by a bullet. We were able to prove this on our own improvised test range near Valencia.

I tried to make the dangerous dynamite "safe," by adding machine oil and potassium nitrate, but without success. My homemade "safe" dynamite could not even be reliably detonated with a blasting cap or with a booster charge (a cartridge of jellied dynamite). Willy-nilly, we just had to make use of what we were given.

Pepe took his place behind the wheel of the dynamite-laden Ford, and I sat beside him. The pedantic Pepe inspired more trust in me than the dashing Rubio. We had to cover more than 200 kilometers, of which 150 kilometers were on mountain roads. Alfambra, like Teruel, was more than nine hundred meters above sea level. It was a sunny day, and the little stone houses of the village seemed as though they were bleached white. Local inhabitants, especially children, looked at the arriving Republican troops with curiosity.

The next morning, the sirens wailed: air-raid warning!

The vehicles clustered in the village began to drive around in all directions, but Pepe didn't lose his head: he started up his Ford and drove it into a field. High altitude bombing didn't present a genuine threat to troops.

Because of the lack of space in Alfambra, Domingo started to look for better accommodations for us in a neighboring village. We finally got settled in Orios, and from there we went to report to the Teruel sector commander, an anarchist named Benedito who was festooned with all sorts of weapons. He received us with extreme ill will, and in a thunderous voice, he declared that the offensive, which he had prepared, would go down in history!

When the commander finally shut up, Domingo requested permission to brief him on our plan of action. The captain proposed the use of the demolitions group to cut the rail and highway lines of communication in the Teruel-Calamocha sector and to derail enemy troop trains. The commander threw up his hands in despair: no, he didn't believe in the possibility of successfully derailing enemy troop trains. The demolitions group ought to be ready to sever the enemy's telephone and telegraph lines, capture "tongues" (Translators note: a "tongue" is a Russian military expression for a prisoner who is forced to provide timely intelligence information) and if there was any time left ... well, maybe they could take a shot at blowing up a railroad.

"Is this an order?"

"Yes, it's an order. Top priority to severing telephone and telegraph communications."

"When do we start?"

"In two days."

"How do we get the necessary guides?"

"Find them yourselves among the local inhabitants."

"And what about your scouts?"

Without realizing it, Domingo had hit a sore spot with the commander: almost no scouting or patrolling was done there. The commander angrily repeated that we'd have to find our own guides.

After picking up two guides, both anarchists, we returned to Orios, and found a really picturesque scene in our unit: some of the men were warming themselves by the fireplace; others were smoking, sitting on the boxes of explosives; and smack in the middle of everything, Rubio was making fuses! These people were obviously contemptuous of the rules for handling mines and explosives. Whose responsibility was that, if not mine?

The operation got started later than was originally planned. The commander called for Domingo a second time and ordered that we should cut all lines of communication between fifteen and twenty kilometers to the north of Teruel, and also to blow up the auto and railroads linking Teruel with Calatayud.

"Are you going with the demolitions team?" Obrucheva asked me.

"Sure. I've *got* to."

"Are these people really so badly trained?"

"That's not the point. What kind of an impression am I going to make on the troops if I don't go?"

"And I'm supposed to wait here, in Orios?"

"Well, you don't really have to stay in Orios . . ."

"Forgive me, but I don't agree. I'm your interpreter—I will be with *you*. Without me, you're a deaf mute: you hear, but you don't understand what the Spaniards are saying; you can talk to them, but they can't understand you. Without me, the group won't be any use to you, especially at night."

I had to agree. But when he heard that Luisa was going with us, Captain Ungria threw up his hands in despair. "Women don't go behind the lines!"

"Sorry, Domingo, *they do*!" I answered. "Get the people ready. We're taking twelve men and leaving six in reserve."

After we had loaded ourselves down with explosives, we set out for the defensive positions of the company through which we had to pass to penetrate the rebel lines. The demolitions team changed their leather boots for cord sandals, known as *alpargatas*. You don't go far in the mountains in boots. Everyone was armed with a pistol and a knife. In addition, Rubio carried a submachine gun for any eventuality.

It was getting on toward nightfall. The guides went ahead; behind them Captain Ungria, Anna, and I; and after that—all the rest. On each person's back was a white rag to which was attached a piece of decaying wood with glowing fox fire so that they wouldn't lose each other in the darkness. One of our men, Marques, had put on the red-and-black anarchist scarf so that our anarchist guides, who had been doing a bit of anarchist propagandizing among our troops, would think their propaganda had been successful and would be more inclined to behave reliably.

Domingo and I both had binoculars. We carefully scrutinized the area. For nighttime use, we established "caution" and "halt" signals. Night in the mountains falls suddenly. Now Antonio and Rubio were striding along beside the guides. Enemy posts were in the vicinity.

It was necessary to move in absolute silence, but our men were insufficiently trained for night movement.

After two hours, we rested. By my calculations, we had traveled about ten kilometers. And there were many more to go.

A strange feeling overcomes you when you pass through enemy lines at night: it's as if you're walking on a narrow bridge over an abyss: one false move and—it's all over.

But now the front lines were behind us: we walked more cheerfully, and by three in the morning we arrived at the Teruel-Calamocha highway. We lay down about one hundred meters from the roadbed, caught our breath, and had a snack. Then, we split into two groups: the men led by Antonio were to mine the railroad, Domingo's group was to set charges to blow up twelve telegraph poles on the highway and blow up the bridge.

The automobile road was wide and had an asphalt surface. The reinforced concrete bridge was unusually solid. We clearly did not have enough explosives to destroy it. In order to increase the effectiveness of the explosion, I advised Domingo to place the charges close beneath the beams, using rocks to support them, and then I went off along with Antonio's men.

It was about five hundred meters to the railroad. Not a soul was around, but we had very little time: soon the explosions would start. Fortunately, the bridge at that point was extremely easy to blow up. We worked standing in a dried-up streambed. The charges were set perfectly, on the sides of the metal beams.

After the bridge had been mined, we hurriedly got busy on the telegraph poles. As always, when you hurry, something or other doesn't go right, but there was no time left. We lit the fuses of the charges on the bridge and began to move off. The first explosions thundered as we reached the highway. The dark night was pierced by brilliant flashes of light. We quickened our pace, and it was a good thing that we didn't linger! Explosions rang out on the highway as well. Flames shot into the night sky above the reinforced concrete bridge. The earth shook from the deafening detonations.

At the assembly point, joy reigned, but it was still a bit early to rejoice. I was afraid that the enemy would send soldiers to the site of the explosions and begin a search. We saw the lights of vehicles speeding to the damaged stretch of road. We had to clear the area—and fast!

It was easy to get going for the return trip. Satisfied with their success, the men didn't feel tired. By sunrise, we had already entered Republican positions. Domingo sent his demolitions men off to rest, and he and I went to report to the sector commander. We were admitted only after midday. The commander, waving his hands, began to reproach us for having done little but "make noise."

"The enemy got reinforcements! His lines of communication still work!" the commander shouted at the top of his voice.

Domingo responded sharply that the mission had been completed precisely, and on time.

Our artillery adviser. N. N. Voronov,[3] who was present during this conversation, seizing the opportunity, said: "You've got to consider the commander's mood: the offensive is not going according to plan, and his troops are sustaining heavy losses."

"Why should we take the blame? Can a small demolitions team really guarantee the success of an entire offensive?"

"Certainly not."

The commander nevertheless pressed Domingo hard.

"You obviously didn't blow up anything, and you certainly didn't destroy communications!"

Fortunately, one of our guides was an anarchist. He began to yell at the commander, arguing that the bridges had, in fact, been

3. N. N. Voronov subsequently rose to the rank of Marshal of Artillery during World War II. His field interpreter was Nora Pavlovna Chegodayeva, a classmate and friend of Anna/Luisa.

destroyed. With desperate gestures, he showed how the fragment of the bridge had flown through the air.

I don't know whether he convinced the commander or whether the commander just got bored with the argument, but we were finally permitted to leave, and told to prepare for another sortie into enemy territory. I was really depressed. The fate of the offensive certainly didn't depend on our group's operation, but we could have done more. That is, we could have, if we had been given more independence in assuming responsibility and risk.

At the same time, why in hell blow up telegraph poles when everybody knew that the rebels used field radio sets? You can bet it wasn't difficult at all for the Fascists to repair the damage we inflicted on the lines.

We were also wasting our time on bridges: what sense was there in busting a bridge over a dried-up stream? It was much more advantageous to set automatic mines on railroads and highways. That way, you'd use up less explosives, and the effect produced might be even greater: the first vehicle or train that was blown up would force the enemy to halt until a careful check could be made for a significant distance down the road.

When I returned to my students, their initial excitement over the events of the immediate past had already subsided. The troops looked exhausted, and almost all of them had foot injuries.

"Todos esta bien." Domingo lied bravely, looking at the questioning faces of his comrades in arms. "And they're expecting more from us, so now off to sleep!" The captain didn't want to discourage his demolitions men, but he could hardly hide his own dejection from them.

"What's the matter with you, then?" Rubio asked on behalf of everyone.

"The matter?" exploded Domingo. "They didn't take Teruel, that's what's the matter!"

The soldiers looked at each other. The reason was sufficiently weighty to explain the bad mood of their commander. But in spite of initial failures, the command kept trying to take Teruel. The International Brigade managed to penetrate right into the city itself, and other Republican units advanced behind it. At the time, the enemy didn't counterattack, and this allowed us to hope for success.

The men had foot injuries, and yet they were supposed to walk more than forty kilometers on those feet, so Pepe suggested that we use vehicles for sorties behind the lines, mentioning that in the event of danger it was easier to escape by car. He had already tried out the idea on Anna, and she suggested bringing it to me

The idea captured the fancy of the other chauffeur, Juan, and he strongly supported Pepe. Domingo was also excited by the new idea, and we decided to risk it.

We set out on the operation: Domingo, Obrucheva, myself, Pepe, Juan, Rubio, the brothers Antonio and Pedro, and seven men from an army unit that had taken up the defense around the village of Perales. At noon, three vehicles entered a grove in no-man's-land and headed for the Teruel-Calamocha highway. At first, we jolted along, dry shrubbery lashing along the sides of the vehicles, but finally, four kilometers from our jump-off position, we came out onto an unpaved road and picked up speed.

Silent hills stood all around us. Stunted grass yellowed in the sun, dark boulders were visible in the distance. There were neither wild animals nor sheep flocks; the only movement was the occasional cloud, soaring high in the sky. A squat *cortico*—a shepherd's hut—built of stone, was visible on a flat area, a whole kilometer away. Taking cover, we sent out a scout. The signal came back: okay to proceed!

There was no one at the hut, but a saddled horse nibbled at the grass not far away. Raising its head in alarm, with a frightened cry, it shied away from the soldiers. On the saddle, dried blood was visible. We looked in the hut: it was empty. Some kind of tragedy had occurred here, but what exactly had happened? Did it represent a threat to us? After we drove our vehicles into the shade of the grove beside the hut, we carefully reconnoitered the vicinity with our binoculars. All around, everything was quiet. We still had farther to go. But we hadn't gone more than two kilometers when we noticed a group of armed men on a nearby mountainside. We weren't successful in our attempt to slip by and hide around the bend in the road. Shots rang out, bullets whistled by us. The troops followed orders precisely. Tumbling out of the vehicles, they took cover and returned fire.

Juan blasted away with short bursts from his submachine gun. Our fire was very heavy and clearly not without results. The enemy fell silent. Then the people on the mountainside began to withdraw, making short rushes from cover to cover. But toward the east, in the direction of the Republican positions!

Domingo yelled at our people to hold their fire. Could it be that we had run into our reconnaissance people? Why had no one warned us of the possibility of such an encounter? At the staff, they had told us that not a single Republican unit was behind enemy lines.

We waved a red scarf, and the group on the mountainside responded in kind. Juan asked that we send him for a parley. We

agreed and awaited with sinking hearts to see whether the un
known group would send someone out to meet Juan, or whethe
a single, fatal shot would ring out. But Juan kept on going. A mar
appeared from behind a bush and began to cautiously descend to
ward Juan. After a minute, Juan turned toward us and merrily
waved his arms. We got up from the ground, and the "enemy" be
gan to extricate themselves from behind the shrubbery. Everything
was straightened out very quickly: we had run into a reconnaissance unit of one of the anarchist columns.

In this ridiculous encounter, neither they nor we were at fault
When we found out from the recon unit that there were no Fascis
detachments up ahead, along the automobile road, we resumec
our drive. About a half hour later, after we had camouflaged ou
vehicles in the brush, we were observing the traffic on the Teruel-
Calamocha highway.

We looked down on a lifeless railroad: it seemed as if the trains
ran very seldom. There were no guards on the automobile high
way, and traffic consisted mainly of single vehicles. Occasionally
a convoy of ten to fifteen trucks appeared, sometimes with sol
diers, sometimes with freight. We *could* have driven out on the
highway, found a place in one of the convoys, and made some
fireworks for the rebels! Instead, we approached the road in the
open, to a distance of about five hundred meters, and turned so
that it would be convenient to open fire.

It never occurred to the Fascist drivers that the cars along the
road might be Republicans. Waiting until a long column of vehi
cles loaded with some kind of cargo appeared, we took them
under heavy fire. Some of the trucks skidded off to the side of the
road, and the drivers jumped into the ditches; some trucks caught
fire, and the rest stepped on the gas and fled toward cover.

Once we had withdrawn from the road, we set a matchbox
switch (exactly like the one I had shown to Tukhachevskiy the
year before) in a rut and placed a good charge of TNT in the
bushes on the roadside, in order to delay possible pursuers. Our
precautions didn't appear to be out of place, because the deafen
ing roar of an explosion soon reached us. Obviously, the Fascists
had stumbled upon the fougasse (Translators note: fougasse is a
commonly used French military term for a buried antipersonnel
mine that disperses fragments, small bomblets, or incendiary ma
terial) and would refrain from pursuing us.

Our sortie was considered successful, but I returned in an un
happy mood. I had seen with my own eyes that the rebels were
able to quickly repair the damage from our mines and fougasses
not only on auto roads but on the railroads. Was the sector com-

mander really right? Did this mean that the demolitions men couldn't do the things that we had intended, that they would be of no value to those troops who were engaged in fierce fighting at Teruel?

On the following day, Domingo and Antonio led two groups behind enemy lines to set mines. Domingo crossed the front lines at the usual place; Antonio crossed farther south, at the point where the Teruel-Calatayud railroad passed not more than twenty kilometers from Alfambra. In the sector where Antonio's group was operating, the density of Fascist posts seemed to be greater, and our people could only move at night. Crossing the automobile road, the demolitions group noted that the road was being patrolled quite energetically and that the railroad was also guarded.

Nevertheless, after they had studied the guard system, our troops set up two mines with ampule detonators in the ruts of the roadway. When he heard the noise of an approaching train, Antonio himself ran to the railroad bed and set up a mine with a wheel switch. The train passed over the wheel switch, but nothing happened. Now all their hopes were pinned on the ampule mines—and they worked well. The first one went off—the train continued. The second went off—and the train just kept going! Totally undisciplined gunfire began to pour out of the car windows, searchlights twinkled along the road, and flares shot into the air. They had to move out in a hurry. About a kilometer away from the railroad, the demolitions men heard another blast. Later it was learned that this was set off by the wheel switch. It didn't go off under a train, but in the hands of a Fascist who picked it up.

I was discouraged by what I heard. Mines, which worked faultlessly in tests, didn't give a good account of themselves in combat. All the work, all the risk, and we only blew up a road!

Returning from the mission, Domingo also looked gloomy. And something else was wrong. Looking him over, I saw that his uniform was burned.

Nothing could explain the torrent of awful curses that my friend hurled at the rebels, the high command, the weather, and all the Spanish saints. When he had calmed down a bit, Domingo told me that he had not been successful: the capsule mines which he was able to set were detected by the patrols, and the wheel switch didn't work. The only thing that Domingo's group did was to capture a Fascist fuel truck on the return trip and set it afire.

In this particular action, Rubio stood out. He'd gone out onto the asphalt with a red light. The fuel truck stopped immediately. The driver and his helper, dressed in Falangist uniforms, sensed something out of the ordinary, and grabbed for their weapons, but Rubio was one step ahead of them. Then he opened the tank, lit his handkerchief, and tossed it into the spreading pool of gasoline, along with a box of matches! The demolitions group hadn't been able to run far enough away. Many of them had their uniforms singed, and some their hair as well.

"Here's the carburetor from the fuel truck," Domingo said gloomily. "We're out of luck, Rudolfo (Starinov's cover name in Spain), absolutely out of goddam luck."

The New Year, 1937, arrived, and on New Year's Eve, we moved from Alfambra to Orios. Midway en route, we were stopped at a checkpoint by a column of anarchists who demanded our vehicles. Domingo charged out of the cab like a raging lion. Cocking his weapon, he shouted for the anarchists to clear the road. Juan and Rubio stood beside their commander, weapons at the ready; Pepe snatched a grenade. The anarchists backed down, but obscenities and threats were hurled at our backs as we passed.

In Alfambra, as always, our reception was not the warmest. Teruel continued to remain in Fascist hands so the anarchists were bobbing and weaving, looking for someone on whom to blame their failure. "The rebels are bringing up reinforcements by railroad, and you did nothing about it!" the sector commander shouted. He was dead wrong, of course, but we couldn't think of defending ourselves.

Domingo knew that our people were in no condition to move: after a fifty-kilometer march, the majority of them had bleeding feet. Not wanting to risk another auto trip into the enemy rear, he nevertheless tried to reach the railroad with twenty men on horseback. He wasn't able to reach the objective and returned with his group the same night.

Then an order arrived: "Relieved from the front. Report to Valencia."

When the secretary of the Provincial Committee of the Communist party of Spain, Comrade Uribes, heard our report, he tried to soothe us with comforting sentiments.

"Comrade Uribes advises you not to be discouraged," Obrucheva interpreted. "He says that the operation fell through because of insufficient forces, an absence of cooperation, and a lack of discipline on the part of the anarchists, who were only courageous when they were in the Republican rear."

"Well, that may be," I said. "But we've had a lot of failures. Tell Comrade Uribes that tomorrow's what's worrying me."

Interrupting Anna, Uribes anxiously inquired how we had evaluated our own operations.

"Our people performed superbly, even those who were going behind enemy lines for the first time. Take Juan, for example. You ought to see how that boy sets mines and directs fire. He'll make a great demolitions man. And the rest displayed good skills, as well. The troops are convinced that we can penetrate to important rebel targets, and strike the rebels on the roads. These convictions are very valuable. Now, however, equipment is worrying me."

"What happened?"

"The men haven't mastered it yet."

"They have to master it! Don't be discouraged. Don't lose any time, and I repeat, don't be discouraged! We believe in you! We're relying on the demolitions men for outstanding performance!"

We were inspired when we left Comrade Uribes. I have to admit that when we went in, I'd been afraid that they were finally going to say "good-bye" to our demolitions men. But what was the problem with the mines? Why in hell wouldn't they work the way they were supposed to?

Domingo met us on the threshold of our new quarters, which had been confiscated from fleeing Falangists, and the captain's wife invited everyone to the table. "Let's wait for Juan," I said. "He's putting the car away and will be right up."

"What did Uribes say?" Domingo asked.

Before I could answer, shooting erupted outside the windows. When we reached him, Juan was lying in the driveway alongside a gleaming Ford. On the asphalt around him a thick dark stain was spreading. His right hand seemed to be protecting his heart, which had been shot through.

The two murderers were already being pursued, but we joined in. When we caught them, however, they resisted, shouting. Domingo knocked the pistol away from one of them, and the other was disarmed by troops who arrived on the run.

At the staff, everything became clear: the killers belonged to the anarchist column.

"We needed the car, and your driver put up a fight . . ." The scumbags didn't even consider themselves to be guilty of anything!

We buried Juan the next day. His relatives placed his body in a niche in the stone wall, and the cemetery workers cemented over the lid. It was after the interment that Juan's brother, Vicente, volunteered to join the unit as his replacement.

Destination: Jaen

Since the night before, everything had been turned upside down in Captain Ungria's quarters. Steam rose in clouds above washbasins and pans. Eight-year-old Antonio endured a few unnecessary smacks. Clothing irons hissed.

"Blessed Madonna! Why was I ever born on this earth?" the captain's wife constantly exclaimed in a martyr's voice. At eleven o'clock in the morning, everything suddenly grew still. The señora appeared from the bedroom in a dress with a black-lace mantilla. In her highly-piled hair, a mother-of-pearl and tortoise-shell comb gleamed, and in her manicured fingers a splendid fan fluttered. Behind her marched an unusually clean Antonio.

Even Captain Ungria was dressed in holiday attire. His shirt, with a colorful tie, was dazzling in its brightness. The creases in his trousers were sharper than the edge of a Spanish switchblade.

Today was the day of the corrida—the bullfights!

Franco's cutthroats were at the very gates of Madrid and had even captured part of the university campus in November 1936. At Teruel, hundreds of soldiers were being lost in the bloody operation that had begun in December 1936 and was to last until August 1937, but today—there's a corrida!

In the empty lots behind the house where we had our school in Paterna, a suburb of the city, we heard shots at night: the anarchists were shooting their victims, taking the law into their own hands. When we went out to the firing range in the morning, we often found bodies along the target berm: young and old, well-dressed men and women, children and the elderly, and poor folks with calloused hands. The anarchists claimed that they were shooting counterrevolutionaries, but in fact, the anarchists also shot people whom they had robbed.

But today—there's a corrida!

Enemy aviation bombed Valencia more often. On the streets there were starving, exhausted people. There were food shortages here and there, and on the southern flank, the enemy was preparing to launch an offensive.

But today—there's a corrida!

Yes, there was a corrida today, and Captain Ungria with his

family, Antonio and his young wife and brother; the fiery-haired
Rubio; little Pepe; and even Vicente, Juan's disconsolate brother,
who had become a regular driver for our group—all of them hurried to the center of town. There, a large, gay crowd of Valencia's
residents had already gathered: they simply didn't have the
strength to deny themselves the pleasure of watching their beloved
toreadors.

Despite all entreaties, I remained at home. One corrida had
been enough for me: I just didn't want to be a witness to beautifully choreographed killings of innocent animals.

In no particular hurry, I strolled along the empty streets to
Vicente's little garage, which we had outfitted as a mine laboratory where we constantly tested our equipment. We had already
sorted out the cause of our failure at Teruel: The fuses of the
wheel switches were twenty years old! In exercises, we placed
them under slow-moving trains, and the contact with the wheels
pressing down upon them was sufficiently prolonged so that the
fuses worked faultlessly. But fast-moving trains did not ignite the
fuses. I did manage to get new fuses, but with great difficulty.

Something was also wrong with the ampule mines: their delay
time was too great. We spent a lot of time correcting that short-
coming, cutting apart the blasting cap. After three days' work, we
conducted a test of new wheel switches and ampule mines on the
railroad near Valencia. The effectiveness surpassed our expectations.

At that time, we also made electric mines, which could be detonated by trip wire or pressure. These were fitted with timed
safety devices to allow safe installation. The safeties cut off ten to
fifteen minutes after the mines were set, thus permitting the demolitions men to withdraw a sufficient distance. However, I had not
taken into account the peculiarities of Spanish character: Safety
devices insulted their self-respect, and the troops simply ignored
the precautionary measures!

There was no time to waste preaching safety sermons, so I invented a backup system, which made it impossible to set the electric detonator without installing the safety. Let the demolitions
men say and think whatever they wanted, but that was why we
had no accidents in mining operations, and that kind of record
was exactly what I wanted.

The troops were trained to use a blasting plunger as a power
source, but also were able to use regular flashlight batteries instead. They also knew methods of controlling mines with simpli-
fied detonators.

Our recent failure at Teruel had forced us to thinking about developing a mine to set between the rails. It would hopefully explode five to six meters ahead of an engine. One-and-a-half to two kilos of explosives would guarantee the derailment of the train. In practical exercises, we were able to completely vindicate the wheel-switch mines. Our troops called them *rapidas* because they could be set so quickly: in fact, it was possible to set the *rapidas* less than a minute before the appearance of a train.

One thing still disturbed me, and that was the total carelessness of some of the demolitions men with their explosives. People like that can't be given the kind of dynamite that explodes from friction or from a sharp blow.

At about this time, I found the time to travel to the naval base in Cartagena. When I had delivered a note from Berzin to N. G. Kuznetsov,[1] I tried to beg five TNT-loaded depth charges from the sailors. Those sailors were great! The rebels were never able to blockade the Republican shoreline of Spain. Vessels of the Republican Navy selflessly carried on patrol operations. In spite of the piratical activities of the Italian fleet, they managed to convoy many freighters to Cartagena and other Republican ports.

N. G. Kuznetsov complained that we were disarming him: the depth charges were needed for antisubmarine warfare, but when he learned that the TNT was to be used for operations in the enemy rear, he made the necessary formal arrangements with the command. He only asked one favor: that we not forget about the enemy airfields when we sortied behind rebel lines.

I brought the depth charges to Valencia and melted more than two tons of TNT from their casings. This was a painstaking job, but absolutely necessary. Now we had an explosive far more reliable than dynamite.

The day before the corrida had been payday, and I had bought two pocket watches to use in making time fuses. So while the demolitions men goofed off at the corrida, I could probably finish off that job.

Teruel really hurt our reputation . . . Domingo's men were being treated like stepchildren. The commander even had to concern himself with food supplies and storage of unit equipment. I was certain that more would be heard from the demolitions men. It was just a shame that nagging little details and the general Republican disorganization impeded training.

After the New Year, I got some current Soviet newspapers and

1. Capt. 1st rank—later Fleet Admiral of the Soviet Union—Nikolai Gerasimovich Kuznetsov, cover name "Admiral Nicolas," was senior Soviet naval adviser to the Republican regime and later Soviet people's commissar for naval affairs during World War II. He played a major role in the theft and exportation of the Spanish treasury to the USSR.

learned that Pavel Rychagov, who commanded a flight of pursuit planes, and some other volunteers who distinguished themselves in the performance of especially important missions, had been awarded the title of Hero of the Soviet Union.

I reported the news of Domingo, Rubio, and the other demolitions men. They heartily congratulated us, the Russians. I was also very pleased for my countrymen. But the feelings of pleasure and pride for my comrades-in-arms was mixed with a feeling of bitterness for my own failures. That feeling has never left me, even today. The only good thing was that time passed quickly in my work on homemade grenades and engineer mines.

And so, I busied myself in Vicente's garage until he appeared in the door to order me to go to dinner. While Vicente talked about the corrida, I tried to clean my hands, but metal dust had virtually impregnated the skin, and you almost had to scrape it off with a knife. Señora Ungria would again look at me askance. She considered me a bad role model for her son.

Information about the enemy preparations on the Southern Front were confirmed. The rebels began their offensive, and Domingo's group was ordered to report immediately to the Southern Front. Six "old-timers" were to handle the training of the novices. The rest of us got ready to travel. We were taking with us about a ton of TNT, a half ton of dynamite, all our new mines, and barbs for puncturing automobile tires. Our old trucks and the five autos that we had acquired both legally and illegally were filled to capacity with these items.

As usual, little Pepe drove the vehicle with the dynamite. With a telling glance, my interpreter indicated the new group cook, Rosalina. The girl hadn't been with us long. She was a dressmaker, but she had mastered mine warfare quickly. However, when she noticed that the troops were eating any way they could, and sometimes even eating cold food, she agreed to act as cook. "But with one condition, Domingo!" she said. "You must let me go on missions, just the same!"

Now Rosalina had found a place in Rubio's car. Miguel, a stocky Andalusian with deep eyes, had settled in beside her. It seemed we might soon have another set of newlyweds among us.

Señora Ungria waved after us, her stern, but increasingly sad, face held high. Our vehicle column left Valencia. The route lay to the southwest—to Jaen. I don't know how much time it might have taken to get to Albacete—the first large city on our route of march—if there had not been a good asphalt road.

There were many good roads in Spain, their frequency exceeding that of railroads by a factor of four. This time, the automobile road net simply saved us: the prolonged January rains were beginning, the sky was almost sagging under the weight of the clouds; the grass, beaten down by showers, clung to the sodden roadsides, and the dark lonely fields swelled with moisture.

How different this trip was from my trip to Cartagena! Then, the sun was shining, and at Alicante, I even went swimming. But here, I was involuntarily wrapping my jacket around me and pulling my beret down farther. There, oranges glowed like fire on the branches and under the trees. Here, the fruits were only dimly visible through the rain-darkened leaves, and possibly for that reason there seemed to be fewer of them. The empty fields added to the feeling of melancholy. Could it be that everything around me seemed so dreary because I was nervous?

Jaen was to be the last chance for the demolitions men! If we didn't live up to the expectations of the command there, it would mean that my troops and I hadn't earned our keep for the republic.

And here was Albasete, where we made a short stop. The troops got out to stretch their legs and check the vehicles. On the street I ran head-on into an old acquaintance—Ya. N. Smushkevich![2] We hadn't seen each other in more than a year and certainly hadn't thought that when we met again it wouldn't be in Moscow, Leningrad, or in Belorussia, or even in one of the Black Sea resorts, but thousands of kilometers from the motherland, in a small but famous town in Spain.

"You're not going any farther today," Smushkevich said decisively.

"How do you work with the demolitions men here?" I asked. "Usually we're supported on the supply allowances of the units in the sector where were are operating . . ."

"We'll get it arranged," Smushkevich said soothingly. "I think that the Spanish command will not refuse a small request from their aviation adviser. Come with me!" And they didn't refuse Smushkevich's request!

We found quarters for our people, had dinner, sent Rosalina and Anna off to rest, and sat down together with Smushkevich around a high fireplace, a a fire burned to ashes. "Here's how we fight," he said with a sigh. "We've only got a few planes, damn few. Our eagles are plenty brave, but they're too few. And how about you?"

2. Smushkevich, known as "General Douglas," survived the purges, rose to the rank of lieutenant general, and received two Hero of the Soviet Union awards—before being arrested and executed in the early days of World War II.

I described to him the Teruel experience, our plans, and then told him that it was difficult to use female interpreters in our operations.

"Listen—we have the International Brigade reinforcing us. There are lots of Czechs and Poles among those boys. Probably some of them know Spanish, right? Today we'll clear up this problem and get some volunteers for the demolitions team."

When they learned that we needed people who knew Russian for work in the enemy rear, the first who appeared were two Yugoslavs: Ivan Kharish and Ivan Karbovants. Kharish was short and stocky; Karbovants was thin and tall. Their comrades in the International Brigade called the two friends Pat and Patashon. Later, in Captain Ungria's detachment, Kharish and Karbovants were nicknamed Juan Pequeño and Juan Grande—Little and Big John respectively.

Both had been sailors in the past; both spoke English, French, Spanish, and Russian, and Big John also knew Italian.

After the Yugoslavs, a handsome, smiling Czech, Yan Tikhiy, arrived; he was followed by the American Jew, Alex[3]; and the Bulgarians, Pavel and Vasilin. Then, we were simply overwhelmed: there was absolutely no getting rid of International Brigade volunteers who wanted to strike the enemy rear! Germans, Austrians, Frenchmen, Finns, Italians, Hungarians—all came to us.

"We've *got* to take these people," Captain Ungria whispered to me feverishly, his bright eyes shining with excitement. "Look at them! What people! Where will you ever find such guys! And when would the regular forces ever give us reinforcements anyway?"

I certainly wasn't going to refuse this gift of fate. When I had finished negotiations with the staff responsible for recruiting the International Brigade, I hadn't just gotten two interpreters at Albasete, but more than twenty outstanding fighting men!

Anna seemed quite unhappy about the arrival of these Russian- and Spanish-speaking replacements from the International Brigade, who she thought would render her services unnecessary, but I told her that I wanted her to serve as my deputy and not just as my interpreter. The Southern Front was too big for one person to handle alone, and with her knowledge of the language and the

---

3. "Alex" is Alex Kunslich, an American who was highly regarded by the Republicans. Although not physically robust, he was extremely brave, and performed many dangerous missions. On one such mission behind enemy lines, he was injured and became separated from his men. He was rescued, hidden, and cared for by a peasant family, and fell in love with their daughter, Conchita, who subsequently became an underground operative for the partisans. Conchita's brother also became a partisan. Subsequently, Alex's group was surrounded by Franco forces, and he was captured and shot.

people, and the training and operational experience that she had already gained, she could often fill in for me and direct operations independently, sending groups across enemy lines on her own.

At Granada

Jaen clung to the side of the foothills and from a distance seemed to be buried in greenery. First appearances were deceiving, however, because gardens and groves only surrounded the city. Even in the outskirts, we already encountered gray stone. In the narrow, canyonlike, medieval side streets, there was neither shrubbery nor grass. Grass timidly poked up only here and there in the squares in the center of town, along with carefully tended evergreen trees in orderly rows.

This petrified city of almost sixty thousand inhabitants was strange. With the frenzy of a fanatic monk, it repelled the tender boughs that were extended to it from the orange and mandarin groves, and stubbornly refused to listen to the thrilling rustle of the olive trees.

The inhabitants of Jaen certainly didn't remind one of monks, however. Even though the front lines passed within twenty-five to thirty kilometers, the people noisily enjoyed all the available pleasures of life. I think that, in the evenings, the marvelous Spanish music even managed to penetrate the high walls of the huge convent! In Jaen, Domingo and I went off to visit the Provincial Committee of the Spanish Communist party, the secretary of which was Comrade Nemesio Pasuelo, a member of the Central Committee of the Communist party of Spain. He greeted us warmly and introduced us to another secretary who was there with him: Cristobal Valensuela. Valensuela's secretary was a friend of Anna's from the Lenin Institute in Moscow, which did not hurt our reception. All questions concerning the arrival of the demolitions group were quickly resolved, i.e., billeting, communications with the unit commanders, and logistics.

After a few days, Comrade Pasuelo gave a dinner, which was attended by almost all the local Party workers; our adviser on the Southern Front, Vil'gelm Ivanovich Kol'man (Vil'gelm Ivanovich Kumelan) a shaven-headed Latvian colonel, with his two interpreters, a radioman, and a cipher clerk; Domingo; Vicente;

Obrucheva, and me. This was my first meeting with Jose Aroca and Pedro Martines, both members of the provincial committee. Martines was another graduate of the Lenin Institute who remembered Anna very fondly. Martines was directly responsible for all the needs of our special unit. It was interesting to watch Kol'man's two interpreters (he referred to them as his "transformers"), in action. One was a Russian-French interpreter and the other a French-Spanish interpreter: neither could translate directly from Russian to Spanish, or vice versa. When Kol'man spoke, the first interpreter translated his Russian into French, and the second then retranslated the French into Spanish. All Spanish communications to Kol'man had to follow the same process in reverse, from Spanish to French, and then from French to Russian. Inevitably, both interpreters sometimes made inaccurate translations, resulting in significant misunderstandings.

We learned much about the accomplishments of the provincial Communists. Since the very first days of the rebellion, the Spanish Communist party, led by Pasuelo, had fought against the rebels. In Jaen there remained only one member of the committee: Martines, who was an invalid. An enormous workload had fallen on his shoulders, and partially because of this, he was unable to resist some twists and turns in agricultural policies. Only when the remaining members of the provincial committee returned from the front, was it possible to carry out some agricultural reforms in the interests of the poor; and even then, although the members were present, the reforms had to be put through in secret session.

We also learned about the heroic struggle of miners and the metal workers of Jaen Province. Later, by order of the Party provincial committee, these metal workers from Linares and Ubeda made casings for small mines, which we loaded with homemade explosives and homemade fuses.

The comrades from the Party provincial committee prepared accommodations for us right alongside the convent. When he looked at the cloister, occupying a broad expanse almost in the center of the city, Vicente made a logical observation: "We won't be disturbed in a neighborhood like this. The Fascists will never drop bombs there!"

He was wrong—in the first air raid after our arrival, a bomb struck in the vicinity of our house.

About that time, we got some very important information about partisan detachments behind Franco's lines in Cordoba and Granada, including a large group in the mining region of Minas de Riotinto. These partisans carried out attacks on the enemy every day. Continuous communications weren't maintained with this detachment, or with the others, however. Attempts at creating an organized underground in the enemy rear were unsuccessful because all the inhabitants of some cities and villages had fled to Republican territory.

Nevertheless, we believed that our unit could operate successfully because there was no continuous front. In the mountains, there was lots of cover, and small groups of demolitions men could hide easily during the day. Moreover, many of the enemy's most important lines of communication were located so close to his own forward positions that we could easily reach them and return on night sorties.

I mentioned this to Kol'man, the military adviser, whom I visited during the very first day in Jaen. A fine fellow, calm and reasonable like nearly all Latvians, Kol'man completely agreed with me.

"Domingo's group must operate in the Granada, Cordoba, and Peñarroya regions," he said, bending over the map and outlining these points with his pencil. "The Front commander requires that we limit the enemy's capability to systematically bring up reserves. We also need to divert the maximum number of troops to guarding the lines of communication. At the same time, the demolitions men are to collect intelligence and capture tongues. Think you can do it?"

"With our people, it's easier to blow up a few cars or derail a troop train than to capture a tongue."

"And how about organizing demolitions in supply dumps and airfields?"

"That we can do!" Domingo exclaimed enthusiastically.

"Then let's define more precisely what you intend to do, and identify top priorities . . ."

The military adviser threw down his pencil and energetically rubbed his high forehead.

"I've gotta admit, I'm tired," he said with a guilty smile. "So many problems . . ."

One day, when I returned from an exercise, I noticed that Juan Grande was not present among the troops. Juan had been grumbling a few days earlier, saying that he had made a mistake when he joined the demolitions men. "I thought they had called me to fight, but here we are, fooling around with kids' toys. They're even trying to makes us interpreters, too! I'm a soldier, not an interpreter!"

Juan had threatened to return on foot to Albasete, to the International Brigade. "On foot or not, he took off," said one of the soldiers confirming my suspicion. "He packed his gear and headed for the station before the exercise."

At that instant, a distraught Yan Tikhiy appeared before me. Was he also planning to leave?

"What's up? Does Jaen bore you, too?"

"Don't get mad, Rudolph, but I've got to have a serious talk with you."

"Speak: I'm listening."

"You've got to understand. You're fascinated with demolitions equipment and tactics. You load us down with information, and that's great, but you're forgetting about the human spirit. We came to Spain to kill Fascists; you only send your old-timers behind rebel lines. We just get taught and taught some more! It's an insult . . ."

"The old-timers have more experience."

"It's better to get your experience in combat—word of honor! Juan just couldn't take it any longer. He's an emotional guy."

"I want to train you well. Do you think Juan has already run off?"

"I don't think so. There's been no train since morning."

"Let's go to the the station."

"You won't convince him now!"

"Let's give a try anyway!"

Vicente quickly drove us to the station, where, in the waiting room, Juan sat plunged in gloom.

In place of a hello, he said "I'm going to Albasete!"

"Listen to me. Tomorrow, your buddies are going off on a mission, and you're cutting out? I've relied on you a lot. I thought we'd be going together on this operation."

Juan Grande turned to us with an embarrassed look: "Really?"

"Yes. Didn't it occur to you that your comrades might think you'd chickened out?"

Juan didn't know where to put his huge hands. Then, uncertainly, he looked at me.

"Put on your gear, Pat," Yan Tikhiy said, "put on your gear, and let's go to the car. Enough of this. But just remember: there are no movies over in Albasete."

"Go to hell!" barked Juan Grande. "So okay, I'm ready. If we're going to fight tomorrow, then I guess I'll stay . . ."

The time that we spent in Jaen was not wasted. In comparison to the Teruel operation, we now had impressive forces at our disposal and were able to operate with many groups. Domingo reported to the Front commander that the troops were ready for combat. The demolitions men were immediately given several missions. They were sent to Cordoba, to Granada, and to the area north of Granada. We were to blow railroad and highway bridges, set up derailments of troop trains, blow up enemy vehicles, wreck aircraft on airfields, and destroy production facilities.

Other groups got the mission of finding people in the enemy rear area who were sympathetic to the cause of the republic and ready to help in destroying important military targets. While we were thus engaged, Kol'man took the opportunity to attempt to entice Anna away from my unit. He claimed that his two "transformers" made communication with Spanish officials virtually impossible, which was certainly true, and he pointed out that I already had two additional interpreters on whom I could rely. He also derided the conditions of our lifestyle that Anna had to share, for example, the ever-present explosives—she kept dynamite under her bunk—and the physical hardships. In my absence, Anna talked over his offer with some of the men of my unit, and on their advice, decided to remain with us.

While Kol'man was engaged in his recruiting effort, I took Juan Grande with me to Granada, as I had promised. Captain Ungria went north to the famous Guadalquivir River, on whose banks stood Cordoba. The positions of the Republican troops in the north approached to within eight to nine kilometers of Granada, and halfway surrounded the town. There was one railroad at the rebels' disposal at that time, connecting the garrison of Granada with those of Seville, Cadiz, and other strongpoints occupied by the Fascists in southern Spain. The automobile highway, heading west, was also in their hands.

By order of the command, on a night in the near future, the special unit was to blow the railroad bridge at about ten kilometers out of Granada and to reduce the city's production of electrical energy for military purposes.

We arrived at the designated jump-off spot at midday. We had to leave the cars a few kilometers back, not because we were afraid of ambushes or artillery bombardment, but because the prolonged rains had rendered the roads impassable. We had not yet unloaded the explosives from the cars. The necessary guards were left beside them, and the rest of the troops I led to the command post of the battalion that was defending the sector which had been assigned to us. Stuck in the mud, we finally found the CP, four kilometers from the road.

The battalion commander, a hefty, forty-five-year-old former sailor, had been previously informed of the arrival of the demoli-

tions team, and he was waiting for us. He was not troubled by our
gentle hints that we were short on food.

"I'll feed you, I'll get you warm! But we don't have villas here
for rest and rehabilitation, however. You'll have to sleep without
fires and mattresses!" he said, joking along. Suddenly, staring at
Juan Grande, he asked: "Are you a sailor?"

The battalion CO was really pleased to have guessed Juan's
profession. They pounded each other on the back, got right down
to informal terms of address, started recalling familiar ships, ports,
and the keepers of every tavern and fleshpot from London to
Lima. I realized that our efforts wouldn't be wasted here. A sailor
will never let another sailor down: he might have to put himself
out, but he'd do what had to be done!

Which is exactly what happened afterward: the battalion commander provided us with supplies, selected outstanding guides,
and also detached some of his soldiers to take part in the group's
sortie.

But, at the outset, the battalion CO caused us a little grief: it
appeared that the battalion didn't do any patrolling.

"Why, Commander?"

"*No hai ordenes* (There are no orders)!" he said, shrugging his
shoulders.

It wasn't the first time that we had heard that damned "no orders" in Spain!

We had to do our own reconnaissance against the enemy, just
as we did at Teruel, and we just resigned ourselves to it.

That evening, the battalion commander accompanied me and
some other demolitions men to the first line of trenches. The
trenches were poorly dug: the sides, where the clay was unstable,
were not reinforced, and in many places had collapsed. Water
squelched under our boots. We climbed out of the communications trench and went up the hill. The sky was totally black, but
down there in the hollow, sparkled a glittering field of hundreds
of bright constellations: the lights of Granada

The battalion commander stopped, turned toward the glowing
points of light, and tugging on his leather belt, he said: "Granada
. . . leave her alone, you swine!"

At nightfall the following day, our group quietly passed through
the battalion outposts, loaded down with explosives. Antonio and
his men had already left before nightfall.

The battalion commander accompanied the demolitions team to
the foremost outposts, excitedly wishing us luck.

Darkness. Silence. More mud clung to our puttees with each
step. There were ditches, furrows of some kind, and stones under

foot. But down there in front of us lay all the glittering lights of Granada.

Granada! No other city in Spain has so won the affection of Russian poets! The immortal Pushkin dreamed of your beauties. In our own times, Mikhail Svetlov dedicated noteworthy verses to you. For the Russian people, Granada became a symbol of passionate love and great bravery.

The marchers were tired. We had to take a break. I asked Yan Tikhiy to remind the troops once more what to do in the event the enemy attacked while we were working on the bridge. Our biggest danger was probably the threat from the direction of the highway. Ten kilometers from the bridge, there was a strong rebel garrison from which they could rush reinforcements. We had to act swiftly, in absolute silence.

We reached the bridge over the Genil River undetected. The scouts reported that the bridge was unguarded.

The evening passenger train from Granada had already passed by. The next one was expected in the morning. It had already been established that we would take no chances of derailing the passenger train with a mine. Kol'man had warned us to make sure we did not blow a passenger train!

At 10:30, the demolitions men got to the bridge. Some men under Juan Grande got busy with the lower belt of girders, and others began to fasten TNT charges to the upper belt. Sanchez and a group of soldiers went to set mines under the rails. We worked in silence: conversation was forbidden. One charge, a second, a third, . . . now only one left, and then: all done!

The silence was abruptly broken by a shot from the direction of the highway, followed, a moment later, by another rifle shot. A flare soared into the sky. Pale light flooded the railroad embankment, and I saw Juan Grande's men running and dropping their explosive charges.

The flare died out, and the night immediately grew darker. We had to blow the bridge, but it might be too late! A second rocket illuminated us. Invisible marksmen opened up heavy rifle fire. The demolitions men took cover from the rifle fire behind the embankment. The bridge was clear of our people, but the mining wasn't completed. It was a good thing that those were TNT charges, and not dynamite: a chance shot would have blown us all right out of this world.

Vicente activated the igniters. The two of us inserted them into the charges, and then crawled behind the embankment where the rest of the unit was waiting. The medic was bandaging three wounded. The enemy continued to illuminate the area with flares, and occasionally shot at the bridge. We had to get farther away from the bridge and cross the highway before the rebels received reinforcements! We sprinted along the embankment, jumping across the railroad bed in short dashes, and after about three minutes managed to cross the automobile road.

We had to force the enemy to give up pursuit and divert his attention from our group, and so we left some delayed-action grenades on the road.

On the bridge, bright flame shot up, and a powerful explosion reverberated through the air, but the bridge received only insignificant damage: it didn't even sag! The explosion did encourage our troops, however: they hadn't gone through all this for nothing!

The Fascists, who had followed us in vehicles, reached the bridge. The noise of the motors stopped, and in two to three minutes, a heavy machine gun furiously opened up from the embankment. As one man, the troops threw themselves into a ditch. I waved my hand in a northerly direction: "Crawl that way!" Stopping to catch a breath, I was able to look back. Fascist soldiers were running across the fields and along the roads, shooting at us. From behind the embankment, a new group of Fascists showed themselves. Where had they come from?

Two hundred meters from the ditch, we again set delayed-action grenades, and took off toward an isolated cottage with a garden

About that time, the grenades that we had dropped along the road exploded, and the enemy fire slacked off. We rejoiced, but somewhat prematurely. Up until this time we had been covered from the light of the flares by olive trees, but now we had to cross an open field . . .

In the garden of the empty cottage, we set two mines and five more delayed-action grenades, and managed to get out into the field. In some places, it was covered with stubble, in other places, it was rocky, but the going got easier. Then in the garden, the grenades began to explode and firing began. The Fascists had obviously surrounded the cottage. I warned everyone not to return the fire. Soon the enemy lost us.

I decided to check whether everyone got out all right, and found that Yan Tikhiy and Miguel, Rosalina's fiancé, were missing. Rubio set out to look for them. We didn't have to wait too long before we could make out the bits of fox fire attached to their clothing, gleaming like fireflies. Rubio and Tikhiy came up, carrying Miguel. The medic rushed to the wounded man, but Miguel was already beyond medical help. Then, the lights of Granada, serving as a beacon for us, suddenly died out. It was as if the city had just dropped off the face of the earth. The deafening roar of an explosion reached us. Antonio's group had struck!

The troops, who had seen us off not long before, hurried out from the battalion positions. They carefully took Miguel's body. The battalion commander thrust a flask of wine into my hands: "We didn't think you'd make it back!" he said.

Antonio returned about an hour later. His group sustained no losses. Clutching the battalion commander's seemingly inexhaustible flask, the radiant Antonio excitedly told us how he had successfully put out the lights of Granada.

The demolitions men had passed through the enemy lines unnoticed and had arrived at the electric power plant precisely on time. Both buildings of the power plant, the upper one on the dam and the lower one by the standpipes, were brightly illuminated. Not far away, there were dark silhouettes of armed men, but there was no guard around the standpipes themselves. Taking Pedro along with him, and giving orders that the remaining troops cover him with fire if necessary, Antonio crawled up to the standpipes. When they had mined both standpipes, placing five-kilo charges of TNT on each, Antonio and Pedro crawled back to their party: the igniters would work within five to six minutes.

The two blasts occurred almost simultaneously, and the lights went out in Granada. There was no pursuit.

"We were really worried about your safety," said Antonio. "We heard a real battle breaking out around the bridge. What was going on there?"

"They spotted us. Miguel's dead. Three wounded."

"Miguel?" Antonio was about to lift the flask to his mouth, but he didn't quite make it.

In our house in Jaen, peace and quiet reigned. Anna Obrucheva called out loudly: "Rosa! Rosa! They're back!"

"Wait!" I tried to stop my interpreter, but the radiant Rosa already stood at the door.

"*Salud*, Rudolph! You got back quickly! I didn't even have time to finish sewing his shirt!" When she looked at me, Rosa understood everything without my saying a word. Crumpling up Miguel's unsewn shirt, she hid her face in it.

Before we left for Jaen, I had begun attempts to train intelligence people. Our experience at Teruel clearly showed that we needed our own sources of information and could not rely on the intelligence supplied by the Front staff. We encountered more problems training intelligence men than we did training saboteurs, however, because we were often working with illiterate or at least poorly educated peasants who certainly were not lacking in bravery, but had difficulty writing down what they had learned about the enemy. Before our departure for the Southern Front, Domingo had introduced me to Capt. Francisco del Castillo Sain de Texado who commanded a battalion of twelve hundred men and controlled a large network of Republican partisan, underground, and intelligence personnel, operating in the enemy rear. Del Castillo needed assistance in organizing communications for his network and in evaluating and analyzing the mass of data that it produced. As soon as we got to Jaen, Domingo and I began to devote a lot of attention to organizing a true partisan intelligence service, using del Castillo's assets. I immediately encountered the language barrier, which is a constant in all foreign intelligence work. My personal participation in the development of our intelligence service was limited from the start by my inability to speak Spanish. All Anna's efforts to teach me Spanish had been in vain: I'd acquired only a very limited vocabulary, and never could grasp basic grammar. For example, I always used the infinitive form of the few verbs I knew, which exasperated Anna who was a perfectionist in grammar. While I may have been hampered by my inability to speak Spanish, Anna was perfectly suited for it. She had native fluency in Spanish and a fine background in subversive work at the Lenin Institute, where she had trained Latin Americans in illegal activities of all kinds, including secret writing, organization of clandestine communications nets, and the tactics of subversion. She was already fully familiar with the technical Spanish vocabulary of this type of work. Soon after we got to Jaen, she became indispensable to our intelligence program, making "meets" with sources; collecting, translating, and analyzing material from dead drops; and even tasking agents. Anna worked very well with Captain Ungria's sixty-year-old intelligence deputy, Agustin Fabregas, an old Communist. Soon we had a completely covert, illegal organization, extending back one hundred kilometers into the enemy rear, with agents at all important bases and facilities, including major airfields. These agents not only collected and reported intelligence on enemy activities but they carried out sabotage, initially using homemade delayed-action mines, and later, magnetic mines. In addition to her intelligence activities, Anna also solved many of our logistics problems: she found that Spanish notions of chivalry made it difficult for Republican officers on the Southern Front staff to refuse requests from a woman, particularly an attractive Russian military woman. Accompanied by Domingo, she made frequent visits to the staff and was always successful in getting them to release all kinds of essential supplies—ammunition, fuel, explosives, and other equipment—even though she had no authorization! This kind of deception was necessary because ours was an illegal and unofficial organization, not even carried on the republic's military supply allowances.

Recognition at Last!

I'm reading over some newspapers of those remote and disturbing days: newspapers of that heroic and tragic spring of 1937. Familiar names of people, and cities, and rivers pass before my eyes.

On 8 February, government troops shelled the bridge at Alcolea in the Guadalquivir, 15 kilometers from Cordoba. The cities of Montoro and Lopera were occupied by troops of Republican units.

On 8 February, the Fascist rebels, with superior forces, successfully occupied Malaga . . .

On 12 February, the fiery Dolores Ibarrury spoke in the Olimpia movie house in Valencia, calling for the rear to be strengthened and cleansed of all idlers and enemy agents . . .[1]

On 21 February, the Republican government of Spain announced the mobilization of men between the ages of 23 and 27. About 150,000 men will flow into the ranks of the army.

On 25 February, aircraft of the Fascist interventionists carried out a savage attack on the city of Andujar. There were many civilian dead and wounded.

According to a "Havas" correspondent, Italian troops in Abyssinia used poison gas.

And here is a March report which is particularly memorable for me:

On 11 March, Republican troops on the southern front blew up bridges at Alcolea and Las Pedroces, paralyzing enemy troop train traffic . . .

1. The "cleansing of the rear area" involved mass executions carried out by military and police, and the barbaric peasant tribunals described by Hemingway in For Whom the Bell Tolls. It also involved operations by Republican guerrilla groups operating in the Republican rear.—Transl.

On 25 March, Republican troops successfully beat off an enemy attack at Posoblanco ...

Defeat of rebels and interventionists at Guadalajara! An impressive victory for Republican troops! Large numbers of prisoners and captured weapons ...

On 25 March, a munitions train was blown up by Republican troops at Montoro. The bridges at Bélmez and Espiel were destroyed ...

I sit over the yellowed newspaper pages, but I see neither the headlines on the stories nor the lines of the reports. From across the miles and the years, a vision comes back to me, a vision of a road, flooded in spring sunshine, the road leading from Jaen, via Andujar and by the monastery of La Virgen de la Cabeza, to the battalion command post. Vicente accelerated, and we flew past the "sacred place" in fourth gear. From the walls of the monastery, belated shots rang out.

I see clearly the little town of Andujar, all crunched together as though it were a single, very antiquated building. I see a room with a fireplace where Colonel Peres Salas, commander of the Southern Front, received us. He was tall and sharp, an old-fashioned ladies' man. He had been a professional officer of the Spanish Army, but he was one of those officers who stayed loyal to the Republic. And now Peres Salas was invested with great authority.

Courteously inclining his graying head, the colonel listened to Obrucheva who was interpreting my presentation. He was extremely friendly with the interpreter (she was, after all, a woman, and he was a Spaniard!) but always curt with me.

What was going on? If this was going to degenerate into some kind of personal conversation between the two of them, I couldn't even begin to convince this self-assured fellow that a small group of demolitions men could easily derail a troop train carrying an enemy infantry or tank battalion.

The colonel was smoking and obviously getting a little nervous.

Right from the start of our meeting, Peres Salas took great pains to give me no reason to doubt his negative view of the military advisers and volunteers, regardless of their nationality. He, the commander of the Southern Front, considered that he needed neither advisers nor volunteers. He only needed weapons! If weapons and equipment were provided, the Republican Army would gain victory over Franco without the help of volunteers. All of this was always expressed quite categorically and directly.

I intentionally ignored the colonel's views, however, and tried to prove to him something that, in my view, needed no proof.

Waiting until I paused, the colonel politely asked Obrucheva: "Excuse me: are you also Russian?"

I had spent enough time in Spain to understand that question without an interpreter.

"Yes, I'm Russian," responded Obrucheva.

"Blessed Mary!" The colonel threw up his hands in mock despair. "I am an unredeemable ignoramus! I thought that there was nothing else in Russia but polar bears, bearded Bolsheviks, and volunteers! Apparently, charming girls live there as well!"

"I'm a volunteer, too," said Obrucheva, blushing.

Peres Salas looked at her sadly: "Everywhere, young people are searching for adventure! Such rash impulses, such ardent hearts! And Spain is so picturesque in novels . . ."

"You're mistaken, Colonel. Your compliment pleases me, but unfortunately, I'm not as young as I look. I have an eight-year-old daughter."

"You went off to war, leaving your daughter?! Do your wives also accompany husbands on their trips?"

"Wrong again, Colonel. I'm just an interpreter."

Peres Salas was silent. What he had just heard did not fit in with his perceptions of the world and of people.

They offered us coffee: the colonel began to inquire about the Soviet Union. Taking advantage of the opportunity, I led the discussion around to my own people. Relying on the experience of Teruel, I tried to explain that cutting the enemy's lines of communication and attacks on bridges were less effective than derailments of troop trains:

"I'm aware that the command is considering employing the demolitions men for attacks on bridges, stations, enemy ammunition dumps, and airfields. And if we're ordered to, we'll do all of that. But casualties appear to be significant, and the effectiveness of such operations is doubtful. In any case, that is a completely different story from destroying enemy equipment and soldiers while they are being transported. Setting up train derailments with mines, you will be operating truly . . ."

Peres Salas forcefully shoved aside his demitasse:

"I absolutely forbid you to set up derailments on sections of track where there is passenger traffic! Mistakes are possible, and then public opinion will turn against us! Fascist propaganda does not lose the opportunity to portray partisan operations as banditry!"

"What public opinion are you talking about, Colonel? There's not a single honest man in this world who would dare to blame the republic! I hope that you haven't forgotten that the Fascist swine destroyed thousands of noncombatants of Madrid and other cities?"

"We are not Fascists! We do not have the right to subject a peaceful population to risk!"

"Excuse me, but it's not clear to me about whom you're concerned. All the noncombatants have fled from the immediate frontline area into Republican territory, so who do you think is riding passenger trains? I'm sure that the rebels are not using the railroad to take noncombatants on picnics at the front!"

"None the less . . ."

"When the air force bombs supply dumps, stations, and even troop trains, there is also a threat to noncombatants. The bottom line is this: the war goes on."

"The air force is one thing, but demolitions is another. In short, I categorically forbid you to set up derailments on sections of track where there is passenger traffic. Your mines cannot distinguish a train carrying noncombatants from a troop train. It's better to let the demolitions men blow bridges and stations, and shoot up troop trains."

Domingo only smiled when he learned about the results of our visit with the Front commander. "We'll see!" he said enigmatically. "We operate behind enemy lines. The rules are different there."

The vision of my visit with Colonel Peres Salas, is replaced by another vision: again, there's a road, bathed in sunlight. In a Mercedes, we are trying to make way against a flood of refugees heading in our direction. The enemy had attacked Posoblanco, and so the inhabitants fled. Squeaking, high-wheeled carts crept slowly along, carrying crying, confused children and downcast women. The mules anxiously twitched their ears, and the eyes of these mild animals were filled with fear. It was as if even the animals in Spain had come to know what kind of danger lurked in the sunshine!

Flushed with anger, Vicente drove us to Andujar. We didn't recognize the little town, which was hidden by a thick cloud of brick dust. The house where we had met with Colonel Peres Salas, simply did not exist anymore. The air raid had just ended. Women cried mournfully, searching for their children. Some of them were on their knees in the middle of the streets, hurling curses at the sky. We unloaded the dynamite and turned over the car for use in carrying casualties.

Around a half-destroyed house, a small group of people worked with crowbars, makeshift levers, and spades. The group was commanded by Jimenes, the secretary of the Andujar Party committee. From beneath the wreckage, you could hear children crying and audible moans.

"Enough!" yelled Jimenes, and climbed into an opening that had been outlined in the ruins. Several tense minutes dragged by, and then Jimenes lifted a sobbing boy, two or three years old, from a crevice between some stones. They saved the child, but the mother was already dead.

Pepe found us only after an hour. He had driven eight severely injured children and women to the hospital. Two of the kids died on the way. There were few trained medical personnel available, so Anna's knowledge of first aid proved invaluable. She immediately offered her services at an emergency field-dressing station, working desperately to handle the long lines of casualties awaiting attention.

All this notwithstanding, in the meeting that followed, Colonel Peres Salas reconfirmed his ban on derailing trains. The enemy battalions, tanks, and weapons would be allowed to pass undisturbed to the front so that they could then destroy Republican soldiers and noncombatants.

My visions of the past continue to change, one following the other: this time, it is evening: olive branches are clearly silhouetted against a purple sunset. Rubio whistles while packing dynamite into a tin can. Beside him is a whole pantry full of tin cans that will be transformed into grenades.

"Listen, Domingo, didn't Pepe tell you about our idea?" Rubio asked the commander.

"What idea?"

"We want to take a little stroll around behind enemy lines. We're going to cross the front lines, capture a couple of Fascist vehicles, and go for a ride. Maybe we can do something or other over there . . ."

Rubio was right. It might damn well be possible to do something over there, like set mines on highways and railroads, and blow up bridges!

"Let's think about it, Rubio."

It's early morning. There's a delicate aroma of earth and vegetation.

An energetic knock comes on the door. It must be Captain Ungria. And there he is! Unshaven but happy, he stands on the threshold, flashing a smile. "*Salud!* Our group put an electric power line out of commission at Cordoba. At the same time, we also selected an outstanding location for a covert partisan base. Want to come see?"

"You really can sit down if you like. Is it far?"

"Not very: several kilometers west of Adamuz. Actually, it's pretty close—just across the front lines. With the binoculars, you can see the Fascist electric power plant from there. Let's go organize another base with a laboratory in Villanueva de Cordoba!"

"Listen, Domingo: why did you bring your wife and son?"

"She came of her own free will, damn her, and a kid who's a soldier's son from childhood ought to be accustomed to our life by now! So—are we going to Villanueva?"

"We'll have to go."

Images of the past! So many of them.

Now I'm reading Spanish and Italian Fascist newspapers of February 1937. Many columns are outlined in funereal black, denoting heavy Fascist casualties. Do all these papers deal with the same war? Yes, they do.

In the spring of 1937, Republican demolitions men carried out many sorties into the enemy rear just when he was launching an offensive. They were successful in establishing several covert bases in the rebel rear, like the base west of Adamuz, which I just mentioned. The roads and military targets of the enemy were located rather far behind the front lines. It took the demolitions men a lot of time to reach them, and they often had to spend two to three days there. Well-camouflaged bases right in the enemy's rear area not only gave our people the opportunity to take cover during daylight hours but to carry out several operations on one sortie without crossing the front lines each time.

We set up the base at Adamuz on the premises of an abandoned creamery, surrounded by a dense olive grove. The presence of this base permitted small groups to reach the Peñarroya-Cordoba or Montoro-Cordoba rail lines in the course of one night, mine them, and disappear without a trace.

There were no inhabitants in the immediate area of the creamery: all the peasants had fled to Republican territory. It was Capt. Francisco del Castillo who steered Captain Ungria to the best place to set up our base. We had worked with del Castillo on the Southern Front. In addition to the battalion he commanded, del Castillo controlled a large clandestine sabotage and intelligence organization behind enemy lines. He was well acquainted with the situation there, and had made more than one dangerous sortie across the front lines himself.[2] From the small but dense grove that surrounded the abandoned creamery, we could clearly see the road leading from Cordoba to the electric station, which was situated three kilometers from us.

On the highway below us, enemy vehicles passed peacefully. Soldiers walked along the roadside, and not one of them even suspected that we were close by. And we just kept watching . . .

There was definitely a danger of being detected, but we were very careful. We posted the necessary military security on all possible approaches to the creamery. On the most dangerous paths leading to the base, command-detonated, rock-throwing fougasses were set; at night, we supplemented these with pressure or tripwire mines. We kept movement on the base premises to a minimum: the little creamery looked empty. We maintained an alternate base in the vicinity, and if the Fascists discovered us and attacked during daylight hours, we would withdraw to that base, leaving delayed-action grenades behind us as we went. If an attack came at night, we planned to withdraw across the front lines. This might seem very straightforward, but you have to remember that there were no continuous front lines, and it was often very difficult to know whether you were in friendly territory or not.

It was from this abandoned building that groups, including those commanded by Rubio and Alex Kunslich, the American partisan, departed to derail a munitions train east of Montoro, to blow up a train in the tunnel on the Peñarroya-Cordoba line, and to blow several bridges in the same area.

The tunnel was put out of commission by means of a "pickup" mine, of a type tested at Kiev in 1932. The engine pulling the munitions train picked up the mine from the tracks outside the tunnel and dragged it into the tunnel where the mine exploded, exactly as we had calculated. The road was heavily damaged, and the tunnel was blocked. It took the enemy almost five days to fully restore traffic there. The Fascists attacking Posoblanco were much in need of that road because it was used to bring up troop reserves. The catastrophe was quite unexpected because after our first attempt to blow the tunnel, the rebels had stationed almost an entire battalion to guard it. They would never guess that the mine had been carried in by the steam engine itself!

I must state that Colonel Peres Salas, when he had given the order to blow the tunnel, generously offered Captain Domingo a company of soldiers and a ton of dynamite. Actually, all we

---

2. Castillo survived the civil war and escaped to the Soviet Union, where he fought in World War II, and retired on a pension.

needed to do all that was nine demolitions men and fifty kilograms of explosives.

"The Front commander knows regulations very well, but he's completely unacquainted with partisan equipment," Domingo said afterward. "Otherwise he wouldn't have been so free with his resources. So here we are, with a ton of dynamite on our hands!"

"Didn't you try to talk to the colonel about setting up train derailments?" I asked.

"I did try once to explain to that deaf monarchist that we've got to blow up enemy trains! I'd have had more luck explaining it to his horse!"

"Look, let's get it straight, Peres Salas is no monarchist . . ."

"I don't care! He's a—how do you say it in Russian?—a *poputchik* (a fellow traveler, i.e., a Communist sympathizer). Sure, sure! He's a fellow traveler. But mark my words, he's untrustworthy." (To the credit of Colonel Peres Salas, I must note that he remained loyal to the republic to the end and was executed by the Fascists in 1939.)

Domingo was so excited that I thought I wouldn't be able to stop him. But the captain was obviously protesting too loudly: after the explosion in the tunnel, Peres Salas began to treat the demolitions men better. But he never permitted the derailment of trains in areas where there was passenger traffic.

Well, orders are orders! Nevertheless, the demolitions men violated them once . . .

On a moonlit night, we left the base at Adamuz with three groups and set out for the railroad junction of Cordoba. Some kilometers out of the city, far from the road, one of the groups came upon an abandoned *cortico*—a fieldstone shepherd's hut with a low earthen wall. Around dawn, it was raining heavily, and the troops were exhausted, so we decided to rest. We left Marques, a Spaniard, on guard. Juan Grande stretched out next to the door, his carbine in his hands. Rubio found a place on a bench, under the window. The rest lay down on the floor, and sleep instantly overcame them. The only people awake were Antonio, fussing with his Mauser, and two new recruits, Aldo and Emilio, Italians from the Garibaldi Battalion, who were softly chatting about something or other. I began to doze off, but they woke me up quickly.

"A shepherd is coming to the *cortico*. He's herding goats and sheep," Group Commander Marques whispered. Hiding behind the window, we began to follow the owner of the *cortico*.

The shepherd was obviously brave. He saw our tracks, but plodded right on toward the hut. We'd be getting acquainted soon!

We revealed ourselves to the old fellow, and asked him to tell us what he knew about Cordoba.

The shepherd sat on the threshold of the hut, just like they sit in Tver or Ryazan, leaning his crook in the corner.

"There are lots of Fascists in Cordoba," he began, slowly. "Very many . . . And they're always on the move, always on the move. Go on about one and one half kilometers, and there's a road: you'll see for yourselves that I'm telling the truth. Their forces are large: lots of men and vehicles, more than enough to do the job. Over there, not far away, they're building an airfield, and that's bad for you boys, believe old Manuel, it's going to be bad. You won't be able to cope with the Italians who are going to run that airfield."

"Looks like the time has come again to send another 'Greeting to Mussolini,' " Aldo said to Emilio.

Sitting on the threshold, old Manuel looked at the speaker in confusion. "An Italian!—Please sir, I'm an old man . . ."

"Our Italians are not like those sitting in Cordoba," Rubio said to calm the shepherd. "These guys are from the Garibaldi Battalion; that means they're friends of the people and enemies of Franco."

The old man arose, unbending his spine with difficulty, and extended his big sun-darkened hands to Aldo and Emilio.

"I am happy to welcome honorable Italians to my home! Thank you, boys, for coming here to us, thanks . . ."

A low whistle was heard from outside: Sanchez, standing watch, was warning us of more danger. A slender girl approached the *cortico*, exchanging smiles with two Fascist soldiers.

"That's my younger daughter, Esperanza," old Manuel mumbled. "Forgive the little sinner, she's really not guilty. The guys are always courting the girls . . ."

The soldiers following along behind Esperanza were disarmed and searched before they knew what hit them. Simple village boys, they had been called up for service with the rebels only a short while before. They served in a reserve regiment in Cordoba, and from time to time, they were assigned guard duty on bridges and crossings. They were drilled hard and poorly fed.

While Marques interrogated the soldiers, our own boys found it possible to calm down Manuel's daughter with compliments. Soon she was happily flirting with them all!

The rain began again. Now it was coming down in torrents. Manuel's goats and sheep bunched up under a huge tree on which grew some kind of pods. The old man looked at the flock with concern.

"You can't do anything about your sheep. Afterward, we'll gather them up. Meanwhile, we can't release you or your daughter. You know—this is war," Antonio explained apologetically to the old man.

The prisoners looked in confusion at each other and then at the demolitions men. One of the soldiers finally couldn't hold back any longer and, not addressing himself to anyone in particular, asked in a voice strained with emotion:

"What's going to happen to us?"

There was silence in the house. As a matter of fact, what *could* you do with prisoners? Night was going to fall soon, and we'd be off on our mission. We couldn't take them with us, but at the same time, we couldn't just release them. Leave them under guard at the *cortico*? That also wouldn't do: we weren't coming back this way.

After a long argument we decided to take the soldiers with us.

"Even though you served the Fascists," said Marques to the soldiers, "we are giving you your lives. Now you prove to us that we haven't made a mistake. We're reconnaissance men. We need to reach the railroad, undetected. At ten o'clock in the evening, a passenger train passes, and then a military train follows. We have to be in place by ten o'clock."

Marques and Antonio tied up the prisoners, who had definitely cheered up. We excused ourselves to Manuel and his daughter for the inconvenience, and took to the trail again.

We got to the railroad on time. The prisoners actually led the group to a stretch of road on a turn where the tracks passed along a cliff. Now all we had to do was carry out our mission. Precisely observing the prohibition set forth by Colonel Peres Salas, we were to let passenger trains go through, but to patiently wait for military trains, and blow them up.

At first, it was suggested that we split into three groups and set mines at three widely separated points on the track. That plan had already been changed in the *cortico*, as a result of the bad weather. It was decided that we'd all operate together.

In the distance, the carefree lights of Cordoba glowed. From the airfield next to the city, aircraft engines thundered. One after another, Italian bombers rose into the sky with loud roars.

The passenger train showed up right on schedule. It buzzed by, illuminating us with its windows, and happily headed for Cordoba.

"Wait for the troop trains," whispered one of the prisoners.

We knew that the troop trains would run next. When we had

waited a few more minutes and made certain that there were no guards about, the demolitions men moved up to the railroad.

They worked quietly: they had learned a lot on the recent sorties, and if a demolitions man is quiet, then you know things are going well. We set two mines, and all our reserve explosives under the outside rails of the railroad track on the turn.

"Ready," whispered Marques, "let's go!"

The rails were already buzzing, and with each second the train was getting closer. We couldn't see it, and even the lights from the engines weren't visible. They only appeared when our troops had withdrawn from the roadbed a few hundred meters.

Suddenly I heard a loud exclamation from Juan Grande, violating every security rule in the book: "Look!" Disappointment, despair, and horror were in his voice. I turned around and went numb. Along the mined stretch of track rushed the gaily sparkling lights of the coaches of a passenger train.

What could we do? In my mind's eye, the stern, unyielding face of Colonel Peres Salas flashed for an instant. Could it be that the colonel was right in forbidding us to operate on lines with passenger traffic? I began to imagine people in the train, gathering up their suitcases before arriving at Cordoba, looking through the windows at the approaching lights of the city. And for some reason, for an instant, it appeared to me that there were no men in the cars, only women. Why would women be going to a city occupied by the Fascists?

Nevertheless, if I wanted to try to stop the train, I wouldn't get anywhere standing around and thinking about it! I was about a half a kilometer from the railroad bed. Signaling with a red flashlight, Juan Grande dashed toward the road, but the engineer didn't see the flashlight. Flames shot up under the wheels of the engine, and the sound of the explosion reached us. In Cordoba, the lights went out instantly . . .

That was a difficult night for me. The future didn't look too bright. I knew that excuses don't help. It would be good if they just simply took me away from this front. But what if they dismissed me completely? Danger hung over all of the demolitions men, over our whole profession. We'd worked so hard to get off to a good start!

"Rudolph! Right away!"

Pepe shook my shoulder so hard, he could have awakened the dead. Pepe was radiant, and so choked with enthusiasm that it was really impossible to understand him.

"Right away!"

I left the dairy. The rain had ceased. Under the olives sat Captain Ungria and some fat old guy with shifty eyes. The soldiers sitting around them smiled happily at me. Juan Pequeño touched me on the shoulder. Captain Ungria ruffled my hair. Confusion and happiness showed in his eyes.

"Here, listen to this yourself . . ."

The fat old bird was the alcalde (mayor) of one of the villages near Cordoba. About half an hour before, he had been picked up by our security guards. The alcalde claimed that he wanted to cross the front lines.

"What motivates you to leave the rebels, Señor?"

"Not long ago, someone from our village derailed a train near our village. The Fascists wanted to arrest me, but fortunately someone warned me."

"And why did you come to *us*?"

"Haven't I told you what was going on back there? I've had enough with all of them! Arrests are taking place in all districts."

"And all because of the passenger train?"

"By the Blessed Virgin! That train was carrying Italian soldiers, officers, and aviation technical personnel to Cordoba. And not one of them survived!"

Rubio slammed Juan Grande on the back and broke out into a loud laugh. The radiant Domingo extended his hand to me:

"And you were afraid of Peres Salas! You were in mourning!"

The alcalde fearfully began to blink his eyes. He didn't know what was happening.

For several days in a row, refugees from Cordoba—railroad workers, noncombatants, soldiers from guard units—had crossed the front lines to the Republican side. "The derailment of the train with the Italian Fascists enraged and shocked the rebels," the refugees confirmed. "They haven't found the perpetrators of the disaster yet. The bandits wreak their savage anger on anyone who falls into their hands."

Colonel Peres Salas learned of the derailment of the train on the same day that we had come back into Republican positions. He listened to the report with indifference. Soon, however, the importance of the event began to dawn even on Peres Salas because reports of the train wreck filled the Fascist and foreign press, and we managed to get copies of local Fascist papers with the obituaries of their fallen heroes. Correspondents of progressive papers began to arrive at the partisan-demolition team base in Villanueva de Cordoba. Typewriters began to rattle away, and camera shutters began to click. The demolitions team base turned into some kind of a conference hall for a while. We wondered how the journalists had found the base, but learned that they had been directed to it by the Southern Front staff. Operational security dictated that we be very careful about what we told these journalists; after all, the war was still going on, and we didn't want to give out any information that would help the enemy. I kept away from the journalists and told the soldiers not to reveal true identities of our men or the tactics they employed.

The demolitions men were especially happy to meet Mikhail Kol'tsov and Ilya Ehrenburg.[3] Kol'tsov spent a long time visiting with Captain Ungria, Rubio, Juan Grande, Pepe, and other men. He was delighted with the bravery and grit of the people.

Ilya Ehrenburg arrived exhausted, and spent the night with the demolitions men. I recall that he was delighted with our mounted couriers, and especially with the youngest of them all, the eight-year-old son of Captain Ungria.

Ehrenburg briefly described the derailment at Cordoba in a sketch printed in *Izvestiya* on 23 March 1937. Although he was careful not to reveal details concerning our personnel and tactics, his article clearly indicated to the enemy that the train wrecks and other acts of sabotage behind enemy lines were not the work of local partisans, but of special Republican units that operated across the front lines, and this caused concern for Captain Ungria and me.

The attention of the journalists and writers was naturally flattering to the demolitions men. They felt others might finally cease to regard them as a dubious burden on the army. I was also happy that we had fulfilled the specific request of the Republican infantrymen and sailors to remember to strike at enemy aviation. Finally, we all understood that now, after the flood of articles and sketches, Madrid and Valencia would also remember the demolitions men.

That's how it turned out. First, they sent us our pay for the past three months, and we paid our debts. Further, the leaders of the demolitions group were called to the general staff of the Republican Army. When they had heard Captain Ungria's report, they decided to form a special battalion for operations behind enemy lines. The troops of the battalion would receive regular army pay and aviator's rations. The supply service got orders concerning the issuing of uniforms and fuel.

We were celebrating: now, at last, we could undertake ex-

3. I. G. Ehrenburg covered the civil war for *Izvestiya*. An extreme sensitivity to Stalin's whims, coupled with highly elastic loyalties enabled him to elude the purges and the repressions of World War II, even though many of his associates were killed. After Stalin's death, he wrote in support of some political reforms and revealed some details of his personal knowledge of Stalinist terror. Kol'tsov was arrested during the purges and shot in February 1940.

tremely active and wide-ranging operations behind enemy lines! Peres Salas had to quietly acknowledge his mistakes.

Equipment in Action

In Spain, spring of 1937 was marked by new, heroic exploits of the people and new acts of treason by the venal generals, anarchists, and Trotskyites. The most difficult event of February was the surrender of Malaga. The most important port and city of the country fell into the hands of the enemy with the consent, and even the agreement, of the then deputy minister of war, General Ascensio. This happened at a time when Malaga could have been successfully defended, when enemy forces could have been tied down there, and the enemy rear threatened. The popular indignation forced Largo Caballero, who had earlier defended General Ascensio with stupid persistence, to accept the general's resignation.

Concentrating their forces, the rebels intended to cut the Madrid-Valencia road and strike at the Spanish capital from the south. In mid-February, the Fascists forced the Jarama River and captured an advantageous bridgehead. In March, they rushed toward Guadalajara, but suffered a crushing defeat on all fronts. In those days, Guadalajara was a synonym for the word *defeat*. Thousands of Italian cutthroats fell there. The removal of General Ascensio and the echo of the victory at Guadalajara sharply raised the fighting spirit of the struggling Spanish people.

Events inexorably unfolded. The rebels threatened to capture Posoblanco. The enemy intent was clear: capture Posoblanco, develop an offensive in the direction of Ciudad Real, and straighten out the front line between Montoro and Toledo.

Our military adviser on the Southern Front, Kol'man, tried with all means at his disposal to convince Peres Salas not to abandon the town and withdraw his troops to a "more favorable position." When he learned of this, Kol'man sped off again to see the Front commander, taking Anna with him. Although I was away at the time and had left her in charge, Kol'man told her that he would take full responsibility for taking her away from her assigned duties, and assured her that her assistance was essential. He claimed he did not want to risk working with his two "guardians," as he called his two interpreters, and that he needed someone who could communicate directly with the colonel without fear of misunderstanding. It was beginning to look like he was also interested in Anna from a personal viewpoint! Arriving at the Front headquarters, Kol'man had Anna interrogate two prisoners concerning conditions in the rebels' rear area, and got some fresh intelligence that they could use in arguing with the stubborn colonel.

When they got in to see Peres Salas, they did not take up the matter at hand immediately but, instead, talked for a long time about Russia, Russian arts and literature, Latvia, Leningrad, etc. When Peres Salas was in a good mood, Kol'man got to the point of the visits, and they were able to convince the colonel to stand fast at Posoblanco for reinforcements, which they promised were on the way. Later, Kol'man made yet another play for Anna, offering her the opportunity to join his staff and replace his "transformers," but she refused once more.

Early in the morning on the following day, the Fascists, preparing a decisive attack, subjected Posoblanco to heavy aerial bombing. Immediately after the air raid, however, a fresh battalion of Republican troops drove into the city. In the stubborn fighting that took place there, Captain Ungria's demolitions men operated successfully, blowing up trains and vehicles behind enemy lines and collecting important intelligence, including capturing "tongues." Posoblanco was saved.

In March 1937, Anna was unexpectedly invited by Kol'man (in my absence!) to meet none other than G. M. Shtern (Comrade Grigorovich),[1] senior Soviet adviser to the Spanish Republican government, who informed her that she had been awarded the Order of the Red Banner (her second!).[2] When she asked why I had not recieved a similar decoration in view of my efforts, Shtern told her that I had been decorated, and directed her to tell me the news, saying that he was sorry that I wasn't around at the time! Shtern wasted no time in trying to pressure Anna into transferring to Kol'man's staff, but she begged to be allowed to remain with my unit, and Kol'man and Shtern regretfully honored her request.

The troops of the special battalion (Translator's note: *battal'on spetsialnogo naznacheniya*, or *spetsnaz* battalion) enthusiastically received the decision of the March Plenum of the Central Committee of the Communist party of Spain, promoting the combat

1. Col. General Grigoriy Mikhailovich Shtern returned to the USSR, and fought with distinction against the Japanese in Mongolia, and the Finns in the Winter War. He commanded the Far Eastern Front and served as chief of air defense forces before being arrested and shot in 1941.

2. It is likely that Obrucheva received her first Order of the Red Banner for work at the Lenin Institute prior to her arrival in Spain. Details are not available.

slogan: "Win the war!" Like the majority of the inhabitants of the republic, they accepted the resolute demands of the Communist party concerning the maintenance of order in the rear area of the Republican Army, and the need to go over to the offensive on the front. The courage and sagacity of the Spanish Communist party was also acknowledged by many socialists and anarchists.

I recall, for example, one of the anarchist battalion commanders on the Aragon front. We crossed the enemy lines in his sector on one of our missions. "We've got everything, but we lack the organizational capability and singleness of purpose of the Communists," the battalion commander admitted in disappointment. "Our leaders are masters of beautiful phrases, and of corruption behind the lines. They ought to be out there, in the trenches."

"Why in hell are you following those kinds of leaders?" Antonio asked. "Either you change their minds, or you throw them out!"

The battalion commander stubbed out his cigarette, examined it, and tossed it away. "It's easy to say. . . . Don't tell me you haven't heard of the anarchist party courts?"

In the spring of 1937, there were many people like this battalion commander among the ranks of the anarchists on the Aragon front, but they limited their actions to griping. The rank-and-file socialists, no less than the Communist fighters, were enraged by the conduct of Largo Caballero. Many suspected that he had entered into a cabal with the anarchists and the Trotskyites . . . against the Communist party.

"That haughty bureaucrat doesn't threaten Franco, but he does threaten Jose Dias!" said the troops bitterly.

But no experiences of this type could prevent true patriots from fulfilling their military duty to the Republic. And they—particularly the Communists—fulfilled that duty, sparing neither their efforts nor their lives.

Almost every day, automatic mines blew troop trains and vehicles sky high. In the Cordoba-Peñarroya theater, men from Captain Ungria's battalion expertly destroyed a large railroad bridge. The successes of our demolitions men in the vicinity of Posoblanco were matched by the combat operations of other units and partisan detachments.

On the Southern Front, I had occasion to meet an old acquaintance, M. K. Kochegarov, with whom I had trained partisans in Kiev in the period 1930–32. It turned out that he also was using the mines we had developed there.

Other Soviet soldiers whom I had known earlier were also fighting in the enemy rear area. For example, the aggressive and energetic B. I. Kremlev-Kiselev was able to organize many brave attacks on rebel and interventionist military targets.

The moonlight season had arrived. The moon rose higher and remained longer in the cloudless sky. This nighttime illumination assisted the enemy. The demolitions men cursed violently at the moon. Soon, however, we learned how to work even in those conditions, although on one of those nights, I certainly had a close shave.

In the moonlight, I picked up a satchel of explosives from a severely wounded demolitions man and made a careless move. Everything turned out relatively happily: the electric detonator went off, but luckily, the main charge didn't. I nearly lost my right hand and had a few fragments penetrate my hand, face, and chest. No one else suffered any injuries.

This unfortunate accident brought me together with a member of the Jaen Party Provincial Committee, Comrade Frederico del Castillo, who was chief of the military medical service on the Southern Front.

"They say that a demolitions man makes only one mistake!" Frederico remarked as he was picking a long fragment out of my bloody hand. He was a remarkable doctor and a charming fellow. People like Valensuela, Aroca, Martines, and Frederico del Castillo dreamed of traveling to the USSR after the victory. All of them, except Martines, died at the hands of the rebels and interventionists.

Derailments continued on the enemy railroads. The demolitions men derailed a troop train carrying Moroccan cavalry. Out of thirteen cars, not one remained undamaged. The rebels were beside themselves. They assigned several battalions to guard the railroad, and carried out constant sweeps for engineer mines.

Our troops were ready for them. We already had mines that would explode upon the first attempt to remove them from the roadbed. The mining parties also changed their tactics: they changed their areas of attack more frequently and used the wheel switches more heavily.

When they had let a "vigilance" patrol go by, the demolitions men would move out to the railroad one to two minutes before the arrival of a train, set the wheel switches, and the train would be wrecked, *right on schedule*! In this way, for example, a munitions train headed for the Franco forces at Montoro was wrecked in the second half of March 1937.

Our people pulled off that operation under very difficult circumstances. It was impossible to approach the road from the south because there was no cover. We couldn't carry out the sortie on a single night because it was too far from the front lines. From the north, the railroad was protected not only by guards but by the swift Guadalquivir River, and in addition to our mines and weapons, we had to carry with us two canvas boats. I had crossed the Dnepr River on such boats in the early thirties, but that was only on a training exercise.

This operation was led by Ruiz, a sailor. West of Montoro, the river was not guarded, and the demolitions men crossed it undetected. They were able to set up two mines and to witness the derailment. During the day, the rebels tried to carry away munitions from the derailed train using vehicles. But they weren't even able to do that: aircraft under the command of Soviet pilot K. M. Gusev made a surprise attack on the cluster of enemy vehicles. Many of them burned or exploded right there by the wrecked train. It must have been possible to clearly observe that scene from the Republican positions on the mountains. Comrade Pasuelo, arriving from Jaen, turned out to have been a witness to that unforgettable spectacle.

Almost simultaneous with this, our troops blew up two small bridges. One, at Belmes, the other at Espiel. By the end of March, Captain Ungria's demolitions men had brought railroad traffic on the Cordoba-Peñarroya line to a virtual standstill. The Franco forces then began to send their freight along the highway, and so Captain Ungria's men turned to the highway. Soon they had sharply reduced the movement of enemy columns on the road net, especially at night. Because of this, several rebel infantry battalions never reached the front: they were assigned to guard highway installations and the road itself.

Comrades Pasuelo and Valensuela, secretaries of the Jaen Provincial Committee, as well as Comrade Martines, did not forget about the demolitions men. They even sometimes appeared in our workshop where we made engineer mines, hand grenades, and other devices. In the shop, a small team led by Sastre accomplished the most painstaking and sometimes dangerous work. Translated, the word *sastre* means tailor, but Sastre himself was an excellent electrician and later became a pyrotechnician. All of his feelings showed instantaneously on his broad round face. Given his unusual stoutness, Sastre was unusually agile. This man, who appeared on first glance to be a nervous fellow, actually worked very calmly and reliably.

Sastre learned how to make all the mines and grenades that we in the Soviet Union had used during the war against the foreign interventionists and "White Guards," as well as those which we had invented during the period of partisan training at the beginning of the thirties, and he even began to improve these devices. When he had mastered our "potato" and "apple" mines, Sastre suggested his own "orange" delayed-action mines. I must admit that this invention turned out to be most precise. Our miners received antitrain mines and other types of delayed-action mines, which had to be set on moonless dark nights, with lengthy, precisely calculated delays, so that they would explode in the full moon.

Sastre also took part in the development of the first small magnetic mine, later perfected by the English. These mines of ours stuck well to metal and, depending on fuse length, they exploded within five to thirty seconds after they were placed, knocking jagged holes in tank cars. Well-tested *bombas de mano*—hand grenades—and the explosives for them, were in greatest demand, however.

These weapons could be made on Republican territory, or in covert bases behind enemy lines. We carried only the fuses and the explosives with us, but the metal for the bodies of the grenades we picked up locally. For this purpose, we used pieces of water pipe or tin cans, stuffed with barbed wire or nails, or just simply barbed wire. We needed only detonator caps and Bickford cord for fuses. Since there weren't enough caps, we started to make grenades with black powder and other explosives, which would explode without the caps.

We demonstrated our hand grenades to Comrade Pasuelo and other workers of the Jaen Party Provincial Committee. In terms of the strength of the explosion and the lethal radius, they were better than factory-made grenades, but a bit heavier. We were hampered by a lack of caps and, especially, Bickford cord, but when we mentioned the problem to Comrade Pasuelo, he was able to rectify the situation.

"Here's something I really understand—a modern Jaen arsenal!" remarked Pasuelo when he entered the shop. Our troops worked fast: some, with the help of a special device reminiscent of a manual bread slicer, cut the Bickford cord into lengths; others coated the cord with an inflammable compound. Rosalina prepared the grinding tools, and Sastre himself forced the cord into the detonators with a special press.

Explosives made at Jaen were used on several fronts. Who would have thought that we'd be making them again, only four years later, but on Soviet soil?

The situation at the front was improving. Rebel attacks were beaten back, and Republican units went over to the offensive. The demolitions men were sent on one mission after another.

The special battalion was now completely manned. It was based in three locations: Jaen, Villanueva de Cordoba, and Valencia where the shop work continued as did the training of all the new groups. The battalion staff reported for duty, headed by a Yugoslav, Captain Ilyich. Neat and sharp, Ilyich did something no one could teach Domingo to do: he produced detailed documentation, painstakingly gathered information about group operations, and drew conclusions for the command. He had previously been responsible for handling supply problems. Later, after the battalion had grown to brigade size, Ilyich kept the position of chief of staff but also commanded the second battalion.

"A paper war!" growled Domingo. "Why do people need so much paper? How can you sit over paperwork, when you could be going behind the lines?" But Domingo's cutting looks and grumbling didn't faze Ilyich who quickly mastered sabotage tactics and technology as well as the intricacies of code. Soon, Domingo and I were able to leave Ilyich in charge during our absences. We began to form the second battalion and decided to assign one battalion to operations behind enemy lines on the Southern Front, while the other battalion was to be used wherever it was needed. We had plenty of rations and had captured plenty of weapons and ammunition from the enemy to outfit the second battalion.

At that time on the Southern Front, the special battalion had several bases in the enemy rear, where we sent the equipment and personnel for attacks on enemy lines of communication and other objectives. Captain Ungria's people were already familiar with the areas, and the approaches to all the important objectives. In accordance with the orders of the provincial Party Committee, they also had established contact with local people who would assist in sabotage and propaganda work. These bases were located in mountainous areas, with thick, high ground cover, about ten to twelve kilometers from the front lines. When taking up positions at one of the bases, our troops always waited to see if the enemy was aware of their presence before going out on operations. When leaving the bases, everything possible was done to cover our tracks, but we learned that this was impossible in the majority of cases. The enemy occasionally found signs of our presence, and for this reason we tried not to return to old bases. Instead, we set up observation posts near them, watching for the appearance of enemy soldiers or spies whom we captured.

When we were at these bases, Domingo and I often spent time studying the intelligence data our covert network had collected and transmitted to us through a system of dead drops. Often this information caused us to revise our plans at the last minute. Anna played a critical role in this intelligence work not only in translating the documents but in interpreting my advice to Domingo as we planned operations. Our intelligence function was so important that our senior Soviet advisor, Maj. Khadzhi-Umar Mamsurov, otherwise known as "Ksanti,"[3] actually forbade Anna and me to go behind enemy lines except in situations when we had to quickly analyze and respond to the information from our secret "postal system." On one of these trips, I had to leave Anna and return to our lines immediately with some intelligence that required Ksanti's immediate attention. A large enemy hunter-killer group appeared in the vicinity of the base, but Domingo, Anna, and the group managed to escape in a hectic withdrawal that involved a night swim across a reservoir. As they withdrew, they inflicted heavy casualties on the enemy by the skillful use of mines and delayed-action grenades, and sank a patrol boat on the reservoir, killing its entire crew. When the group returned to our lines, I was already off on another mission into the same general area. Due to the lack of two-way communications capabilities, they could not warn me that the enemy would be on the alert after the beating Domingo and his group had inflicted on the hunter-killer group. Anna was quite concerned by the time I returned; it seemed something more than common professional interest was developing between us.

In the second half of April, a very happy event took place for me: Gai Lazarevich Tumanyan and the elusive Ksanti came to visit.[4] Ksanti's arrival also pleased Domingo who had heard a great deal about Ksanti's sorties behind rebel lines. Ksanti directed the operations of the majority of the partisan and *spets* groups on other fronts, as well as our detachment, which later became Captain Ungria's special battalion. Prior to the creation of the special battalion, Ksanti had sent down some advisers to the unit, as well as urgently needed equipment. We were still lacking proper radio equipment, however: sometimes we had radio receivers but no transmitters!

"How tall he is! Look how he sits his horse!" he said in admiration. "He's a born cavalryman!"

I informed Domingo that Ksanti was not only a cavalryman but

3. A famous Soviet GRU special forces operator, Khadzhi-Umar Dzhiorovich Mamsurov later fought in the Winter War with Finland, won a Hero of the Soviet Union award in World War II, and rose to the rank of colonel-general. Mamsurov played a major role in Republican special operations, and was appointed senior Soviet advisor to Ungria's unit after it was designated as the XIV Special Battalion.

4. It is likely that Mamsurov was making a command tour of the units that he advised as well as escorting Tumanyan, who seems to have been in charge of recruiting and assigning Soviet special purpose forces advisers for the Republican Army.

a genuine Ossetian *dzingit gorets*, i.e., a trick-riding mountaineer, and Domingo immediately decided to show our guest the cavalry demolitions platoon that he had formed at Villanueva de Cordoba. Ksanti and Tumanyan got acquainted with the demolitions men, talked with them a long time, and shared their experiences. Together, we toured the bases at Jaen and Villanueva de Cordoba, and even visited the covert base in the enemy rear, west of Adamuz. Tumanyan and Ksanti were quite comfortable with the results of their trip. When we parted, they remarked to me that some groups might be transferred to other fronts in the near future.

Recalling those days, I can't refrain from recounting a combat experience, which occurred in the hot days of April 1937.

I have already mentioned the monastery of La Virgen de la Cabeza, which had long been occupied by the rebels. Several Republican attempts to clean them out had been unsuccessful. Neither artillery bombardment nor air attack could substantially harm the garrison of the cloister: thick walls and the strongly arched basement ceilings protected the enemy.

The rebel garrison in the monastery stuck into Republican territory like a painful splinter. We had to get rid of it, but how? Somebody got the idea of using demolitions men to capture the monastery. They were supposed to enter the monastery at night and blow out the stone wall. Domingo objected to this absurd venture:

"First, our troops would be destroyed if they even tried to approach the walls. Secondly, a small group is simply physically incapable of dragging up the required amount of explosives to the monastery."

"Are you saying that the demolitions men are powerless?"

"What do you mean 'powerless'? Let's think about this a while."

The demolitions men continued to observe the monastery, thought the whole thing over, and proposed their plan for its capture.

"What are you counting on?" they were asked skeptically.

"We are relying exclusively on the rebels' complete ignorance of classical literature," calmly responded Sastre, the head of the mine shop.

A week later, a rider appeared on the road from Andujar to the CP of the battalion which was besieging the rebel nest. Fearfully looking at the monastery, he rudely urged on his mule, which was loaded down with two cases of cartridges. A few shots from the monastery wall forced the rider to slide off his saddle and hide in a ditch. A few more shots, and the rider began to crawl away, abandoning the mule.

The animal, having lost its rider, began to nibble on the grass. On the roadside, the grass was withered, but up by the monastery, a broad green carpet could be seen. The mule rushed right up there to graze.

"This took place in the evening. In the morning, the mule was gone: obviously, the rebels brought it inside with them," Domingo related.

They patiently waited two more days. On the third day, the battalion besieging the monastery got ready for the attack. A rider appeared once more on the road from Jaen to Adamuz. He was also traveling by mule, and he also carried two cases. This time, however, we had specially selected the mule. About a month before, this mule had run off from the rebels. We learned from the peasants that the mule had been raised in the monastery.

In one of the cases loaded on the mule there were explosives: twenty kilograms of dynamite surrounded with barbed wire and pieces of iron. This case was fitted with detonator switches. The other case contained bad cartridges.

The rider cheerfully urged the animal along, but shots from the monastery also forced this "unsuccessful" fellow to slide off the saddle. Released, and completely on his own, the mule leisurely wandered up to the monastery wall.

The demolitions men didn't see just how the mule got into the monastery, but they knew when that had occurred from the roar of the explosion. The battalion immediately rose to the attack, and got almost all the way to the monastery, at the price of only a few wounded: the confused rebels were unable to open fire in time. Two days later a white flag flew over the cloister: the rebels gave up.

"Frankly, we didn't hold out much hope for the success of your venture, but it actually helped us a lot," said one of the Republican military leaders.

"You obviously didn't think that an Andalusian mule could become a Trojan horse, did you?" Domingo grinned, "but dammit, wasn't that mule more destructive than Homer's stallion?"

At Madrid and Zaragoza

On 2 May, Ksanti and I saw off Gai Lazarevich Tumanyan on his return trip to the USSR. When we had returned to the Barcelona hotel, I felt sick. The thermometer showed around thirty degrees Celsius.

Ksanti ordered me to rest, locked the room, and took off to get some medicine. He had only just returned when shooting broke out in the city. These weren't the isolated shots to which we had become accustomed; they were bursts and volleys. Heavy machine guns were rattling away. Somewhere near the hotel, a grenade exploded, then another . . .

Ksanti turned off the light.

"What's going on?"

"It's probably the anarchists attacking," he said calmly, gazing out into the dark night. "We have to phone . . ."

But we couldn't phone anywhere: in place of the usual female operator, we heard only male voices. When they heard us on the line, they rang off immediately. The firing intensified. After an hour spent behind barricades with the hotel staff and guests, we found out that an armed coup by anarchists and POUM members was under way. They were demanding the removal of the Catalonian government, immediate dissolution of the armed forces, and the transfer of all power to the anarchists and Trotskyites.[1]

They had been able to capture the barracks of the mountain infantry battalion, the telephone station, and the telegraph, and to gain control over the railroad station and all the city transportation. The area where the building of the United Socialist party of Catalonia was located was the target of particularly heavy firing. Obviously the bandits wanted to take it as well.

1. According to Prof. Robert Conquest (see: *The Great Terror: a Reassessment*, New York, Oxford Press. 1990, pp. 409–410) this uprising was a provocation engineered at Stalin's command by the Soviet consul-general in Barcelona, senior NKVD officer V. Antonov-Ovseyenko, whose brutal terror tactics in suppressing the Tambov "Greens" have already been referred to in the introduction. According to Conquest, Stalin wanted the POUM liquidated because POUM officials were criticizing the Soviet purge trials, and were possibly trying to bring Trotsky to Spain. Eradication of the POUM and the Trotskyites would permit the Communists to seize power in Barcelona. It appears that the Spanish Communists actually initiated the uprising by forcibly seizing the telephone exchange from the anarchists who controlled it. This precipitated the fighting, which was then falsely labeled by the Communists as an anarchist coup attempt.

To leave the hotel was unthinkable; anyway, I could hardly stand up.

We believed that the anarchists and Trotskyites would be put down without delay, but the government of Catalonia was completely disorganized. The anarchists took their battalions out of the front lines with impunity, and settled down in the city. When they saw that they were unable to draw the majority of the workers to their cause, they attempted to provoke the people by shooting at noncombatants.

The central government sent an air force squadron and tanks to put down the rebel coup, which finally brought the rebels to their senses. During the night hours of 6 May, the anarchist-Troskyite putsch was put down, but Barcelona had to suffer through three tragic days. Hundreds died in street fighting, and many women and children were among the dead.

During those days, it was unbearable for me to be unable to take action. But as soon as I got better, Ksanti, his female interpreter, and I took the risk of escaping and rejoining our own people.

Vicente drove the car, avoiding the streets that were still blocked with barricades and those neighborhoods where there was still firing. Somehow we managed to get out of Barcelona. Within a day, I was looking at Rubio's happy face, the cunning eyes of Juan Grande, and the imperturbable Pepe.

Events occurred with dizzying speed. After the refusal of Largo Caballero to discuss the national military and political situation with the council of ministers, the Communists pulled out of the government. Caballero thought he'd just wait them out, but the majority of the influential socialist ministers announced that there could not be any government without the Communists. After several convulsive, clumsy attempts at forming a so-called "trade union government," he was forced to resign.

A new government arose: the government of Doctor Negrin. It included three Socialists, two Communists, two left-wing Republicans, and one representative each from the Catalonian and Basque nationalist parties.

As a sign of support for Largo Caballero, their friend in the struggle against Communism, the anarchists refused, at first, to participate in the new government. However, their defiance didn't last long. When they realized that the government not only existed but was operating without their support, the anarchists came begging. But they were unable to reassert their former influence, and their authority declined drastically.

The Negrin government accepted the decree on agrarian reform worked out by the Communist minister Vicente Uribe. This decree quickly gained popularity among the people: it protected the peasants from the so-called uncontrolled elements and halted the forced collectivization of agriculture, which had been created by the anarchists.

The Spanish Communist party quickly gathered increasing momentum. Its readiness to fight on aroused a fresh enthusiasm among the masses. Although the civil war was now entering into a period that was characterized by infinitely more serious conditions than had existed at the beginning (the rebels now controlled the majority of the territory, and food and weapons were in short supply) the Republicans were hoping more than ever for victory.

A series of brilliantly executed operations proved that their hope was well founded. It was not enough to remove some generals and dismiss a few bankrupt politicians from the government, however. Wherever they were hiding, the remaining traitors should have been exterminated, down to the last man, and the passivity and routine of the staffs should have been overcome.

Alas, these things just didn't happen.

In an attempt to ameliorate the situation in the northern provinces, the republic launched an offensive in the summer of 1937 in the area of Brunete. The best units of the army joined in this operation, first of all the units of the 5th Regiment. The operation was commanded by Generals Lister and Modesto, popular heroes of the Spanish people.

It was necessary to destroy the enemy capability for bringing up reinforcements on the railroad that connected the rebel grouping around Madrid with the provinces that they had occupied in southwestern Spain. The command gave Ksanti the mission of cutting the section of railroad between Talavera and Navalmoral de la Mata. The strike at these vital communication lines was timed to coincide with the beginning of the Republican offensive operations around Madrid. The rail lines were to be disrupted for no less than five days.

A unit from Captain Ungria's battalion was diverted to this operation. At the end of June, we found ourselves southwest of Talavera, fifteen kilometers south of the Tajo River. The Tajo is a quiet river, about 150 meters wide—200 meters wide if you measure from bank to bank. The Republicans held the southern bank of the river while the Fascists occupied the northern bank.

It was decided to infiltrate five or six small groups of demolitions men carrying engineer mines across the river on the first night, and after that to infiltrate two or three groups per day for a week. The people, equipment, and boats for crossing were carefully prepared. Finally, the time to act arrived.

The light boats were put into the water without a sound, and the people embarked in silence. Soon the boats disappeared from view. Seconds passed, then minutes . . . and on the north bank a flare shot up: we diligently searched the river, but the boats weren't visible.

Later that night, upstream to our right, two more flares blazed forth, almost at the water's edge. From the northern bank, machine-gun and rifle fire broke out, and Republican units returned the fire. It turned out that the alarm had been triggered by two local inhabitants, trying to swim out to our side. Finally on the north bank, the long-awaited signal gleamed: we got ready to receive our returning demolitions men and to provide them with fire support if they were being pursued.

Several tense minutes passed. The first boat quietly beached on our side of the river.

"Everything went well!" reported Erminio, the commander of the returning group. As if to confirm those words, a loud explosion was heard from the north, at the railroad.

Unfortunately, the other groups had yet to return, and the enemy was already aroused. Far away, flares gleamed in the night, and on the opposite bank, the enemy started to get restless. The river was not only an obstacle, but an arrow pointing toward safety. Our troops knew that their friends were on the south bank. Not far from the water on the opposite side, a hand grenade exploded. No doubt about it: a firefight was starting up over there. More grenades went off. One of the groups swam back from the opposite side. The soaked demolitions men climbed silently out of the water and immediately cleared the riverbank.

In the morning we added up the score. No one was killed or missing, but we had two wounded. On the railroad line west of Talavera, however, fourteen instantaneous and delayed-action antitrain mines had been set. On the first night, these mines had blown up an enemy troop train, and then sent another train sky high . . .

The demolitions men worked for five days in a row against the rail line east of Talavera. The troops completely forgot about their own needs. They grabbed bites of food here and there. Their eyes were all sunken and red. Even Rubio's hair was tousled and faded, and Jan Tikhiy's joking had ceased, but they had accomplished their mission: railroad traffic was paralyzed.

The Republicans took Brunete!

After this victory, Domingo literally caught fire. Taking one company along with him, he decided to operate along the enemy lines of communication to the north and northwest of the enemy groupings around Madrid. After five days, I joined him, bringing another of his demolitions groups, and we worked together, right up to August. It was at Madrid that I saw the Nazi pilots who had been shot down at night by Spanish fighters; in the prisoners' eyes there was only fear and servility.

The next big operation in which the troops of Captain Ungria's special battalion participated took place at Zaragoza in August 1937. That action also began successfully. In August, on the Aragon front, the tone was set by Lister's units. The influence of the anarchists was totally at an end, and the ringleaders of that group had fled the country. In the course of the offensive by Republican troops, Belchite was taken. This forced the Fascists to take troops from other sectors of the front and throw them in on the Aragon front, which had been considered secure up to that point. Domingo's men got another chance to show off their skills: Marques attacked a vehicle convoy from ambush; Antonio was busting bridges with a daring born of desperation; Alex, the American, derailed locomotives and entire troop trains; Juan Pequeño's group destroyed an enemy troop train almost sixty kilometers behind the lines. The wreck was set up with such coolness and consummate skill that few survivors emerged from the wreckage.

I was really pleased for my comrades. They'd become demolitions men: creative, daring, refusing to accept hopeless situations, able to capitalize on the slightest enemy blunder. There were many examples that confirmed my assessment of their abilities. I will describe only one, in which Rubio's group, including the nineteen-year-old Nogues from Barcelona, blew up a heavily guarded bridge over the Albercia in broad daylight, destroying a column of troop and munitions trucks that was passing over it. I choose this incident not because it was any more striking than the others, but only because in the complicated situation which had arisen, Republican troops worked together well with men of the International Brigade.

I have already mentioned that in 1937 Rubio got the idea of taking over the automobile roads behind enemy lines. Together with his comrades, he had then carried out the first daring raids on Fascist highways at Peñarroya and Cordoba. In the summer of 1937 our "driving club" broadened its area of operations, appearing first on one front, then on another. The group, consisting of Rubio, Nogues, and Carrillo, became skilled at capturing isolated cars. With these cars, they often spent hours driving around the enemy rear area. Once they sensed danger or saw a checkpoint ahead, the demolitions men would destroy their "requisition," and head for the mountains. They would then reappear on new highways, capture new autos, and continue their "walkabout" behind enemy lines. Once they returned from a prolonged foray with several "liberated" suitcases and briefcases, containing documents, operational maps, photos, notebooks, officers uniforms, toilet articles, books, and even a Telefunken radio receiver.

Not one of us ever thought that captured autos could be used to blow bridges, but then . . .

After we wrecked the railroad line at Talavera, enemy traffic on the automobile road net increased sharply. As a rule, movement took place at night in columns. Bridges, which were the most difficult to restore, were heavily guarded. Under these conditions, the use of spikes for puncturing tires, and single mines, would obviously not have the desired effect.

Then one day, chatting with the group commander before a routine sortie behind enemy lines, Ksanti suggested:

"Friends! You already have experience in capturing cars. Try exploding a captured car on a bridge; you'll take out the guard and wreck the bridge at the same time."

That night Rubio's and Nogues's groups safely crossed the Tajo River and reached the automobile road. No suitable targets appeared, and they had to spend the day hiding in the Sierra de San Vicente.

"What are we going to do?" Nogues complained. "There are hundreds of vehicles going to Madrid, but almost no single cars . . ."

All day long, the demolitions men remained glued to their binoculars. The road in the area of the bridge east of Talavera was as visible to them as the palms of their hands. From the mountain, it was clear that the majority of trucks and cars crossed the bridge without stopping. The way to get onto the bridge was thus quite clear, but how would you blow the bridge if you were speeding across it?

While they were working out the best way to proceed, a military truck with a field-kitchen trailer appeared on the road. The driver was more than happy to stop to answer a question from a "gentleman officer." Sitting next to him was the cook.

"What's in the pot?" asked Rubio.

"Soup."

"Pour it out on your damned mother! We've got something else to put in . . ."

They tied and gagged the prisoners and laid them to rest on opposite sides of the road. Falling in at the tail end of a convoy, the field kitchen calmly approached the target, and drove out onto the bridge. Suddenly, right in the middle of the bridge, the trailer was uncoupled from the tractor.

The trailer blocked traffic on the bridge, and a sentry rushed to drag it off to the railing. He immediately sensed something funny was going on: the aroma coming out of the pot was not that of soup, but of burning Bickford cord. Old soldiers were well acquainted with that smell, and the sentry was undoubtedly an old soldier. He didn't panic, but began trying to push the trailer over the rail. He wasn't strong enough to do that alone, however, so he began to ask the drivers to give him a hand, but neither the drivers nor the soldiers of the bridge guard had figured out what was going on. Suddenly, flames shot up, accompanied by a thunderous explosion, and the truck, which had lost its trailer, was able to disappear without a trace.

Our demolitions men learned how to operate skillfully along the enemy communication lines. In the spring and summer of 1937, they received repeated expressions of gratitude from the command.

Unfortunately, Anna wasn't with us to share in these exploits. She had become seriously ill following her night swim in the frigid mountain reservoir when Domingo's group successfully eluded pursuing Fascist forces. Fever, chills, joint pain, and general lethargy incapacitated her. Frederico del Castillo advised prolonged rest in the Soviet Union. Kol'man of course, did not lose the opportunity to point out that her condition resulted from her association with the partisans. He promised that she would not have to take any cold baths if she transferred to his command! She was sent to Valencia for a rest and further diagnosis, and Kol'man even pursued her there, pressing his offers of more suitable work. It appeared that she really needed prolonged rest, and homesickness was also beginning to set in, so she decided to return to the USSR. The return was no pleasure trip however: she was assigned to assist Nikolai Nikolayevich Serebryannikov[2] in courier duties, carrying secret documents. For this mission she was given a new identity with a complete false biography—a "legend"—that of a Bulgarian-born Russian citizen. Domingo and I had the opportunity to bid her farewell at Murcia in early June while we were on our way to the Talavera operation. She and Serebryannikov left from Cartagena immediately thereafter on a freighter loaded with Soviet volunteers, all traveling under cover.

2. Serebryannikov was an NKVD officer.

The voyage was quite eventful: the captain and crew of the ship were anarchists who had to be constantly watched lest they betray the passengers to Franco's forces, the Italians, or the Moroccans. In addition, they had to run the naval blockade of Cartagena mounted by Franco and his allies, and avoid detection by their aircraft and naval surface units and submarines as they crossed the Mediterranean. They also had to pass through customs at Istanbul without revealing the presence of passengers aboard. After ten days of constant tension, Anna returned to Soviet soil and a much-needed stay at a sanatorium to repair the damage done by her partisan exploits.

Sometime during the last ten days of June, I returned from Jaen and visited our military adviser, Kol'man. We talked about this and that. I noticed that Kol'man was acting as if there were some secret matter that he had decided not to discuss with me.

"What's going on?" I asked directly.

"You haven't been reading the newspapers from home for a long time, have you?"

"Where in hell would I get newspapers?"

"And you haven't been listening to the radio? . . . and you don't know anything?"

Kol'man looked around as if he were afraid that someone was listening to us.

"On 11 June, Tukhachevskiy, Uborevich, Kork, and Yakir were tried. They have been carrying on sabotage, trying to set up our defeat in the coming war. They wanted to establish a government of landowners and capitalists."

"What!"

"Here are the papers. Read them."

Yes, everything had happened exactly as Kol'man said.

"All the accused confessed completely to the crimes that they had committed . . ." I read on, with horror.

Kol'man handed me one more paper, from 13 June.

"Look here . . ." The lines jumped out before my eyes: "On 12 June of the present year, the court sentenced the villainous traitors and turncoats to the supreme punishment: death by firing squad. The sentence was carried out."

As in a waking dream, I saw Yakir's face before me, saying: "You have been given a most important task by the Party, Comrade Starinov. I hope that you will justify our trust . . ."

I saw the forest at Olevsk, the airfield at Kharkov, the night training exercises where Yakir spoke with pride about Soviet military equipment. Was this man a traitor and turncoat? And was Marshal Tukhachevsky a Bonapartist? And Eideman, Uborevich,

Primakov, Putna—all renowned heroes of the civil war—were they all enemies of the people too?

Kol'man carefully took the newspaper from my hands. "How could this be?" was all I was able to say.

"This is a monstrous wrong," the adviser agreed. "It's impossible to believe. But you saw it yourself. . . ."

"But how would there be any profit in betraying the Soviet Union? The government which they themselves had established? The government for which they had shed their own blood?"

"Keep your voice down . . . This is some kind of savagery . . . I myself don't know what they were counting on . . . what the capitalists could possibly have given them . . ."

"Nothing! If Yakir or Primakov fell into the laps of the capitalists, they would be the first to be shot!"

"Look, they're writing about an attempt to take power . . ."

"But they themselves *were* the power!"

"Nonetheless, the facts are right here, before you . . ."

Yes, the monstrous facts were before me, and neither Kol'man nor I could afford to doubt Stalin or the court. I couldn't afford to doubt it, but my mind simply couldn't accommodate all that had occurred.

When I read in the papers that Vyshinsky had been decorated with the Order of Lenin "for strengthening Socialist legality," and I ran across the name of Yezhov, and the cartoons of Yezhov's iron hand holding the writhing enemies of the people, I was overcome by deep depression.

Not for a minute had I forgotten that I had worked with Yakir, that I had often escorted Primakov and Tukhachevskiy.

"And how will *you* reply when they ask if *you* knew Yakir or Primakov? What awaits *you* on *your* return to the motherland?" I asked myself over and over. "How will *you* respond?"

"Rudolph, you don't look very well," Domingo said when he met me. "Are you tired?"

"Yes, my friend, I'm just tired. . . ."

How else could I answer the captain?

Fate had spoiled the demolitions men too long without finally giving us one of those little gifts which she might better have kept for herself. This isn't a matter of superstition. We worked with dynamite, which even under peacetime conditions can give you some nasty surprises. It can blow up at the first spark or from the first hard knock.

Up until this time, however, you might say that it had never misbehaved for us.

Near Teruel, at Alfambra, Pepe had come under aerial bombardment with a car full of dynamite but was able to drive the car into the woods. The dynamite didn't explode, even though one bomb landed very close.

One day in Alfambra I caught troops calmly sitting, smoking, on cases of dynamite that had been pulled up next to the fireplace. No explosion occurred there either.

In Jaen, the dynamite was stored under the cots of Anna and Rosalina. But when a Primus stove blew up one night in the next room and streams of burning kerosene spread out across the floor into the women's bedroom, they were able to throw blankets on the flaming liquid before it could reach the explosives.

Our vehicles carrying dynamite were frequently under fire; the demolitions men carried dynamite on their backs across the front lines, and everything somehow came out all right!

But at Zaragoza everything *didn't* turn out all right.

I was at the command post of an infantry battalion, preparing Lieutenant Padillo's group to sortie behind enemy lines. Groups were crossing the line in other sectors as well. Padillo had already lashed up his knapsack, when we heard a loud explosion from the direction where the group sent over by Captain Ilyich, our chief of staff, was supposed to be operating. The medics were already scurrying around the scene of the explosion when we got there. A stray bullet had hit a knapsack containing dynamite that was being carried by one of the soldiers. The unhappy victim was scattered about in pieces, and three others were seriously wounded. Captain Ilyich was among them. He had not yet entirely recovered by the time I left Spain in the late fall.

Together with the remaining Soviet volunteers, I tried to transmit to the Spaniards the experience of partisan warfare which had been accumulated in our nation during the civil war years. In addition, I taught them what I had learned in the early thirties under Yakir and Baar. In my opinion, the successful application of engineer mines along Franco's lines of communication was only possible because of the energetic development of those frightening weapons that we had undertaken in the motherland during the early thirties. In Spain, the tactics and techniques of mining worked out by Soviet-led partisans were more sophisticated than those employed by the enemy for minesweeping. The rebels could not guarantee the security of their rear area, even though they frequently threw in a regiment of soldiers to guard a one hundred–kilometer stretch of road. They never did learn how to find several types of our mines, and those that they did find, they could never disarm, except by exploding them.

German and Italian sappers tried to learn about our equipment, but we constantly gave them new puzzles to work on. Sometimes we set booby traps for them, or fit mines with fuses that couldn't be removed without detonating the mine, or used magnetic mines, which were unfamiliar to the enemy. The enemy only learned that our mines had been set when they derailed his troop trains. It became apparent that Soviet military leaders really had known what they were doing when they tried in every way to stimulate the research of military engineers, technicians, and commanders of engineer troops to make mines for partisan use!

In the final analysis, though, no matter how good mines may be, they will not confer a significant advantage if they aren't placed in reliable hands.

The operations of the special partisan units of the Republican Army were most successful when they were closely and skillfully coordinated with attacks by regular troops. They were successful only because they were performed by people who were inspired by the ideals of the struggle for freedom and democracy.

In the ten-month period since I arrived in December 1936, the special group had rapidly expanded, first becoming a detachment; then a specially designated battalion; then a brigade; and finally, a corps under the command of Capt. Domingo Ungria. This unit carried out 239 separate sabotage operations, 17 ambushes, and 6 raids; as a result of which 87 trains were derailed, 112 vehicles were destroyed along with a significant quantity of fuel and lubricants, and 2,300 enemy officers and men were killed or wounded.

Our own losses were fourteen men: of these, one was killed setting up a mine, another was killed crossing enemy lines, yet another was killed by the anarchists in Valencia, and the rest were killed on raids.

In the course of the partisan war in the rebel rear area in Spain from 1936 to 1939, not only did we test the sabotage equipment that we had created in the USSR between 1925 and 1934, but innovations were produced, including the magnetic mines, improved versions of which saw wide use in the German rear during World War II.

In the corps, thousands of Spaniards were trained and gained experience in partisan warfare, as did hundreds of people from other countries who had come to the aid of the republic. The cadres of officers and specialists trained by Soviet advisers helped organize and conduct the partisan struggle in World War II in almost all German occupied nations and on the occupied territory of the Soviet Union. These trained cadres increased both the scope and effectiveness of that struggle. When the republic fell, a significant portion of the Republican Army wound up in jail. The only exceptions were personnel of the XIV Partisan Corps, a significant number of whom escaped from the enemy rear area into France, while the rest were able to sail to Algiers.

Veterans of this corps fought in partisan ranks in Italy, Belgium, and Poland; and later in Algiers and several Latin American countries.

Wherever they went, the knowledge and experience that they had gained during the partisan struggle in Spain was of great advantage to them. When World War II began and the Nazis occupied a number of countries and a large part of France, soldiers of the Republican XIV Partisan Corps who were sitting in French jails jumped the fences, overran their guards, and broke out of the camps to take an active role in the partisan war in the German rear, most importantly in France, where the XIV Partisan Corps was reconstituted. In 1943, in France, the strength of the reconstituted corps was greater than it had ever been in Spain. At that time, the corps consisted of twenty-seven brigades divided among nine partisan divisions, and its area of operations covered two-thirds of French territory.

In World War II, Ivan Kharish ("Juan Pequeño"), who later rose to become a major-general in the Yugoslav Army and a national hero of Yugoslavia, certainly distinguished himself. Fighting in Spain throughout the entire war, and accomplishing many difficult and dangerous missions in the enemy rear, Ivan Kharish began his career as an interpreter for the adviser to detachment commander Domingo Ungria, and ended as adviser and senior instructor for the sabotage brigade of the XIV Corps. After Hitler attacked France, he escaped from a French camp and, posing as an itinerant machinist, he crossed Germany to reach Yugoslavia, where he derailed his first train on 9 September 1941. The echo from that explosion aroused the Yugoslav people to intensify their struggle against the occupying forces. His group grew to a detachment, then a division, eventually carrying out about thirty-two hundred sabotage operations in which some twenty-one thousand enemy officers and men were reportedly killed. Irreplaceable losses suffered by the Kharish unit were only seventy-eight men over a period of forty-five months. Enemy losses resulting from the operations of Kharish's partisans may have been overstated, since the population hated the occupation forces and may have frequently exaggerated the body count. Nevertheless, the actual losses inflicted on the enemy by Kharish and his partisans were great, and clearly numbered in the thousands.

Domingo Ungria, his son Antonio, and some of his partisans traveled to the USSR via Algiers, bringing with them the XIV Corps flag. Many of the soldiers of the Spanish Republican Army found a second homeland in the USSR and fought in World War II, including about three hundred Spaniards who fought with partisan units which the author of these lines happened to command. These included Domingo Ungria, Leonardo Garcia, Jose Bravo, Juan Menendes, Juan Otero, Francisco Guillon, Manuel Belda, and many others who not only fought behind Fascist lines but also trained partisan cadres, making use of the experience which they had gained in the struggle against Franco's rebels.

Return

The freighter left Kronshtadt astern. Ahead, in the dark haze of an unusually fine fall day, the outlines of the Admirality and the Peter and Paul Fortress at Leningrad began to appear. I was returning from Spain with several comrades. Happy and enthusiastic, we looked at the dark green water of our Gulf of Finland and at the golden needle of the well-known spire.

Behind lay a difficult year in Spain; a remote nation, which was yet painfully close in other ways. We had buried many countrymen there, but we had also found true friends, and the earth had soaked up our blood.

When the bow and stern lines had been hauled in, the steamship gently came to rest against the dock. Our first steps on land were timid and uncertain. It seemed that the earth was moving beneath our feet, just like the ship's deck. But the sensation didn't last long: the earth was firm, just as it is supposed to be.

The road from the port to the hotel was stunning in its immutability. Everything that I loved, everything that was dear to me, had remained as before. It was as if I had left that changeless city only yesterday.

The granite-lined banks unfolded peacefully and smoothly along the swift Neva; the rostral columns stood at attention. The

horses on the Anichkov Bridge reared up furiously on their hind
legs. The Nevskiy Prospect majestically and confidently clove
through the city.

Leningrad!

How beautiful you looked to me on that fine fall day in November 1937!

I had seen Madrid, Barcelona, Paris, Antwerp, and Brussels.
They were all beautiful in their own ways, no arguing on that
point. I had also changed my initial impressions of Paris when I
saw it on my return trip from Spain, in the early morning when
people were hurrying off to work and the noisy street urchins,
searching through the crowd, stuffed copies of *L'humanite* into the
hands of passersby.

But you, Leningrad, are the most beautiful of all cities!

I walked along the streets, restraining myself with difficulty
from the temptation to press my cheek against the rough stucco of
every wall. Then, when I could restrain myself no longer, I went
on, first touching a bridge railing, then the wet bark of a sapling,
and then the cold iron of a streetlamp post.

"Staying long?" asked the desk clerk at the hotel.

"Just twenty-four hours," I responded.

I didn't tell her that these twenty-four hours weighed on my
conscience, and that when they had expired, I'd have to give an
explanation of why I stopped over. After having just set foot in
Leningrad, however, I really couldn't leave town immediately, until I got some things straightened out.

It all started with telephone calls. It might seem strange, but the
home and work numbers of many of my acquaintances and colleagues were firmly fixed in my memory.

For this reason, once I was alone, I literally hung on the phone.
But what a disappointment! Wherever I phoned, complete strangers answered. Could I have confused the numbers? Nothing like
this had ever happened before. Unsure of myself, I dialed the
number for the Directorate of the Military Commandant of the
Moscow-Leningrad Station.

"This is Chernyugov, duty assistant to the commandant . . ."

At last, a familiar voice! But even *he* sounded a bit different.
During my time there, Chernyugov, a military clerk, had answered
loudly and cheerfully, and having become the assistant to the
commandant, he certainly wouldn't have become more restrained.
But that was then: now he was different . . .

"Greetings, Comrade Chernyugov! Starinov here!"

The line went silent for some time. Then Chernyugov diffidently inquired: "Which Starinov? Is this Comrade Military Engineer Third Class[1] Starinov?"

"Most certainly! In the flesh! Don't you recognize me?"

The line went silent again.

"Can you hear me, Comrade Chernyugov?"

"Yes, I hear you ... Where are you calling from, Comrade Military Engineer?"

"Right now, from the hotel," I said, laughing. I recognized the characteristic note in Chernyugov's voice and was becoming amused by his apparent bewilderment. I hastened to reassure him: "Everything's fine with me! I'm alive and well! How are things there with you?"

"Everything is normal, Comrade Military Engineer."

"Listen, Comrade Chernyugov, I'm calling specifically to find out where Boris Ivanovich Filippov is now."

There was no response.

"Did you hear me?"

Yeah, Chernyugov heard me, all right.

"Right now ... he's ... at a health resort ..." There was either scorn or condescension in Chernyugov's voice.

I heard the other phone ring on the watch officer's desk.

"Excuse me, but I have another call."

Holding the silent receiver in my hand, I slammed it down onto the hook.

Boris Ivanovich certainly chose an inappropriate time for a trip to a health resort! People who are concerned about their health do not go south at the end of October. All the same, Chernyugov's tone was quite disrespectful. Had the promotion gone to the poor bastard's head?

I shrugged my shoulders and made another call: this time to the Military Transport Service Directorate of the October Railroad, to my old buddy Kolya Vasil'yev. He'd be able to explain what was going on.

Kolya answered, and it was the first time that I had ever heard the terse, frightening phrase: "They took him!"

"They" took him? "They" arrested Boris Ivanovich? Gentle Boris Ivanovich Filippov, who was always trembling in fear before the chiefs? Sincere, simple Boris Ivanovich? This was inconceivable!

I had learned from the newspaper that Yakir, Tukhachevsky, Uborevich, Kork, and Primakov had fully confessed their crimes. Was it clear that they actually had given something to the ene-

---

1. A rank for military technicians, it was the equivalent of major.

my, that they were actually hatching some kind of a plan? What could Boris Ivanovich have been planning? The biggest risk he'd ever taken was to get an extra pass to a health resort for his wife. And then he might have even tried to save the doctor's certificates since, as he said: "In paper there is strength, dear boy!" Inconceivable!

Did this mean that his friendliness, his concern, his simplicity, were all just camouflage?

Suddenly, I became disgusted with myself. What in hell had happened to me? Was I becoming afraid of something? How could I have dared to doubt Fillipov?

Then, the merciless voice of conscience asked me: "Didn't you also doubt Yakir? You knew him, too, didn't you? Fillipov was arrested by the same authorities. Why do you doubt them now? Do you think there's been another mistake? Knock it off! You thought exactly the same way when you first heard about Yakir's arrest!"

Totally confused, I decided to call one more friend, N. S. Frumkin. He had met me at the dock and appeared to be very sad for some reason or other. Frumkin said that he would call on me in person. He refused to talk on the phone.

After that I didn't go near the phone.

Now I could guess why strangers were answering on familiar phones. This meant that the rumors of mass arrests in my motherland—rumors that had reached Spain!—were true.

I left the hotel and wandered about the city for a long time, trying to figure out what was going on. One persistent thought kept boring away into my brain: Tomorrow I must go to Moscow. What news awaits me there? I returned to my room late at night. I didn't want to spend any time, alone, one-on-one with the black phone. Once again, the earth beneath me seemed to be moving beneath my feet . . .

On the following day while waiting for the train, I couldn't restrain myself and dropped in at the headquarters of the Moscow station. Chernyugov closed the door behind me and informed me in a whisper that Appoga, the chief of Red Army military communications, and Kartayev, the chief of communications for the Leningrad Military District, had both been arrested during the summer.

"Enemies of the people!" he told me fearfully. "And Filippov was an accomplice of Kartayev."

I saw that Chernyugov was burning to give me additional details, but felt that I had already heard enough. On the train, I couldn't fall to sleep for a long time.

Exhausted from lack of sleep, physically and mentally worn

out, I reported my return to the Moscow authorities. They gave me quarters in the Balchug Hotel and said that they would call me. I took a Pyramidon tablet and fell asleep. I awoke toward evening. A depressing stillness filled the hotel corridors. Suddenly I had a bright idea: I ought to go immediately to my old chief from Kiev, my close friend, Ivan Georgiyevich Zakharov. This was someone with whom I could share my alarm; here was someone who could resolve my doubts! I thrust the key into the housemaid's hands, took off down the stairs, hopped into a taxi, and headed for Zakharov, stopping on the way to get a bottle of wine and a cake.

Grief awaited me at my friend's house. His wife met me with tears and mourning. She recounted a frightening story: during recent weeks, Ivan Georgiyevich had been living in endless anxiety, expecting something really bad to happen. Two of his immediate superiors, with whom he and his wife were also family friends, had been arrested. Zakharov feared the slightest noise and became withdrawn and irritable.

One day, early in the morning, there came a hasty and persistent knocking on the door. Ivan Georgiyevich got up, but cried out and collapsed on the spot with a fatal myocardial infarction! As it turned out, the knock on the door was just a duty officer from the unit bringing some kind of telegram.

I don't remember how many hours I spent wandering aimlessly around the city. I came to myself when I saw that I was standing before the house of one of my oldest friends: we had served together for eight years in the same regiment.

I climbed to the fifth floor of the old house with difficulty, afraid that even here I would find tears. I rang the bell: in the apartment I could hear the soft sounds of footsteps. They stopped at the door. After a minute, a muffled voice was audible: "Who's there?"

"A friend!" I shouted with pleasure.

"Who are you, friend?"

"It's me, Starinov!"

"Starinov? Oh, yeah! Hold on, Ilya, I'll open the door for you." Bolts clanked: one; two; three. The door finally opened slightly.

"Come on in," said my friend, fearfully looking past me into the hall. When he had closed the door, he sighed in relief, extended his hand to me, and smiled, but his face was still strained. "You . . . where are you coming from?"

"Returning from special detached duty."

"Why are you dressed like a foreigner?"

"Well, you see, I was out of the country. I haven't gotten new clothes yet."

"Overseas? Could be a problem!"

We were standing in the entrance hall. No one had even suggested that I take off my coat.

"Look—it's only me! Have I come at a bad time?"

My friend focused his gaze on the toes of his bedroom slippers. "Forgive me, Ilya . . . But you know what these times are like . . . Between us, they've arrested our friends not long ago. They took Yuvko and Lermontov. Those guys were never part of the Opposition: they always followed the general Party line." He dropped his head so low that his chin almost rested on his chest.

"It's clear, then," I said. "If they weren't in the Opposition, and weren't following any particular group, they'll be acquitted!"

They didn't try to stop me leaving . . . the door shut silently behind me.

Descending the stairs, I was choked with rage. I went out onto the sidewalk.

"Ilya, wait a minute!"

Buttoning up his jacket as he went along, my friend came after me. He wore a guilty expression. He clutched at my hand, "Ilya, don't be angry! Please understand! It might have been different if you had come from the Far East . . . but then, God knows where you've come from . . . See, I work on secret documents, and in all my security questionnaires, I've written that I have no friends or relatives who have ever been overseas or who are overseas now."

"Go home. They might see us talking."

"You *do* understand?"

"Get lost!"

It was getting very cold at night. The streets emptied quickly. The usual crowds could still be found only in the city center around the movie theaters and restaurants. Lyubov' Orlova smiled happily from the billboards, touching her hand to her captain's hat, and in the Metropole, *Volga-Volga* was being shown.

Ivan Georgiyevich Zakharov was dead.

I never had a better friend . . .

Three days later, I had an appointment with Marshal of the Soviet Union K. Ye. Voroshilov. I arrived at the meeting together with the chief of Red Army intelligence (GRU), senior major of State Security,[2] S. G. Gendin. When he heard my report on Spain, and how I had trained soldiers for a special unit, Voroshilov

---

2. The Chief Directorate for State Security (GUGB) was created in 1934 as a replacement for the OGPU, and was subordinated to the NKVD. From 1937 to 1938 the NKVD, the GUGB, and the GRU were all controlled by one man: Nikolai Ivanovich Yezhov, the architect of the "Great Terror."

thanked me for my thorough mastery of my military duty. "You deserve a high decoration," he said. "I think, Comrade Division Commander [he referred to Gendin in this fashion!],[3] that Starinov has earned a promotion. We also need to give him work in his speciality which is commensurate with a higher level of importance."

Coming out from behind his desk, Voroshilov firmly shook my hand: "Await your assignment, Comrade Starinov!"

Within two weeks, however, Gendin had been arrested as an enemy of the people and shot, and I was still at the Balchug Hotel, awaiting assignment.

My meeting with the people's commissar for defense had initially reassured me and cheered me up. There certainly were no sins in my past, or at least no one had entered any on the record, and they had even thanked me for my service! Of course, I soon realized that reassuring myself in this way was like renouncing my old comrades and betraying the memory of the dead who had probably not committed the monstrous crimes that had been entered on their records. My depression returned, and my confusion intensified.

Time passed. No one called me to go anywhere, and no one proposed any "important work."

Every new day brought me more bad news.

I visited the family of Konstantin Shinkarenko, former commander of the legendary Kotovskiy Brigade.[4] Shinkarenko was a friend of mine from the partisan school in Kiev and was among the first in the republic to be awarded the Military Order of the Red Star and to receive the Distinguished Revolutionary Weapon award (Translator's note: this award was a specially engraved sword or a revolver, presented for outstanding combat service). It appeared that they had taken Shinkarenko.

I learned from his wife that many of Kostya's friends had also been arrested. These were partisan leaders whom I knew and with whom I had set up the secret partisan bases to be used in the event of war.

"Kostya is an honorable man: he is not connected with any enemies of the people. I wrote to Comrade Stalin, and I'm trying to get a meeting with Comrade Voroshilov," Shinkarenko's sobbing wife repeated endlessly.

She got no meeting: she got nothing at all. Konstantin

---

3. Gendin's rank of senior Major was equivalent to a division commander, or general, in the rank system employed at that time in the Red Army.

4. The Kotovskiy Brigade was an elite partisan unit named after Grigory Ivanovich Kotovskiy, an organizer and leader of civil war partisan units, and later commander of Red Army formations.

Shinkarenko was only released and rehabilitated after the death of Stalin. He left the camp in serious condition, with only enough strength to reach his native Moldavia, where he quickly died.

In the meantime, the clouds had thickened over my head.

I finally got a call, but it wasn't to the ministry of defense—I was called to the NKVD—at the Lyubyanka Prison. It was for what they used to call an "interview with prejudice."

The light was positioned so that it hit me right in the eyes, but the face of the investigator was in darkness. "Don't be afraid," I heard. "We are calling you as a witness. We only want one thing from you—a totally sincere deposition. That is the interests of the state as well as in your own interests."

"But of what am I a witness?"

"Can't you guess?"

"No."

"Good. We'll help you, then . . ."

I do not recall the exact course of the interrogation. "We" were constantly worming out where I had served, how close I was to this or that fellow, how often I had met with M. P. Zhelezhnyakov or with A. I. Baar . . .

I answered the questions directly. Yes, I knew the people who were named. Yes, I carried out their orders. What else was I supposed to do? These were orders from my immediate superiors.

"Well, now . . . And for whom were you setting up the secret partisan bases in the 1930s, one hundred kilometers away from the border. For whom were you training these so-called partisan detachments so far from the border?"

I understood the direction in which the investigator was heading. If I had answered in a confused or evasive fashion, my status would have immediately changed from "witness" to "accused." He wanted me to admit the illegality of the actions taken in the thirties and to discredit my former chiefs. From the stories of the wives of friends who had been arrested, I already knew that the partisans trained by us were being being accused of two crimes: "lack of belief in the power of the socialist state," and "preparation for hostile activities in the rear of the Soviet Army."

The investigator looked at me almost affectionately. A pike probably doesn't feel any particular animosity for a carp, which he already considers doomed . . .

"The bases were actually established within one hundred kilometers of the border, but the fortified regions were established at one hundred kilometers or more from the border, and they cost hundreds of millions and billions of rubles!"

"Leave the fortified regions out of this! They're irrelevant!"

"What do you mean, 'irrelevant'? If that amount of money was spent on construction of the fortified regions, then it must be because it was planned to let the enemy penetrate into the country as far as these lines. And if that's the case, then it's logical to prepare everything possible for the unleashing of partisan warfare between the border and the line of fortified areas. I trained partisans to fight the enemy. The measures we're talking about were taken in the interests of the motherland."

I can only speak briefly about the interrogation, which actually lasted about three hours; recalling any aspect of it disgusts me. The investigator clearly didn't have a warrant for my arrest. When he put my papers to one side and signed my pass, he said: "We'll stop for today. In view of your military record, we're not going to touch you. However ... it's just possible that we might meet again. You ought to think things over. I advise you to write down everything that you know about the participants in the cases of Yakir, Baar, Zhelezhnyakov, and the rest of that crowd. Don't hide anything. This will simplify your situation."

After my "conversation" with the NKVD, I understood that all the advance preparations to prepare partisan bases and partisan detachments for use in the event of war had been liquidated: the partisan cadres had been destroyed, the detachments liquidated, and anyone who had even the slightest relationship to these matters was viewed either as an enemy of the people or as an accomplice thereof.

I was seized by fears such as I had never felt at the front, or even behind enemy lines. I had risked my life in war, but in combat, everyone, even the closest friends and the most upright people, were in equal jeopardy.

There was only one way out: I had to personally address myself to the people's commissar for defense, tell him about my concerns, and ask him to defend me against these unfounded accusations. Through contacts with the son of A. D. Tsyurupa[5] and Voroshilov's adopted son, I was able to get an appointment.

Voroshilov received me, but this time he was stern and withdrawn. "What's up? What do you want to tell me?"

Frightened and confused, I described my recent experiences to the marshal. "Comrade People's Commissar, I simply fulfilled the tasks given me by the Central Committee in training for partisan

5. Aleksandr Dmitriyevich Tsyurupa, commissar of food supply during the civil war, was responsible for the forced expropriation of food from the peasantry, which initiated the "peasant war." The exact connection between Tsyurupa, his son, and Voroshilov is not clear, except that Voroshilov was undoubtedly extremely familiar with Tsyurupa's efforts in support of the Red Army.

warfare, and the weapons caches were prepared on your direct order."

Voroshilov seemed embarrassed. "Don't get upset . . ."

Then, after a brief hesitation, he picked up the phone:

"Greetings, Nikolai Ivanovich![6] Yeah, it's me. Say, there's a guy named Starinov sitting here with me who's recently returned from Spain. He's been interrogated about carrying out the orders of Yakir and Berzin to train partisan bands and cache weapons for partisan use . . ."

There was a pause. An unnaturally coarse voice was audible on the other end of the line.

Voroshilov spoke again: "Sure, he carried out the orders of enemies of the people. But look, he's just a little guy—he couldn't even have known the true nature of the problem."

Another pause. Then the marshal spoke again:

"But he distinguished himself in Spain, and he's atoned for his sins, to a significant degree. Leave him in peace. We'll take the appropriate measures, ourselves . . ."

I don't intend to comment on that scene.

We now know that between 1937 and 1938, around forty thousand officers and political officers of the Red Army were shot. This number is four times greater than the number of German officers killed in the first year of the war on the Western Front.

The *History of the Great Patriotic War* states that: "between May 1937 and September 1938, almost half of the regimental commanders; nearly all commanders of brigades and divisions; all corps commanders and commanders of military district troops; members of district military councils and district chiefs of political directorates; the majority of political officers at corps, division, and brigade levels; a third of the regimental commissars; and many instructors in the higher and intermediate institutions of education were shot."

Among the forty thousand officers and political officers who were victims, were nearly all of those who had experience in partisan warfare during the civil war or who had received partisan training at the beginning of the thirties. *Several times more partisan officers and specialists were killed during this period than were killed as a result of enemy action during all of World War II.*

In this way, the number of well-trained and experienced military officers was reduced—not long before the outbreak of World War II! Personnel who lacked the required training and experience

6. Yezhov.

began to be promoted. For example, in November 1937, captains were commanding three divisions in the Transcaucasus Military District. These included an Armenian division that was commanded by a captain who had neither experience as a regimental commander nor even as a battalion commander, but had previously only commanded a battery. In the words of the Transcaucasus Military District commander, A. V. Kuibyshev: "There weren't any better people available." In answer to the question put by People's Commissar for Defense Voroshilov: "What's become of all your officers?" Kuibyshev responded: "All those who are left have been transferred to the control of the People's Commissar for Internal Affairs (NKVD) without any specified duties." The district commander added that the Georgian Division was commanded by a captain who, in the previous two years, had only commanded a company and had no command training of any kind beyond that level. Corps Commander N. V. Kuibyshev was shot soon after this conversation.

As promised, on the third day after my meeting with Voroshilov, Brigade Commander (Combrig) Kryukov, chief of Red Army military communications summoned me. The anticipated meeting concerned me. Aleksander Yevdokimovich Kryukov and I had shared years of service together in the 4th Korosten' Red Banner Railroad Regiment. How would he greet me? Did he know that my attention had long been focused on partisan activities? Would he be pleased about my return to a railroad troop regiment after such a long interval? Not likely!

In my concern, I imagined a lot of things, but I couldn't have predicted what actually happened: the combrig received me in the presence of Comrade Barinov, the commissar of the directorate.

"Outstanding!" Kryukov said, smiling broadly. "The prodigal son returneth! Let's decide on your assignment."

Pausing to direct a meaningful glance at the commissar, Kryukov's smile didn't fade as he said:

"I discussed the matter with Comrade Barinov, and we decided to offer you the post of chief of military communications for a district."

For a minute I was struck dumb and was only able to move my jaws. Finally, the power of speech returned:

"With your permission, Comrade Combrig! How can you make me a district chief of military communications? I'm a commander of railroad troops, a demolitions man; I trained partisans, and after the academy, at my own request, I was not assigned to military communications organizations. The work which you have offered me is beyond my capabilities . . ."

"That's no answer, Comrade Military Engineer Third Class," interjected Barinov. "Look at the comrade combrig [and he nodded in Kryukov's direction]: the most that he's done to date was command a railroad regiment, a half year ago, and now he's chief of military communications for the whole Red Army. And he's not working out too badly! There aren't enough cadres, and we have to advance young officers to leadership positions before they're ready."

Barinov solemnly intoned the last phrase as if he were reproaching me for my faintheartedness.

I was in a most ridiculous position. On the one hand, the post of chief of military communications for a district would raise me to incredibly dizzy heights in the hierarchy: on the other hand, it was absolutely clear to me that I wouldn't be able to handle the assignment well—it fit neither my knowledge nor my inclinations. What could be worse for subordinates, or for an officer himself for that matter, if he is in the wrong assignment?

"What are you thinking about?" the combrig asked with concern. "Two railroad regiments will be subordinated to you. Directing the military communications services of two railroads, you'll be able to live in a large city."

"If you aren't otherwise forbidden to do so, it would be better to assign me as commander of one of the two railroad regiments," I implored.

"Enough of this modesty, Ilya Grigor'yevich!" Kryukov shook his head. "Many of your messmates are already chiefs of railroads or district military communications chiefs, and all you can say is: 'Gimme a regiment!' Now, regimental commanders are people who got their commissions in the thirties, not the twenties. They were platoon commanders when you and I had companies!"

"You've got to believe me! I'm not prepared for that kind of job."

"You keep on harping on this 'I'm not fit! I'm not fit!' business! Fine! If you want to be stubborn about it, then we won't talk about a district-level assignment. But it's not going to be a regiment either! The lowest level of responsibility that we can offer is the post of chief of the Central Scientific Test Range at Il'ino. Does that suit you? Just remember one thing: the range is far away from cities, in the woods . . ."

I had to take the best of two bad alternatives. After consideration, I agreed to become the chief of the proving ground.

"We'll cut your orders," Kryukov said happily.

I stood up with Barinov and headed for the door.

"Wait a moment, Comrade Starinov," Kryukov called out. "Stay a bit . . ."

We were left alone.

"Why don't you come home with me for dinner tonight," Aleksander Yevdokimovich suggested, using the familiar form of address like the old days. "Seems like I haven't seen you for a century. My wife and sons would be pleased to see you . . . You haven't by any chance gotten married yet, have you?"

"Well, almost . . ."

Kryukov's eyes got big: "Great news! Who *is* she? I've got to meet the woman who could tame you!"

"I'll introduce you, Aleksandr Yevdokimovich."

Kryukov threw up his hands:

"I know you. At the last instant, you'll run away from her. Well, you come on over, we'll expect you."

That night, around the Kryukov's family table, Aleksandr Yevdokimovich and I talked with complete candor. First, we talked about Spain; but the conversation imperceptibly turned to other things. We'd had a couple of drinks when Kryukov asked me point-blank: "What do you think? Do you think it's easy for me to fill the role of chief of Red Army military communications? Ilya! You know yourself that I'm a field soldier; I've got no experience in the military communications bureaucracy. You're sailing in waters with submerged rocks and shoals all around; you've got to look out, or you'll be destroyed. And then one person after another is designated an enemy of the people, and the cadres are being thinned out. I'm running around like a squirrel in a treadmill. You probably did the right thing by selecting the post at the test range. We're sending a group of academy graduates there: bridge builders and machinists. Maybe we can expand the operations there."

"But the test range is an entire city in the woods, with its own economy.[7] I'm afraid that the job of running it all will simply devour me," I said.

"It won't devour you! You've got deputies and assistants. They'll run the economy, and you spend your time with your equipment and your mines. Nobody will bother you. Right now, more scientists are being taken to the test range than you think. You'll get all the required funding and the time to do what you want."

Kryukov said all this sadly. Anxiety, discouragement, and it

---

7. A poorly organized national-level system for production and transportation of food forced many Soviet military units, installations and facilities (particularly those in remote areas) to maintain vegetable and livestock farms for their own use. The practice continues today (1995).

seemed to me, fear, resounded clearly in his voice and could be read in his eyes. It was not as much the words as the tone in which they were said that led me to drop my guard.

That evening, agonizing doubts and fantastic forces were bearing down on me. I pushed my drink aside. "Aleksandr Yevdokimovich! How could people serve the Soviet power for twenty years and then suddenly betray it. And what people! People to whom the nation owes everything, absolutely everything! Now they're enemies of the people? And who are they anyway? Bourgeois? No way! They're first-rank Red Guards, and Red commissars. What were they hoping for when they committed treason? Tell me, what? How was it possible to fool us? We knew many of them from the front, from work . . ."

Aleksandr Yevdokimovich sighed heavily.

"Cut it out, Ilya: Comrade Stalin personally handles the cadres, he has taken over that concern, and he does not accuse innocent people. It's not by accident that he advanced Yezhov to head the NKVD, right? Why do you sit there in stony silence? Let's have another drink!" Aleksandr Yevdokimovich suggested sadly, adding: "Just remember, you and I haven't buried anyone." Kryukov bent over the table, and I noticed tears on his face.

He took my hand: "Once, you saved my son, so I'm entrusting to you a family secret. At the end of last year, my brother, Lt. Col. Andrey Kryukov, was dismissed from the Red Army. I'm sure that this was a mistake: he is an honorable man, and I'm convinced that it'll all be sorted out and that he'll be reinstated. But now what's going to happen to me?"

I was struck by Aleksandr Yevdokimovich's openness, and couldn't immediately respond. Kryukov was the first to regain self-control: "Drink up, Ilya, to the health of Comrade Stalin! He doesn't unjustly accuse the innocent!"

On 17 February 1938, I was promoted to the rank of colonel,[8] and on 20 March of the same year, i.e., four months after my return from Spain, I was appointed chief of the Central Scientific Test Range. The first person whom I informed about this change in my fortunes was my friend Anna Obrucheva, whom I married not long after. Anna's life since her return from Spain had not been easy. Following her recuperation at a sanatorium, she applied for a position in the People's Commissariat for Education (*Narodniy kommissariat prosveshcheniya*, or *Narkompros*). This organization had been gutted by the purges: four out of five of the directors and deputies had been condemned as enemies of the

---

8. At this time, the rank of lieutenant colonel did not exist in the Red Army system.

people during 1937 alone, and the remaining staff was short-handed, inexperienced, and terrorized. Her first assignment was as chief of children's homes and special schools (schools for the handicapped), but she found that her lack of knowledge in these specialized areas made it difficult for her to be effective. At her request, she was finally put in charge of Spanish children's homes where children of Spanish Communist refugees were being raised. There she could at least use her language skills. The pressures of her work and the purge atmosphere had already taken their toll, however, and she suffered a relapse. On doctor's orders, she left the Commissariat for Education after ten months.

Since I had to go to Kislovodsk for medical treatment, I didn't go to the test range immediately. Before my departure (I was still living in the hotel) I decided to bring some of my things over to an old friend, Yevseviy Karpovich Afonko, with whom I had worked from 1926 to 1930, preparing barriers along the Ukrainian border. Beginning in 1932, Yevseviy had worked in Metrostroi (Translator's note: Metrostroi = Moscow Metropolitan Subway Construction Agency). He was just as much a cheerful, physical guy as he had been when I knew him in the army.

"Leave your junk! Leave it!" Yevseviy said. "Whenever you return, take it away with you. But, mind you! I won't keep it for free! You've got to bring a bottle of dry Caucasian wine!"

The first thing I did when I returned from the rest resort was to dart off to Yevseviy's. Her hands hanging along her thin body, Afonko's wife stood silent in the open door.

"It can't be true . . ." was all that I could say.

The next time we saw Yevseviy was twenty years later. As promised, I brought him a bottle of dry Caucasian wine.

"Just a little late," joked Afonko, "but I'll accept it. You're in my debt!"

I was struck by my friend's cheerful tone and appearance. He had hardly changed during those years. His eyes looked young; his grip was like iron.

"So? Are you surprised? Do you want me to lift a two pood dumbbell (Translator's note: a traditional Russian unit of weight, one pood = thirty-six pounds) with my little finger?" smiled Afonko. "No, brother, I didn't knuckle under in the camps."

He uncorked the bottle.

"Ilya, I survived so much that it's better not to remember, but I do remember. You can never forget such things!"

Yevseviy Karpovich had suffered in prison. In true partisan fashion, Afonko paid back the first interrogator who laid a hand on him by knocking the guy right off his feet. For that, he got twenty days in solitary, but he survived the icy solitary cell and the subsequent interrogations.

Sitting in Lefortovo prison, where the investigative units of the NKVD were officially permitted to torture the prisoners, Yevseviy Karpovich wrote to Stalin every ten days, as prisoners were then permitted to do:

> Dear Iosif Vissarionovich, those who have been arrested are being tortured: they cannot endure it, and so they incriminate themselves. They are then required to name their accomplices and, without holding back, they incriminate their friends. The most recently arrested don't hold back at all and "confess everything." For whose benefit is this required?

And they didn't condemn him to death for letters like this!

Even some torture and humiliation didn't drag false statements out of Afonko. In the complete absence of any material evidence of a crime, and without even a trial, they tossed him into the camps for eight years for "espionage on behalf of an unknown nation"!

"And then, brother, I stopped writing to the Great Leader," Yevseviy Karpovich sadly admitted. "I stopped, because I was convinced: *Stalin knew about everything . . .*"

At the end of April 1938, I arrived at my new duty station at the Il'ino test range and was told that my predecessor, Colonel Chumak, had been arrested as an enemy of the people. No one knew the nature of his crime.

"Did you have a major reorganization after Chumak's arrest?"

"Hmmmm. We turned over his house, with the veranda, to the day-care center . . ."

I began to acquaint myself with the work of the proving grounds, with testing equipment for railroad troops, and with the exercise schedule. But changes *hadn't* been limited to reassigning the house with the veranda! I found that work on a whole series of equipment prototypes had been interrupted; the inventors and authors of the designs had also been declared to be enemies of the people. Their names had been stricken from the work program. Often even the suggestions that they had made for new types of equipment had also been stricken. This was absolutely illogical. But as they used to say: "Where will you go, and whom will you tell about it?" Clearly, what was happening on the proving grounds was also happening everywhere else.

When I think about those days, I ask myself: isn't that why the development of so many remarkable kinds of new equipment was brought along at a snail's pace in the prewar years? Isn't this why, at the beginning of the war with Hitler's Germany, there were so few outstanding weapons ready for serial production in the armories of the Red Army?

And I answer myself: "Yes, that's precisely why!"

It's true that not all valuable specialists were sent to dig gold in Kolyma or to rot in the swamps of Siberia, they even let some work in prison.[9] These "happy ones" perfected their designs in solitary cells, isolated from the world. Above them hung the constant threat that any mistake would be taken as an act of sabotage, any failure would result in a worsening of their conditions of confinement. It was difficult to receive the necessary scientific information, to learn about the latest developments in science and technology. One might say that the milieu didn't exactly foster creativity!

At Il'ino, imprisoned specialists were delivered to the test range and experimental fields under heavy guard. Only the chief of the test range, the commissar, and the head of the NKVD special department knew about their arrival. I remember that, in the spring of 1939, they delivered to us, in the same secret fashion, some kind of aircraft design engineer whose name I never learned. The railroad car with the prisoner and the guard was diverted to a branch line across the test range. By that time, State Security operatives had already put up tents in a small woodland clearing and had surrounded them with two high barbed-wire fences. It was only later when I finally met the designer of the excellent Pe-2 dive bomber, V. M. Petlyakov, that I learned exactly who my proving ground "guest" had been.[10]

Even under those difficult conditions, the test-range staff worked in a harmonious and friendly fashion. My commissar, Aleksandr Vasilyevich Denisov, deserves a lot of credit for that: he was the kind of guy who was able to get deeply involved in professional matters and rally people behind him. However, even in my friendly staff, things sometimes heated up a bit.

Soon after my arrival, my deputy for material and technical support, Dmitriy Ivanovich Vorob'yev, was accused of Trotskyite connections. The sole basis for this appeared to be Vorob'yev's friendship with the chief construction engineer of the Saratov rail-

9. These include such personalities as the well-known engineer, A. N. Tupelov; S. P. Korolev, the space vehicle and rocket designer; K. I. Stakhovich, a jet designer; and Aleksandr Solzhenitsyn, who worked on various scientific projects because of his background in languages, physics, and math.

10. Petlyakov survived his imprisonment and designed other successful Soviet aircraft including the Tu-7 (Pe-8) heavy bomber, only to perish in a possible accidental air crash in 1942.

road bridge, Col. I. M. Ipatov, who had been declared an enemy of the people, not long before.

In a Party meeting, engineer P. I. Martsinkevich and Vorob'yev's assistant, V. N. Nikitin, who was a Knight of the Order of the Red Banner, tried to defend Dmitriy Ivanovich. But the meeting was filled with malevolent people, and Vorob'yev was thrown out of the Party.

On 8 December 1938, Beria replaced Yezhov as people's commissar for internal affairs, and then a purge began throughout the NKVD[11], so they never got around to arresting Vorob'yev. He got his Party card back after nine months. A threat also hung over Aleksandr Yevdokimovich Kryukov. The cadres department of the general staff sent me a request to provide a detailed Party evaluation report on Communist party member A. Ye Kryukov, specifying his behavior for the period under discussion.

I wrote a very positive reference.

Aleksandr Yevdokimovich got off unharmed, but in September 1939, he was relieved of his duties.

Starinov's tour at the test range was extremely productive: working night and day through all seasons of the year, he made good use of his resources,—including an experimental shop, an eighteen-kilometer railroad line, a company of his own troops, and railroad troops arriving periodically for exercises—to develop new methods of destroying and rebuilding railroad bridges and wrecking trains. He spent a great deal of energy on the development of mines that were reliable, safe to transport and plant, would not attract enemy attention, and could remain functional for long periods of time under difficult environmental conditions. Particular attention was given to delayed-action and quick-detonating antitrain mines and to the development of methods to use these weapons to deny an enemy use of a railroad net. Research was also conducted on countering minesweeping methods, including research on burying mines and the development of earth augers for that purpose. In addition to the development work, Starinov's staff prepared, with the customary innumerable rewrites, a regulation on railroad barrier operations as well as a set of performance standards on that subject. Starinov also wrote a dissertation entitled "On Mining Railroads" in which he set forth methods for mining operations that would deny an enemy use of a railroad for up to six months but would permit traffic to be quickly resumed once the road fell into friendly hands

11. Prof. Conquest estimates that 20,000 NKVD men died in the purge.

again. The motivation for this work was not only "love for the art," as Starinov says, but the increasingly threatening international situation, e.g., the Italian invasion of Albania, Germany's move into Sudetenland, Japanese incursions in the Soviet Far East, the fall of the Republican government in Spain, and the German invasion of Poland. The USSR was not inactive during this period, either: in the spring of 1939, the Soviets concluded a nonaggression pact with Germany, deciding in advance on the partition of Poland.

Following the German invasion of Poland on 1 September 1939, Soviet troops reoccupied the Baltic States, western Belorussia, the western Ukraine, and eastern Poland, recovering most of the land that the USSR had lost during the civil war.

On the Karelian Isthmus

In mid-November 1939, I was ordered to Leningrad on a special mission to prepare for the attack on Finland, which began on 1 December 1939. The chief of staff of military communications of the Leningrad Military District was forming a special group of seven men to organize large-scale mine clearing along the roads, and I was designated senior man of the group. Anna remained behind at Il'ino, hoping that the war would be over quickly.

The Finns didn't spare their mines, and some of their mine layouts were definitely deceptive. We immediately ran into booby traps of the most diverse types as well as antipersonnel mines and metal antitank mines of a type completely unknown to us, which sometimes even exploded under just a man's weight.

How were we going to disarm these mines, right on the spot, without removing them? In the mine detonators and around them, there was either granulated or compressed TNT. Poured TNT is not dangerous, but compressed TNT is another story ... we'd have to melt out the compressed TNT in order to begin the study of the types of mines that were unknown to us.

We got hold of a cooking pot and put in it mines that we had found. Then we suspended our "saucepan" in a somewhat larger pot that we had found in a Finnish border-guard bath. We poured water into both pots and fired up the heater until the water in both pots bubbled. "Now, maybe, we'll be able to do it," I said to Col. Vladimir Nikolayevich Podozerov. Nodding in agreement, Podozerov asked whether we had much of a future, working together in this business. Despite his clear concern, he was a wonderfully cool fellow! I was convinced that we had done everything correctly and that the mines would not explode, but I nevertheless hesitated in my response. I hesitated until I was absolutely certain that nothing adverse would happen. I don't know what was going on with me—it was probably a lack of faith in my own ability.

I carefully unscrewed the detonator from the mines, and the disassembly and study of the "boiled" mines began. By evening, a staff typist had already typed up our first instruction on disarming Finnish mines. The instruction reached the troops immediately, and the troops devoured it! Mines were everywhere on the roads, the bridges, railroad tracks, and in abandoned homes. Mines were concealed in the snow, hidden under woodpiles, under boards that seemed to be carelessly thrown along the roadside, under the wheels of abandoned carts, and even under the bodies of dead enemy soldiers.

We went off to the frontline units not only to advise but to work.

On one of the first days of the war, I saw Army Commander (Commandarm) First Rank G. I. Kulik at the front. His car had overtaken a unit that had been bogged down. The army commander hopped out of his car with an unpleasant expression on his face.

"Why have you stopped?"

I was the senior officer present, and I reported that a car had been blown up by a mine up ahead and that another car had hit a mine trying to get around the wreck of the first car.

"So what? Are you just going to stand around?"

We did not have mine-clearing personnel at that time, and there were no demolitions men in the vicinity, and so, naturally, I got the task of clearing the mines myself, assisted by an adjunct professor from the Military Transport Academy, N. F. Avramenko. Hastily throwing together a trawl, fitted with grapnel hooks, we destroyed all the antipersonnel mines, which had pressure and trip-wire detonators. Then we found, safely extracted, and by Kulik's request, disarmed an antitank mine of the type we had already gotten to know, right there on the spot.

Shortly after this, I was sent to the Kirov plant, where they were to begin the manufacture of a suspended mine trawl that I had suggested. A prototype model of the trawl was put together in a single day with the assistance of the famous heavy-tank designer, Zhosef Yakovlevich Kotin, a Hero of Socialist Labor. Unfortunately, the first tests did not produce the anticipated results, and while the factory got busy improving the trawl, I returned to the front.

They were very difficult days. Our troops were only able to enter the territory protected by the so-called Mannerheim Line on 30 December. The attack to break through the main Finnish defensive line began on 11 February 1940 and was completed after twelve days. After that, we still had to cross a second defensive line, but I was not destined to participate in that operation. An enemy sniper, lying in wait for a group of demolitions men, put two shots through my right arm. The medics, who came on the run, applied a tourniquet and started to bandage me up, but my sleeve continued to fill up with blood. It was almost impossible to evacuate me from the area where I had been wounded. My comrades were concerned because I was losing so much blood, and reported on my condition to General Chibisov, commander of the Leningrad Military District.

They sent a military transport plane from Leningrad: unfortunately, it crashed upon landing on a frozen woodland lake, injuring the pilot. They then had to send another transport plane from the district, this time for two wounded: the pilot of the first plane and myself. This plane quickly returned us to Leningrad.

By the time they started to operate, I had already lost consciousness.

I spent two months in the hospital. It seemed as if the hospital surgeons did everything possible to save my arm, but when I was finally discharged from the hospital, I could hardly move my fingers. Prolonged treatment by specialists was required in order to restore the functioning of the nerves in the hand, but it was impossible for me to receive treatment while running the test range. My friends once more showed touching concern for my welfare. I was still on convalescent leave when I learned of my new assignment—chief of the Barrier and Mine Department of the Directorate of Military Engineer Training of the Main Directorate of Military Engineering of the Red Army. This new assignment both alarmed and pleased me.

Experience gathered in the war with the Finns clearly showed that the most primitive but well-deployed mines were capable of inflicting serious casualties on attacking troops and of interfering with the use of lines of communication and undamaged buildings. One would have thought that this experience would have put an end to the underestimation of the importance of mine-barrier operations and would have opened broad perspectives in our work.

The main mission of Starinov's understaffed and overworked department was to bring Soviet mining and mine-clearing capabilities up to the level of other nations. Starinov soon found that this was an impossible task: the work that had been carried out in the late twenties and early thirties to strengthen border defenses—the demolition charges that had been cached at major strategic points, the special units that had been created for mining and demolitions, the partisan detachments, the reserve stockpiles of mines and demolitions—all had been "liquidated." The Ulyanovsk special equipment school, the only school in the USSR that trained officers to use radio-detonated mines, had been converted to a communications school. The bloody shadows of the purges were still everywhere, and any military developments associated with purge victims were avoided with an almost religious horror. This was especially true for developments in the fields of mining, minesweeping, demolitions, and partisan operations, all of which were officially associated with Starinov's late chiefs, Tukhachevskiy, Yakir, and Berzin. Stalin and his entourage remained deeply suspicious of many initiatives in mining and demolitions and preparations for partisan war. The official line was that such defensive measures or preparations were unnecessary: in the event of an attack, the USSR would immediately carry the war to enemy territory. Paradoxically, Starinov notes, Soviet borders had been stronger in the twenties and thirties, when the potential enemies were weaker than they were in 1940 when the USSR faced Nazi Germany. Starinov's department, nevertheless, charged boldly ahead, revising existing regulations, instructions, and norms for mining and mine clearing; working on the reconstruction of border fortifications and developing new types of mines, including a new delayed-action antitrain mine. Starinov was asked to estimate the numbers of mines of all types required if the existing 1939 Field Service Regulations were to be followed. The numbers thus derived were five to six times larger than the planning figures used by the Ministry of Defense and were rejected as fantastic. With permission of his superiors, he made an "end run" around the military chain of command to the Central Committee of the Communist party and succeeded in attracting Party attention. Although higher planning figures were finally accepted, actual mine production was never initiated to meet the planning requirements. At the beginning of 1940, a total of only one million antitank mines had been issued to Soviet units, as opposed to the 2.8 million figure required under planning norms. There were almost no delayed-action mines or booby traps, and only half the required minimum number of engineer mines were in storage. Maneuvers in the Moscow Military District in the fall of 1940 were planned to yield important results concerning mine and barrier operations, but failed to do so since many of the rank and file were recently inducted conscripts who were not familiar with mine technology and could not use it. Starinov made a valiant effort to overcome the psychological impact of the purges and the reactionary behavior of military bureaucrats to convince the Soviet general staff of the necessity for strengthening mine and barrier capabilities, but in the end, he admits that his efforts were like "a drop in the ocean." Meanwhile, the international situation decayed as Germany prepared for Operation BARBAROSSA, *the invasion of the Soviet Union. By this point in Starinov's narrative, World War II had been underway in Western Europe for nearly two years, since shortly after Hitler concluded his agreement with Stalin.*

Trip to Brest

I arrived at Brest on the evening of 19 June 1941 on maneuvers with the troops of the Special Western Border District. The streets were blossoming with young girls and women in bright dresses. Ice cream vendors screeched at passersby: "It's going to be very hot here!" At a trolley stop on Mayakovsky Square, a young fellow dressed in an apache shirt was trying to pick up a leggy girl, but she just turned up her sweaty nose and kept a haughty silence. A trolley sailed majestically along past beautifully decorated windows, flower stalls, and carefree crowds on the evening sidewalks . . .

My companion—the stout, round-faced Lt. Col. Zakhar Iosifovich Kolesnikov, deputy chief of the Directorate of Military Engineer Training of the Main Military Engineer Directorate—was wiping his bald spot with his handkerchief and constantly sipping from a bottle of Narzan mineral water. "It's better if we travel by night," he said, puffing. "In the daytime, we might be burned to a crisp!"

Moscow receded farther with each kilometer that we traveled.

The train sped along past quiet groves and fragrant meadows on which stacks of fresh-cut hay grew dark.

"It's a paradise here," Kolesnikov said. "Right after the test, I'm going to take some leave and head off to the countryside for some fishing. You like to fish?"

"When I've got time, I fish."

"How about hunting?"

"I'm not really interested."

"That's a mistake. Only in hunting, Ilya Grigor'yevich, can you comprehend the beauty of the world. You see that it's alive . . . You really ought to get into hunting weapons."

"I didn't catch the hunting bug in childhood, and now it's really too late."

"Nonsense! Beauty can get you, even in your seventies."

It was time to hit the sack. Kolesnikov was in dreamland almost as soon as he hit the pillow. I couldn't sleep, however: I was thinking about the upcoming exercise, and was looking forward to meeting my old comrades. I was pleased that I would be seeing the chief of the district artillery, Gen. Nikolai Aleksandrovich Klich, who had been my friend in Spain on the Ebro River. I was also curious to see the district commander General of the Army D. G. Pavlov. He fought as a tanker in Spain, had a dizzying rise in rank after his return, and now was commanding one of the most important military districts.

How would Pavlov receive me? Had he changed drastically since that time when I saw him at Belchite, pale and shaken because a tank attack had bogged down in the swampy river flood-plains?

I fell asleep with these thoughts.

The conductor's voice awakened me: "We're approaching Minsk, Comrade Officers!"

In the square in front of the railroad station a car awaited us. Along still-peaceful streets, illuminated by the early morning light, we set out to visit the district staff.

"It's a paradise here, a paradise!" Kolesnikov tirelessly repeated, looking out on either side of the vehicle. "It's a beautiful paradise!"

At the Belorussian Military District staff headquarters, the first order of business was to meet with the chief of the engineering directorate, P. M. Vasil'yev. He also arrived in high spirits. When he had reported that everything in the maneuver area was ready for the exercise, he took us to get acquainted with the district chief of staff, V. E. Klimovskikh. Klimovskikh was clearly not interested in us, frequently picking up the phone, listening to some report or other, scowling more and more, his face growing increasingly gloomy.

Vasil'yev bent over my shoulder and spoke confidentially: "There are constant reports about German spies and aircraft violating our borders. He's getting panicky."

Klimovskikh excused himself and sent us off, saying that the matter of setting up mines and barriers in the maneuver area should be obvious. Leaving the chief of staff's office, I asked Vasil'yev if it might not be impossible for us to visit the commander right then.

"Impossible? Why? Let's go!"

Pavlov actually received us very quickly. When we entered, he was talking on the phone, and he greeted us with a nod. He spoke sharply into the phone, with irritation: "It's nothing . . . Just hang in . . . I know, they've already reported! Hang in there!" Finally, Pavlov put down the receiver. Almost as an afterthought, he extended his hand to us. Hastily familiarizing himself with the test program, he observed that, in his opinion, far too much attention was being given to the construction of antitank barriers and far too little to developing ways of overcoming those barriers.[1]

The telephone began to buzz again:

"I know; they reported," he responded firmly, but it was obvious that he was having a difficult time retaining his composure. "I know; I already passed the word," he repeated, "I know . . . but up above, everything is quite obvious to them. Everything!"

With a futile gesture, he replaced the receiver. Klimovskikh, the chief of staff, came in. He gave us a hostile stare. "Excuse me for interrupting your meeting, but there's a very important matter—"

"Well, Wolf," General Pavlov said, calling me by the cover name I had used in Spain, "we'll get together during the exercise! There'll be more free time there, and then we can talk about everything. By the way, I have a version of the new mine trawl . . . But right now, you'll have to pardon me, I'm busy."

We left the district staff with troubled hearts. It was clear that things on the border were not as peaceful as they were being represented in Moscow in the quiet offices of the Second Building of the Ministry of Defense, where the Main Directorate of Military Engineers was located.

I went to see my old friend, General Klich.

"Wolf, damn you! Good to see you! Here for an exercise, are you? Well . . . I'm afraid there's not going to be an exercise."

---

1. Soviet military doctrine of that period stressed offensive action to carry the fight onto the enemy's territory.

I couldn't help admiring Klich. He was still the same: tall and thin, organized, confidence in his every movement. He'd been a tireless favorite of the Spanish artillerymen.

Nikolai Aleksandrovich invited me to sit down. I had hardly done so when we began talking about the situation on the border.

"What's going on here?" I asked directly.

"Very bad things are happening."

"Specifically what?"

"Specifically . . . the Germans are moving their troops up to the border and bringing up tanks and artillery. Their aircraft are always overflying our territory."

"And what are *we* doing?"

"We are reorganizing and rearming our troops. Shooting down enemy aircraft is strictly forbidden. TASS announced that on 14 June. I don't know how to evaluate that. It definitely calmed things down a bit on our side, but at the same time, it lowered our level of combat readiness."

"What do you think?"

"I think we'd better keep our powder dry, particularly when we're dealing with those German swine."

"You're holding something back."

Nikolai Aleksandrovich looked at me reproachfully. Normally restrained, he suddenly became excited: "You have to understand why I'm upset . . . I have many artillery pieces, but the artillerymen are mostly youngsters, and they're insufficiently trained. What's more, they've gathered up vehicles from many artillery regiments to use in the construction of fortified areas. Even the tractor prime movers have been taken away. Our artillery has no prime movers. Do you understand? Our artillery can't move!"

"You reported this to Pavlov, didn't you?"

"Yeah, I reported to Pavlov, and I phoned Moscow, too, and I always got the same answer: 'Don't panic! Calm down! The Boss knows everything that's going on!' "

Neither Klich nor I had touched upon the contents of the speech given by Stalin at the graduation of the military academies on 5 May 1941. This speech was not published, but many had heard it, and some excerpts had even been reprinted in reports about the international situation. Stalin asserted that the Red Army had been reorganized and completely rearmed. In fact, the rearming had only just begun. But we couldn't talk about that, even one-on-one.

The phone brought an end to our reunion. Klich had been called to report immediately to the district commander.

On Saturday, 21 June, Kolesnikov and I had already arrived at

Brest. It was another marvelous, sunny morning. The sun shone down on the heaps of coal along the railroad track and on the stacks of glistening new rails. It was the very picture of tranquility.

On the train, I met an artillery colonel who was familiar with the maneuver area. The colonel told me with alarm, that even after the TASS announcement of 14 June, the situation on the other side of the border had not changed. But *our* troops had begun to relax. He nodded in the direction of soldiers with suitcases who were walking along the station platform.

"Not so long ago these guys were sleeping with their boots on, and now they're getting ready to go off on leave! Why? The TASS announcement!"

On the road, we stopped at Kobrin where the staff of the Fourth Army was quartered. We looked up the engineer chief, Col. A. I. Proshlyakov. He put us up in his own office and promised to send a car around in the morning, so that we could travel to the maneuver area together. Proshlyakov confirmed that the Germans had been bringing up equipment to the western Bug River all through June, that they had set up camouflage screens in front of open sectors in their lines, and that they had erected observation towers.

"We were warned that the German military might attempt a provocation and were ordered that we were not to respond to any provocation," Proshlyakov said calmly. "That won't happen. There are no nervous nellies on the army staff."

On the warm evening of 21 June 1941, the staff offices of the Fourth Army, which was covering the approaches to Brest, were following a typical Saturday routine. We had been told that the exercise had been canceled,[2] and we wandered around the picturesque town for a long time. Then we returned to the office of the chief engineer, wished each other a good-night, and happily stretched out on the staff couches.

---

2. The reason for canceling the exercise is obscure. The exercise would have at least provided an excuse to maintain larger forces than usual in the field near the border, in a situation where an attack was obviously imminent. Even if the exercise had been canceled, there was no need to release troops on leave and not to provide senior personnel with emergency contingency orders and plans. Although it is claimed that the Soviet leadership was trying to avoid provoking a German attack, senior Soviet military personnel on the scene were clearly alarmed and reporting to Moscow, and Soviet intelligence had acquired the plans for Operation BARBAROSSA. All reports of the threat seem to have been rejected by Stalin. One wonders if Stalin was baiting the Germans, cynically planning to use the unprovoked attack as a means of uniting the nation, in the misguided assumption that Soviet forces would score a quick victory. If so, he clearly did not anticipate the energy of the German assault, nor did he accurately assess the ability of his own purge-crippled forces to defend against this assault.

22 June

I awoke with a start; explosions were rumbling through my dreams. Everything was quiet all around, but through the open window, growing brighter in the dawn, floated a droning, straining rumble of aircraft engines. I looked at my watch: it was 4:20 A.M. Kolesnikov also got up. He rummaged around on the chair that he had pulled up to the head of the bed, searching for his watch.

Not far away, a loud crash was followed by an explosion. The house rocked, and the window glass whined plaintively.

"What's that, demolitions work?"

Kolesnikov listened carefully. "More likely a bomb dropped from a plane."

But where in hell were the pilots coming from? I didn't finish the thought because more explosions followed in a few seconds, merging into one deafening roar, followed by silence. Then, we heard the roar of aircraft engines once more, now growing, now decreasing in intensity. That sound reminded me of Spain: it was the roar of Junkers dive-bombers. Kolesnikov and I rushed to the window: the sky over Kobrin was peaceful and blue; a few fleecy clouds were drifting along. On the other side of the wall, we heard boots clomping about. Along the corridors flew the order: "Everyone outside! Immediately!" In the empty offices the ringing of telephones was deafening.

"Zakhar Iosifovich, something's going on!"

Kolesnikov knew that without my prompting. Hastily pulling on our uniforms on the run, we ran out onto the street just as a squadron of planes headed straight for the staff offices. Somebody yelled: "Aiiirrrraiiid!" We dashed across the square, jumped over some kind of ditch, and flung ourselves into a garden. Watching the planes as we ran, we saw small, pointed shapes separating from the black fuselages.

Bombs fell with piercing shrieks, and the army staff building, from which we had just fled, was enveloped in a cloud of smoke and dust. Powerful explosions tore the air, making our ears ring.

Yet another flight of aircraft appeared. For more than an hour, German dive-bombers dove unopposed on our defenseless military base.

When the attack was over, thick, black smoke rose above the ruins. Freshly broken timber cluttered the streets. A part of the staff building had been destroyed. Somewhere, in a high-pitched, drawn-out shriek, a strained female voice, desperately and disconsolately wailed: "A-a-a-a . . ."

When I learned from a surviving duty officer that the Fourth Army staff was going to transfer to the alternate command post at Bukhovichi, Kolesnikov and I decided to go to Brest. There, among the representatives of the Ministry of Defense and the general staff who had arrived for the exercise, we ought to be able to find people who were well informed about what was happening and get orders.

We got into the first vehicle that came down the street. Ahead of us on the highway, officers ran about, hurrying off to their duty stations. Along the roadside, women trudged with bundles and baskets, dragging hastily dressed, sleepy kids. They were leaving the military base.

The streets of Kobrin, so serene the night before, reeked with the smell of the first fires. In the square, people crowded around a loudspeaker mounted on a telegraph pole. We stopped to listen, too. The people looked hopefully at the black, saucer-shaped loudspeaker. The familiar call sign of Radio Moscow brightened up the listeners' faces. Taking a breath, the city of Kobrin waited to see what Moscow had to say.

"Moscow time: six o'clock! We bring you the latest news . . ." We hung on every word, but we heard a series of announcers about the successes of Soviet labor, the great harvest, the overfulfillment of the Five Year Plan, the celebrations in the Mari ASSR, and this, and that . . .

"The German news service reports . . ." began the loudspeaker. The girl next to us rose on her tiptoes to better hear.

Nowhere, and never after, have I ever heard such silence as reigned in that moment in the Kobrin square.

But the announcer went on to talk in an official tone about the sinking of British ships; the German bombing of cities in Scotland; the destruction of seventeen German planes over England, according to Reuters; and the war in Syria, and then went silent. *There was not a single word about the German attack on our nation.* The news broadcast ended with a weather report. The girl alongside us was no longer standing on tiptoes. Sullen, she glanced at the loudspeaker and then at the remaining townspeople.

"Let's wait: maybe there'll be a special bulletin or report," Kolesnikov said uncertainly.

But right on schedule, the morning physical exercise program began on the radio. Our driver spat on the ground and slammed the car doors. People began to scatter; the girl next to us looked around in confusion and then ran off. Vehicles carrying crying women and children were already rumbling through Kobrin, heading east. Some of the kids might already have become orphans in the few short hours of war that had already passed.

And it seemed as if the announcer, with his cheerful voice, was almost giving them some parting advice: "Extend your arms out to the side! Sit down! Faster! Stand up! Sit down! Faster! That's it! Very good!"

The Junkers dive-bombers approached the town again. Their howling and the frightening screams of the bombs finally drowned out the voice that was calling us to "jump up, jump as high as you can . . ."

Over fifty years have passed since that June day, but I cannot forget Kobrin Square, the black saucer-shaped loudspeaker hanging above it, and the ill-starred exercise class.

When we learned from refugees that German troops had crossed the border in the Brest area and that fighting was going on in Brest itself, Kolesnikov and I set out for Bukhovichi to the Fourth Army staff. There, they told us that when enemy bombers were approaching the city, they had received a telegram from the staff of the Western Special Military District warning of the possibility of a German attack during the period "22–23 June." The telegram ordered that Soviet forces were "not to be fooled by any provocation, and to forcefully challenge any further complications of the situation." At the same time, the order stated that German troops would be confronted by a state of full combat readiness. The fact that the war had actually begun, and that we had to operate without fear of consequences, became clear only after we received a telegram sent by the district staff at 5:25 A.M. "Raise troops and carry on combat operations."

We decided to return to Minsk, the headquarters of the Belorussian Military District, for orders.

We traveled through Pinsk, arriving there almost at midday. On the military airfield near the city, pilots and personnel of the airfield service units rushed about, among burning aircraft, trying to save those things that remained undamaged by the bombs. Pinsk itself had not yet been bombed, but the city was completely alerted: the streets were unusually busy, and there was a crowd of men around the military commissariat (Translator's note: the military conscription office, where volunteers were being enlisted at this time). In the offices of the Municipal Party Committee, they asked questions that neither Kolesnikov nor I could answer. But then no one in the Municipal Committee could believe that the enemy would get to Pinsk, located as it was some two hundred kilometers from the border! We climbed aboard a truck bound for Minsk, carrying military dependents being evacuated, and arrived there on the following morning. In the city outskirts we came across livestock that had been killed by shrapnel. In the city itself, smoke rose everywhere.

The staff of the Special Military District had already been redesignated the staff of the Western Front.[1] General Vasil'yev, now chief of Western Front engineers, was nowhere near as calm as he had been two days earlier. He stated that no one knew what the situation was at the front: lines of communications with our forces had been systematically cut. "We have one thing to be glad about," the general said. "This morning, our troops launched a counterattack, following a directive of the people's commissar for defense"

Obviously, the chief of engineering troops was nervous because he didn't notice that his statement about the loss of communications with our forces did not agree with his statement about our counterattack!

From Vasil'yev's office, we got in touch with Moscow, with the Main Military Engineer Directorate, where Col. M. A. Nagornyy, chief of the Directorate of Combat Training, ordered us to return immediately.

Regular railroad traffic to the capital had already ceased, but General Vasil'yev gave us a car. Seeing us off, he asked us to expedite delivery to the front of explosives and mines; most importantly, antitank mines.

On 24 June 1941, at midday, we were in Moscow. The capital had changed noticeably: there were fewer civilians and cars on the streets but more military personnel, and everywhere camouflage work was going on. They were attempting to change the appearance of the city from the air, camouflaging buildings, and building dummy facilities.

We arrived at our duty station in the second building of the

---

1. In the USSR, a military district was a peacetime territorially-based organization in which local formations and units, military training establishments, and military facilities were subordinated to a single commander who was responsible for combat readiness, training, upkeep, logistics, and recruitment in his district. Districts located on the borders of the USSR were designated as Special Military Districts. Such districts also had responsibility defending against enemy attacks and supporting intelligence and partisan operations in nations bordering on the USSR. There were sixteen military districts in the former USSR, many of which continue to exist in the CIS. A front is an operational and strategic formation of armed forces, usually created at the beginning of hostilities for the purposes of carrying out operational and strategic missions in one or several strategic directions in a continental theater of operations. In this case, the Special Military District, with its staff and all its assets, was simply transformed into the Western Front.

Ministry of Defense around lunchtime, but there was no such thing as a lunch break anymore. We were immediately shown in to see Colonel Nagornyy, and together with him we set out to see Gen. I. P. Galitskiy. Galitskiy had recently been discharging the duties of the chief of the Main Engineer Directorate, and in the first days of the war, he did everything possible and, it seemed to me, many things that might have been impossible, to improve engineering support of Red Army combat operations. We reported to him on the situation on the Western Front, and transmitted the request from the chief of engineer troops for more explosives and mines.

I wasn't able to get home, although I passed almost right by the place, but I did have the chance to call my wife. Anna was a brave person: she'd been with me in Spain and had gone behind enemy lines with my demolitions men. Nevertheless, she was relieved to learn that I had survived the attack and was home from the front.

Two Days in Moscow

A communique of 23 June reported that the enemy advance had been beaten back with heavy losses for the attackers. Supposedly, our troops had destroyed three hundred tanks, and captured more than five thousand prisoners. Brest and Lomzha had been abandoned, however.

Overnight, our directorate was transformed into the Red Army Engineer Troops staff, with all the responsibilities that followed from that transformation. It was necessary to form new units, organize courses for training specialists in the use of mines and explosives in barrier operations, and to position the forces and equipment that were at our disposal. We wanted to believe that the enemy had already been stopped and was on the point of being driven out, but the situation on the front got worse and worse. The enemy occupied more cities, important transportation and communications centers. Mobilization plans for significant parts of the Soviet Union were upset.

On the morning of 26 June, Colonel Nagornyy called me and unexpectedly announced:

"Ilya Grigor'yevich, prepare yourself for a new command!"

I looked at him inquiringly.

"The minister of defense has ordered immediate assistance be given to troops in setting up barriers. Engineer operations groups (Translator's note: *operativno-inzhenernye gruppy*) have been created, which are not based on normal tables of organization. You have been designated as chief of the group on the Western Front. We recommend Col. Mikhail Semenovich Ovchinnikov as your deputy. Agreed?"

"Certainly. What will you place at our disposal?"

"Four demolitions experts from the command group, three sapper battalions, six thousand antitank mines, twenty-five tons of explosives . . ."

"Twenty-five tons? That's not enough for one day's work."

"Then we'll deliver more. But mine operations won't be in accordance with the norms previously applied in training exercises. We haven't the explosives." It was clearly sickening to Nagornyy to have to say that. He swore, and had a few bad things to say about I. A. Petrov, who had been managing the orders for mines and the development of explosives reserves.

That day, 26 June, General Galitskiy brought us—officers and engineers divided into operational groups—to meet the people's commissar for defense, S. K. Timoshenko.[2] I had seen Marshal Timoshenko more than once, on the Karelian Isthmus for example, and on exercises. He was always a self-confident, loud fellow, but he had changed; he looked very tired, and it seemed as if his voice had actually been shattered. He listened to General Galitskiy's report with an unnatural calm. Only when Ivan Pavlovich cited the small number of available antitank mines did the marshal's expression harden. Then the marshal enunciated just one sentence with his usual energy: "Don't wait for orders from above! Act on your own initiative!"

And that's the way we were given broad authority to destroy military facilities ahead of the attacking enemy. It seemed strange that when he saw us off, the defense commissar did not once mention Stalin.

After leaving Timoshenko, we visited Maj. Gen. G. K. Malandin at the general staff. Pale, with dark circles under his sunken eyes, Malandin was more animated than the defense commissar. He stated, with restraint, that the situation was becoming difficult, but then he refused to give specific information about the actual

2. Semen Konstantinovich Timoshenko, Marshal of the Soviet Union, held the position of People's Commissar for Defense from 1940 to 1941. Thereafter, he held various high-level posts, including representative of the Stavka of the High Command, Front commander of several fronts, and commander of the defense of Stalingrad.

situation at the front. We got only the most general kind of information: the enemy was continuing to push on to the east, on several important axes of advance: "I won't give you the details, you'll get them on the spot. Just remember—and make sure all your troops and officers remember—*you are covering the strategic axis of advance to Moscow*! The strategic axis of advance *to Moscow*, comrades!"

We were given a mandate, signed by the minister of defense, which permitted the bearer to mine and blow up bridges and roads and to erect various kinds of barriers.

From the general staff, I returned to Nagornyy's office. He and I were informed that a group of reserve armies had just been formed under Marshal S. M. Budenny by a 25 June directive of the defense commissar. This group was to prepare and occupy defensive positions along the line: Sushchevo-Nevel'-Vitebsk-Mogilev-Zhlobin-Gomel'-Chernigov, and farther along the Desna River. This line extended more than five hundred kilometers inside the boundaries of the Western Front! On two hundred of these kilometers there were no significant water obstacles or other natural obstacles to enemy tanks. According to very hasty calculations, a mine barrier in that area would require about two hundred thousand antitank mines, even more antipersonnel mines, and a minimum of six thousand delayed-action mines. Disregarding these numbers, we began to calculate the minimum antitank mines necessary for erecting barriers in the zones that could be most quickly prepared, from the Barents to the Black Sea. We came up with a number of about 1.2 million units!

Unfortunately, that many antitank mines simply did not exist in the European portion of the Soviet Union. And who could say how many still existed on 26 June? Neither Nagornyy nor I could give even an approximate answer to that question.

Once more, Nagornyy had some bad words to say about General Petrov, the chief of the Main Engineer Directorate; for my part, I cursed Marshal Kulik. General Petrov was not only exceedingly cautious, but was indifferent to the duties that had been assigned to him and obviously didn't even know the significance of mines and explosives in wartime barrier operations. You could talk with him about something pleasant—about hunting or fishing—but not about mines. With Kulik, however, it didn't even do any good to talk about fishing.

On the night of 27 June, I received the three sapper battalions that had been placed at my disposal. Not only were they below full strength, in two of the battalions there was just one rifle for every three soldiers, and in units below battalion level, there were no digging tools besides spades. Early in the morning of 27 June, we loaded our engineer operations group onto vehicles and headed west, down the Minsk highway, toward the battle.

Another group, commanded by Maj. I. V. Volkov, was to follow along behind us.

Frontline Roads

I was well acquainted with only three of those people who rushed with me to the front in the green pickup of the engineer operations group: the old mine warfare expert Col. Mikhail Semenovich Ovchinnikov, Maj. A. T. Kovalev, and Lieutenant Semenikhin.

I had frequently had the occasion to meet the slender, short, and at first glance, shy Mikhail Semenovich on field exercises, in my department, and on various commissions. He was an ardent supporter of mines and demolitions. In the spring of 1941, he became quite fascinated by calculations of the probabilities of tanks hitting mines in various minefield layouts. For this purpose, Ovchinnikov cut out models of tanks from cardboard and drove them endlessly over minefield layouts.

I had become acquainted with tall, slender Lt. G. V. Semenikhin on the Karelian Isthmus, where he had quickly mastered the difficult and dangerous work of mine warfare. He represented a happy combination of caution and tenacity. When he heard about my assignment as chief of the engineer operation group, Semenikhin announced: "I'm ready to go."

I knew Major Kovalev best of all: he had worked as the chief of the first section in our department. Kovalev loved his work and was an unflappable and careful officer. I now gave him responsibility for most of our concerns for training and logistics.

Other officers from our group—Maj. L. N. Afanas'yev, Maj. P. N. Umanets—were less well-known to me, but I wasn't worried about them. They were both considered outstanding specialists of some kind, and neither was a novice in the army. While we certainly had to be concerned about the undermanned and poorly equipped battalions that we had been given, there was one consolation: our soldiers were all good Soviet citizens. You're going to have to spend every free minute with them, and everything will work out all right, I thought, sitting in the cab of the pickup alongside my redheaded, blue-eyed driver.

I had only the most vague impressions about this guy. His pals called him Volodya. He was obviously lively and quick-witted. He seemed to be from a cultured family, but I'd seriously erred in not even taking the time to learn his last name. "What's your family name?"

A blush slowly spread across the driver's clean, open face. Red spots appeared on his cheeks. Without taking his eyes off the road, only bending a bit over the wheel, he responded with a strange defiant tone: "Shleger—my family name is Shleger, Comrade Colonel."

The tone of the answer surprised me. "What's with you? Don't you like your family name?"

Volodya became as red as a lobster. His knuckles turned white on the steering wheel. "I suspect that it's you, Comrade Colonel, who does not like my name."

"It's a mistake to worry about what I think," I said, smiling, and rapidly changing the subject, I began to talk about a Jewish fellow with whom I had served in Spain.

"You're wrong . . . I'm not a Jew," Volodya interrupted me. "I carry my father's family name, and he was German. But in the last war he fought against the Kaiser, and when the Red Army was created, he was elected to be an officer by the soldiers . . ."

"Keep your eyes on the road!" I warned.

Perplexed, Shleger returned to a calm tone of voice.

"Everything's all right! Don't worry! Is that clear?"

Volodya Shleger nodded. "Clear, Comrade Colonel!"

Together, we traveled many tens of thousands of kilometers on wartime roads. His combat career began in the capital and ended on the banks of the western Bug River in 1944. My conscience would bother me, however, if I didn't assert that during all that time, Shleger's nationality never caused any problems for him, or for me, for that matter. I myself wasn't bothered by the fact that Shleger was a German, because I recalled that I fought alongside antifascist Germans in Spain. In those days, however, to some people the word *German* was a synonym for Fascist.

My driver didn't lose heart, however, and didn't hold a grudge. He learned to handle our equipment very well and afterward taught mines and demolitions to the partisans, carrying out a series of complicated special missions. Shleger's nimble pickup was able to slip through many difficult places in which even the highly acclaimed Willys jeeps got hopelessly stuck. Shleger's son also became a distinguished soldier: he finished commissioning school and became a military pilot, as his father dreamed he would.

Approaching Vyazma, we noticed a truck convoy standing on the side of the road. There were fifty or so vehicles in the convoy, and all of them were empty. On the highway, a tall senior lieutenant raised his arm and shouted, as though warning us about something. He explained that he was the chief of the column. "I am going with my vehicles to Belostok, to my unit," he nervously explained, "but have you heard what's going on up there ahead?"

Ahead, bombs thundered.

"Do the German dive-bombers really have such a large operating radius that they can fly all the way to Vyazma from Poland?" said the senior lieutenant in bewilderment. Actually, the operational radius of the German dive-bombers was definitely not that great. Obviously, they were no longer flying from Poland.

But I didn't begin to try to explain that to the senior lieutenant. I was having great difficulty in taking my eyes off the *fifty empty trucks*! In Vyazma, we might be able to load seventy additional tons of explosives onto those trucks! "Why did they send you off empty?" I asked. "We'll have to correct that mistake, on the move. Here are my papers. You're going to continue, but now you'll be carrying a load."

The senior lieutenant looked at the mandate signed by the defense commissar, and saluted.

Pleased at our auspicious beginning, I smiled at Ovchinnikov: "We've got a great mandate!"

About sixty kilometers west of Vyazma on the Minsk highway, there is a bridge across the Dnepr. We sent vehicles with sappers and explosives on ahead, and Colonel Ovchinnikov and I decided to inspect the Dnepr bridge. If the German offensive was to continue, the bridge would have to be prepared for demolition. We presented our papers to the chief of the bridge guard, and explained our intentions.

"Well, well . . ." said the chief of the guard, taking us in with a quick glance and then focussing once more on our papers. "Going to blow it up, eh? . . . well, well . . ." Then, he unexpectedly shrieked: "Pa-tro-ol! To arms!"

We were immediately disarmed and seized.

"Comrades, what are you doing? Haven't you seen our documents?"

"Doc-u-ments," the guard chief lingered over the word, mocking me. "You just called them 'man-dates'!"

"Yeah, a mandate! You've got our mandate in your hands."

"You see," intoned the guard chief, turning to his subordinates.

"You see how crudely the Germans work? He doesn't rely on a cannon, the snake! How do you like the signature that they slapped on it? People's commissar for defense! He tries to impress you!"

He turned again to us, surveying us with contempt: "Your fuehrer's really slipped up! They let you down! They really weren't paying attention. They didn't even know to whom the bridge guard was subordinated. That's the end of you!"

Dumbstruck, Ovchinnikov and I looked at each other. The chief of the bridge guard was right about one thing: the bridge guard was subordinated to the NKVD. Moscow had been a bit too hasty when sending us off and had not gotten proper clearance.

Seeing our confusion, the guard chief called, "Petrov, Sidorov! Tie them up!"

"Comrades: this is all a misunderstanding!"

"A misunderstanding!" one of the troops shouted. "Now we're going to swat you, and then there won't be any misunderstanding. Why are we wasting our time with them, Comrade Chief?"

But the guard chief had already decided that it was a bit too soon to "swat" us. Better to interrogate us first! Shouting at the soldiers, he ordered that the prisoners be taken to the district NKVD. Gun drawn, he sat in the truck next to Volodya Shleger who was completely bewildered.

The chief of the district NKVD greeted us with undisguised glee. He had already received information about two colonels who were engaged in inspecting the highway facilities, and now he finally had the "saboteurs" in his hands.

The absurd roadside events were threatening to lead to even more unpleasant consequences, and we understood that, and so we turned from explanations to threats. A firm and severe tone of voice, the driver's itinerary, and the signature of the people's commissar all worked to produce the desired effect.

The chief of the district department began to waiver. He nevertheless made up his mind to communicate up the line to the regional directorate.

Ovchinnikov and I sat in an empty cell and waited. The wait was unpleasant. An hour passed. Then, the chief of the district department himself opened the door. Smiling in embarrassment, he made a helpless gesture, and with further gestures, invited us to come out. The scene reminded me of something from a silent movie! We exited the cell. Milling, embarrassed, around the door were our recent prisoner escorts.

The chief of the regional department finally found the gift of speech.. "Comrades, excuse me . . . It is a disturbing misunderstanding . . . I hope that you will not take offense . . ."

We damn well did take offense, but at that time, we were only interested in getting back our documents, weapons, and pickup, and catching up with the group as quickly as possible.

The pickup stood by the porch, and a smiling Volodya rushed to start the engine.

"Maybe you can carry us back to our duty station," asked the chief of the bridge guard. "It's a really long way on foot . . ."

I waved my hand: "Get in!" The soldiers were pleased; they stretched out on the truck floor, and the pickup rushed away from that place and sailed on down the road.

To tell the truth, we really had no reason to feel offended. The population was on the alert from the first day of the war. As it turned out later, not one of our inspections of bridges and other road installations went unnoticed, even though some of them were not officially guarded. Local inhabitants *always* informed the nearest military or militia units of our presence. Our case was really just an unfortunate misunderstanding. But the country was being flooded with real Nazi spies, and if these spies resisted, they were mercilessly destroyed.

Before we reached Orsha, I had to leave my column to Major Afanas'yev again while Colonel Ovchinnikov and I went to the Front staff, accompanied by our liaison. Two of our pickups drove along a woodland road, bouncing along over pine-tree roots and carefully avoiding potholes. The early summer sun gilded the tops of the trees, but had not yet warmed the undergrowth. In the depths of the forest, under shrubs, it was still dark. There was a sharp fresh smell of moist earth. An oriole sang. Such quiet, such peace . . .

Suddenly, short bursts of automatic-weapons fire and several pistol shots rang out up ahead. And then, just as unexpectedly, everything went quiet again.

Maybe there was nothing to worry about, but I knew that caution was necessary in war, regardless of the circumstances. I stopped the vehicles, transferred all the soldiers to my pickup, and gave the order to proceed slowly.

"Comrade Colonel, looks like a policeman is running away in the woods!"

With weapons at the ready, we cautiously approached a bend in the road. In the high, dewy grass, two wide, dark tracks were clearly visible: the tracks of a vehicle that had been driven down into the woods.

We listened. Everything was quiet. We'd probably never be

able to identify the vehicle, or to know why the policeman ran off into the woods. It was doubtful if that was even necessary, at this point.

"Forward!" I ordered Shleger, and the pickup moved farther.

After about a kilometer, on the next turn of the road, we were stopped by a towheaded kid of about fifteen, holding the age-old national Russian weapon: a pitchfork.

"Comrade soldiers! There are German parachutists over there in the woods! I saw them myself when they jumped from the airplane and got together over there in the woods. I was nearby, herding the livestock."

"Shall we comb the woods?" Ovchinnikov asked.

I didn't have time to answer before a tall woman rushed out of the bushes. "Good thing help is here! Comrade officers, give us a hand! They've got submachine guns, and all we've got is these things!" She was also brandishing a pitchfork. That young collective-farm woman was a beauty, her three-cornered kerchief hanging down on her shoulders, resolutely going against enemy submachine guns with her pitchfork.

"Wow!" exclaimed one of the soldiers, unable to restrain himself.

The woman threw a glance at the guy, frowned: "Well, why are you standing around? Move it! They're not far off!"

"Get in the car," I said to the woman and the kid. "Just show us where to go." We had to turn around.

Soon we were met by another kid, just as towheaded as the first. "Auntie Anya?" he whispered "They're over there. They're fooling around with the vehicle over in the brush."

Six of us soldiers, together with "Auntie Anya's detachment," left the truck and went deeper into the woods on foot. Through a gap between the trees, we could see a clearing, in the middle of which stood a black Red Army staff car and three men dressed in police uniforms with traffic patrol armbands on their sleeves (Translator's note: ORUD = *otdel' regulirovaniya ulichnogo dvizheniya*, traffic control division).

A tall fellow wearing the rank of a police sergeant major crawled out from under the car. Wiping his hands with a rag, he said, "Get them out quickly! Let's get out of here!" The sergeant major spoke Russian, but his companions were dragging the body of a man dressed in a Soviet officer's uniform out of the staff car.

"Halt! Hands up!" I yelled. The "policemen" jumped away from the car, but four shots echoed almost simultaneously. Two of the Nazis fell among the hay bundles, and two dove for cover, attempting to crawl away and hide.

"Stop, you snakes!" I heard the voice of Sgt. Sergey Koshel. "Stop!!"

Recklessly exposing himself, he pursued the bandits, firing on the move, and right after him came Auntie Anya, the other soldiers, and the kids.

Ovchinnikov and I ran to the car. One of the bandits had been killed outright, but the other was only wounded. When we had disarmed him, we rushed over to the fellow who they had been dragging out of the car. He was one of ours—a Soviet captain—and he was dead. There was one more body in the staff car, that of a soldier who had obviously been his driver.

At about that time Sergeant Koshel and Auntie Anya appeared out of the woods, carrying a wounded "policeman."

"Where's the other one?" I asked.

Sergey Koshel drawled: "The second guy put up a fight, so we just took away his Lebensraum (Translator's note: ironic reference to the Nazi concern for gaining Lebensraum—living space—at the expense of other nationalities)." Auntie Anya wiped the sweat from her high forehead.

"What's your family name?" I asked.

"My name? Shmatkova. Why do you want to know, Comrade Colonel?"

"Because I have to know who caught the saboteurs. Supposing that you put together a list of the people in your work detachment, Anya Shmatkova."

"It's a really great work detachment! What do you want this for?"

"I am going to report to the command."

Anya Shmatkova straightened her kerchief, blushed, and looked around in confusion: "We should have put one together! We never had name lists. We've really got to gather some hay. Hey, fellows, let's go!"

"Listen!" I tried to keep Shmatkova from leaving, but she extended her hand. "Until the next time! We've got to gather hay!" And she left.

I never saw or heard of Anna Shmatkova again, but I never doubted, and I do not doubt now that she and her young friends took away the Lebensraum of more than one German during the occupation.

It was people just like her who entered the partisan movement.

On the Western Front

The correlation of forces on the border in the opening days of the war changed markedly in the favor of the enemy. Directive No. 3 of the people's commissar for defense, requiring that troops of the Northwestern and Western fronts carry out active offensive operations against the enemy, appeared at an inauspicious time. The offensive operations that we undertook on June 23, 24, and 25 produced negligible results, but the losses inflicted on our troops were extraordinarily heavy. The unjustifiable attempts to go over to the offensive at a time when we should have been organizing our defenses, only exacerbated a situation that was already bad. The Nazis certainly understood that, and feverishly attempted to develop and consolidate their successes.

We arrived on the Western Front when the Front command post was situated northeast of Mogilev, in the deep woods not far from the Dnepr. The weather was warm and dry. Staff officers set out tables right under the trees. Here and there were tents covered with tree branches. Telephone wires were strung everywhere.

We didn't find the Front commander, D. G. Pavlov, at home: he was up with the troops.

The Front chief of staff, General Klimovskikh, listlessly extended his hand to take my official report. He looked totally worn out. When he read the report, he sighed heavily, and slowly shook his head.

"It's not enough."

"We can't get any more, Comrade General."

Klimovskikh acknowledged with a nod. Grinding his teeth, he looked at the report again.

I held my tongue. What was I supposed to say? We had brought with us three times more mines and explosives than we had been given in Moscow. On my own authority, I'd taken charge of a lot more mines and explosives along the road.

"Throw all your forces into mining and cutting all the main auto and rail lines on the axis of the enemy advance," Klimovskikh said. "And don't take your time! Right now, every minute costs us."

"Request permission to acquaint myself with the situation."

"See Operations about that; oh yes, and definitely get together with the engineers."

I first went to see the chief of the Front engineer directorate, and I wasn't particularly encouraged by what I found. The only remaining assets of the Front engineer troops were two pontoon bridge battalions and three sapper battalions. The rest of the engineer troops had been encircled, and communications with them had been lost.

The chief of the engineer directorate and I distributed our modest resources and equipment along the highways on which we would have to erect top-priority barriers. I split my group into three detachments.

To Colonel Ovchinnikov and Major Afanas'yev fell the task of erecting barriers in the triangle defined by the cities of Vitebsk-Polotsk-Lepel'. I placed a three-company battalion of sappers at their disposal, along with several tons of explosives and several hundred antitank mines, Bickford cord, and detonators. They also received other accessories for demolitions work, but as with everything else, we didn't have enough of those either. Ovchinnikov immediately decided that he would operate along the Vitebsk-Polotsk line. Major Afanas'yev took the Lepel' line.

In the center, we deployed a detachment under the command of Major Umanets. He was to erect barriers along the Minsk-Borisov-Orsha line. The third detachment, led by Major Kovalev, was to cover the Mogilev-Minsk direction. Umanets and Kovalev also received several tons of TNT each, along with antitank and antipersonnel mines. We gave more mines and explosives to Umanets because his sector appeared to be more dangerous.

I placed a quantity of explosives and TM-35 antitank mines in reserve. We carefully camouflaged them in the woods near Orsha and set up our command post there, under the supervision of Lt. G. V. Semenikhin.

In those tragic days, we often had to visit the Western Front staff. With my own eyes, I could see the staff had recovered from the shock that they received in the first hours of the war. I saw how quickly the staff officers acted, how they set up communications with the troops. They already knew the situation better and were better able to predict developments. I recall that it was on the second or third day after I arrived that I got the opportunity to present myself to the Front commander, D. G. Pavlov. He had grown noticeably thinner and hollow cheeked, but was happy about our barrier operations.

"Go to it, Wolf!" he said. "Use everything available to erect barriers. Do you have enough equipment? Not enough? Try to get some more, by hook or crook. Mines! We need mines! Do you hear me? Mines!"

I couldn't stop thinking of my earlier conversation with Pavlov, when he had complained that in the upcoming exercise too much attention was being devoted to erecting mine barriers and too little devoted to breaking through such barriers.

Releasing me, the commander promised to see to the support of the engineer operations group, and in fact, the Front services helped us in every way possible.

But General of the Army D. G. Pavlov was not destined to command the front—or even to live—for much longer. On 1 July 1941, the commander of the Western Front was replaced by order of the State Defense Committee. Klimovskikh was replaced by Major General Malandin, and Lt. Gen. A. I. Yeremenko temporarily assumed command of the troops.

Pavlov was arrested by Khadzhi-Umar Mamsurov—Ksanti of Spanish civil war fame—and I was present at the moment of his arrest. It seemed as if this totally exhausted, almost wretched, man experienced a feeling of long-awaited relief. He had been relieved at last of the responsibility for the entire front, a responsibility that had been clearly beyond him. But whose fault was that? Not one of the officers who had known Pavlov for a long time considered him to be sufficiently well prepared to take that high post that he had occupied for two or three years. But he had served faithfully and correctly, and had strictly obeyed even the last order from above. "Do not respond to any provocation."

Now, they had taken him away. Obviously the Front commander supposed, in his naiveté, that the punitive hand of Stalin would stop there, and go no further. Dmitriy Grigor'yevich never thought that not only he himself but also his closest assistants would be immediately sacrificed, simply to save the authority of the "greatest and wisest visionary," who had actually made a complete ass of himself.

As soon as they arrested Pavlov, they shot him. His bitter fate was shared by the Front chief of staff, Major General Klimovskikh; the front artillery commander, Lt. Gen. N. A. Klich, and a whole series of other undoubtedly distinguished officers.

Klich's arrest hit me particularly hard. I was convinced of his honesty and his innocence. It was from Klich that I had heard, not two weeks before, about the complacency of the upper echelons. Wasn't it he who had said that mortal danger hung over the nation and the army, and that the careerists and the blind men did not want to see that danger?

Klich had done everything in his power to raise combat readiness of the district artillery, but when they took his prime movers away, he was unable to move his artillery pieces. And they took away his people from their positions for work on defenses, gathered up his old cannon and ammunition, and instead, sent him new guns—*but without any ammunition*.

What in hell could Klich do?! Protest? He protested all right, but they simply smoke-screened, stupidly repeating that "Comrade Stalin knows all, and is taking care of everything." Would Klich have disobeyed orders? No, Klich wouldn't have been able to do that. He was obligated to obey them.

In the Western Front staff, confusion and despair reigned once more. The arrests took the ground right out from beneath people's feet. No one could be sure of living to see the next day. Everybody remembered the 1937 purges all too well.

The butchery of the Western Front command had a bad effect on the troops because it was impressed upon them that Pavlov was a traitor. Naturally, the soldiers began to suspect other generals as well.

As tense as the situation was, I ought to mention one tragicomic episode: on the day when Pavlov and other officers were arrested, it was a long time before I could find anyone to report to about my work on barrier construction. Finally, I made my way to the office of the new Front chief of staff, Major General Malandin. But he was occupied with other problems, and he sent me off to one of the staff officers. This officer was talking with some major whom I didn't know.

"Permission to speak, sir?" I announced myself. The officer raised his head: his face blanched, and a nervous tic distorted his cheek. The unknown major sprang to attention. Perplexed, I hesitated and then took a step forward to present my brief.

And then the officer to whom I was going to give my report suddenly began to babble: "I was with the troops, and did everything I was supposed to! I'm guilty of nothing."

He was looking past me. I turned to peek over my soldier, and was thunderstruck: behind me, my two NKVD border guard escort officers stood staring into the tent. Because of the disaster on the bridge at Vyazma, I had stopped traveling anywhere without border guards to help coordinate with the guard units at important military objectives. Even strong-willed, experienced officers, who had never cracked in the toughest combat situations, completely lost their self-control, at the appearance of people in the green garrison caps of the NKVD.

And I could understand that.

Combat Days

We had already spent several days on the Western Front. To me, the situation didn't seem to be very encouraging. I have already mentioned the absence of radio communications with the detachments. The wire communications net of the Front could seldom be used successfully; first, because our detachments were rarely deployed near military telephone centers and telegraph terminals, and secondly, because telephone and telegraph were not always secure. Further, there was nothing resembling a staff in the group. Only Lieutenant Semenikhin remained with me, performing the duties of communications officer, assistant for matériel and technical support, adjutant, and senior administrative clerk. The lieutenant was exhausted from the multitude of responsibilities that had been heaped upon his head. Now and then, he would fall into a state of near prostration when he sat down on a stump to work.

It was our good fortune that we had been able to increase the size of our motor pool on the way to the front. It was only because of this that the battalions assigned to the group were able to complete their missions across the three hundred–kilometer operational area and keep me informed, in a more or less timely fashion, of the work they had completed.

Maj. P. N. Umanets, who had a two-company sapper battalion at his disposal, distinguished himself. The battalion had been formed on the very eve of the war, manned mainly by drafts from other units, and certainly was not noted for cohesiveness. But it was their task to operate on the highway from Moscow to Minsk, the most critical line of all.

I have already written that I had not previously known Umanets. However, once I saw the major at work, I knew I could rely on him, and I wasn't mistaken, either. He conducted his operations with daring, and didn't lose his head in tough spots. North of Borisov, for example, his sappers had only partially damaged a bridge over the Berezina: one of the girders was left up but sagging. When Major Umanets arrived at the bridge, a firefight was already going on behind him. Umanets quickly had the sagging girder shelled by artillery, and it collapsed right in front of the enemy. All told, in Umanets's operational area, from Borisov to Orsha and from Orsha to Krasniy, more than forty bridges were blown.

Highway bridges were generally heavy reinforced concrete structures up to fifty meters wide. The sappers didn't have the time or the tools to build niches or chambers to hold mines. It was necessary to blow up the massive concrete girders with cutting charges. This required the expenditure of a large quantity of explosives and sometimes repeated mining of the same structure. This was the case, for example in Loshints: the twenty-meter reinforced concrete bridge didn't collapse after the first explosion, and Umanets had to start all over again from the beginning. Already under enemy fire, Major Umanets and his sappers placed another five hundred kilograms of TNT, and set off a second explosion, which was successful.

Unfortunately, the destruction of massive reinforced concrete bridges with the expenditure of large quantities of explosives did not always yield the anticipated results. It was the dry season, and small, shallow streams did not represent serious obstacles to the enemy.

During the first days after our arrival at the front, it was difficult to know where the Germans had managed to penetrate and where our units were engaging them, but Colonel Ovchinnikov and Major Afanas'yev worked very creatively under such conditions.

Several kilometers from the Berezina, Afanas'yev and a sapper company ran into enemy tanks. They began to withdraw to the Berezina, blowing bridges and mining bypasses. Right at the Berezina, on the Minsk-Lepel' highway, however, they ran into more enemy tanks, which fired on the eastern bank of the river, cutting the electric lines from which the wires led to the charges beneath the bridge. Afanas'yev called for a volunteer to swim under the bridge and light the fuse on the backup ignition system. A volunteer was found immediately. He successfully completed the mission and returned, uninjured, to the trenches. And just as the first German tank appeared on the bridge, the explosion roared. The tank fell into the river, together with the fragments of the bridge.

Our units had already left Lepel'. Enemy troops were just about ready to enter the city. This time, Afanas'yev blew the bridges without waiting for the enemy to appear.

I should note that when mining structures before the arrival of the enemy, Afanas'yev and Ovchinnikov always left some of their people behind (around two men per detachment), depending on the significance of the structures and the threat posed by enemy capture. Hidden not far away, a car would wait for them. After the explosion, the demolitions men were easily able to reach their companies, or, following previous orders, they would head for another target.

As a rule, volunteers were given the task of blowing up bridges directly in front of the enemy, and there was no shortage of volunteers.

On the right flank, M. S. Ovchinnikov always operated very successfully. The colonel, who was growing thinner and even more stoop shouldered all the time, complained about the shortage of mines and demolitions materials at every one of our meetings, but he didn't just sit there with hands folded: wherever it was possible, he personally scrounged his own mines and explosives. Afanas'yev and the others complemented each other. Ovchinnikov had great experience and definite creative talents. He knew exactly where explosives were to be found, and was capable of organizing coordination with combined-arms officers. Major Afanas'yev distinguished himself by his inexhaustible energy.

I can't pass over in silence another of my most creative assistants from those days: Major Kovalev. Fate inflicted many trials on him, but he handled himself honorably in each difficult situation. Kovalev was once on the bridge over the Drut' River, on the Mogilev-Bobruisk highway. From the west bank of the river, a female telephone communicator arrived on the run, saying that the senior officer present was being called to the phone. The major hurried to pick up the phone, and he heard something like this: "I am the commander of the Mogilev garrison. I am ordering you not to blow the bridge over the river Drut', under any circumstances, without my permission."

The speaker had a foreign accent. When Kovalev dropped the receiver, he darted off to his sappers and accelerated the work. The bridge was ready to be demolished before nightfall. At midnight, when the enemy opened a heavy fire from behind the riverbank and sent tanks across the span, they went in the air. Major Kovalev received a slight head wound, but he didn't leave his post, and when he learned that we still had some troops west of the Drut', he was able to get them to the east bank of the river on a low floating bridge that was undamaged.

While on a mission at Mogilev, Major Kovalev fell into an encirclement. Fighting their way out of the encirclement, the defenders of Mogilev were to blow the Dnepr bridge on the automobile road. The sappers rushed off to carry out the order, but the electric lines seemed to be damaged, and two soldiers were killed in attempts to repair them. The situation appeared hopeless. And then Kovalev's lucky star smiled down on him.

The sapper company had recently adopted a twelve-year-old orphan boy. This desperate kid began to ask if they would send him to fix the damaged wires. Kovalev hesitated a long time, before he agreed. "My heart bled as that little guy crawled out," Kovalev admitted to me later. "But I was relying on one thing: he was so tiny, maybe they wouldn't notice him and wouldn't shoot at him." And the Germans actually didn't notice the Tom Thumb demolitions man. He made it all right to the bridge, found the problem, and fixed it.

Detachments of our groups operated together with railroad units.

At the Tolochin station, I met an old acquaintance, Maj. G. A. Krasulin.

"No explosives! Help us out!"

Krasulin had a small detachment of railroad troops with him. I helped the major as much as I could. He got busy on a highway bridge, and we took it out right under the enemy's nose.

Soon after that, I was called to the Front staff. I traveled in an extremely good mood, and there was every reason to feel good: it seemed as if we had gotten our work down pat. But I knew from the tone of voice of the duty officer that there was some kind of unpleasantness afoot.

I was sent immediately to the acting Front commander, Lieutenant General Yeremenko. I wasn't even able to finish introducing myself: "When will you finally carry out my order and stop leaving undamaged bridges for the Germans to use?" Yeremenko interrupted. "Who was supposed to blow the bridge on the highway at Tolochin? Why was it left to the enemy? Where in hell have you been?"

"Comrade General, the bridge was blown before my very eyes!" I answered calmly when he finally paused.

"How in hell could enemy tanks appear east of Tolochin if you had already blown it up?"

No arguments could convince the general that we had cleanly blown the bridge. He looked at me with such hostility that I began to think that he would call a representative of the military tribunal and order a court-martial. The situation was desperate.

And suddenly I was saved by the telephone bell.

It was the commander of Front aviation on the line. Yeremenko's face grew progressively brighter the longer the conversation lasted. Smiling, he motioned me to sit down. Then he gave an order to bomb some enemy concentration or other, and when he had replaced the receiver, he turned to me. "Well, mistakes happen." He raised his hands. "The bridge seems to have been destroyed, but the Germans built two new ones next to it. They're small, and poorly built, and vehicles are clustered around them. Now our aviation is going to cover them!"

I felt quite relieved.

Two months later, I again appeared before Gen. A. I. Yeremenko. He had already taken over command of the Bryansk Front. He received me to discuss matters related to the training and arming of partisans. This time, the meeting was most pleasant. Andrey Ivanovich did everything he could to help me. He even suggested that I accompany him to watch tests of Molotov cocktails, and I certainly didn't refuse.

In the very first days of the war, we realized that the antitank mines in the army inventory didn't contain enough explosives, and that in the absence of antitank artillery, we could no longer stop the advance of enemy tanks. Exploding beneath the tracks of an enemy tank, the mines only damaged two or three links in the track. If they were not hindered by artillery fire, German tankers could repair that damage in about a half hour.

Attempting to increase the power of the mines, the sappers of the engineer operations group sometimes put two of them together, and often increased their strength with an additional charge of TNT. Even then, the mines only damaged the suspensions of the enemy vehicles, and could not put an enemy tank and its crew permanently out of action. Primarily, however, we set such beefed-up antitank mines in small quantities, and mainly for strengthening our troops' field fortifications. For mining the highways and areas where we assumed flanking movements might be made, we were never able to avoid using the standard antitank mines. These could only be set on the roads after our troops had withdrawn, and it frequently happened that the enemy advance guard was following right on the heels of our rear guard. Delayed action mines would have helped us out so much in that situation!

I remembered Spain, remembered Rubio, the master at making grenades out of food cans, tea containers, punctured gas cans, and other junk. I remembered Capt. Domingo Ungria and the fougasses we set on the roads at Cordoba and Granada. And now it was starting all over again: the troops of the engineer operations group were beginning to assemble homebuilt, delayed-action mines and grenades. In the beginning, no one believed that our homemade creations would be of any value. But later, they had to thank the sappers. The homemade explosives came in very handy for the partisans. I particularly liked our rock-throwing fougasses, which were very simple. Hemp wicks, or cotton fabric wicks of the kind used in kerosene lamps, burned at the rate of one centimeter every two minutes. Knowing that, we prepared a large quantity of igniter tubes made of sections of Bickford cord from three centimeters to five centimeters in length, attached to wicks which were between three centimeters and twenty centimeters long. In this manner, we got fuses that provided delays ranging from five minutes to thirty minutes. We set charges of varying size, well in advance, in front of a section of road that had been demolished. These were placed under heaps of road gravel or under isolated boulders, with a well thought-out system of delayed fusing.

The application of these simple, rock-throwing, delayed-action mines permitted troops and demolitions teams to break contact with advancing enemy units. The rock-throwing mines were especially effective against enemy motorcyclists.

The Nazis attempted to disarm them, and it wasn't really difficult to spot them because of the smoke from the burning fuses. But no one was really able to disarm them: the fuses were constructed so that they would blow up at the slightest attempt to lift the rocks off of the charge.

In the first days of the war, we always carried with us in the pickup another one of our inventions: powerful homemade, delayed-action grenades made from food cans filled with pieces of barbed wire and nails. Inside the can were chunks of TNT of varying weight. We used these grenades as substitutes for the mortars and machine guns we didn't have, and we carried between ten and thirty of them on every trip that we made along the front. They were especially useful in setting up roadblocks. Usually roadblocks must be set up after your own troops withdraw. The rear guard fells trees and sets up mines. It's important to delay the enemy approach to the roadblock for as long as possible, however, and it was precisely at that point that our homemade, delayed-action grenades came in handy. The demolitions men distributed them along the roadsides when they were firing their last shots and pulling out. Explosions thundered in front of the advancing enemy, and he would either slow his advance or stop it entirely. The Germans opened fire into the woods and bushes, thinking that the grenades had been thrown from there.

"Comrade Colonel, is it true what they say, that you were in Spain?" Sgt. Sergey Koshel once asked me. This was the same Koshel who helped me capture the enemy saboteurs who had been tracked down by the collective farmers.

We were heating tea by a little campfire. Curiosity glowed in

Koshel's blue eyes. The other soldiers raised their heads. They were exhausted: each of them had borne burdens that were far too heavy during the previous days. The soldiers' cheeks were covered with stubble, and after weeks of uninterrupted combat, even the faces of the youngest soldiers seemed to have aged. Soldiers' curiosity always had a deep significance for me; it testified to their high morale because a person who was defeated wouldn't even have been interested in such things.

Now, Sergeant Koshel and the other sappers wanted to know if it was forbidden for us to use our mines and explosives in ways that would inflict even heavier losses on the Nazis.

I knew that it was possible to do so, and so I described our combat operations at Cordoba and Teruel and the feats of Captain Ungria's demolitions men. The sappers listened attentively. When I finished my description, somebody asked me: "What about us going behind Nazi lines and attacking the roads?"

"Everything in good time," I responded, "but for now, let's continue attacking here." Around that campfire, they asked me the same questions that I had asked myself more than once.

One day when I happened to be visiting the Western Front staff, I saw Voroshilov. Accompanied by some unfamiliar general and two colonels, the marshal was on the way to the tent of the political directorate. When he noticed me, he stopped, motioned to me to approach, and asked me what I was doing. When he heard my response, he showed considerable interest in whether I was training partisans.

"Partisans? Not by any means, Comrade Marshal . . . strictly speaking, that is."

"Good, good. I'll call you and get you involved with that issue. You're free to go, now . . ."

That meeting was encouraging: it indicated that I was remembered, and that partisan training was going to start! They realized they needed partisans after all!

Of course, at that time, I didn't know about the Central Committee and Council of Ministers directive of 29 June, which informed the leaders of Party and Soviet organizations of the need to unleash partisan warfare in the enemy rear. I first learned about the Party's call to unleash partisan warfare three days later from Stalin's radio address in which he said:

"In the areas occupied by the enemy, we must create mounted and foot partisan detachments and sabotage groups for combating the units of the enemy army, for kindling the flames of partisan warfare everywhere and anywhere, for blowing up bridges, roads, telephone and telegraph poles, for burning forests, warehouses, and carts. In the occupied areas, we must create intolerable conditions for the enemy and his accomplices, pursue and destroy them at every step, and frustrate all of his plans."

This performance surprised me because I didn't rule out the possibility of further orders, specifying the missions and tactics. Stalin's address didn't even mention the basic missions of the partisans: to cut off enemy troops from their supply sources! Setting fire to the woods in the enemy rear would be harmful to the partisans and useful to the enemy. If anyone other than Stalin had called upon the partisans to set the forests ablaze, he would have been labeled a provocateur. If the partisans had actually obeyed that order, then the forests in the areas under enemy control during 1942–43 would have been destroyed, and the partisans would have deprived themselves of their own cover. Furthermore, the partisans couldn't blow up highways and set fire to warehouses. Destruction of highways requires a lot of time and explosives, and the partisans didn't have either. It's almost impossible to burn carts: they don't carry fuel.

Partisan operations in the rear of a powerful enemy, especially one trained in counterpartisan warfare, requires comprehensive training of partisan forces and optimum planning for their employment. Stalin certainly didn't foresee anything like that in his address. After Stalin's address, there was an intensification of the hasty insertions of inadequately trained partisan detachments behind enemy lines, and a corresponding increase in partisan casualties. Stalin's recommendation to engage units of the enemy army cost the partisans dearly. As sad as it seems, we were fighting as if our people really had no experience at all in partisan warfare.

I had temporarily abandoned my plans for penetrating the enemy rear area. But then, working in the defensive positions of the Twentieth Army, I somehow had a chance to talk about it with the army chief of staff, a natural-born intelligence man, General Korneyev. He was immediately carried away with the idea of sending demolitions men into the enemy rear. And so we decided to sortie detachments of volunteer demolitions men behind enemy lines!

I put Sergeant Koshel in charge of a composite detachment. Penetrating enemy lines, the volunteers were to mine a section of the highway that had been restored by the Germans, several kilometers east of Kakhanovo.

"That's a well-known section of road. We worked on it ourselves and are familiar with the general area as well. We'll accomplish the mission!" Koshel said to me when I saw him off. "Don't worry, Comrade Colonel!"

I worried about the mission, not because I doubted the people or because I felt that the situation was too complicated for them. My concern was that Koshel's group might be caught behind enemy lines, as frequently happens with demolitions men. If our sapper group disappeared, we would have to inform the Front staff, and I knew only too well the consequences that that would entail *for me*. I accompanied the volunteers to the forward area. One by one, they slipped off into the darkness. The long hours of waiting began.

The deafening explosion that echoed across the front lines was totally unexpected.

"There's Koshel!" I said to the representative of the army intelligence department who was sitting with me on the outskirts of the village of Russkiy Selets. He looked at his watch and checked the time. He was perfectly calm, but then, he wasn't the one who was responsible for Koshel.

All he had to do was get intelligence from Koshel and his people when they returned and report it to the staff.

Again, the time passed with agonizing slowness. At dawn, when I heard some rustling in front of the trenches and saw the indistinct figures of the returning sappers, I was happier than I had been in a long time.

Filthy, and pale from fatigue, the soldiers tumbled into the trench one after the other. Koshel was the last. His thin face was almost gray. "May I report, Comrade Colonel?"

I put my hand on his shoulder. "Good boys! Everybody sit down. Did you get them mad?"

"We got 'em mad, Comrade Colonel!"

The army intelligence representative smiled as enemy fire fell all around us. Everyone was interested in learning how the men crossed enemy lines, how they fooled the enemy, how they attacked. But Koshel was laconic: "Everything went off without a hitch. We waited in the woods. At night we set the mines in a crater that had been refilled by the enemy. We also set two antitank mines with clock fuses to go off in the daytime. We saw these mines destroy a truck in a large column . . ."

"Didn't the Germans shoot at you?" someone asked.

Koshel threw the inquirer a tired look: "Of course they shot at us!" Then he said: "You could give us a smoke, boys. We haven't had a smoke since yesterday. We're worn out . . ." Immediately, several hands extended tobacco pouches to him.

The tempo of the enemy advance had slowed. Why not take advantage of the greatest vulnerability of the Nazi army? The Germans had penetrated our territory, mainly along highways and railroads, but they did not control the huge woodlands, swamps, and plains between the roads, and would never be able to control them. Given those conditions, supposing we were to transfer our demolitions operations into the enemy rear area? The enemy was most vulnerable in the rear area.

I developed these thoughts, and wrote them up in a letter that I sent to Marshal Timoshenko, asking, unsuccessfully, for an appointment. I also shared them with the chief of the Military Engineer Directorate of the Western Front, Major General Vasil'yev. "Go behind enemy lines?" he asked me. "Well, it's possible, but you're going to have to talk it over with Comrade Army Commissar Mekhlis, the Supreme Headquarters representative to the Front.[1] Yes, yes! You can't resolve such questions without Mekhlis. Go to see him and tell him the whole thing yourself."

A meeting with Mekhlis wasn't a laughing matter. I hadn't forgotten how I had gone to see him one time to try to help out a sapper officer who had been arrested for no reason at all and who was being threatened with execution.

But I had no alternatives. I absolutely had to go a second time to see this man for whom I held such a deep aversion.

Mekhlis listened attentively to my suggestions: then he looked me over suspiciously, from head to toe. "Not long ago, you were complaining that there were no mines, and now you want to poke around in occupied territory? Strange . . ."

"Permit me to explain, Comrade Army Commissar First Rank! Mines, which are set . . ."

"Where is your family?"

"In Moscow."

A long pause ensued. He had obviously decided that I had asked to go behind the lines because my family was in occupied territory. My face flushed with anger, the kind you'd get if someone spit in your eye. Mekhlis was looking off to the side, obviously pondering something else. He changed the subject.

"Get me full particulars on all those who have asked to go behind enemy lines."

"May I leave?"

"Leave."

1. Lev Zakharovich Mekhlis—one of "Stalin's own creatures," according to Professor Conquest—was an old Bolshevik and veteran of World War I. During the civil war, he served as a political officer in large Red Army formations in the Ukraine and held the position of chief of the Main Political Directorate during the purges of 1937–38, during which he distinguished himself by his tireless and highly successful efforts to exterminate the command structure of the army in which he himself had served. Relieved from that post in 1940, he was again chief of the Main Political Directorate in 1941 when Starinov dealt with him, and no less dangerous than before.

When I finally calmed down, I decided that I would never give Mekhlis any information about sappers who had expressed the desire to go behind enemy lines. If one of them disappeared in occupied territory, his family would pay for it. This cynical tyrant would remember everything.

I briefed General Vasil'yev on the results of my meeting with Mekhlis. "Well, now," the general said, "this means that the army commissar has other more urgent matters on his mind. But have you called on Comrade Ponomarenko, the member of the Western Front Military Council? Pantelemon Kondrat'yevich is the First Secretary of the Communist party of Belorussia and is certainly concerned with partisans as a matter of Party business!"

General Vasil'yev's idea raised my hopes! But was it worth going to a member of the Military Council empty-handed? Wouldn't it be better to show him models of mines that could be made anywhere and under any conditions since the components used in their manufacture were generally available? After a while, I assembled two such models, and wrapping my "souvenirs" in an old newspaper, I called on Ponomarenko on the afternoon of 11 July 1941.

The first model demonstrated a delayed-action antitrain mine (PMS). I explained its construction and how it should be set. Ponomarenko held the mine and tested the functioning of the firing switch, which was made from the bulb of a pocket flashlight and a battery instead of a regular detonator.

"It works! But I think it's pretty complicated. Look how many times you have to turn the safety switch."

"With this kind of construction, Comrade Member of the Military Council, the mine is absolutely safe to set up, and because it is detonated electrically, it does not attract the enemy's attention—there's no noise or smoke before the explosion."

Ponomarenko set the PMS aside without responding, and turned his attention to the other model. I described the second one and began to talk about other mines that could be made out of any available materials, about homemade hand grenades, and incendiary devices. "Not bad, but you've only got a few models and some stories, and you don't have many mines in stock."

"Comrade Member of the Military Council, if we have models, we can start production right at the front! The people only need to know what to do!"

"Don't try to convert me," Ponomarenko said. "I'm on your side! Get more fuses and detonators of all kinds, give them to trained officers, and let's go supply the partisans!"

"I have no specialist officers, Comrade Member of the Military

Council, and we're short on mines and explosives. But not long ago, in the thirties, there were partisan schools."

"Schools?"

"Precisely. In them, we trained people in the tactics of partisan operations, showed them how to make every possible kind of mine, and how to use them in the enemy rear. Would it be possible to organize such schools now?"

Ponomarenko hesitated for a moment, touching the model mines with his fingers, and then he raised his head squinting at me: "That's an idea! Establish a school! But it's better to give it some kind of a misleading name, so that it doesn't draw attention. Let's call it a Training Center. Right! That's it! Training Center! I want you to prepare a report to go immediately to the people's commissar for defense with a draft of the appropriate order for his signature."

In the course of our conversation, we turned to the question of the amount of time needed to prepare partisan formations, and we began to argue about the time needed to train detachments and groups. When I told Ponomarenko that it had taken from three to six months for specialized partisan training of trainees who already had no less than a year of general military training, and that in Spain, it had taken a month and a half with combat soldiers, he looked at me attentively and said:

"You're just exaggerating. Study Comrade Stalin's decree, and it will become clear to you that in the enemy rear, partisan theory dictates that you have to kill Germans, and kill them wherever you actually have the chance. Out there, you don't have to think about it. There, you have to strike at the right time; there, you have to carry out ambushes where the enemy least expects it. There, life itself generates the tactics of the partisan movement. Our mission, however, is teach the people to shoot and to set mines, *and for that you only need three to seven days.*"

I was stunned. Before the war, it took two to three months to train partisan units composed of people who had either finished their military obligations or had completed basic premilitary training.

"Why are you hesitating?" asked Ponomarenko. "Five or six days—that's really nothing. Look, we took only two hours to train the partisan detachments that Voroshilov spoke to."

There was no arguing the point. That was the position of the member of the Military Council.

The next morning, I handed Ponomarenko a memo to the people's commissar for defense (Marshal Timoshenko), and a draft order for the commissar, directing the organization of a special training center on the Western Front. Ponomarenko read through both documents, made some corrections to the text, and the papers were retyped. They were signed on the following day by Marshal Timoshenko who had left the position of people's commissar for defense and had taken command of the Western Front.

On 13 July, the minister of defense designated me deputy chief of the first Front partisan school, officially known as the Western Front Operational Training Center (OUT = operativnyy-uchebnyy tsentr). The flames of people's war had been ignited on territory occupied by the enemy. Well-trained demolitions men, radio operators, and intelligence men had to become partisans. I began to train those cadres in the latter part of July 1941.

"Get to work!" said Ponomarenko, when I signed the order after reading it. "Go to Roslavl. There you'll find a training facility for Front partisan detachments, and you'll be able to accommodate the Operational Training Center there. Lots of luck!"

The First Students

About 6:00 A.M. on 14 July 1941, Semenikhin, Shleger, and I found the buildings of a turf-cutting directorate about five kilometers from Roslavl, in the midst of swamps and deciduous forests. According to our information, Belorussian Communist party workers were quartered at the directorate, and we hoped that they could tell us where the partisan cadres training base was located. The duty officer, mystified by our arrival, stubbornly repeated: "Everyone's asleep."

Through the open door of the room, I could see a row of people sleeping right on the floor. But this was important, and we insisted that the duty officer find and awaken Comrade Eydinov, secretary of the Central Committee. The duty officer went into the room. Eydinov was sleeping on a short Viennese sofa, his knees pulled up. He sat up, rubbed his face energetically; he took the letter from Ponomarenko, read it through, and then began to energetically rub his face some more. "Excuse me, but we finished work very late last night."

The partisan training base was in a Pioneer camp on the outskirts of Roslavl. Along the way, Eydinov brought us up to date: there were no specialists in partisan tactics and equipment at the camp, but detachments had been formed, and people had been given specific missions: to kill Nazi soldiers and officers, to destroy various kinds of military targets and railroads, and to hinder communications.

"How are they going to do that? Were they trained?"

Eydinov shrugged his shoulders. "I guess they taught themselves!"

At the former Pioneer camp I met the chief of the training base, Ivan Petrovich Kuteynikov, who had formerly been the head of the military department of the Council of People's Commissars of the Belorussian Soviet Socialist Republic. Ivan Petrovich admitted that he had no clear idea of either partisan warfare in general, or of partisan tactics, or of the tactics and equipment of sabotage work. He threw up his hands. "I never wanted to be a partisan. But if it's a matter of clothing, or food, or unit logistics in general—that kind of thing—yes, that I can do.

"We've got problems with weapons," he added. "There aren't enough rifles, we have no machine guns, and you just can't get any hand grenades. And you're talking about fuses, and stuff! There isn't a single living soul who might even be able to understand even a tiny piece of this demolitions business. One thing we were able to do: we restored drill rifles. We soldered shut the holes bored in the tops, and it's not bad—we can shoot!"

"Do you mean that the partisans don't have mines?"

"What in hell do you mean, mines? Praise God they even learned to solder those holes!"

"That's too bad. Mines, by the way, are substitutes for artillery for the partisans. Look, Ivan Petrovich . . ." I began to explain the advantages of engineer mines.

At the end of my impassioned talk, Kuteynikov put down his fork. "You mean you have these mines with you? Hey, show us!"

The mine models, incendiary devices, and hand grenades—all these were revelations for Kuteynikov. "A little thing like this can wreck a whole train? It's that powerful?"

We met with the future partisans right after breakfast. I saw many careful, guarded looks; I saw faces stamped by fatigue, anxiety, and concern. I knew what was going on in the minds of those people, who had selflessly offered to make their way into the enemy rear, but who were nonetheless disturbed by the lack of weapons and communications gear.

I didn't waste time on generalities, just started to demonstrate the equipment I had brought with me. Soon the guarded expressions began to change. After the training session, the students hung around for a long time to see the mines and grenades up close, to touch them. We were bombarded with questions. I was beginning to feel some concern myself. I had demonstrated the partisan equipment, but how was I to explain to those people that we only had a few models of that equipment at our disposal, that there was no documentation on how to make mines, that we didn't even have the mines themselves in production, and that there was no other sabotage equipment on the front at the time?

There was only one way out: go immediately to Moscow to the Main Military Engineer Directorate: that was the only place we would get relief. In the afternoon of the same day, Shleger's pickup was speeding toward Moscow. I say "speeding" because, traveling on the old Warsaw road, we reached Moscow before dark. The city had a strange appearance—if the shadows had not been tinged with the red rays of the setting sun, you might have thought that the Moscow day was just beginning: there were far too few people on the streets.

My chief, Colonel Nagornyy, was in his office. He congratulated me on finishing my work with the engineer operational group and indicated that he expected me back in the office. I let him read the order from the People's Commissariat for Defense, which appointed me chief of the partisan school.

"Do you intend to sit on two chairs—serve both here and there—at the same time? You'll never be able to do it!"

However, after he had heard me out, he agreed that it was imperative to assist partisan training in every possible way. With the help of Nagornyy and Galitskiy, we quickly got orders for the ingredients to make mines, grenades, and incendiary devices, but we couldn't get any radios. Loading our booty into the pickup, we drove back to Roslavl late in the morning of the next day. There we found a dumbfounded Kuteynikov: on the night of 16 July, he had already received an order to send one hundred men behind enemy lines.

"Did they say you're supposed to send them off empty-handed?"

"They told us that was our business!"

After I had hastily considered what we might do, I grabbed the deputy by the shoulder: "Is there a pharmacy around here? Is it open?"

"There's a pharmacy in town, and it's open. Aren't you feeling well, Colonel?" Kuteynikov asked.

"I won't get better if the pharmacy lets me down. Let's go!"

Since I had no prescription, the pharmacist raised his eyebrows, and tried to delay a bit. I presented my identification card, and explained what I needed. The pharmacist was in a good mood: "So, you guarantee that the patient is in extremis?"

"I guarantee it."

"Then I'll prepare as much medicine as you need!"

Leaving the pharmacist and his assistant to fill our huge order, I returned to the Pioneer camp and immediately began training the partisans. I went to the field with them, to the highways, and to the railroads. I showed them how to set up mines under various conditions, and acquainted them with other methods of disrupting enemy communications. They successfully manufactured several kinds of homemade grenades, friction igniters, and explosive mixtures. Meanwhile, Lieutenant Semenikhin had received information that there was still some ammonium nitrate at one of the nearby collective farms, and brought three tons of it to the Pioneer camp. Ammonium nitrate worked just fine as the raw material used to make homemade ammonal.

Using the hastily requisitioned explosives and homebrew materials, we were able to outfit the departing group with grenades, igniters, and explosives. Our next problem was to ensure that the friction igniters and the homemade ammonal did not get damp while the group was traveling behind enemy lines. We also came up with a solution to that problem, but our huge new demands plunged the Roslavl pharmacists into turmoil. Even so, they didn't let us down.

At dawn on 17 July, I received an order to transfer the operational training center to Chonka, near Gomel': the enemy had taken Smolensk the night before, and the situation was decaying.

The permanent party of the operational training center (OUTs) and the personnel of the Central Committee of the Belorussian Communist party reached Chonka via Mglin. The streets of Mglin, filled with refugees and mooing cattle, reminded me of the streets of Valencia in 1936. We didn't slow down at Mglin, just turned in the direction of Unechi, and only stopped in Klintsy, where the evacuation was also in full swing.

When we arrived in Gomel', we were quartered in the so-called Regional Committee villas. It wasn't a bad place for training; there were woods and a railroad quite close by.

Training began as soon as we had unloaded the vehicles and found accommodations for the people. We allocated sixty hours for training for partisan formations, *fifteen times* less than was allocated in the early thirties. But there was nothing we could do about that . . . this was war and the situation was very serious.

We began by training instructors. Training generalist instructors took too much time, so we began by training instructors specifically for sabotage groups: Lieutenant Semenikhin, K. S. Mikheyeva, F. P. Il'yushenkov, and several others.

Semenikhin had led a very hard life. He was the son of a cavalry regimental commander who was a colleague of M. V. Frunze, and was orphaned at the age of nine. He and his sister were raised in a children's home in Leningrad. In 1930, he went to work as a metalworker in a factory. He wanted to become an engineer, so without leaving his job, he enrolled in and completed a course of study at the Leningrad Institute of Engineers and Mechanics of Socialist Agriculture.

Right after the Institute, Semenikhin was called up for service with the railroad troops. He finished the one-year course and was assigned to cadre troops. In the winter of 1939–40 on the Karelian Isthmus, I'd already had the opportunity to evaluate this daring officer who combined high initiative with the right amount of caution, and as I became better acquainted with him, I understood that he could become a pretty good instructor for partisans.

Semenikhin quickly mastered sabotage equipment, which was totally new for him, learned the tactics of partisan war, and began to instruct students. Within a year, he was deputy chief and, later, when the Central Staff of the Partisan Movement was created in 1942, he became the chief of the partisan school.

At Gomel', the OUTs staff met young, blue-eyed Klavdia Semenovna Mikheyeva. Klavochka, as she was called by her friends, worked in a match factory, but she was interested in incendiary devices suitable for partisan work, and helped us in many ways.

After seeing her at work, I suggested to her that she transfer to the shop at the training center, but Klavochka reddened and refused! She seemed offended!

"Comrade Colonel, please do not talk with me about such things in front of witnesses," Mikheyeva said, speaking rapidly and not raising her head. "And, people should not know about my association with your subordinates."

"Do you have reason for such a request?"

"Yes."

There had to be a very important reason. I had some hunches about reasons and spoke about Mikheyeva to the Central Committee. As I had supposed, she had been designated to stay behind in Gomel' for underground work when Soviet forces withdrew. I showed them that it would be impossible to cover up Klavdia Semenovna's association with the Operational Training Center, and that to leave her now in the underground would be quite risky, so they transferred her to the OUTs. But after just ten work days there, Klavochka asked to be sent behind enemy lines.

After the initial training of the sabotage-tactics instructor group, we began to train instructors in partisan tactics. In the outline of the draft order for the creation of a training center, I planned to request at least twenty-five NKVD border guard officers for the center. Experience showed that they were the most valuable workers: because of their work, border guard officers were already well acquainted with many of the measures and methods used by partisan forces.

And the border guards who were sent to the OUTs justified our expectations. F. P. Il'yushenkov, P. A. Romanyuk, T. P. Chepak, S. I. Kazantsev, and F. A. Kuznetsov, and all the other comrades of the first draft turned out to be fine operaters, and became outstanding tactical teachers.

When the war began, Stalin quickly gave the NKVD the tasks of raising partisan units to fight behind German lines as well as ensuring the security and political reliability of partisan personnel and units being trained by Party organizations and the GRU, since such units obviously represented a potential threat to Stalin's regime. The presence of NKVD officers in Starinov's school may possibly have been due in part to Starinov's choice, but also indicates that Starinov's operations had been immediately penetrated by the NKVD. After July 1941, the NKVD ran partisan operations throughout the war through the Fourth Directorate (Partisans) of the People's Committee for State Security (NKGB), which was subordinate to the NKVD (See, Dziak, J. J. Chekisty: A History of the KGB. *New York. Lexington Books. 1988. Appendices C and E). The NKVD operations in the enemy rear—involving partisan units,* spetsnaz *units, extermination and hunter units, and singletons—were conducted independently of the operations of partisans controlled by the Party or the GRU, and sometimes at cross-purposes to those operations. The Fourth Directorate (Partisans) was under the command of Gen. Pavel Sudoplatov and Naum Eitingon, both of whom had remarkable careers in Soviet special operations, including experience in Spain, and were personally highly regarded by Stalin. Following Stalin's death, both were imprisoned (for twelve and fifteen years, respectively), by the anti-Beria faction. It is unusual that Starinov makes no specific reference to either of these important figures since he almost certainly had to deal with either or both during his tour in*

Spain. As pointed out above, however, it is possible that General Ivon was Eitingon.

Exactly one month after the beginning of the war, the OUTs staff learned of the secret Central Committee decree of 18 July 1941 entitled: "Concerning the Organization of the Struggle in the German Troops Rear Area." The decree attributed extraordinary significance to the struggle in the German rear and directed the partisans to make unbearable conditions for the occupation forces by disorganization of their communications lines and their troop units, foiling their plans, and killing occupation forces and their Russian collaborators. Every effort was to be made to raise partisan cavalry and infantry units, sabotage units, and extermination units, and to spread a network of underground Bolshevik organizations in occupied territory, which would direct all operations against the Fascist occupation forces. Republic, regional, and district Party organizations were to take part in organizing and training partisan and sabotage groups in areas threatened by German invasion. The important role that this decree assigned to Party organizations was unfortunate because Party organizations could only survive in the enemy rear if they moved into partisan-controlled areas. Underground organizations composed of known Party workers and Communists were always vulnerable to German countermeasures, and the 18 July order ultimately led to the death of many brave people who had been sent to organize networks in the enemy rear.

But the decree had even more insidious impact: by placing the responsibility for partisan warfare in the hands of the Party, it alienated many professional military leaders—including members of the general staff—who avoided involvement with partisan warfare because they remembered how Stalin had settled accounts with those who had trained partisans in the thirties. The negative influence of the Party continued even after a Central Partisan Staff had been created, because the Central Staff and the regional and republic staffs were unfortunately staffed by "partocrats" who lacked the requisite military and specialized training to direct war in the enemy rear.

The decree also overlooked major questions of partisan organization, training, communications, and logistics, as well as the questions of how to utilize the large numbers of Soviet military personnel who had been bypassed by the rapid German advance and still remained behind German lines. Nor did the decree assign to partisan forces their most important mission: that of cutting off German troops from their main sources of supply! Perhaps most important, the decree completely ignored the experience of the civil war, the thirties, and the Spanish civil war, which indicated that operational control of partisan forces could only be exercised through a military command and control structure, located not on occupied territory, but on our own territory, and equipped with powerful radio communications centers. As far back as our own civil war, V. I. Lenin and the Central Committee of the Party (which had been the main staff for directing partisan warfare), took steps to establish a centralized military-operational leadership of partisan activities. For this purpose, the Central Staff of Partisan Detachments was established by order of Lenin in the operations department of the People's Commissariat for the Army and Navy. After the Brest-Litovsk peace treaty was signed, the staff was renamed as the Special Intelligence Department of the Operations Department, for purposes of cover. The former chief of this department, S. I. Aralov, wrote in his memoirs: "V. I. Lenin attributed great significance to the work of the partisan staff, and later to the work of the Special Intelligence Department." A school for training demolitions men was set up, under the Special Intelligence Department.

Thus, the 18 July decree didn't solve a single problem in enhancing the effectiveness of the partisan struggle in the German rear. Moreover, it led to an increase in the numbers of poorly trained and badly armed partisans who were being dropped behind German lines without radio communications. There was no central operational command structure responsible for establishing communications with operating detachments and providing them with logistics support. Party organizations, the NKVD, and Red Army intelligence (GRU) were hastily training and inserting people into the enemy rear. It sometimes turned out that partisan units or underground organizations would successfully infiltrate people into the enemy's command structure, only to have them "liquidated" by other partisans or underground workers who viewed them as collaborators.

At this time, a special commission was created by order of the Red Army Main Political Directorate. This commission was charged with responsibility for training underground workers and raising partisan formations in areas threatened by German occupation. This directive, dated 19 August 1941, called for the establishment of special sections and departments in political directorates at the Front and army levels, to work with the local population in developing partisan and underground resources. In September, a section was also formed for this purpose in the Main Political Directorate. The Front and army sections could do little to help, however; they lacked the trained personnel and equipment necessary to carry out their mission. Although I was the chief of the partisan school and later assigned to the central partisan staff, I didn't even know about this development. Ponomarenko never mentioned it to me, nor did he mention it in his memoirs. In addition to the special commission, a Directorate for Activation of Partisan Units, Detachments, and Groups was created in the fall of 1941 in the Defense Commissariat's Main Directorate for Unit Activation. This directorate was staffed by incompetents, however, and was dissolved in December 1941.

Time passed, and the front moved inexorably toward Gomel'. We had to hit the road again, this time with only hours' advance warning!

The school graduates had acquired a firm knowledge of partisan work. They were constantly reminded that Hitler's army was totally dependent upon the delivery of reinforcements, munitions, and weapons from deep in the German rear; and that partisans could completely paralyze German transportation by massive sabotage, leaving the enemy formations at the front without ammunition or fuel. In order to protect Soviet people, we recommended that sabotage be conducted as far as possible from settlements whose residents helped the partisans. I must also note that it was explained that large-scale sabotage is the most reliable way to effectively force the enemy to refrain from retaliation upon the peaceful populace.

Some of the organizing groups, sabotage groups, and the partisan detachments that we raised in areas that were threatened by the Nazi invasion were left in place. Others were inserted across the front lines into the enemy rear.

Soon the OUTs opened a partisan school at Mozyr', and a group of instructors headed up by Chepak and Kazantsev was sent there. They picked up instructors from us for other schools as well. It seemed that things were getting off to a good start! But there were still an inadequate supply of weapons, a complete absence of radio communications gear, and training blunders. It became clear, for example, that dressing up partisans and border guard guides as "local inhabitants" did not bring good results. Disguised as local inhabitants, our people dropped in at settlements, hid their weapons, and then took some time off without putting out proper security. As a result, they took casualties. It was then decided that all our people would have to wear military uniforms, and they were never allowed to hide their weapons without a very good reason. Those who couldn't get uniforms sewed a strip of red bunting on their headgear. Good results were soon evident: the appearance in the enemy rear of uniformed, well-armed detachments, inspired the local population, terrorized traitors and turncoats, and made the occupying forces jumpy. It even helped to discipline the partisans themselves, forcing them to practice vigilance: during the day, they either remained in the woods, or if they called at a village, they put out security, not relying on their "costumes" to protect them.

People voluntarily came to us all the time—people who otherwise could have gone to Siberia or the Far East to escape the horrors of war but preferred to go behind enemy lines on dangerous missions.

New Schools

Soon after our move to Gomel', the shop at the operational training center ran short of parts for the mines. We were also running short of flashlight batteries, without which you can't make mines with electric detonators. We couldn't find parts or batteries in Gomel'. We might have solved the problem by a trip to Kiev, an industrial capital city, which was only two hundred kilometers away, about four hours by train, each way. But the idea of a trip to Kiev had scarcely arisen when another idea popped up: along the way, why not search out the officers and demolition specialists whom I had known in the thirties? They certainly all couldn't have been scattered!

The shortest road from Gomel' to Kiev passes through Chernigov. There, I ordered Shleger to drive to the district Party committee offices: the situation was very threatening, and in the district committee they would certainly be preparing to conduct partisan war. I guessed that they'd be running into problems: no partisans had been trained around Chernigov, and it might have never dawned on anyone that the enemy was right on the other side of the Dnepr and the Pripyat.

In the waiting room of the office of Aleksey Fedorovich Fedorov, the first secretary of the Chernigov District Committee, sat a fifty-year-old man. The secretary's assistant took my mandate and passed through a high door upholstered in brown leather. After two or three minutes he threw it wide open: "You arrived at a most opportune time!" Fedorov said, greeting me in an unexpectedly friendly fashion. "Couldn't be more opportune! Here we are, getting ready to play partisan, and we haven't got knowledgeable people! Sit, sit, Comrade Colonel! I'm not going to let you go so easily!"

Returning the documents, Aleksey Fedorovich said that the people for the partisan detachments and groups were already selected and armed with rifles, and that there were also grenades and machine guns, but all that they knew about partisan war had been learned from books. He wanted to know if I could conduct a training session the next morning. I told him I had to be in Kiev immediately, but left a summary of a lecture about disrupting the enemy rear, and promised to send instructors.

After a meal at Fedorov's cafeteria, we parted, and by evening the golden dome of Kiev's Saint Sofia cathedral was blazing before the windshield of Shleger's car; bathed in the red rays of the sunset, it looked like melted copper. The expanse of the Dnepr flashed like blue steel, and Kiev's gardens and parks were encircled with patches of dark green and light green. We got into town just after 3:00 P.M.

But on the streets where I once used to wander with girls and pals who were dear to my heart, trenches were being dug; at familiar crossroads, welded antitank hedgehogs were being hastily thrown up, and on house windows, white paper strips—protection against shock waves—had been pasted, as if crossing out the past.

We stopped around No. 25 Kreshchatik Street. Near here lived Nikolai Vasilievich Sliva, a veteran from the Kotovskiy Brigade and twice recipient of the Order of the Red Star. In the thirties, he had been trained to be a partisan brigade commander. An unknown woman told us he'd moved to Moldavia the year before. She didn't know the address.

There wasn't a soul on the square in front of the Ukrainian Communist party Central Committee building. The sun was declining, twilight was creeping in: maybe this was why the vague echoes of artillery fire from the west seemed even more clear.

In the access control department, they found out who I wanted to visit, got in touch with the chief of the Military Department of the Central Committee, Petr Ivanovich Zakharov, then carefully scrutinized our documents, and finally issued us passes.

The corridors of the building, covered with carpet runners, were empty. Zakharov listened attentively to our requests for ten thousand ampules of sulphuric acid, two thousand batteries and bulbs for flashlights, and—as a little something extra—his assistance in finding the mining and demolitions officers and specialists whom I had known from my previous work.

Petr Ivanovich decided we had to see Comrade Burmistenko.

The face of Mikhail Alekseyevich Burmistenko, secretary of the Central Committee of the Ukrainian Communist party, was gray, and there were dark, heavy bags beneath his eyes, but his glance was intent and tenacious. "The old partisan bases are long gone," Burmistenko said after he had heard me out, "but the people should still be around. We'll try to find any of them that you can remember. But as far as batteries are concerned, that's a lot easier: we'll certainly get them to you!"

Zakharov mentioned that I had brought some model mines with me, and Burmistenko asked to see them, noting that he hoped we weren't going to try to sabotage the Central Committee building. I replied that our mines had no charges in them but that there were live electric blasting caps in the mines and that our model incendiary devices were also live. Burmistenko ordered that my models be brought in. While I brought in two suitcases, about fifteen people assembled in the secretary's office to see the demonstration.

I showed how the mines worked and also demonstrated how the incendiary devices functioned, taking the precaution of placing them in giant stone urns, which had been brought in from the corridor. Burmistenko was impressed: he requested that we give him the equipment and announced his intention of asking Ponomarenko to detail me there within five days so that he could start a partisan school.

On the following day, I visited the offices of the Central Committee again, but this time with a list of former partisan commanders and mining demolitions specialists whose full names I'd been able to recall during the night. He promised to get started right away searching for these people and ensured that my request for supplies had been met. Then he bid me farewell, noting that they were awaiting my return.

Ponomarenko was very encouraged with the results of my trip to Kiev, and accepted Burmistenko's request to send me to Kiev on a training mission. Two days later, I was on the road again. This time there were four instructors in the pickup, among whom was the twenty-three-year-old border guard officer, F. P. Il'yushenkov, whom I had chosen as an assistant. Il'yushenkov was black-eyed, slender, smart looking, and quick in his movements, with a remarkable memory.

In the young officer's thick chestnut hair, silver threads glistened—a souvenir of the first days of the war when he'd been serving in the border guard detachment at the Lithuanian city of Mariapol. He had seen cowardice and confusion, but had also seen the unwavering bravery of soldiers and officers, and had demonstrated his own bravery in the sad days of the retreat eastward. I could rely on Il'yushenkov.

I recall the date of my second trip to Kiev quite precisely: it was 1 August, when the Central Committee of the Ukrainian Communist party held a conference for the command parties of two Kiev partisan detachments, as well as one each from Donets and from Kharkov. Coming straight from the road, we found ourselves in the meeting.

Those were disturbing days! The artillery cannonades were drawing closer; in various parts of the outskirts of the city, one could hear aerial bombs; the blue sky overhead was filled with the straining sounds of fighter plane engines; and the sharp, jarring cracks of the antiaircraft machine guns and cannons could be heard.

Nevertheless, we set up a display of sabotage equipment in the foyer in front of the meeting hall, where I met Leonid Petrovich Drozhzhin, the deputy of the cadres department of the Central Committee: a lively, energetic, and affable fellow. Zakharov informed me that a place had been selected to set up a partisan school at Pushcha Voditsa, that in the future, Drozhzhin would be the man to see regarding questions of partisan personnel and supply. Burmistenko and other colleagues spoke.

That meeting was the very first time that I recall where questions of partisan tactics were discussed from every angle, where the civil war experiences were discussed, and where the partisan training of the thirties was recalled. We also discussed operations carried out by detachments that had begun to operate in the enemy rear.

That evening, I went to Pushcha Voditsa with my instructors. Training in the partisan school was to begin the next day. In the shops, they would learn how to prepare partisan equipment, in the field, they would learn how to set mines along highways and railroads. And training would be twelve hours a day. It was a good thing that I was familiar with the city and its environs: I didn't have to rack my brains over such things as where to set up ambushes or which march route to take for a night movement. And the students easily mastered the material because many of them had either intermediate or higher educations. By 6 August, the partisan school at Pushcha Voditsa was going full blast.

The time allocated for my detached duty was flying by. Soon it was time to say farewell to Pushcha Voditsa and to Kiev. Before my departure, Mikhail Alekseyevich Burmistenko called me in for a serious discussion, mainly relating to basic questions of underground work and urban partisan activity. At the same time, he told me that he had not been able to locate any of the partisan officers on the list that I had given him. Some of them had been shot as enemies of the people, others sent to camps as accomplices of enemies of the people, and a third group had taken off for parts unknown.

A chill shot through me. I knew all of those people to be true patriots; many had participated in the civil war, and some had been decorated with the Order of the Red Star. The rest had served with distinction in the ranks of the Red Army or in civilian labor. Now they were enemies of the people!

"Well, you certainly couldn't have known who you were actually training as partisans and saboteurs. Later, Comrade Stalin taught our organs of security how to unmask enemies of the people," said Burmistenko in a flat, toneless voice. He said that he knew that I was trustworthy, and he asked me to help him get instructors for his school at Pushcha Voditsa. He got what he asked for: in the course of five days, we had tried to train a group of saboteur-instructors drawn from people with basic and higher civilian educations. And we'd at least started production of homemade mines and grenades in Kiev.

We said a fond farewell to Burmistenko. "Until the next time!" he said, with emotion. But there was no "next time"; M. A. Burmistenko died behind enemy lines.

Keeping our promise, we returned along the Gomel' road, stopping at the Chernigov regional Party committee offices. We met with Fedorov who wisecracked that he'd gotten tired of waiting for us, and showed us a revised version of the old lecture outline that I had left for him, which he had printed up in a small edition. Fedorov said that the Chernigov regional committee had already gotten partisan training underway and asked whether we had any new inventions to share. When we mentioned that we had some delayed-action incendiary devices, he assembled six or seven people for a demonstration. The devices ignited after varying intervals, and burned brightly. I began to explain the construction of the devices. Aleksey Fedorovich took one of the spheres as a "souvenir," and it suddenly burst into flame!

"Never mind," said Fedorov, trying to reassure me and the other comrades. "It's my own fault, but it payed off because I found out, firsthand, how these damned cigarette lighters really burn! What saboteurs! What chemists!"

We had just returned to the OUTs when personnel from the regional and district Party committees of Belorussia arrived. They were to be left behind to work in the German rear. The enemy was approaching Gomel', and there was barely enough time to show them the partisan equipment and its operation, and to have them read through the lectures on the principles of underground organization.

In mid-August, P. K. Ponomarenko informed me that the Belorussian Central Committee had decided to relocate the OUTs to the Orel region. Ponomarenko requested that we immediately leave for Orel. Giving me a letter to the first secretary of the Orel regional committee, V. I. Boytsov, Ponomarenko said that I should arrange with Boytsov for accommodations for the OUTs and should help him start partisan activity in the Orel area.

At that time, I gave Ponomarenko a memo about the need to establish a special military command-and-control organization to direct partisan and sabotage groups. This organization would be based either on unoccupied Soviet territory or in territory controlled by the partisans. This memo was based on lessons we had learned in Spain. I also suggested organizing a military underground in occupied cities and towns, and pointed to the need for thorough training for all participants in such activities. Ponomarenko agreed with all my basic recommendations, excepting the one concerning the creation of sabotage units. He asked me to rework the report and resubmit it to him, which I did two days later, after consultation with a number of experienced underground workers. He was still unhappy about my recommendations for raising special sabotage units and my recommendations to increase the length of training to a three- to six-month period, but he accepted the report and promised to rework it and send it on himself. Then, he told me to get busy on fulfilling the requirements of the 18 July decree: we had to hurry!

Our conversation took place under the overpowering rumble of bombardment and the sharp cracks of antiaircraft guns. In literally two or three hours, we started off down a new road with a small group of border guards from the OUTs. The next day, we reached Bryansk, stayed overnight in a hotel, which was empty because of uninterrupted bombardment, and in the morning we hurried on.

I had not been in Orel for seven years. I was struck by the smokestacks and shops of new factories, the new houses, and the streets. The majority of the smokestacks were no longer smoking, however, and the streets were nearly deserted: Orel had also been evacuated. In the regional Party committee, V. I. Boytsov immediately arranged with the command of the military district to provide food for future partisans. To ensure that the school would not suffer from lack of personnel, funds, and matériel, it was set up in the staff of the military district as a subordinate unit of the operational training center of the Western Front, the OUTs. We found a place for the school, a bit over ten kilometers outside town, not far from the airfield where outsiders had no business at all. Initially, the regional committee sent twenty-six people who were to be trained as instructors, and by 18 August, the school was completely staffed. For cover purposes, the school was called a "firefighters' school."

A calm, reasonable Party worker, I. N. Larichev, was made head of the school, and his deputy for operations was D. P. Belyak, a Communist. The chief of staff, a Communist named M. S. Yevseyev, was an unusually civil individual who was really cut out for staff work.

The operational Orel workers constantly helped the regional committee in establishing the school and training the partisan cadres. These workers included: G. Bryantsev who became a popular young writer in the postwar years, M. M. Martynov, V. A. Cherkasov, and their comrades. The chief of the regional NKVD directorate, K. F. Firsanov, also did much to help the school.

Among the future instructors sent to the school by the regional committee there were workers from the Party and from the Soviets, NKVD operatives, agronomists, teachers, and even one leading baker! From the "ladies team" of six female instructors came the famous partisan Ol'ga Kretova, who fought on the Southern Front, and Mariya Belova, who taught sabotage techniques and methods of partisan warfare to hundreds of people during the war years.

In September, groups from Kursk and Tula arrived at the "firefighters" school, sent there by the local regional Party committee.

My assistant Il'yushenkov continued to work out well during those days. It fell to his lot to train the detachment led by the secretary of the Bryansk Municipal Committee, D. M. Kravtsov, a detachment that was later to become quite famous. This Kravtsov showed his initiative in helping to start the massive production of engineer mines and grenades in Bryansk. In addition to Kravtsov, other partisan commanders who were later to distinguish themselves were also trained in the firefighters school. These included M. P. Romashin, A. D. Bondarenko, and Hero of the Soviet Union Gen. M. I. Duka.

But I spent only a few days at Orel because an order arrived from Moscow directing me to return to the Main Engineer Directorate immediately.

Do You Recall Operation ALBERICH?

Colonel Nagornyy threw up his hands: "Look here! Denis Davydov dropped by! Well, are the partisan efforts on track?"

"Am I really supposed to get it going all by myself?"

"On your own! But now, those efforts are going to have to get along without you. You're needed in the department."

The summer was ending, but Nagornyy's face showed no signs of a tan.

"What's the matter? My face isn't exactly radiant, is it?" he smiled. "I know ... these are tough times, Il'ya Grigor'evich ... You're going to run barrier operations at Moscow."

"At Moscow?"

"Yes, and don't make any mistakes. By the way, let's go, and I'll introduce you to the new chief of the directorate, General Kotlyar."

Major General Kotlyar repeated to me what I had already been told by Colonel Nagornyy. For several days, I took part in the raising of new units, traveled along the defensive lines outside the capital, and even viewed them from the air in order to determine where and how to strengthen the barriers. Then, a new order arrived: go to the Western Front and check on the defensive lines around Vyazma. I spent three days in Vyazma, and on the fourth day, the Front staff called: Report immediately to Moscow! I wasn't even able to say good-bye to my mine-laying comrades, and there I was—back in Moscow, in the familiar yellow walls of the Second Building of the People's Commissariat of Defense. General Kotlyar was waiting. He explained that there had been a change in plans, that Kiev had been evacuated and that the enemy was threatening the Kharkov industrial region and the Don basin. Kiev evacuated? The voice of Kotlyar sounded hollow and remote. What I was hearing was not sinking into my consciousness: four armies were in trouble; they were escaping an encirclement, and fighting with their formations broken up; the troops were unable to hold on to new defensive lines, and heavy fighting was going on along a three hundred–kilometer stretch of the front.

The chief of the directorate brought me back to reality with the sternly uttered words that the Stavka of the Supreme Headquarters had decided to assist the troops of the Southwestern Front in the defense of the Kharkov region by means of massive mine and explosives barriers. In the case of further enemy advances, it would be necessary to mine and destroy all facilities in Kharkov that had any military significance. The words "all facilities" meant the most important factories, shops, bridges, railroad roundhouses, airfields, etc.

Kotlyar told me that I had been appointed to command a special engineer operations group which was being sent to Kharkov. He asked me to assemble an equipment list, keeping in mind that time would be limited. He called the Stavka and set up an appointment. Late that night, we were met at the Stavka by the chief of the general staff, Marshal of the Soviet Union B. M. Shaposhnikov. I had not seen the marshal since 1936, the day of my departure for Spain. Then he had been smiling and cheerful; now he looked gloomy. It wasn't difficult to understand the reason for Shaposhnikov's mood: the enemy had encircled Leningrad, was rushing toward Odessa and Moscow, and had just taken Kiev. Germans were flooding Belorussia, and our position not only looked difficult but downright threatening. When he had outlined the situation that was developing on the Southwestern Front, the marshal looked me in the eye: "Do you remember Operation ALBERICH?"

Yes, I recalled that operation well from my reading in military history: in March 1917, in the course of carrying out a forced withdrawal from France to take up positions behind the so-called Hindenburg line, the kaiser's troops had conducted massive demolitions and mining in an area approximately four hundred thousand square kilometers in a period of about five weeks. Military historians considered Operation ALBERICH the most significant mining and demolitions operation of all time.

"Now, you're going to have to destroy and mine an even larger area in the Kharkov region, and we won't be able to guarantee that you'll have five weeks to do it. You'll have to work fast, Comrade Colonel!"

Turning to General Kotlyar, he asked: "Have you prepared the equipment requisition?"

"Exactly as you requested, Comrade Marshal!" Kotlyar responded.

I handed Shaposhnikov a sheet covered with writing. Picking up a pencil, the marshal became absorbed in reading. He shook his head: "My dear fellow: we've got to make do with reserves! You know that things are going badly with equipment and manpower!" The pencil was crossing out items on the list. "We'll approve it, but in this abbreviated form," the marshal said firmly, signing the requisition.

It was impossible to discuss the corrections made by Shaposhnikov: he arose, indicating that our audience was at an end. "Collect your people, draw the necessary matériel, and go immediately to Kharkov!" he said, seeing us off. "Just remember: I don't want a single unhappy incident. The mines must not endanger our troops."

I dared to remark: "On such a scale and with such time limits—"

Shaposhnikov interrupted: "You are personally responsible for seeing that our troops are completely safe from your mines. I wish you luck."

Three days later, traveling through a steady downpour, our group arrived in Kharkov. One important unit had been lost along the way, however, the one bringing the radio-controlled mines, commanded by Lieutenant Khomnyuk.

On 4 October, Marshal Timoshenko approved the plan for barrier operations in the area of the Southwestern Front, to be known as Operation PITFALL. This plan included the use of our radio-controlled mines, which were still lost someplace along with Lieutenant Khomnyuk and his people. Timoshenko was no longer interested in the fate of the engineer operations group, which I commanded while simultaneously performing the duties of chief of the mine and barrier department of the Red Army's Main Engineer Directorate. He directed me to get the approval of N. S. Khrushchev, a member of the Military Council. Khrushchev made substantive revisions in approving the plan: he increased the number of mine casings that were to be produced in the Kharkov industrial plants from two thousand to five thousand in order that we might set more fake mines. Khrushchev knew about my participation in training instructors in the partisan school at Kiev, and he also knew about the training for partisan warfare that was conducted in the Ukraine during the late twenties and early thirties. He was told about this by Col. M. K. Kochegarov who was already training partisans in Kharkov. I recall that Khrushchev surprised me by his composure. Unlike other highly placed Party workers, Khrushchev did not appear to be gloomy and nervous in those difficult times: on the contrary, he was cheerful, a quick and energetic worker.

Wait, Find a Way, and Succeed

The staff of the engineer operations group was set up in the buildings of a chemical technical institute not far from the Front staff in Kharkov. When I had locked up the operations plan and the requisition in the safe, I set out for the Kharkov Regional Party Committee to resolve some questions about production of equipment and mining the city's commercial enterprises. They had advised me to do this at the Front Military Council.

It was late night. Vehicles with darkened headlights crawled along the city streets, the wheels of two-horse carts rumbled, troop units advanced to the front, and one could hear, as if far away, the horns and whistles of the special trains and locomotives on the railroad. They were carrying reinforcements and munitions to the front, where the Thirty-eighth Army under Maj. Gen. V. V. Tsyganov was defending the city, and carrying to the rear the equipment from factories and institutes, and evacuating the families of workers, engineers, and military personnel.

In the impenetrable darkness, I almost had to guess the location of the House of Plans and State Production. The wide doors of the entrance that I used opened, to uncover a rectangle of surreal bluish light, then slammed shut, merging once more with the surrounding darkness. Despite the late hour, there were quite a few people in the reception room of the secretary of the district committee, A. A. Yepishev. Yepishev's assistant told me that I wouldn't have to wait long, and I didn't. Quickly briefing the secretary on the barrier plan, which had been approved by the Military Council, I handed him a requisition for drills for boring holes to set mines and for casings for delayed-action mines and booby traps.

"You could have come a bit earlier with this kind of a requisition, but your order will be filled," said Yepishev. "If there's a problem, the city committee will help you out. Maintain liaison with them."

Trouble doesn't travel alone. It wasn't enough that the vehicle column with the radio mines had disappeared: our electrochemical blasting caps also presented us with a surprise. The day after we arrived in Kharkov, military technician N. K. Leonov reported that in each box of detonators some had gone off during transit.

Electrochemical detonators are not watch mechanisms, and quickly testing their reliability under frontline conditions was an almost hopeless task. But there was no other alternative; I ordered the testing of one hundred detonators with varying delay times. Problem was, even if we reconditioned all the electrochemical detonators in the switches, we still wouldn't know if they'd work correctly. The answer could only come with time.

A second concern was people. Where would I find them? The number of sapper battalions that were subordinate to the front was inadequate. I visited the Military Council, and they recommended that I join forces with the independent railroad brigades working in Kharkov. An excellent idea! The railroad brigades had the people, and we had the experienced instructors and the equipment, and in a number of cases, we could actually conduct on-the-job training. The commanders of the railroad brigades immediately agreed, detailing several of their men to take courses organized by our group. Later, with the assistance of these trainees, they set up the most advanced delayed-action mines available at that time.

When I arrived in Kharkov, I had also taken the first opportunity to visit my old advisee from Spain, Domingo Ungria, who was working in the tractor factory there. We didn't have time for a long visit. After we drank some hot, strong Spanish coffee, he explained that there were twenty-two former Republican Army soldiers in Kharkov, and they were all dreaming of getting into the Red Army. "Help us, Rudolfo!" he begged me. "We are not on the register of the Military Commissariat, and no one even wants to talk to us about enlisting in the Red Army. But you know damn well that we can fight the Fascists!"

The same evening I spoke with General Nevskiy telling him about the past activities of the troops of the Republican Spanish *spetsnaz* brigade and about the commander of the XIV Partisan Corps, Lt. Col. Domingo Ungria. The general was impressed by their feats, but could see no way to get them into the Red Army since they weren't on the Commissariat register.

"I'm afraid that no one in Kharkov will be able to resolve this problem for you. You might have to go to Moscow," Nevskiy said. But the question was resolved without Moscow's help, right there in Kharkov. I simply turned to N. S. Khrushchev, and he, as a member of the Front Military Council, permitted me to enlist the Republican Army veterans directly into our battalions.

The Spaniards were happy when they learned that they had been enlisted into the Red Army. And they immediately began to help us mine the most difficult and complex facilities. Later, they ran sorties into the enemy rear and operated in other sectors. During these operations, the Spaniards distinguished themselves, fighting in frost and snowstorms far more violent than one encounters in the Pyrenees.

While all this was going on, the engineer operations group got started setting delayed-action mines on the roads and in other facilities of military significance in the immediate vicinity of the front lines. This was required in view of the worsening military situation. Now all we had to do was trust that the mine-laying parties didn't run out of mines.

On the morning of 5 October, I set out with a group of subordinates to visit the city industries. I've got to admit that I didn't expect very much, but I was certainly surprised. The Kharkov workforce was making rifles, machine guns, solid rocket motors for Katyusha rockets, and aerial bombs; they were also repairing aircraft and tanks and outfitting armored trains, and doing all this under heavy bombardment. It was going to be complicated for them to master some of our mines, to set up the production of the hermetically sealed mine casings, to produce the drills and nonremovable detonator circuit switches, and to make some of the small machined parts and electrochemical detonators for mines. We were therefore elated when we learned that the designers of Kharkov's Miner's Lamp electromechanical and locomotive factory, and the factory that produced mine surveyor's instruments had already worked out designs for drills and mines, and had already begun to produce mine casings!

The visits to the factories were certainly encouraging; it seemed as if we'd be getting everything that we wanted, right on time. We still had no clarification, however, on the status of the electrochemical fuses, and we still hadn't heard a word about the lost convoy carrying the radio mines. Arriving late in the evening at the Thirty-eighth Army staff, I was getting ready to dine when the group duty officer reported that there was some lieutenant or other looking for me. . . . Khomyak? . . . . or Khomnyuk? I pushed back the chair and ran out down the stone stairs to the empty vestibule of the chemical technology institute, where a boyish, tall, slender lieutenant stood in a mud-splattered tunic, with a canvas map case on his hip. Next to him, in a similarly splattered tunic, stood a sergeant.

"Comrade Colonel, request your permission to report! The special equipment is all in order, we sustained no losses, and we're ready for combat assignment!" Both of them, Lieutenant

Khomnyuk and his assistant, Sergeant Sergeyev, were so exhausted they could hardly stand.

"Thanks, Comrades!" I said, discarding the official form of address. "Good boys! But how did you get here? Where were you?"

They had managed to arrive because they understood that it was forbidden to go slow delivering the special equipment. They hadn't waited for the rain to stop, but had driven their vehicles as far as they could, through nearly impassable mud to Kupriansk where they had asked for assistance from the military commandant. He had the sappers loaded onto railroad cars and hooked them up to the first troop train heading for Kharkov. They had arrived just in time; the antiaircraft guns were rumbling once again, beating back a routine air raid.

Now that the operations group had been completely assembled, it might seem as if I could at last breathe freely and feel confident that all would go well, but that wasn't the way it turned out!

Right from the start, it appeared that despite all the efforts of the people of Kharkov, we would not be able to get enough delayed-action mines, and that instead of the required three hundred tons of explosives, we would receive not more than one hundred tons. Then, military technician Leonov reported that one of the electrochemical delayed-action fuses that had been sent for testing had gone off too soon. It was necessary to design and build reliable safety devices with longer delay times, otherwise it would be impossible to set delayed-action mines around military facilities in our own rear area! In a meeting of the Military Council, we were reproached for our sluggishness and inadequate preparations. Khrushchev said that troops should always have explosives ready for use in barrier operations. I replied that I had tried for many years to get just such equipment, but without success. Khrushchev then directed me to prepare a report to the State Defense Committee on the experience gained in the Kharkov mining operations. General Nevskiy and I got busy on the report and presented it to the Front Military Council immediately. There wasn't any time to lose: the Sovinformburo reported on 7 October that the new enemy attack was developing in two new directions: one for Bryansk and the other for Vyazma.

About that time, we also saw indications that enemy agents were observing the work of our mine-laying parties, and we immediately took steps to deceive the enemy. First of all, we increased the use of dummy mines that were carefully camouflaged to resemble the real thing. These would confuse the enemy and force him to disperse his forces in minesweeping operations. They would also dull the vigilance of his best sappers and help us to inflict casualties on them.

During that time, we were also carefully setting radio-controlled mines in the city and its suburbs. After 7 October, we set a radio-controlled mine in the military district staff building, at the Kholodnogorsk and Usovsk overpass, and in other places as well. In the daytime, the sappers gave the impression that they were digging pillboxes or bunkers, while at night they brought in explosives in sacks, bottles, and cartridge boxes. They buried the explosives deep in the earth, set the complicated radio-control devices, and fitted them with fuses and switches to ensure that the mines would be detonated if they were detected and disturbed by the enemy. On October 3, Khrushchev had ordered me to set a radio-controlled mine in the house at 17 Dzerzhinsky Street. On 10 October, General Nevskiy reminded me of Khrushchev's order. The Dzerzhinskiy Street house was a villa built at the beginning of the thirties for the secretary of the Ukrainian Communist party, Stanislav Vikent'yevich Kossior.[1] After Kossior's fall from grace, the house was turned into a day-care center, and after the evacuation of the city, number 17 had been taken over by some leading officials of the Party and the Ukrainian government. The reason for my delay in carrying out the order to mine the house was that the officials—including Khrushchev—were still living and working in the building. We were therefore limited to examining the building from the street, and estimating the quantity of explosives necessary to destroy the Germans who, we supposed, would be attracted to the building. We made our calculations and stopped worrying: certainly no one would dare to put 250 kilograms of TNT under the feet of the Communist party and government of the Ukraine! On 12 October, however, Khrushchev once more asked me why his order to mine the building had not yet been carried out, and categorically ordered me to do it with a radio-controlled mine. I tried to warn him. After all, radio-controlled mines were still new, the city was under aerial bombardment, and an irreparable accident might result from the strong earth tremors, but Khrushchev wouldn't accept any delay.

Six men, including myself, were cleared to enter the building to carry out the necessary work. The house was located right in the city center, in the midst of a garden among big oaks and lime trees. The trees, with their luxuriant foliage, would effectively screen the sappers from observation from the sides, even if the observers were higher than the stone wall and the high iron gate.

1. Kossior, a member of the Communist party since 1907, was arrested in the last round of purges in April 1938 and shot shortly thereafter.

We went through that gate on the night of 12 October. The house stood on a high brick foundation, and a balcony ran along the first floor. In the lower portion of the building, there were subsidiary accommodations and a small boiler room. When we had removed the coal from part of the boiler room floor along the inside load-bearing wall of the house, we dug a shaft to a depth of more than two meters. We carefully poured the back-dirt into sacks. In the first sack went the first layer of earth; in the second sack, the second layer; in the third sack, the third layer, etc. On each sack we put a serial number to ensure that we would make no mistakes when we refilled the shaft, and that the original succession of strata in the earth would be preserved to the extent possible. This was done in case Nazi sappers tried to look for the mine.

After they had dug the shaft, the miners took turns going down into it, hollowing out a niche under the internal load-bearing wall for the radio receiver and a large explosive charge. This was difficult, exhausting work. It was only at noon on 14 October that we began to lower the TNT crates into the shaft. The charge was a big one: we had to kill all the occupants of the building, and take out the external building security force at the same time. And, of course, to reward Nazi sappers for attempting to remove the mine, we fixed the radio-controlled mine so that it could not be removed without detonating it. After that, we carefully camouflaged it and removed all traces of our work. All that remained was to "reassure" the enemy by dangling a few "terrible Soviet mines" in front of him, because we understood all too well that if the enemy did not find any mines in such a beautiful building, he would become suspicious and most probably not occupy the building. We therefore set a decoy mine in the boiler room. In the corner, under a heap of coal, we sacrificed some very expensive explosives, and set a complex delayed-action mine, equipped with various backup detonating devices. All these devices, which were in good condition, were assembled with great cunning and gave the appearance of being very dangerous. They were actually totally safe, because the dry-cell batteries that powered them were dead!

When they finished this task, the miners restored the floor of the boiler room to its original condition, hollowed out the ceiling, and covered it with fresh plaster and whitewash. When the building guards came into the boiler room to check on the condition in which we had left the place, they turned their attention to the ceiling; not to the walls, nor to the floor, which was hiding a 350 kilogram charge of TNT, nor to the heap of coal in which our decoy mine was hidden. Nothing aroused their suspicions.

Sappers Are the Last to Leave

Artillery fire was getting very close to Kharkov. At night, the sky above the western suburbs was red from the flashes of guns and fires: the enemy was furiously attacking.

Three weeks before it had seemed unthinkable, impermissible, to mine this wonderful city, but now that Kharkov was crammed with mines, we wanted to emplace even more of them. Even the concern that each mine might possibly be fatal for our own people seemed to fade. During the last days before we pulled out of town, the sappers worked tirelessly so that the Germans would not be able to use the local industrial facilities and to prevent the Kharkov airfields from being used. Beneath the floors of factory shops, we buried many dozen powerful delayed-action mines, and smaller mines were emplaced everywhere in the most unexpected places, such as ventilator shafts and office chandeliers. We didn't have enough explosives to completely destroy Kharkov's four airfields; that would have taken 180 to 200 tons of explosives, and we had only about 25 tons, including some "field-expedient" explosive substances. We used up the rest of our explosives on delayed-action mines. Since we couldn't completely destroy the runways, we set mines along the sides of the runways, in areas where aircraft would probably be dispersed. We decided to blow up some of the hangars, and to further deceive the enemy, we faked unsuccessful demolition of several hangars.

After October 20 there was fighting in the suburbs of the town. The cosy villas on Ivanov Street and Basin Street, for example, were evacuated. Since we couldn't be sure that the Nazi leadership would select the mined house at 17 Dzerzhinsky Street for their residence instead of one of these houses, the military council approved the decision to set decoy mines in the best of them.

Starting on 19 October, Shleger's pickup, which by this time had become familiar to the population, brought our miners to the entrances of these houses in broad daylight. The miners carefully lifted out boxes of "explosives" and spent a long time carrying them inside the buildings, and then came out and drove on. In the space of three days, our people visited more than ten houses. In the evening of 24 October, we visited the house at 17 Dzerzhinsky Street for the last time, in the company of the secretary of the city Party committee, V. M. Churayev. The gate was closed, and no one was visible behind the fence. Shleger jumped over the fence and opened the gate. We went into the house, wandered around the rooms, and wound up in the boiler room. Outstanding! We'd left the impression that the inhabitants of the house had just left, in a hurry.

From Dzerzhinsky Street, we drove to Rudnev Square. Stopping on the bridge, which had been prepared for destruction, Churayev got out of the car, stood at the iron fence, and touched the cold railing.

The Germans were breaking into the city. Directly in front of them, our men, among whom were the Spanish volunteers, mined the highway at Belgorod. On the main highway from Kharkov to Chuguyev, a special group of miners was waiting for our last troops to withdraw so that they could add real mines to the many dummy mines that had been set.

We anxiously awaited Stalin's speech of 6 November 1941—the 24th Anniversary of the Great October Revolution. The speech was a great disappointment: to raise national morale Stalin seriously understated Red Army casualties and grossly exaggerated those of the Germans. He placed the blame for the Red Army's lack of success on the failure of the Allies to create a second front in Europe, and on our supposed lack of tanks and aircraft, of which we actually had plenty, but never mentioned the real causes: the purges of 1937–1938 in which nearly the entire command cadre of the Red Army was exterminated, including well-trained partisan cadres. Stalin mentioned that the Germans had overextended their supply lines and had been forced to exist in a hostile environment that had been ravaged by our partisans, but he failed to draw the proper conclusion from this, namely that we had to paralyze the enemy rear area. If he did draw that conclusion, he certainly took no steps to implement it.

After our withdrawal from Kharkov to Voronezh on 5 November, we immediately began to look for information about how well our mines worked in Kharkov, and plenty of information was available: our troops were still continuing to come out of the encirclement of Kiev; our underground was sending intelligence reports, and civilians were escaping from behind German lines, bringing information about the hellish conditions there. Unfortunately the information we received was contradictory! According to some reports, the Germans deactivated our mines with impunity; according to others, they suffered casualties trying to remove them.

On 10 November, our intelligence delivered to the staff of the Southwestern Front a copy of the German command's order No. 98/41 of 8 November 1941, which stated that on the approaches to Kharkov, and in the city itself, a large quantity of Russian mines had been observed, some of which were delayed-action mines with clock mechanisms and electrochemical fuses. The German command was informing its troops that the Russians had buried mines to a depth of 2.5 meters, and made use of wooden casings, which would render the mines undetectable to mine-sweeping devices. In spite of this, the order affirmed that "the incompetent setting and camouflaging of the mines permitted experienced sappers to operate, even without the use of mine-sweeping devices."

I got the order with a note, written in an unfamiliar but forceful hand, by someone in the Front Special Section (NKVD military counterintelligence): "These mines, which are so easily detected and disarmed, were set under the direction of Col. I. G. Starinov." I was more than a little disturbed, even though I knew that after our delayed-action mines appeared, there would probably still be instances in which the enemy would miss some of them, especially when we had used the devices in such large numbers.

We were hardly able to recover from the impact of Order No. 98/41, when new and important information arrived: "The German garrison commander, General Braun, and his officers, are quartered in the house at 17 Dzerzhinsky Street. German sappers have removed some kind of 'special' mine from the basement of the house."

This was very encouraging news for me. General "Hangman" von Braun installed in a house that we had mined! After we received the captured German document that alleged easy removal of the mines, I was "invited" to visit the Special Department, and then I was called in to see Khrushchev. After the interrogation at the Special Department, which was fairly polite, I went to see Khrushchev with even greater trepidation. To my surprise, he received me cordially and even smiled.

"I read the German document describing the ease of sweeping our mines in the Kharkov area. I know that the Nazis actually found a mine in the villa at 17 Dzerzhinskiy Street and that the commander of the German garrison has moved into that house. If they only found *one* mine there, then this means that the 'hangman' has fallen into the pitfall. Can you think of another interpretation?"

I pointed out that the large decoy mine had been carefully dressed up to make the Germans think that they had found the only mine that was supposed to blow up the building and to convince them that they had no need to search further. Khrushchev agreed: he said that they had already received information that German generals had been killed by mines; that tanks and vehicles had been destroyed, and that there had been explosions on the airfields. He knew that these were only the mines that we had set with relatively short delay times. I was very pleased with Khrushchev's trust in me, and I decided to try to talk to him about my recommendations to conduct mining operations in the enemy rear. I pointed out that the enemy was digging his own grave, that his supply lines were overextended, and that there were enormous opportunities in the enemy rear for specially trained demolitions men. He ordered me to write a memo to Stalin on the subject, and promised that he would personally send a request to Stalin to receive me, so that my recommendations would not get lost by incompetent bureaucrats in Stalin's chancellery. General Nevskiy and I wrote up the memo which contained suggestions for mine warfare at the front and in the enemy rear. Our proposals pointed to the need for greatly increasing the numbers of antiauto and antitrain mines and delayed-action mines to be used in mining installations, since only massive, planned application of mines in defensive operations would prevent the enemy from using highways, railroads, and airfields, even after obvious damage had been repaired. This would involve only limited expenditure of our own forces. For this purpose, we needed hundreds of thousands of delayed-action mines, and we needed to be able to cleverly employ the best mine in the world at that time, our radio-controlled mine. At that time, having driven deep into our country, the Axis armies were clearly pausing for a breather. The enemy would soon be stopped, and we would begin the liberation of temporarily occupied territory. The greatest significance had to be attached to the mining of the enemy lines of communication. For this we needed special mines. These should be simple to prepare, and to produce in the required quantity. There were many Soviet citizens who, after the necessary training, could cleverly employ those mines to close down railroads and destroy automotive transport. In brief, we needed *spets* units! Prior to my departure for Moscow, Khrushchev gave me a personal letter to Stalin, asking him to receive me.

The officers of the engineer operations group and I were all extremely tense throughout this whole period, however. The captured German order, the cover note that accompanied it, and the news about No. 17 Dzerzhinskiy Street cost us many sleepless nights. For two days, I lived as if I myself were sitting on a mine that could not be disarmed: suppose that the Germans, by some miracle—or just by pure luck—had been able to find and disarm the radio-controlled mine? Had the beast fallen into the pitfall, or not?

This tension continued until 13 November when I got a call from the Front Military Council to destroy the German "viceroy" of Kharkov and to detonate several other radio-controlled mines.

Late on the night of 13–14 November, I went to the Voronezh broadcasting station with General Nevskiy and Major Chernov, the chief of the engineer department. I had the ciphers for the mines with me. We sent the signals on various frequencies, in different ciphers. A separate receiver, located in Voronezh, was used to check the signal strength, and it was found to be sufficiently strong, but how strong would it be in Kharkov, three hundred kilometers away?

In Voronezh, I was unable to get the information that I desired about the success of our operation. An aircraft photoreconnaissance mission was flown over part of Kharkov. The pictures confirmed that many of our radio-controlled mines had detonated, but the house at 17 Dzerzhinsky Street wasn't in the pictures; it was impossible to determine whether the mine there had exploded or not. Nevertheless, the results that we obtained in Kharkov and its environs before we withdrew included forty-six bridges wrecked and destruction on the airfields and other important military facilities. It was impossible, however, to determine the effectiveness of our delayed-action and radio-controlled mines until the city was finally liberated by the Red Army in 1943.

Returning to Kharkov after its liberation, as I looked at the place where the villa had stood and saw the miserable wreckage and the huge rectangular crater, filled with water, which had been excavated by the explosion, it is not hard to imagine what I felt. Beneath a heap of concrete blocks, the remains of a flattened luxury car were visible. A few trees, standing far away from the villa, managed to survive. The old chestnut trees standing closest to the house were charred and broken by the force of the blast wave, and all the leaves on their branches had been removed. But the leaves on the trees that stood farther away rustled happily in the breeze, and there were kids playing beneath them.

So the radio signals sent from Voronezh hit the target, but exactly what happened in Kharkov after those signals were sent, and what was the impact of the radio-controlled mines? The entries in the diary of George F., a German officer, give a good idea of how the Nazis felt about the mining of Kharkov.

Here is the entry for 20 November 1941, reproduced with a few abridgements:

The houses are still burning. This huge, deserted city is most unsettling. We drive around to inspect the former second capital of the USSR. Suddenly, we hear the rumble of a mighty explosion. A horde of bicyclists rushes to the place where the blast occurred, and we drive there too. The site of the blast is surrounded. Another mine or "devil's machine" has exploded, set to go off after a predetermined delay period. . . .

In the evening, mines exploded not far from our house. After several mines went off, with the loss of several officers and men, we were ordered not to move into uninhabited houses. There were supposedly sufficient quarters in inhabited houses in the city. . . .

Mines were exploding everywhere . . . but the most frightening thing was the mining of the roads and the airfields. On the airfields, between three and five mines explode every day, and no one knows where the next one will go off. . . . Once, a powerful mine went off in a hangar where repair work was going on, and key technicians were killed. We are forbidden to use this hangar any longer. Mines go off in areas of the airfield not far from aircraft dispersal areas; there are casualties among the pilots, and the planes themselves are damaged. The damage is a result of clods of earth falling on the aircraft.

Every possible means is being used to find the mines. Captured sappers are being interrogated. . . . We have told the populace that they will recompense us for every mine and that they will face execution for concealing them. Unfortunately, the population has only revealed an insignificant number of mines to us. . . . Destruction of mines is being conducted only with prisoners.

In the city and surrounding area, many vehicles and some trains have been destroyed by mines. Hundreds of soldiers, who had escaped death for two years, were killed by mines. Mine explosions are not becoming any less frequent; with each passing day, it is becoming more and more difficult to find them, and, according to the prisoners, some have clockwork mechanisms set to detonate only after four months.

Only one month has passed since the invasion . . . Even now, the losses due to mines exceed all losses directly connected to the occupation of the city. . . .

Our first encounter with planned mining cost us dearly. We ought to get new mine-clearing gear, or else we'll have to build new highways, railroads, airfields, and warehouses, right here in the occupied territory. Our mission really ought to become mine clearing. If we can't overcome the mines, we'll never be able to move and operate freely.

The German officer came to the most logical conclusions in the last sentences of his notes, but the Nazis were never able to "overcome" our mines. Although his diary described the general situation in Kharkov, I had to wait until 1944 to get firsthand information about the effectiveness of our deception at 17 Dzerzhinskiy Street and the impact of the radio mine, which we set there.

Of 315 delayed-action mines set by units of the 5th and 27th Railroad Brigades, the enemy was only able to find 37. Of these, they were only able to disarm fourteen, and the remaining twenty-three had to be detonated in place by the German sappers, resulting in destruction of the roads.

The enemy had planned on using the Kharkov airfields, which at that time had the most modern concrete runways. They were blown up! The explosions of the delayed-action mines in the aircraft dispersement areas, the explosions of powerful fragmentation mines on the airfield itself and in the hangars prevented the occupying forces from using the airfields until spring of 1942.

Moscow at Our Backs

When we had finished Operation PITFALL, we returned to Moscow. We'd been away from the capital for only about fifty days, but the city had changed! In the outskirts of town, no smoke cloud hung above factory chimneys, and downtown the cheerful trolleybuses had disappeared. On some streets, you saw hardly anyone. The apartment houses looked uninhabited, their windows were empty and dirty. Locks hung cheerlessly on the doors of many stores and gusts of ground wind blew snow around the stairwells in the entrances of many buildings.

My miners grew quiet: there was pain in their eyes. I didn't stop anywhere, but went straight to the Central Committee of the Communist party and handed over the envelope with the letter of introduction from Khrushchev to Stalin, requesting that he allow me to brief him on my recommendations for improvements in mine warfare and partisan operations. At the Central Committee, they warned me that the arrival of the letter would be reported up the chain of command and that I should be ready to report immediately to the Kremlin, whenever I was called. "Take our phone number! If you are called out of Moscow you must tell us where you're going, and for how long."

The warning wasn't out of place, because from the next day on, I was involved in construction of barriers around Moscow once again, and had to make frequent use of the number that they had given me.

Leaving the Central Committee, I went straight to the Main Engineer Directorate. The Second Building of the People's Commissariat of Defense was half empty. Most of my directorate had been transferred to Kuibyshev with some others. In my department offices, I found one of my assistants, Major Vakulovskiy. When he saw me, Vakulovskiy took off his thick glasses and hastily wiped them, and came to a semblance of attention, but seemed to be a little more stoop-shouldered than usual. I asked him for the keys to the safe. The aging major's face reddened, displaying such inner confusion that I became alarmed and asked what was wrong with him.

"I wasn't in time, Comrade Colonel ..." mumbled Vakulovskiy.

"You weren't in time for what? What happened?"

"I didn't have time ... I got back from the sector, and it was already over ... In two stoves, you understand. . . ."

"What—in two stoves?"

"They were burning documents, and they burned almost all of ours."

I rushed to the safe. The massive steel door swung wide open. Nothing! Not the summaries of lectures on tactics and techniques of sabotage, which I had developed before the war; not my dissertation; not the instructions and handbooks for saboteurs; not the documents for the engineer operations group that I had commanded on the Western Front.

Vakulovskiy, his head in his hands, explained that when he left the office, there had been no warning of an evacuation, but that when he had returned from the sector, a crew was loading up sacks with documents in the courtyard, and right on the premises another group was burning documents that they said had "no value now."

I stared into the empty safe. You really couldn't blame

Vakulovskiy for anything, but I wasn't able to comfort him. "Well, all right," I said, "now I want to hear about the barrier operation on the Moscow approaches."

Vakulovskiy got the map and began to report. All of the generals of the engineer directorate were at the front, except General Kotlyar. Massive barriers were being constructed all around Moscow by a large engineer operations group under the direction of General Galitskiy. Ten sapper armies were being raised, and the construction of defensive lines had begun in the city itself.

I raised my head: "In the city?"

Vakulovskiy didn't respond immediately, almost as if he had to swallow a lump rising in his throat:

"The situation is most grave, Comrade Colonel."

I should remind the reader how tense the situation had become in the last half of November 1941. Planning to defeat Soviet forces on the Vyazma-Moscow and Bryansk-Moscow directions, to bypass Moscow from the north and south and to seize it in the shortest possible time, the Nazi command tried to attain these goals by means of two successive encirclements enveloping the capital. They intended to carry out the first encirclement to defeat Soviet forces in the areas of Bryansk and Vyazma. The second encirclement, and capture of the capital, was to be by means of a deep flanking movement around Moscow from the north through Klin and Kalinin and from the south through Tula and Kashira, in order to close the armored pincers in the vicinity of Noginsk. In implementing that plan, the Germans spared neither men nor equipment, and reconciled themselves to accepting any losses.

Only on 27 November was it possible to repulse Guderian's tanks about ten to fifteen kilometers from Venev, and to grind down the enemy in a bloody three-day battle and force him to abandon his attempt to reach Moscow from the direction of Tula and Kashira. In the north, however, the situation grew worse: on 1 December, the Germans unexpectedly broke through the center of the Western Front and advanced to Kubinka.

Under these conditions, it was naturally inappropriate to dig antitank ditches, escarpments, and counterescarpments. Only mines would help. Even though a portion of the industry that had, until recently, been manufacturing mines was now on German-occupied territory, and part was being evacuated to the east, mines were still being manufactured wherever it was possible to do so. The work of mining on the defensive lines around the capital in the latter part of November was conducted by well-trained engineer units. This had a beneficial effect on the tactics employed in the mining as well as on the quality of the mines employed. All approaches vulnerable to tank attack were closed. A single engineer operations group, under General Galitskiy, planted fifty-two thousand antitank mines. In areas that were difficult to bypass, the highways were cut with powerful fougasses. Delayed-action mines were set on important sectors of the highways and railroads, in station facilities, in buildings of rest homes and sanatoriums, which the enemy might use for quartering troops, and in administrative buildings of the deserted city. The people often had to work under bombardments, under artillery and mortar fire, and had to fight their way out to join up with our withdrawing infantry units.

The antitank mines we had set in the fall caused particular concern. Sudden strong frost could put them out of commission: moisture seeping into the fuses would freeze the compressed spring of the firing mechanism. It was necessary to selectively test thousands of mines. And there was still one more problem— snow! From 20 November, it fell and fell, completely nullifying the mining operations we had conducted in the fall. Buried beneath the deep white covering, the mines had long since been frozen in the ground and were completely harmless to the enemy. There was only one solution: we had to start mining the approaches to the capital all over again, in the fresh snow, on top of the mines that had been set earlier, making a second layer of mines. The mine laying was done in haste, in direct proximity to our forward positions, often in sight of enemy infantry and tank units and under their fire. When General Kotlyar sent Vakulovskiy and me off to the front and demanded that we check on the precise locations of the mines of the second layer in the most dangerous sectors, we didn't know how to respond: no one could give the precise locations of individual mines—there wasn't time to worry about it! You were lucky if you could just put the approximate location of the *minefield* on a map. We were supposed to be setting personal examples, but we couldn't always put together precise maps of the minefields, and were limited to getting bearings of minefields that were emplaced along the main line of resistance. There just wasn't time for anything else.

In those days, Moscow left an unforgettable impression. Yes, the city had been largely deserted. Yes, transportation had decreased considerably, but the workers who remained in the capital were at their posts. At that time, when you could already hear the sound of artillery fire in the western outskirts of the city, when barricades were going up in Moscow itself, the capital appeared to be calm, collected, and confident, like an old soldier.

From the beginning of the war, barrage balloons appeared in

the sky above the capital, and on her boulevards and squares, the merciless stingers of antiaircraft guns pointed skyward; and the elms and lime trees under whose canopy Pushkin and Gryboyedov wandered were covered under the extended fields of fire that branched out from the antiaircraft batteries. The antiaircraft fire was so dense and the barrage balloons so close together that only a few German aircraft were able to penetrate to the capital. In most cases, however, they only penetrated to meet an ignoble death in the skies over Moscow. Concern for relatives and hatred for the enemy strengthened those who remained in the factory shops that were working on the defense of the city. In those days, Muscovites manufactured much of what we sappers needed, including antitank and antipersonnel mines, metal antitank obstacles called hedgehogs, and explosives. It was most difficult to overcome the effects of losing territory and many factories capable of quickly starting up production of large numbers of mines. In the winter of 1941, these factories had been destroyed, had been transplanted to the east, or had not yet had time to get back to work again. The ability to produce mines declined sharply in direct relation to the large area already occupied by the enemy. We got help from Soviet people and mine barrier enthusiasts who got mine production going whenever there was a chance.

And then suddenly things got easier for us: by an order of 28 November, the Stavka introduced the position of chief of engineer troops and created staffs of the Engineer Troops Staff of the Red Army, as well as engineer staffs at the Front and army levels.

Major General Galitskiy was designated chief of staff of the Red Army Engineer Troops, and I became his assistant, while at the same time I retained the responsibility of chief of the barrier department. The department, the post on the engineer staff, *and* the partisan schools—the OUTs! I occasionally take sleeping pills now, but then, to get my work done, I had to take "stay-awake" pills, supplied by the scientific department of the State Defense Committee!

Sometimes night found me in the capital. At that time, at least, there were lots of places to stay. First there were my own quarters; then, there was a room in the Hotel Moscow (in contrast to peacetime conditions there were vacancies, and the rooms also had baths!). Then, there were also accommodations in the basement of the Second Building of the People's Commissariat for Defense, where the staff of the Engineer Directorate had been quartered, a perfect refuge with soldiers' cots, where one could comfortably pass the night. One day, however, I hastened over to the Hotel Moscow: I had been told that P. K. Ponomarenko was stopping there.

The large room seemed comfortless. On a small table near the door, magazines and newspapers were scattered in confusion. Behind another table, cutting a thick link of sausage, sat Ponomarenko. He seemed depressed: his beloved Belorussia was now occupied, and the Germans were just outside Moscow. We talked about the partisan school and its needs for the winter. I had brought a report on my last four months' work with me and gave it to him to read. When he finished, he gave me an inquiring look and said:

"What you've written here is correct, that destruction behind enemy lines is being carried out by Soviet government and Party organizations, by the NKVD, and the People's Commissariat for Defense, without any coordination, and that partisan training, supply, and communications are very poorly developed. It's also true that special mines and demolitions are very powerful items and that they can increase the effectiveness of partisan and sabotage operations many times, but that they are being used in insufficient quantity and often not very wisely."

He looked at the copy of the draft decree that I had written for the People's Commissariat for Defense concerning the creation of a staff for conducting demolitions operations in the enemy rear and the creation of special sabotage brigades. He observed that while he agreed that the partisan school should train the cadres, it would be necessary to think about what one was to call the organization that would command partisans and saboteurs, and to consider the name to attach to the special sabotage brigades. To Ponomarenko, my suggestions amounted to an attempt to militarize the partisan struggle, and this also needed careful consideration.

He asked if I had any information on the effectiveness of partisan operations, and I responded that the intelligence directorate had information about derailments of trains in Belorussia.

"It's too bad that we have no communications with the partisans. I'm sure that many Belorussian partisan detachments and sabotage groups have derailed trains," Ponomarenko said confidently.

I felt a strong desire to talk with him about the need to create a single center for directing the partisan operations and organizing support for those operations. After almost a half year of fighting that was unprecedented, both in terms of the scale of combat operations and cruelty, the enemy had occupied a huge area. Without a single special command center for partisan warfare, there was no opportunity to organize the communications required to support the detachments with the necessary equipment and to plan the partisan operations in coordination with those of the Red Army. That evening, however, I couldn't talk with Ponomarenko about this subject that so concerned me because I was awaiting my meeting with Stalin, who I hoped would immediately resolve all these problems. Ponomarenko asked me to leave the report, which I did, expressing the hope that perhaps Stalin would listen to Ponomarenko on the subject if I didn't get to see Stalin myself.

Two Calls

At the end of November, the ring of hope sounded in the voice of Levitan, the Radio Moscow announcer, as he read the Sovinformburo news: going over to the offensive, troops on the Volga Front were defeating the enemy and had liberated Tikhvin, and counterattacking troops on the Southern Front had liberated Rostov-on-the-Don. Vakulovskiy reported that many enemy tanks had been destroyed at Akulovo and Golitsyno. The Germans were not attacking with the same energy as before, and every day, reserves from Siberia and the Urals were arriving. The day of reckoning for Hitler's boys was getting closer.

Finally, at the end of November, I was called to the Kremlin. The telegram reached me while I was out on the defensive lines at Serpukhov. I returned to Moscow and reported to General Kotlyar who informed me that I had an appointment with Stalin at 2200 hours (10:00 P.M.) sharp. He hurried me off to rest, get cleaned up, and put on my dress uniform, and told me to be back in his office at 2000 hours (8:00 P.M.).

At precisely 2000, shaved and pressed, I was back in his office.

"Well now, you look completely different!" the general said with approval. "Sit down! The Kremlin calls, as I understand it, are related to the letter from the Military Council of the Southwestern Front?"

"I think that's correct."

"Do you recall what questions were raised in that letter?"

"Basically it dealt with the necessity to produce powerful anti-tank mines and delayed-action mines, and we also wrote about the need to use partisans on demolition operations on enemy communications lines."

"Have you thought over what you said, and how you said it?"

"The ideas weren't new, Comrade General!"

"So much the better. Just give Stalin the essence of the problem, and do it as briefly as possible."

"I understand! But there are a series of points that require clarification. It's possible that Comrade Stalin doesn't know . . ."

Kotlyar hastily interrupted me: "Make no mistake, Ilya Grigor'yevich! *Comrade Stalin knows everything!* Remember that! Remember that, and don't get emotional in your conversation. Most of all, beware of raising objections! There may be circumstances that are completely unknown to you, but are perfectly well known to Comrade Stalin. Clear?"

By his intensity, and the emphases of his agitated voice, I could sense the concern Kotlyar felt. "I'll follow your advice, Comrade General!"

I passed through the first Kremlin guard post at 2130 hours.

"Your identification?"

I presented my identification.

"Weapons?"

I had no weapons with me.

The same checks were followed at the second guard post.

At 2130 hours, I approached I. V. Stalin's reception room. Pushing on the shining copper handle of the massive door, I recalled how Stalin had been at the reception for the graduates of the military academies in 1935; how he had smiled good-naturedly, clinked glasses, and drank toasts to the health of those who, in fact, were already dead, who were to be accused as enemies of the people.

Sitting there in the reception room, I was able to convince myself that Stalin would listen attentively to me, that he would believe me, and that he would finally resolve all the questions about the creation of special brigades for demolitions behind enemy lines and about the production of special mines without any delay.

In addition to the receptionists in the cosy, silent room, two people were sitting who obviously had appointments before me. Before each of them were files with papers. A chubby, well-groomed, clean-shaven fellow came in and sat down beside me, one of those guys who greeted the receptionists in a familiar way and sat down without being invited to do so. He drummed on his fancy folder with thick, white, well-manicured fingers, then straightened out the pleats in his trousers with such an anxious look that it seemed as if some important event was dependent on their straightness. Then he began to rustle a newspaper, from which he looked up from time to time to glance at the clock. It was obvious—he was nervous. Meanwhile, time passed.

Suddenly it was as if a faint breath of a breeze blew through the reception room: no one said a word, no one made any kind of announcement, but all those who were "in the know" drew themselves erect and braced themselves. It was clear: *the "Master" had arrived!* My neighbor wiped off the drops of sweat that appeared on his forehead and wiped his palms with his handkerchief.

After a few minutes they began to call people in to see Stalin. A half hour passed. They called my neighbor's name. He blanched once more, wiped his hands on his handkerchief, took his file, and hurried off to answer the call.

Such nervousness made me somewhat uneasy too, and I recalled the parting advice of General Kotlyar: "Don't get emotional during the interview and don't dare to contradict him on anything!"

They didn't call me for a long time: my uneasiness subsided somewhat, and was replaced by a treacherous apathy. I didn't notice that I had dozed off; after three hours of patient waiting it was damned difficult *not* to doze off in the silence of the reception room; all the more so, since it had been a very long time since I had sat in such a comfortable easy chair, in such ennervating warmth . . .

"Comrade Starinov . . ."

What? Did I really go to sleep? Had I slept through my appointment? No: there were still people in the room.

"Comrade Stalin cannot receive you," I heard the flat voice of one of the reception room workers. "Comrade Mekhlis will receive you."

"But I must see Comrade Stalin!" I answered, not yet fully awake.

"Let's just drop in on Comrade Mekhlis," the official insisted.

I looked at the door through which I hadn't been able to pass, and we went off. All my hopes collapsed: I had come so close! Only a few steps separated me from the office of a man, who, if he only knew, would be able to resolve all the problems that troubled me, Nevskiy, and many others.

I didn't expect anything good from a meeting with Mekhlis; I knew him only too well. Nevertheless, I still had to go to see him. How could I avoid going to see him if they had sent me to him from Stalin's office? So I went.

The first thing that jumped into view was the proposal that

General Nevskiy and I had written to the Military Council of the Southwestern Front. The proposal was lying on Mekhlis's desk.

"I'm listening!" he barked at me when I introduced myself.

I began to summarize the report that Nevskiy and I had written, which had been accepted by the Military Council of the Southwestern Front, but Mekhlis leaped out of his chair and interrupted me, accusing me, and the other authors of the letter, of all kinds of irresponsibility. "Don't talk about that! We don't need that now! You say: 'Give me mines,' delayed-action mines, booby traps, even . . . We don't even have enough regular artillery shells . . . we have nothing to load aerial bombs with . . . and you want mines! Now you're talking sabotage brigades . . . and partisans . . . for what purpose?

"Deep enemy rear? Communications lines?" Mekhlis exclaimed with caustic irony. "What the hell are you? Did you fall out of the sky? Don't you know that the Germans are right outside Moscow?"

"Comrade, . . ." I tried to begin.

"It's clear! Enough! Kindly take the trouble to listen and to do what people tell you!"

He sat down again. He abruptly pushed aside our letter with the cover letter from the Military Council of the Southwestern Front.

"Listen to me!"

And rapping out his words, almost as if he was literally forcing the significance of what he was saying into my head, he set forth the plan for the universal devastation of the approaches to Moscow, to include burning the woods in the enemy rear. Stunned by what I was hearing, I sat as though nailed to the spot, struck dumb by Mekhlis's stare.

"Winter is our ally! You must exploit the advantages that winter brings! Completely! We have to freeze out the Nazis! Every forest, every house, every building where the enemy can take shelter from the cold, must be burned down! Do you *at least* understand that much!?"

I responded that you couldn't burn the woods in winter; that the woods were, in any case, the base areas for partisans; and if you burned the villages, you would only be shedding the blood of our own people. My response just threw fat in the fire. Mekhlis branded Nevskiy and me as worthless military theorists, as blind men, and demanded that we pass the word to General Kotlyar that the approaches to Moscow were to be turned into a snowy desert so that the enemy, wherever he might poke his nose, would only find hard frost and smouldering ashes, and finally decide to leave.

Mekhlis got tired, and looked at me as if he was satisfied.

Certainly, winter was our ally. Certainly, winter removed the enemy's superiority in equipment. Any soldier understood that; even *Pravda* had published a good article on the subject, at the end of November. We simply had to make clever use of winter, to take advantage of the abilities of our troops to more steadfastly endure winter's hardships, and certainly more completely utilize their own equipment under winter conditions. And that equipment included mines, which were such reliable weapons when placed in the hands of sappers and partisans.

According to our standard military procedure, when he had finished, I was supposed to repeat the orders he had given me, but I didn't do that: I just sat there silently.

"Do you understand?" shrieked Mekhlis. "The Germans have to be driven out into the frost! They must freeze!"

He reminded me of an hysterical woman. It was useless to try to convince a person like this that the Germans would not be sitting in warm houses if things began to heat up in their rear area, if their communications lines were disrupted by mines, and if their tanks were to be blown up more frequently in minefields.

"The German must encounter desolation everywhere!" Mekhlis demanded. "Snow and ashes! And frost! Is that clear?"

In his tone there was the ring of unquestionable authority, self assurance, superiority, and *power*.

"Is it clear to you, what I've said?"

"Yes. It's clear."

Returning to the Second Building of the People's Commissariat of Defense, I recalled, with horror, that Stalin in his radio speech of 3 July 1941, had called on the partisans to set fire to the forests in the enemy rear. And I had tried to convince Mekhlis that burning the woods would be completely absurd.

Now what would happen to me? I broke out in a cold sweat, and I felt a chill. Depressed and confused, I returned from Mekhlis's office.

Listening to my story, General Kotlyar was puzzled. "Well, I guess things turned out badly, Ilya Grigor'yevich! But don't be discouraged! Things could be a lot worse," he said, obviously having in mind the case of my chief, Colonel Nagornyy, who had been arrested not long before.

Kotlyar consoled me, and I was grateful for that, but the feeling of pressure didn't pass: everything was ruined!

I reported my conversation with Mekhlis to N. S. Khruschev, who said, "Very well. I'll call Comrade Stalin about it."

* * *

The Germans' defeat began when the Soviet troops of the Kalinin Front went over to the offensive on 5 December 1941. On 6 December, troops of the Western Front and the right wing of the Southwestern Front also launched an offensive. The great battle had begun!

Personnel of the Engineer Directorate staff, assisting the attacking formations, were traveling from one sector of the front to the other, and from one army to the other. The roads and fields all looked the same: overturned German trucks, their wheels in the air, their shouts buried in the snow-filled roadside ditches; burned-out vehicles with doors flung open or torn off, tanks with crosses on their turrets and gaping holes torn in their sides, and everywhere corpses in gray-green uniforms, sprawled in the snow, stuck in drifts, twisted in odd positions, their heads wrapped with shawls and scarves over overseas caps and garrison caps, their eyes glazed over for eternity. Ragged columns of prisoners slowly headed to the rear, scarcely able to drag their rag-wrapped legs.

We had the opportunity to study the effects of our antitank mines on the spot. They were working fine, and could destroy a tank chassis, but they still weren't strong enough to totally destroy a tank and kill the crew at the same time. Prisoners confirmed that our mines inflicted serious casualties, but they also confirmed that some of the mines could be easily disarmed, *if there were no complications from the weather*. We knew this; we just didn't have enough mines that were safe for our troops, dangerous to the enemy's troops and tanks, but could not be easily removed by enemy sappers.

In addition to my ideas on improving the mines, I was also reflecting on the partisans. The offensive was continuing, and we were pushing the Nazis farther and farther westward, and some partisan formations were linking up with the Red Army. The partisans were indescribably happy. They said that they had recently been able to increase the effects of their strikes on the invaders, but they also complained about the lack of reliable, fast communications with their own forces, the impossibility of sending Moscow valuable intelligence reports, and about having too little ammunition and explosives.

After 10 December, I found myself in Zavidovo, my old home village. Thanks to our troops' rapid advance, and their penetration into the enemy rear, Zavidovo hadn't suffered much from the German occupation. Some of the houses escaped damage, including the house of my old boyhood friend, Yegor Derevyanin. Yegor was in the army, but I found Yegor's wife, Tatiana, and the children, all in good health. They were cleaning up the mess the Germans had made of their home. When the Germans arrived, Tatiana had moved the children to a village eighteen kilometers away, where the Germans never appeared. She mentioned that the Germans had sent around some arsonists, *posing as Soviet partisans*, to burn houses, but that the people had stopped them after they had burned seven homes![1]

I left Zavidovo, content that my friend's family had survived, and thinking over what I'd heard from Tatiana; it was the final push that I needed to move me to write yet one more letter to Stalin, to talk one more time about the problems of partisan operations and the effectiveness of mining enemy lines of communications. The new proposal, written in rare spare moments, was based on the need for producing mines of various types. It also pointed out the failure to fully utilize the possibilities of partisan warfare and raised the question of the creation of a single unified leadership for partisan combat operations.

I really wanted to get some advice on my letter from someone, either in the military or the Party, but from whom?

Then I recalled Ponomarenko! He was secretary of the Central Committee of the Party of Belorussia, and a former member of the Front Military Council. He had supported the training of partisan cadres, had advanced the idea of the OUTs, and he wasn't indifferent to the needs of partisans! On the first free day that I had, I entered the cavernous hall of the Hotel Moskva. There was the same elevator, the same stairs, and the same paintings on the wall. The same deep easy chairs and divans, the same walnut wood desk for the floor lady, the same room. I knocked. A familiar voice said, "Come in!"

Ponomarenko was standing with his back to the window, with his hands behind his back. It seemed as though he might have been looking at the snow flakes, swirling in the twilight over the city. Time was expensive, so I told him what I'd come for, and handed him the letter. "Read it through, please, and if you have no comments on the substance, please help me deliver the letter to its addressee, Panteleymon Kondrat'yevich."

Ponomarenko took it. "You're a persistent person! Another letter?"

He read it carefully. Then he read it again, but he didn't give it back. "It's good, as far as mines and cadres are concerned. Concerning partisan leadership, however, it's a bit too general, and too brief. That question is not simple. I've got it on my mind all the time."

1. It is likely that these "arsonists" were actually real Soviet partisans, attempting to carry out Stalin's "scorched earth" policy!

"Then perhaps you want me to prepare another type of document in place of my report. You know best."

"I don't know, I don't know." Ponomarenko went to the high window beyond which the snow was swirling. "Leave it here; I'll read it again, think it over, and try to figure out what's the best way to approach this. Don't get yourself worked up."

Two days later I was able to drop in on Ponomarenko. I went, thinking that he'd probably reject all my suggestions! But all my concerns burst like a soap bubble as soon as I passed Ponomarenko's threshold. He smiled broadly, came to meet me, and shook my hand firmly and energetically. He had no questions about anything.

"I've thought it all over," said Ponomarenko. "Sit down!

We talked about our misfortunes, as is the time-honored custom among the Rusi; and we agreed that the most important thing for the partisans was to have a unified command structure, radio communications, training for cadres, and regular supply.

"One thing troubles me, you know," Ponomarenko admitted. "You're sending the letter yourself. They'll start it up the chain of command, and for all we know, it might fall into the hands of someone who doesn't understand partisan needs."

"Then that's the end of the letter!"

"My idea exactly! And you know, Ilya Grigor'yevich, it's very likely that it would be better if I were to sign a letter like this. Don't you understand? I'll send it immediately to Andrey Andreyevich Andreyev,[2] and Andreyev will send it directly to Comrade Stalin. Without unnecessary echelons getting involved!"

Ponomarenko looked at me, awaiting an answer. What could I say? He was right! Actually, it would be better if such an important letter were to be signed by the first secretary of the Communist party of Belorussia and not by Colonel Starinov. It would be better for our common cause. I stood up. "I agree, Panteleymon Kondrat'yevich. Absolutely correct."

"I knew that you would see it my way, so I prepared a draft letter," said Ponomarenko. I read the letter signed by Ponomarenko and addressed to Stalin. It stated the basic propositions I had formulated in my proposal. Panteleymon Kondrat'yevich wrote that he was presenting the thoughts of partisan warfare enthusiasts, and he had included my name among the names of those enthusiasts. In his letter, Ponomarenko retained some of my own sentences, such as: "A tank battalion is a terrible force on the

---

2. Andreyev was a member of Stalin's inner circle and secretary of the Communist party, who had played a major role in the forced collectivization of agriculture and also supported the purges.

battlefield, but when it is on a troop train it is completely defenseless and can be destroyed by two or three partisan saboteurs."

"Thanks," I said to Ponomarenko. "The important thing is that partisan forces should finally be considered comparable to all other kinds of troops of the Soviet armed forces."

"I'll take care of everything," he responded. And in a certain respect he did, because in his memoirs, he claimed credit for conceiving the whole thing, stating that he had prepared the report to Stalin based on his own three-month-long experience in partisan warfare! Although he was quite capable of grabbing the limelight, Panteleymon Kondrat'yevich, later chief of the Central Staff of the Partisan Movement, still wasn't able to carry out the well-founded recommendations that he had stated in "his" proposal.

I returned to the front, conscious of having fulfilled my duty, and certain that within a month or two, no later, a decision would be made one way or another. Within a week and a half, however, I was called back to the Department of Organizational Instruction of the Central Committee of the Party. There, I learned that Stalin had met with Ponomarenko for two hours and that they had discussed Ponomarenko's memo, which was entitled "On the Question of Organizing Sabotage Work in the Enemy Rear." The memo argued that it was necessary to organize a broad well-organized system of planned sabotage, to cut enemy supply lines and force the enemy to withdraw a significant number of troops from the front lines to guard railroads and highways. To achieve these goals, we had to organize a network of partisan and sabotage schools at the Front level, transform the OUTs into a central school, establish a central control for sabotage and partisan activities, and get mass production of mines underway. The centralization of leadership of the partisan movement, which had been raised by all the republics' central committees and regional committees, and even a few Front-level Military Councils, was now considered by Stalin to be both appropriate and timely, and the Central Committee naturally agreed. I tried to argue that military sabotage units should participate in these activities. Because military forces would be participating, I further argued that the centralized command structure should be called the Central Staff of *Partisan Forces*, as opposed to the Central Staff of the *Partisan Movement*. I later learned that Voroshilov had also made the same suggestion, but Stalin sided with Ponomarenko, and chose to call the organization the Central Staff of the Partisan Movement. This title was suggested by Ponomarenko, with the clear intention of securing for himself the position of chief of the Central Staff of the Partisan Movement. He could not have been appointed as chief of a Central Staff of Partisan Forces (a military position) since he lacked the military and specialists' experience. Although a veteran of the civil war, he later became a political officer of railroad troops, attended the Moscow Transportation Institute, and then rose in Party ranks.[3]

When I arrived at the Department of Organizational Instruction, it appeared that work was already under way, putting together a table of organization and authorized manpower positions for the partisan movement staff, determining manpower requirements for the partisan school and brigade staffs, and preparing requisitions for weapons and equipment for partisan detachments. Ponomarenko's letter had gone to its addressee in a very short time, and the decision was made just as quickly!

Several days later, General Kotlyar and I were invited to meet with N. A. Voznesenskiy, a representative of Gosplan.[4] Representatives of the artillery and communications directorates were present at the meeting, as were industry representatives. Back to the Kremlin! Voznesenskiy was a pleasant, polite, young fellow. He told us that we had to make decisions on problems of partisan supply. I was in seventh heaven! The discussion was professional and specific. Kotlyar and I demonstrated mines and fuses that we had brought with us, including a delayed-action mine, components of a nonremovable mine, and vibration and inertial fuses for antitransportation mines.

It was obvious to all that our first priority had to be organizing radio communications with partisan units operating in the German rear. For this reason, from the very first day after the staff was created, we devoted all major efforts to creating a centralized radio school for training partisan radio operators and equipping them with all that they needed, and to setting up a sensitive radio receiving station for the Central Staff. We set up the school in two weeks and got a lot of other organizational and technical problems solved with the great assistance that we received from many other organizations.

Voznesenskiy warned us that the nation's resources were not quite what they were before the war, but promised he'd try to fill our requisitions, and that he'd get his engineers working on mine designs that were safer for our troops. He wished us luck, and his

---

3. To Western readers, the distinction made between "Partisan Movement" and "Partisan Forces" may seem trifling, but semantic differences of this type were accorded great significance in the USSR. Careers, as well as lives, often depended on the correct choice of a term.

4. "Gosplan" was the State Planning Organization of the USSR, the organization charged with the direction of the entire Soviet economy, hence with determining production priorities and allocating specific resources and production facilities to meet those priorities.

wish was granted rapidly: in spring of 1942, the problem of mass production of delayed-action mines and other complicated types of mines was solved completely. Soon our troops and partisans began to receive them. It was about time![5]

As 1941 drew to a close, our information indicated that over two thousand partisan detachments, a total of over ninety thousand people, were operating in the German rear. For the most part, these people not only operated without centralized command and control, but also lacked training, equipment, and communications. The losses sustained by these groups were naturally quite high—in some areas, *over 90 percent of the detachments were destroyed in the first six months of the war.*

A New Mission

I couldn't hang around long in Moscow; on 14 December, Major General Kotlyar ordered me to form a new engineer operations group for building mine and demolitions barriers on the approaches to the recently liberated city of Rostov-on-the-Don, and I immediately headed for the Southwestern Front.

The group included instructors and lab workers from the Western Front partisan school—the OUTs—and along with ten lieutenants who had combat experience and had completed the short course at the Kuybyshev Military Engineer Academy, and former Republican Spanish Army men under the command of Domingo Ungria. I designated Maj. V. V. Artem'yev as my deputy, and Capt. A. I. Chekonin as my chief of staff. On 16 December, the train bearing the freight cars that had been assigned to the group slowly pulled away from the darkened platform of the Kursk station.

I dropped in to see the young lieutenants. A couple of young girls, instructors, Mariya Belova and Ol'ga Kretova, invited me to tea. They had toasted some black bread, and the toast reminded me of home, of my family whom I had not seen in six months.

Steppes, snow, the clacking of the train wheels, the smell of lo-

5. Voznesenskiy was killed in 1950 in a purge that followed the death of Andrey Zhdanov. Zhdanov had been maneuvering to consolidate his own position as Stalin's heir apparent. Zhdanov died mysteriously, however, and his followers—including Voznesenskiy—were purged by Malenkov and Beria, who led the opposing forces in the power struggle.

comotive smoke! When I woke up, I tried to remember what Rostov had looked like in winter. My thoughts changed rather quickly, however, and concentrated on my mission. I knew that so-called defensive belts had been built around Rostov. These consisted of antitank ditches, deployed in three gigantic arcs north of the city, battalion-size defensive sectors, with pillboxes and bunkers and individual rifle pits. The eastern ends of these belts rested on the Don, and the western ends rested on the Don delta. Our group had to mine these belts.

I was really worried: if they had just pinned their hopes on antitank ditches to defend Rostov, that meant that the Fifty-sixth Army under Lieutenant General Remezov didn't have enough antitank mines and fuses. General Kotlyar had also just issued a directive on 5 December ordering that antitank ditches be replaced with less noticeable but more effective antitank obstacles. We'd have to start producing mines locally. But the lack of mines wasn't the main thing that worried me. I was sure that we'd be able to get the mines we needed. I was really concerned about how the Fifty-sixth Army commander and his chief of engineers troops—Maj. E. M. Zhurin—would view our innovative plan for mine operations. Major Artem'yev told me that Zhurin, who had been his boss in the academy, was a sincere, simple fellow, who knew his business very well. But what about the army commander? His views on mine warfare were totally unknown. You see, we wanted to use "covert" mining and "mobile" mining along with "overt" mining.

I'll explain what I mean by these terms: "covert" mining is typical local area mining in which mines are hidden in the earth and carefully camouflaged so that their presence cannot be detected. "Mobile" mining is the quick setting of mines by covert means on sectors where the enemy was able to bring heavy pressure on our troops or where they might punch holes in our defenses with tanks. For mining of this type, in sectors that were vulnerable to armor attack, we had already prepared mine dumps and formed groups of soldiers equipped with their own vehicles so that they could quickly reach the areas where they were needed. "Overt" mining was a completely different matter. In this case, thousands of mines were set in plain view, in tens of thousands of little hillocks, which were easy to observe, even from afar, and to precisely locate with aerial photography. The secret was that by no means all the little hillocks were actually mined, and it was impossible to determine with the human eye, or even with a camera, which hillocks concealed mines.

The enemy was thus faced with a choice: either run over the

hillocks with tanks and be blown up, or avoid the mined areas and accept battle on unfavorable terrain. Clearing mines from the hillocks was extremely difficult, because the mines could be set in hundreds of different ways; there could be five, ten, or twenty mines in a hillock; and no matter whether the hillock actually containing the mines was in the first, the third, or the fortieth row, *you still had to check every hillock!*

Mine-clearing operations were extremely work-intensive and dangerous for the Germans, but most importantly, overt mining required their tanks to await the results of minesweeping efforts while under artillery fire and air attack, which inflicted serious losses on them. It seemed logical for the enemy to shell the hillocks, but the enemy shelled the area where our defensive forces were deployed, occasionally destroying some of the mines that we had set by covert means. There just weren't enough artillery or mortar shells to drop on every hillock.

I also was hoping to reach an understanding on yet another matter with the Fifty-sixth Army staff. The defensive lines of the Fifty-sixth Army principally extended along the Mius River, and rested on the Taganrog Gulf on the left flank. The northern shore of the gulf was held by the enemy. I was certain that the Germans hadn't created a continuous defensive line on the northern shore of the gulf, from Berdyansk to Taganrog. To deceive us, this shoreline was held only by small garrisons, stationed in various settlements, relying on our weakness and on the thirty-plus kilometers of frozen gulf, filled with ice hummocks, that separated our troops from theirs. It followed that the gulf would be an ideal route over which to insert a group of demolitions men behind enemy lines. Explosions on the enemy's roads and destruction of his small garrisons would not only force the Germans to reduce all kinds of transportation operations but it would force them to divert significant forces for the defense of the northern shore and to remove troops from other sectors of the front. That would be great! We had to thoroughly consider the idea of sending demolitions men across the ice of the Taganrog Gulf, weigh all the pros and cons, put our recommendations in writing, present them personally to the command, and see what happened. The Fifty-sixth Army Military Council would make the decision.

We arrived at Rostov early on the frosty morning of 19 December. The city, covered in haze and smoke, was indiscernible from the train window. Looking at the half-destroyed station building from the platform, we prepared ourselves for more ruins elsewhere, but the city was almost untouched. This was easily explained: the Germans had only ruled Rostov for eight days before being booted out by a lightning fast attack. But even in those eight days, the Nazis had time to blow up a few things and, most importantly, to shoot and hang hundreds of Rostovites.

We found Major Zhurin at the Fifty-sixth Army staff. He was in complete agreement with our approach, and after a long discussion, took us to see Lieutenant General Remezov. Remezov was pleased to learn that we could complete the required mining ahead of time and gave us the go-ahead.

My chief of staff, Chekonin, and my deputy, Artem'yev, worked up the plan for the Rostov mine barrier operation, and Zhurin gave valuable assistance. By the morning of 25 December, the plan was ready, and by 26 December, it had been approved by the Fifty-sixth Army Military Council. We intended to set seventy thousand mines, although the Main Engineer Directorate had only released 14,000 to us. An additional 56,000 would have to be produced in Rostov. We began training the miners and setting up mine production.

The Southern Front command had subordinated a lot of engineer troops to the Fifty-sixth Army. They were all fully occupied in building barriers along the Mius, in the Don delta, and in the vicinity of Rostov. Near Rostov, sappers and thousands of city dwellers were digging antitank ditches. Given the prescribed dimensions of these ditches, every linear meter of ditch required moving fifteen cubic meters of frozen, cementlike earth!

The sapper battalions, which were assigned this unpleasant work, were led by elderly, recalled reserve officers and manned by green draftees. With new boots and puttees, and dressed in greasy quilted jackets, the sappers didn't look very impressive. They certainly were nothing like the troops I'd commanded in peacetime, but there were many Communists and Komsomols among them, and the majority of privates had at least a middle school education, which favorably distinguished them from troops of the recent past.

First, we relieved the sapper battalion detachments from their assignments digging the antitank ditch, sent them off to rest, and then started to teach them mines and demolitions. The Rostov Regional Party Committee and the Military Council of the Fifty-sixth Army assigned production of the additional mines that we needed to the factories of Rostov, Novocherkassk, and Aksay.

Before ordering the production of more complicated mines, however, we had to improve them, giving consideration to combat experience. Given local conditions, we also had to work out the optimum technology of production. In short, we had to immediately create a design bureau and a small laboratory-shop. We were really lucky! In the Rostov Communist Home Guard Regiment there were many experienced, capable engineers, including some tool-and-die makers, draftsmen, etc. I requested that an electrical engineer be sent to the engineer operations group, preferably one who had "smelled powder." I got Sergey Vasil'yevich Gridnev, who had been decorated with a "For Valor" medal in the battle for Rostov. Although he warned us that he was an electric power plant designer, he was able to quickly get himself up to speed with the help of our instructors, and he made significant contributions to our effort to develop fuses, particularly self-destructing mine fuses with predetermined intervals, and nonextractable fuses for delayed-action mines. On the same day that he came up with the nonextractable fuse, my Spaniards produced one hundred mines using it.

One episode from those times serves to characterize Gridnev very well: one day, when he was straightening out the safety pin on a "bouncing Betty"—a jumping fragmentation mine—made out of a 100mm artillery shell, Sergey withdrew the firing pin rod too far, and the safety pin fell out into the thick grass. With some difficulty, he held back the firing pin with two fingers, and sat down, hoping to find the safety pin and replace it. Unfortunately, the safety pin was lost. In the meantime, the opening for the safety pin in the firing pin had slipped down into the body of the fuse, and the firing pin itself was slowly but irretrievably slipping in deeper into the fuse. Gridnev's fingers, white from the strain, would soon be unable to hold out the firing pin: the pin would fall, and then—explosion!

Gridnev called for an enlisted man who was helping him. This guy arrived, took one look at what was happening, turned pale, and ran off. Gridnev gritted his teeth. A cold sweat broke out on his brow. The firing pin was slipping from his sweaty fingers. Just then, the enlisted man who had run off returned and handed him a big nail.

Gridnev took the nail and drove it through the skin of his finger, which was covering a second, higher hole in the firing pin of the fuse. He pushed the nail right on through that hole and, finally, was able to secure the firing pin. He then asked for a knife, and when he got one, Sergey cut through the skin of his finger and freed his hand. It's true, however, that after that, he closed his eyes and turned white.

Soon, several Rostov University scholars came to our lab, including M. G. Khaplanov, a mathematics lecturer, and the chemist Miksidzhan, and youngsters from Rostov—mainly female Komsomol members—also began to help the Spaniards assemble mines. They were eager to get into the army, but the boys and girls were not yet of draft age. Unfortunately, many of them never reached draft age: in the summer of 1942, after I had left Rostov, a heavy bomb fell on the part of the university building where the lab was located, and very few of the young mine makers survived. I was very pleased to see that these outstanding youngsters were immortalized during the fortieth anniversary of the Great Victory in 1985.

On the eve of the New Year, 1942, we sent models of the improved mine types to the industrial concerns. The Rosselmash factory made the small parts for the mines and fuses, and Krasnyy Aksay made metal casings for the fragmentation mines. The wooden casings for antitank and antipersonnel mines were made by the Rostov grand piano factory, which is why we used to joke that the enemy wouldn't like modern Rostov music.

We completed mines and demolitions training for the groups that had been sent to us from the sapper battalions. In accordance with tasking from the Regional Committee, we also organized partisan training at a base in the city of Shakhti, and in Rostov itself, we set up a school for training possible underground workers in mines and demolitions. The partisans and underground workers were trained by our NKVD border guard officers—Captains Stepan Ivanovich Kazantsev, Trofim Pavlovich Chepak, and Petr Antonovich Romanyuk—as well as Lt. F. A. Kuznetsov, already known to the reader, and Lieutenants Ivanov and Karpov; the female instructors Kretova and Belova; and some of our Spaniards who had learned to speak Russian fluently.

We also trained groups of people who had been sent to us by the Krasnodar District Party Committee. We taught them methods of partisan warfare to be used if the enemy invaded their district. We later gave the Krasnodar partisans a large quantity of mines and demolitions, which they successfully used against occupation forces. During the first ten days of our stay in Rostov, we set aside strictly limited periods for rest. We even restricted the New Year's Eve celebration to forty-five minutes. Otherwise we'd never have been able to keep up.

A Decision is Made

The Soviet winter offensive continued on all sectors of the huge front. At the end of December, Kozel'sk and Kaluga were liberated, as well as Kerch and Feodosiya. Preparations were also made for offensive operations in the Donbass region. The Military Council of the Southern Front relieved the troops of the Ninth Army, and sent them into the reserves under the command of the Southwestern Direction.[1] The sector of the front previously occupied by the Ninth Army was given to the Fifty-sixth Army. The Fifty-sixth Army thus had to cover a three hundred–kilometer front, two kilometers of which ran along the shores of the Taganrog Gulf and the Don delta.

Considering the thinly stretched combat dispositions of the army, and fearing that the enemy would be able to penetrate the rear of our defending troops across the ice of the gulf, which was thickening under winter conditions, the Military Council of the Front ordered that the construction of defensive lines be accelerated, the shores of the gulf and the Don delta be mined, and that the ice of the gulf be broken up manually, to create *polyn'i*, large areas of open water, to hinder enemy crossings. This was to begin at Azov and Rostov, and continue for 120 kilometers along the southern shore of the gulf.

It goes without saying that we didn't have enough mines, and we had to immediately increase their production, so we went once more to the Regional Committee and to the workers of Rostov, Novocherkassk, Aksay, and Azov. The workers didn't let us down. While the mines were being produced, the sappers and the civilian population were sent out to break up the ice and make *polyn'i*. Soldiers, women, youth, men who were exempt from military service—tens of thousands of people—went out with crow bars, pickaxes, and spades to peck away at the ice of the Don delta and the Sea of Azov. The green, unyielding ice reached almost a half meter in thickness in some places. The crow bars rang and the spades scraped away. It was a miserable job! Besides, in the cruel frost and the cutting winds, even strong healthy men could not break through very much ice. It wasn't enough to just break holes in the ice: in order to keep the *polyn'i* from freezing over again, they had to be covered with branches, and then the branches had to be covered with straw and snow. This was a problem, because there weren't many branches to be found on the steppes.

Zhurin and I considered that the work used in creating *polyn'i* was a waste of manpower, and we reported our opinions on the subject to the new commander of the Fifty-sixth Army, Maj. Gen. V. V. Tsyganov. Tsyganov and Brigade Commissar Komarov, who was a member of the Fifty-sixth Army Military Council, agreed,

---

1. During World War II, Soviet fronts were grouped according to strategic directions. The Southwestern Direction included, at various times, the Southwestern, Southern, and Bryansk fronts as well as naval forces of the Black Sea Fleet.

and reported their views to the Front Military Council. But the Council did not stop the work on the *polyn'i*. Finally, a member of the Military Council of the Southern Front, I. I. Larinov, arrived in Rostov on a routine trip and inspected the shore defenses. He gave the order to discontinue making *polyn'i* and to increase mining operations; to set mines not only on the most dangerous approaches but on any place on the beach that the enemy might land.

At that time, we also strengthened the mining of the most advanced defensive lines of the Fifty-sixth Army, and mined the defensive "belts." General Tsyganov firmly supported the idea of creating a system of trenches, and developed communication trenches along the defensive lines. This system was quickly built in the area covered by the Fifty-sixth Army. After 10 January, when mining operations were going on at full speed along the defensive lines, the Military Council of the army also accepted my recommendation for creation of a *spets* (special purpose) battalion of mine troops for strikes at the enemy lines of communication and strong points on the northern shore of Taganrog Gulf. Tsyganov warned us to wait a while before we got too excited over that development. The repercussions of sorties in the enemy rear might be greater than we expected, he said, and we had to get approval from the Front commander, Lieutenant General Malinovskiy, to discuss with him the manning of such a unit and to arrange for supply of explosives.

The last time I had seen Malinovskiy was in Spain, six years before, in the provincial capital of Jaen, clinging to the slippery slopes of the mountain foothills. There, in one of the narrow, canyonlike medieval alleys, we maintained a haven for demolitions men. Visiting us, Malinovskiy—then code named "Malino"—sat on the sill of a high lancet window. He had flung a fur jacket over his broad shoulders, and the rim of his black beret hung over his left eye.

In the Southern Front staff offices, a heavyset fellow with slicked-back hair and a concerned, puffy face rose to meet me from behind a desk. Of the man I had known six years ago, only the eyes remained, twinkling in a smile of recognition. The Front commander listened carefully to me: he accepted my recommendation to cross the ice of the Taganrog Gulf and carry out sabotage in the enemy rear. To carry out these operations, he decided to use volunteers drawn from units that had been assigned to the engineer group, and also from officers and men of the Eighth Sapper Army. I pointed out that Spanish Republican veterans, with lots of experience behind enemy lines, were also assigned to the engineer operations group. Malinovskiy was concerned that the

Spaniards might not be able to stand the weather, but when I assured him that they had become acclimatized, he approved their use as well, telling me that I should personally look out for them.

We had to select people who were both mentally and physically tough. Lt. Nikolai Ivanovich Moklyakov, at that time commanding the 22d Sapper Battalion, was confirmed as commander of the *spets* battalion. This tall, strong, thirty-five-year-old officer had joined the Komsomol at age seventeen, and joined the Party at twenty-four. Before the war, he had worked as an engineer at the Novo Kramatorsk factory and, if he'd wanted, could have been evacuated with his family far behind our lines. However, on a housing form that had been given to him, he had written, "I am a Communist, and my place is at the front." He took the form to the Military Commissariat and was sent to the front. He gratefully accepted the nomination as commander of the *spets* battalion.

Senior political officer Zakhar Veniaminovich Veniaminov was designated the unit commissar. In the past, he had frequently been elected to the post of Party secretary of some of the largest industrial concerns, and he had a lot of experience with people. He was over forty years old but the commissar never complained about his health! Furthermore, he had enviable self-control, did not accept rash decisions, and one of his favorite phrases was "We'll have to think it over!"

Initially, we intended to select volunteer privates and sergeants for the battalion from the units drawn up in formation. But when the command was given for all volunteers to take one step forward, the whole battalion that Moklyakov had previously commanded took one step forward, and we had to discard our initial intentions. In the rest of the battalions and also in the 26th Brigade of the Eighth Sapper Army, we selected volunteers based on personal interviews with each man.

By the third week of January, the personnel of the *spets* battalion had been assigned. New winter uniforms and camouflage suits had been issued to the officers and men, along with PPSh submachine guns,[2] sapper knives, and sets of tools for working with mines, wire cutters, and grenades. Instructors from the engineer operations group immediately began to teach the novices the arts of mining and operating in the enemy rear.

But that was only the beginning! It was still necessary to decide how the sabotage groups were going to cross the ice hummocks of the Taganrog Gulf, a one-way trip of thirty to sixty kilometers, and how they would maintain communications with their base and

2. PPSh is the Soviet abbreviation for the familiar Shpagin machine pistol (*Pistolet-pulemet Shpagina*), a 7.62 mm., drum-fed, "burp gun" used in World War II and Korea.

with each other. Crossing so great a distance on foot or skis was out of the question, so we had to use sled teams. The army Military Council helped us to get the sleds, and picked out horses for us, but our very first test trip on the ice was discouraging: although they had been very carefully shod, the horses could not make headway, their hooves began to split, and the winds began to turn over the sleds. Jumping off onto the ice, the men tried to help the horses while holding on to the sleds, but the sleds slid away, and the men looked as if they were performing circus pratfalls on the ice. This seemed strange to us because the local fisherwomen went out on the ice without any problems at all! So we went to pay our respects to the fisherwomen. They explained that we needed to attach iron strips to the sled runners in order to cut the ice and to prevent the sleds from sliding sideways. They said that the horses should be reshod with cleated shoes, and that we should attach *buzuluki*, a kind of cleat with three sharp spikes, to the soldiers' felt boots. With *buzuluki* a soldier could not only make his way across the ice but he could clamber up a sheer shore cliff.

We made iron shoes for the sleds, reshod the horses, and acquired *buzuluki*, but then a new problem appeared. We were convinced that it would take more than one night to go on a mission but return to base before morning. An obvious solution suggested itself: depart from our shore at sunset, in order to reach a point within ten to twenty kilometers of the enemy shore by the time that darkness fell, and then to rest a bit before we actually ran the sortie. Since movement during daylight hours could easily be observed from enemy aircraft, we would have to make camouflage clothing for both men *and* horses. So we got white cloth, and covered the horses with wide camouflage horse blankets and hoods. In their new clothes, the horses looked like something out of the age of chivalry! But from a kilometer away, the sleds were indistinguishable against the background of the frozen gulf and the ice hummocks.

For communications between the combat groups and the sled drivers, who would remain at night among the ice hummocks, we issued the drivers pocket flashlights with different color lenses and different colored flares, prepared in our shop-lab. We weren't able to get field radios for our combat groups; even the Front Military Council couldn't help us out on that score: there simply weren't enough available.

Toward the end of January, I reported to the army commander that the *spets* battalion was ready for combat. General Tsyganov assigned us to prevent the enemy from moving freely on the northern shore of the gulf, to destroy personnel and equipment in the enemy rear, and cut enemy communications lines. The operations plan was chopped off by the chief of the intelligence for the Fifty-sixth Army, Colonel Yegnarov; Major Zhurin, the chief of the operations department; Maj. N. D. Saltykov; and me. The army commander approved the plan without changes.

It was a frosty morning in January. The snow-clogged road stretched along the high, steep shoreline. The gulf lay beneath on the right, with the jumbled mounds of ice hummocks sparkling in the early morning sunlight, the dark ice holes surrounded by the toylike figures of the fisherwomen and their sleds. To the left was the steppe, where you could see the frost-cracked earth through the sparse snow granules. In the ravines, the snow lay like fluffy featherbeds with a light rosy tinge in the morning light. Step into those featherbeds and you'd be buried up to your head.

Pushing through the drifts, the detachments of the *spets* battalion were heading toward Yeysk, Shabel'sk, and Port-Katon. An advance guard was up ahead, a pathfinder platoon commanded by the young Lt. Vladimir Dmitriyevich Kondrashev. Behind the advance guard, on good horses, came the *spets* battalion command party. It was followed by the companies, in orderly columns. Then came the smoking field kitchen, with the cook sitting on the limber. Even in the frost, he hadn't stopped pumping his accordion. Then came the sled with the medic, Serdyuk, and then the sled with rations and other provisions.

One company and the NKVD border guard officers went with me to Yeysk, where we would set up the staff for the sortie behind enemy lines. Manuel Belda came along with us: he was a Spanish officer, a hero of many trips behind Franco lines, and he was never discouraged in any situation. He was smiling, and I was sure that he had made some kind of off-color remark to his friends. He was that kind of guy. With him around, you didn't need a political officer! His tales of Spain, of Dolores Ibarrury, and of battles with Franco's forces, raised the fighting spirit of all the soldiers.

The taciturn young Lieutenant Yatsenko also rode with us. He was always the first to notice if one of his comrades was exhausted, or if someone got bad news from home, and he was always able to calm and support his friends.

A former Spanish pilot, now a Red Army soldier, also rode with us. This was Mariano Chico. In Spanish, *chico* means "young boy," but his family name really didn't do him justice. He had the shoulders and chest of a weight lifter or wrestler and the legs of a marathon runner. Chico was a happy-go-lucky fellow from Cuenca whose parents had wanted to see him become a priest. Instead, he joined the Republican Army and became a fighter pilot to preach the truth with the guns of an I-16 fighter plane.[3] And now he was preparing to preach again, this time with mines and a submachine gun.

The battalion marched along. Men from the Don and Moscow; from Cordova and Ryazan; from Valencia and Tula; from Barcelona, from the Altai, and from the Basque country: they all marched and rode together.

When we arrived at Yeysk, following the orders of the commander of the Fifty-sixth Army, I got in touch with the commander of the Azov Flotilla, Rear Adm. S. G. Gorshkov, in order to reach an agreement on coordination between the *spets* battalion and the sailors.[4] We had already had the occasion to meet the flotilla sailors and had run joint missions with them. A bit earlier, the operations group had sent two mine instructors to the Azov area where the shore was guarded by personnel of torpedo boat Detachments 14 and 20. Our instructors and the personnel of the detachments set land mines and sea mines in the Azov area. There, I met the commander of Detachment 14, Tsezar L'vovich Kunikov. Kunikov gave the impression of being an energetic and decisive man. How was one to know who the fortunes of war would bring together? More than a year would pass until that night in February 1943 when a special detachment under the command of Major Kunikov was able to seize a small beachhead on the western shore of the Tsemess Bay near the suburbs of Novorossiysk-Stanichka, which came to be known as *Malaya Zemlya*; "the little land."[5]

When he had heard me out, Rear Admiral Gorshkov asked me to visit him at Primorsk-Akhtarsk, and sent a U-2 biplane for me.[6] The weather was clear, and calm, and the flight from Yeysk to Primorsk-Akhtarsk took about forty minutes. The stout, broad-chested, red-haired admiral looked very young. I even doubted that he had reached his thirtieth birthday. Later, I learned that my

3. The I-16 Moskva, produced by the Polikarpov Design Bureau, was a three hundred mile-per-hour, low-wing monoplane of plywood and metal construction, with a large radial engine, retractable gear, two machine guns, and two cannon. It was an advanced design for its time and performed well in Spain and the Winter War.

4. Gorshkov, who may have had more political and managerial talent than operational capability, was designated commander in chief of the Soviet Navy in 1956, and held that post through the Khruschev, Brezhnev, Andropov, and Chernenko regimes, until finally relieved by Gorbachev in 1985.

5. *Malaya Zemlya* was the site of fierce, prolonged fighting, in which Leonid Brezhnev played a minor role as a political officer. Later, when Brezhnev became chief of state, he wrote a book on the battle, exaggerating his own war record in order to justify the many medals that he awarded himself. A Soviet joke of the period asks rhetorically: "What medals does Comrade Brezhnev lack?" Answer: "Only Heroic Soviet City and Heroic Soviet Mother."

6. The U-2 was a Soviet reproduction of the U.S.–built Fleet biplane. It was used for liaison, observation, and partisan support during the war and was also used by North Korea for night harassment missions against U.S. forces in Korea.

first impression had been almost correct: in 1942, Sergey Georgiyevich Gorshkov was only thirty-two.

After he had read through the letter from the Fifty-sixth Army commander, Gorshkov nodded. "Sorties behind enemy lines— outstanding idea! But, as I understand it, you only have infantry-men, right?"

I confirmed that we had no sailors in the *spets* battalion.

"That's what I thought. And we might have to fight on the sea even though it's frozen. For this reason, Comrade Colonel, I'll have to assign some sailors to you for your sorties. We'll talk about this later: now you're going to listen to my advice."

And Gorshkov didn't spare his advice, for which all of my people, from battalion commanders right down to the drivers, were truly grateful.

Sergey Georgiyevich Gorshkov gave his concentrated attention to our sorties behind enemy lines. He gave the order to form combat groups from ships' companies. These groups were to operate along the northern shore of the gulf with us, as well as independently. He responded immediately to any request we made.

While we were thus involved at the front, other—disappointing—events were taking place in Moscow: at the end of January 1942, in accordance with a decision made by the State Defense Committee, all work on the creation of a partisan staff was suddenly halted! The Central Committee of the Belorussian Communist Party only had the OUTs at its disposal to direct partisan operations. This development raised the question of how the partisan organizations and schools that had already been created would survive. The situation with the central partisan radio school was even more complicated: training had already begun. Now, it would receive reduced financial support and would probably have to be closed. Ponomarenko found a way around the problem, however: he transferred the radio school to the budget of the Belorussian Council of Ministers!

At that time, the Ukranian Communist party, the NKVD, and the GRU (Red Army intelligence) also had their own independent partisan schools, which were concerned with problems of communications with the partisan, sabotage, and intelligence formations that these organizations commanded (without coordinating with each other). Further, the NKVD also had the independent motorized special rifle brigade—OMSBON (*Otdel'naya motostrelkovaya brigada osobogo naznacheniya*)—which was, in fact, neither motorized nor a rifle brigade, but had a partisan and sabotage mission. This unit made enormous contributions to the expansion of the partisan struggle in the enemy rear. If we had only had ten such units in the spring of 1942, we could have cut enemy supply lines completely.

Pass Unseen

Our sorties behind enemy lines across the Taganrog Gulf began with failure. Just when we had all our people billeted, had worked out the route of march for the sortie, and designated the day and hour for the departure of the combat group, strong east winds sprang up, bringing a howling blizzard. We had to sit it out in the huts of the fisherwomen.

The winds died down on 3 February. Moklyakov, the company commanders, and the Spanish comrades asked if it wasn't time to begin. They felt that the people were getting stale from inaction. What the hell could I do? If the weather was clearing up, then it was time! At 3:00 P.M., the sleds carrying the miners went out on the ice and soon disappeared behind the hummocks in the blowing snow. In the evening around 7:00 P.M., however, the sky again turned dark gray: clouds came crawling across the steppe and the gulf. As if to reinforce the clouds, snow began to fall in heavy flakes, and the east wind howled to and fro. That night, no one in the battalion slept. The outpost watched the shoreline until morning, trying to pick out any signs of the group in the blinding midnight swirl of snow. They signaled with the pocket flashlights, but no one saw or heard anything. A mother's worries are boundless when she sends a son off to war, but so are the worries of officers who send their men off on dangerous missions.

The troops of Captain Chepak were the first to return in the morning. He said his combat groups had moved along close to each other, maintaining their orientation by azimuth. The blizzard overtook them when they were halfway to the objective, and the groups only reached the ice hummocks off the northern shore at midnight. After an hour or so, it appeared that the winds were dying down and the snow was not falling as hard, so they started to move ahead. Supporting each other and the horses, falling down and getting up again, they were able to move about six kilometers, when in the snowy haze an enemy flare soared skyward. In its uncertain light, the miners were able to distinguish two ships, frozen in the ice. Then German submachine guns rattled from the unknown ships.

The officers gave the command to withdraw. The return trip was no less difficult. The collective-farm horses had reached their limits and had to be dragged and pushed along. While crossing the hummocks in the middle of the gulf, Captain Chepak lost sight of the other groups. Although his men had fired into the air and even set off grenades, they couldn't find any of the others. We immediately sent out search-and-rescue groups: they penetrated far into the gulf and rummaged around in the area where the *spets* battalion was deployed, but were unable to find anyone in the blizzard.

The wind and the blizzard slackened only in the latter half of the day. Then our long wait was finally rewarded: far off on the ice field, black specks appeared. Fresh horse teams darted off to meet them. They brought back the detachment commanded by Francisco Gaspara. Francisco himself climbed out of the sled with difficulty and with even more difficulty separated his teeth to say, *"Muy frio!"*

An hour later Mariano Chico came back alone. He had gotten separated from his comrades in the blizzard, and stubbornly crossed forty kilometers of ice in a freezing blizzard. Climbing up on the shore, Chico didn't look like the same handsome guy that the young fisherwomen had seen off from Yeysk with such rapturous looks. The earflaps of his cap were pulled down and tightly tied beneath his chin, and his comforter was plastered with thick hoarfrost. His frost-burned face, and a pair of utterly exhausted eyes loomed from the oval outlined by his comforter. Nevertheless, when he returned to shore, he threw back his shoulders and straightened up.

Soon, the Canel' combat group returned, not far from Port-Katon. Canel' himself had been severely frostbitten. His nose was swollen, as were his hands and feet. This was really serious! In order to remove Canel's earlapped cap, they had to massage him with snow, and hold him over a stove! Canel' was immediately evacuated to the Yeysk military hospital. The last to return from the ice and the hummocks were Captain Kazantsev's people. His group reached the southern shore of the gulf, east of the Shabel'sk spit. The shore was too steep for them to scale at that point, and the horses gave out in the deep drifts offshore and had to be abandoned. The people became separated in their attempts to find a convenient way to the shore, and returned in twos and threes.

But one man didn't return, and it was three days before we found his body. This was our Spanish comrade, Manuel Belda. An Andalusian by birth, and a student, he had exchanged his school books for a rifle to defend the republic. An outstanding fighter, he had become a division commander in the Spanish Republican Army at the age of twenty-two, but as a Communist, he'd been happy to get the chance to fight the Fascists again, even if he only held the rank of private! An ardent patriot of his motherland, he had dreamed of seeing Valencia again, but now he had frozen to death on the ice. I had not kept my promise to General Malinovskiy, and even to this day, I really can't excuse myself.

The foul weather stopped on the second day, and from three points, we sent new combat groups behind enemy lines simultaneously. One of the first to reach the north shore was the group led by Junior Lieutenant Yatsenko, which silently crossed the road used by enemy patrols and set mines and destroyed an enemy truck with soldiers. Invisible and silently, Lt. P. A. Romanyuk's group got through enemy lines, as did the group from Barcelona consisting of Hipolito Nogues and Francisco Gaspara; Jr. Lts. F.E. Kozlov and A.V. Korolenko, the former Republican aviators Cano, Esmeraldo, Bravo, Ustarossa, and Hererro; the men from Valencia including Angel Alberca;[1] and the former mechanic, Juan. These were accompanied by Petty Officer M.A. Repin'; Pt. V. Lipnitskiy; the former Donbass miner, Sgt. G. I. Nenepo; Francisco Guillon; and Rafael Estrello.

In order to take advantage of every single winter night and to maintain relentless pressure on the enemy, the miners of the *spets* battalion worked in three shifts. While some were out on missions, others would be preparing for missions, and still others would be resting. Every night, from three to six groups went behind enemy lines. Every night, explosions roared along the north shore, enemy vehicles and tractors pulling artillery pieces flew through the air, and enemy supply dumps went sky-high.

By mid-February, the enemy was forced to reduce night traffic on the shore roads between Berdyansk and Taganrog. In the morning, before sending out their vehicles, the enemy dispatched sapper teams to check the roads and attempted to drag the road surface with heavily loaded sleds. We then began to set mines that were designed to let the sleds through and explode under the armored vehicles that were pushing the sleds. We also set delayed-action mines, which would only become armed one or two hours *after* the road had been dragged. Explosions continued on the roads.

To prevent our movement, the enemy tried to make *polyn'i* along the northern shore, but our miners crossed the *polyn'i* with planks, or appeared where the Germans thought that the bank was

1. The exact Spanish spelling of this name is difficult to determine from the phonetic Russian version. The name might also be spelled in other ways such as, e.g., Alberque, Albergue.

too steep and impassable. The enemy increased the guards along the shore. However, they couldn't put a guard post every hundred meters because they didn't have enough men, and the miners found ways to get through the gaps between the enemy posts. The Germans hurried to mine the shoreline. *That* was very dangerous for us, and in the course of two nights, we lost three soldiers. Then we learned not only to clear enemy mines but to move them and reset them, thus destroying the enemy with his own traps.

One night, the miners had approached the Nazi-occupied shore rather closely. Angel Alberca, leading the patrol, fell in the snow and found that his leg was entangled in barbed wire. A wire entanglement! It was entirely possible that there were trip-wire mines in the barrier. If that were so, then the slightest attempt to pull back his leg would lead to an explosion and death, and the mission would be aborted.

Angel used hand signals to warn his friends: "Stop! Minefield." Grabbing hold of his felt boot by the top, he carefully withdrew his leg. Taking a booby trap from his sack, he just as carefully stuffed it into the felt boot, and wrapped his bare leg with a scarf. He drew on his knapsack over his foot for a makeshift shoe, and continued on patrol. The group arrived in the area of its objective, mined the road, and returned safely to the sleds, which they had left in the hummocks. Only then did the men notice the strange shoe that Alberca was wearing.

"Think nothing of it! The Fritzes will pay for my frozen heel!" said Alberca, laughing it off. A few days later, a Russian who had worked for the Germans as an auxiliary policeman defected to our side and happened to tell us about what happened with Alberca's boot. An *Oberleutnant* who was making the rounds of the guard posts along the shore noticed the strange object in the entanglement and gave the order to retrieve it. The soldiers carefully disentangled the wire that was wound around the boot and carried the trophy ashore. Then, from the boot, they pulled a bundle, tightly wound in string. They cut the string, and—made an unexpected one-way visit to their ancestors! At that time, there was a joke going around the battalion that Angel was able to reach across the entire gulf and kick ass with his boot!

Encountering increasingly clever booby traps, the Nazis began to get jumpy. Every evening the enemy guards shot many rockets into the air, swept the gulf with searchlight beams, and opened up with furious rifle and machine-gun fire at the slightest shadow. Supporting the "burp" gunners and machine gunners, mortars and cannon energetically blasted away at the ice. The Germans had guessed that the miners came out on the ice at nightfall and returned at dawn, and so they sent out fighters against our small combat groups. But this was February 1942, and not June 1941! Enemy aircraft attempting to patrol the gulf encountered our own fighter planes in the air and, as a rule, they had to flee to safety. The German command attempted to run sorties behind our lines with their own units. They also used horse-drawn sledges, and some of the soldiers rode horses. But every time, the Germans hastily withdrew in the face of fire from our units that were guarding the shore. Twice, Nazi combat units ran into ours out on the ice, and fled, refusing to accept combat and throwing away their explosives. Soon, the enemy seemed to abandon the whole idea of penetrating the southern shore.

We certainly had our own failures, as well. Somehow, enemy fighters were able to spot and attack Lieutenant Kozlov's group, which was returning from a mission. One private was killed, several were wounded, and all the horses were killed. Lieutenant Romanyuk immediately came to me with the idea of making decoys of the dead horses.

Romanyuk and his assistant, Jr. Lt. I. A. Naumenko, did good work. Two days later, three sleds set out for the north shore. In the first sled sat Romanyuk's troops, and in the last sled, covered with white shelter halves, lay the decoy horses.

Romanyuk and his troops stopped late at night about a kilometer from the northern shore, behind a snow bank. They got the decoys on their feet, lit the time fuses of signal flares, rushed to their sleds, and drove along the shore so that they wouldn't get hurt by what was going to happen in just seven minutes.

The enemy was jumpy, and fired rockets, but after seven minutes, when the first red signal flares burst into flames alongside the decoys, they panicked! Searchlight beams swept up and down the ice, flocks of flares soared into the air. And then one of the searchlights came to a halt on the horses. All hell broke loose! Machine guns opened up, followed by mortars. There was a great din of gunfire and explosions; columns of water rose above the shattered ice! The Nazis kept up the furious fire for at least a half hour. The fire ceased only after the explosions had knocked over the decoys.

In the morning Romanyuk handed me an outstanding diagram of the firing positions of all the German machine guns and mortars in the sector of the shore where the decoys had been placed. The lieutenant's idea had been very useful! After that, the miners used various types of decoys to locate enemy firing positions, and forced the enemy to waste hundreds of mortar shells and artillery rounds.

We were told by refugees fleeing from the northern shore that our blowing of two bridges near the Budennovsk station, where there was a German garrison, had led the occupation forces to think that our operations were carried out with partisan assistance and that the partisans must also have been helped by the "local civilian authorities," i.e., by Russian collaborators working for the German military government. So we poured some more fat on the fire: we blew up the German headquarters at Budennovsk. The Germans were merciless; they shot all their local Russian *polizei* on the spot.

In the night on 19 February, while carrying out the orders of Gen. Tsyganov, the combat group of Lieutenant Kozlov and Sergeant Lipitsky captured two prisoners. Information obtained from them led us to believe that conditions were favorable for a major strike against the northern shore of the gulf, and the army command decided to destroy the German garrison at the so-called Krivoi Spit. The operation was timed to coincide with the twenty-fourth anniversary of the Red Army. By agreement with Admiral Gorshkov, a composite detachment was created for this operation, consisting of a reinforced company of Major Maloletko's naval infantry battalion, and combat groups of the *spets* battalion.

Before sunset on 22 February, the composite detachment, under Major Maloletko's command, got under way. The German garrison didn't appear to be prepared to repel the attackers, and garrisons from the neighboring towns didn't come to their assistance. The miners cut the communications lines, heavily mined the roads leading to Krivoi Spit, and provided flank cover for the attacking detachment.

The naval infantrymen and the miners took prisoners, blew up two artillery batteries and three searchlight installations, and destroyed all the communications equipment. PO Maxim Alekseyevich Repin's group captured and delivered to the staff of the *spets* battalion a large number of enemy documents, including a thick, common notebook belonging to a German engineer officer who happened to be spending the night at Krivoi Spit and was killed in the battle. The notebook was crammed with diagrams and formulas, accompanied by explanations. I didn't know German, and so I gave the book to one of my officers to read. He didn't find anything very interesting in it, but claimed that it mentioned atomic energy. I didn't throw the notebook away, no matter what my officer said. That notebook didn't gather any dust, I can assure you.

Our successful attack on Krivoi Spit gave birth to an idea for sowing panic in the ranks of the enemy. From scrap plywood, lathing, wire, and matting our craftsmen assembled "tanks," "artillery pieces," "trucks," and "mortars," which even from as close as a half kilometer, looked like camouflaged tanks, artillery pieces, trucks, and mortars. This whole collection of decoys was carried to the northern shore of the gulf on the night of 23 February and set up about three kilometers from the enemy. About four hours after the sleds with miners had pulled back from the dummies, the sparks of self-igniting matches began to twinkle, and the beams of German searchlights finally crossed on the "Potemkin village" that the miners had erected.

The memory of Krivoi Spit was fresh in the enemy's mind: they decided that the Russians were throwing even heavier forces against them this time, and so they opened fire with artillery and mortars. In order to encourage the Nazi artillery, the miners had thoughtfully left mats soaked in kerosene alongside the dummies. A direct hit by the Nazis would ignite the mats. Then the smoke pots set up by the miners went off, too. The smoke, clearly visible in the searchlight beams, gathered thickly over our junk pile, and flames shot up in the midst of the smoke plumes. The Germans figured that they had hit the target and called down a regular firestorm of precise artillery and mortar fire on the burning rubbish heap.

February ended and March came along. Cracks appeared in the ice: the old *polyn'i* widened, and new ones appeared. It became increasingly difficult to reach into the enemy rear. The day of our departure from the Taganrog Gulf was approaching. Rear Admiral Gorshkov took this into consideration and asked us to send instructors to train sailors to carry out sorties into the enemy rear. We sent Chepak and Rafael. At the same time, we prepared for our last big operation on the ice: the destruction of two barges with military equipment in the creeks at Veselo-Vozhnesensk village. It was from these barges that the enemy had noticed our group on its first unsuccessful operation.

We prepared for this last operation very carefully, giving special attention to weapons, waterproof boots, and the construction of telescopic bridges for crossing separations and cracks in the ice. We included the most experienced demolitions men in the group: Sergeant Korolenko, Privates Troyan, Simonenko, Shaposhnikov, Mariano Chico, and Jose. Many people, however, felt very offended that they were not included in the group. First among these was the commander of the headquarters platoon, Lt. Vladimir Kondrashev, who had often been promised that he would take part in a sortie. We had to include Kondrashev in the group. Then it seemed that we couldn't refuse the medic, Serdyuk, who had even made a special study of mines and demolitions.

The local SMERSH representative, Afanasiy Dymov,[2] shook his head when he read over the group roster.

"This won't work."

I was alarmed and grieved.

"What do you mean 'this won't work'? Why?"

"Just because. You've forgotten me! *Maybe you don't trust me?*"

I threw up my hands, and entered his name on the list, too.

Together with the officers of the *spets* battalion, I awaited the results of the group's operation and its return to the observation point at Shabel'sk. At 5:00 A.M., we went out to the shore. Beneath the cliff, the ice loomed dark, distended, and covered with melt water. At 5:11 A.M., two completely silent fireballs of incredible brightness rose out of the darkness above Veselo-Vozhnesensk on the other side of the gulf. I pressed the button of my stopwatch. The thin second hand galloped around and counted off twenty-seven seconds before we heard the sound of two explosions. The sound died away, and the fireballs subsided, and then, all along the northern shore, a chain of twinkling sparks extended immediately. After a minute or two, there were flickering flashes of artillery fire, and then the sounds of the cannonade reached us.

The group returned safely to Shabel'sk. Lieutenant Kondrashev had really distinguished himself on this sortie. He and two other men had crawled right up to the barges, took down the sentries, and opened the way for the demolitions men. When they had scrambled up onto the deck of the barge, which was jammed with boxes of mines and artillery rounds, the miners set delayed-action mines and withdrew undetected.

The temperature and the winds were breaking up the ice, carrying it away, and a sunny blue sky appeared above the twisting roads. It was time to return to Rostov! The staff of the *spets* battalion totaled up the results of their operations: sabotage groups had made 110 sorties behind enemy lines; on enemy roads and patrol paths, along communications lines, and in buildings occupied by the enemy, 744 mines had been set; exploding mines had killed over 100 enemy soldiers and officers, put 56 Nazi vehicles and 2 tanks out of action; cut 74 telephone and telegraph poles, and destroyed 2 bridges, 2 barges, and 4 mobile searchlights. The operations of the battalion and the naval infantry had forced the enemy to withdraw about two infantry divisions from the front lines, just to defend the northern shoreline from Mariupol to Taganrog!

After 10 March, the units of the *spets* battalion left Yeysk,

2. SMERSH (from the Russian *shmert' shpionam* = death to spies) was the designation of the NKVD military counterintelligence organization, from whose ranks rose many of the leading postwar KGB officials.

Shabel'sk, and Port-Katon. The villagers came out of their homes and crowded the roadsides, seeing the miners off as if they were seeing off friends and relatives. We had gotten very close to them during a month and a half! The fishermen had left baskets with fresh fish at the kitchens every day, and the women didn't spare the firewood, or manure briquettes used in place of firewood, to ensure that the nearly frozen officers and men got warmed up. They gave the men returning from missions hot fruit punch, milk, and tea that had been brewed until it was black, and they knitted warm mittens and socks for their guests. In return, the soldiers helped the people with their work, as much as they could.

On the road to Rostov, I dropped in at the home of collective farm woman Yevdokia Ivanovna Pustasheva. The Garcia Canel' unit had been quartered in the Pustasheva hut. The reader will surely recall that Canel' had returned from the first sortie with severe frostbite and had to be hospitalized. At the hospital, they first thought they would have to amputate his fingers and toes. When she heard of this, Yevdokia Ivanovna rushed into her pantry, got some earthenware pots, slipped on her sheepskin coat, and despite her advanced years, crossed the ice to Yeysk to the military hospital. On that day Canel' received his first "transfusion": a pot of goose grease to rub on the frostbitten parts of his body, another pot of sour cream, and a package of fried fish. This woman, whose son was fighting on another front, went to Yeysk two to three times a week, bringing presents to the Spaniard, and setting the doctors straight on how to rub goose grease on Canel's frozen skin. And Canel' returned to duty! From that time on Canel' designated Yevdokia as his Russian mother. So I couldn't leave without saying good-bye to her. I also dropped in at the hut of Ivan Savvich Onoprienko, a fifty-year-old fisherman, who had given a young private soldier his only sheepskin coat. I had to shake a lot of hands, saying good-bye, and there were tears in many eyes when the battalion pulled out. But all along the road, the shout went up: "Come back! Come back in the fall, after the victory! Come back for the grapes and the apples! We'll be waiting!" And they ran along behind the company columns, splashing mud, those kids of Yeysk, Shabel'sk, and Port-Katon.

Returning to Rostov, Starinov found that his subordinates had indeed been busy. His beloved shop-lab had succeeded in initiating production on a variety of new types of antitank and antipersonnel mines. Gridnev had developed a new bouncing Betty antipersonnel mine, detonated by command or by mechanical effects. This device used a homemade ammonal charge to launch a 152mm artillery shell about two to three meters into the air, where it would explode, scattering lethal fragments over a radius of sixty to one hundred meters. Starinov was very pleased by the work that had been carried out on the defensive belts around the city by the Eighth Sapper Army, the 28th Defensive Construction Directorate, troops of the Fifty-sixth Army, and his own engineer operations group, assisted by the civilian population of Rostov. Earthworks and antitank ditches had been improved. Thousands of mines had been set in the belts, and although many of the mines had been damaged by water from spring thaws, they were all being tested and replaced if necessary. Ultimately, thirty-seven thousand antitank and twelve thousand antipersonnel mines were checked and reset, additional reserve stocks of forty-five thousand mines were established in areas that were most vulnerable to armor attack, and twenty-five powerful radio-controlled mines were set.

Starinov's return was not without disappointments, however. While involved with operations in the gulf, he had written a proposal for creation of special engineer guards brigades to operate along enemy communications lines and had sent it to the commander of the Fifty-sixth Army, General Tsyganov. Tsyganov had read the proposal and personally agreed with its recommendations, but had doubts about its reception, and advised Starinov to focus his attention on the Fifty-sixth Army minefields. Starinov's partisan schools were being closed, one by one, and although he defended them by arguing that graduates could be used on any front, he was told that his partisans would operate where they were and that they would get help from the Red Army and the Party organizations. While there were many partisan detachments then operating behind German lines, it was clear that the partisans not only suffered from inadequate supplies of radio communications equipment, explosives, mines, and weapons, but that there was, as yet, absolutely no central direction of the partisan activities.

In the absence of a strong partisan effort, Starinov felt that it was necessary to use regular military forces to strike at the overextended German communications lines. Assisted by Captain Kazantsev and his Spanish colleague, Domingo Ungria, he drew up a detailed proposal for the creation of special brigades for operations behind enemy lines, including detailed tables of organization and equipment, and supply requirements. The proposed units were to cut enemy communications lines, destroy equipment and personnel before they arrived at the front, and attract significant numbers of local partisans to sabotage operations. *The trio signed the proposal and sent it off to Ponomarenko in Moscow. General Tsyganov wanted to keep Starinov and his engineer group at Rostov, and Starinov wanted very much to stay, but Tsyganov was countermanded, and Starinov was ordered back to Moscow to his old position at the Main Engineer Directorate.*

After Starinov's return to Moscow, the enormous effort devoted to the defense of Rostov-on-the-Don ultimately failed. German forces crashed through the Soviet defenses and crossed the Don River north of Rostov on 25 June 1942 on the offensive that carried them deep into the Northern Caucasus and to the banks of the Volga—at Stalingrad.

Single-minded Authority

The Li-2[1] began its descent, its engines roaring, jolting its passengers through turbulence. Fields, woods, ravines, suddenly tilted on edge, and a little stream seemed as if it was flowing straight up, but at the last minute the pilot completed his turn, we leveled off, and everything returned to its rightful place. There was a jolt, and we were on the runway.

Moscow didn't greet me in its traditional drab April garb: there was bright sunshine; warm, dry sidewalks, crowded with people; and lines at the stores. Sunbeams played on the walls of houses and on the windshield of the staff car. Women were washing windows! My God! Washing windows?

When I arrived at the People's Commissariat for Defense, I went to my office. First, I called the chief of staff, but he wasn't in. Then, I called the new chief of engineer troops, Gen. Mikhail Petrovich Vorob'yev, whom I had known since 1940. He invited me to drop by. The meeting turned out to be very unpleasant. Vorob'yev remarked that he had the impression that I'd forgotten my duty as assistant chief of staff of engineer troops since I had spent only one month in the office since my assignment there. I protested that my assignment to the engineer operations group was not my doing, but he was concerned that I had gotten involved in

---

1. Li-2 is the Soviet designation for the Soviet version of the famous U.S. workhorse cargo plane, the DC-3/C-47 Goony Bird. The Li-2 was built in the Soviet Union under license from the United States, and differed only slightly from the U.S. originals.

"partisan problems." He told me that there would be no more engineer operations groups; instead, independent engineer brigades were going to be organized, but that they would be used exclusively for defensive barrier operations. I was to participate in working up the tables of manpower and equipment for such brigades.

Vorob'yev criticized my mining techniques at Rostov, and refused to let me explain or defend my actions. I reported to him concerning the notebook with the mysterious formulae and diagrams which Petty Officer Repin had taken from the dead German officer at Krivoi Spit, and showed him the book. He dismissed it with a shrug:

"No more time now for mysteries and secrets. Send the notebook to the staff of the scientific representative to the State Defense Committee and let them decipher it. Now, you take a rest, and then get busy with your actual responsibilities. I don't dare to be late with the personnel and equipment tables!"

When I got back to the office, I put my other documents in the safe, but left the notebook out on my desk. I called Stepan Afanas'yevich Balezin, the scientific representative of the State Defense Committee. I had known Balezin since the beginning of the war when I had been sent to him by Sergey Vasil'yevich Kaftanov who chaired the committee on higher education. My miners had needed calculations for preparing shape charges and recipes for homemade *plastique* explosives. Balezin gave us what we needed. I called Balezin and brought him the book within a half hour. He promised to send it off for expert examination immediately.

I didn't follow Vorob'yev's suggestion to take a rest, and after my visit to Balezin, I didn't go home either, but went to one of the side streets near the Sokol metro station, where the Western Front Operational Training Center (OUTs) was located. I got a warm reception from my old friend Kuteynikov. I had every reason to rush over to the OUTs. I was very concerned about the future of the center. During its existence it had trained and inserted behind enemy lines almost four thousand partisans, and more than twenty-two thousand mines of different types and twenty-five thousand special grenades had been manufactured in the center's lab. The schools that had been created by the center had accomplished even more! But now, in spring of 1942, according to a letter I'd received from Kuteynikov, a dead calm reigned there. The equipment that the center needed the most wasn't released: all attempts to get radios appeared to be unsuccessful! To insert partisans and saboteurs into the deep enemy rear without a hope of providing them with the necessary direction, of receiving required intelligence, or of dropping explosives and weapons at designated drop zones was simply nonsense. The year 1941 was thankfully past, and we now had to operate in the enemy rear according to a rational plan, fully armed with all necessary skills and equipment. Kuteynikov told me that he had heard that the school would soon be disbanded. Many students had passed the course and had never even been sent out on missions! They were still hanging around in winter uniforms and boots because no one would issue them summer gear. I tried to calm Kuteynikov's concerns but when I returned to my empty quarters nearby, I was alarmed and uneasy.

As far back as the thirties, I had suggested to the people's defense commissar that special units be created and had even worked out manpower tables for them. After the war started, I had often returned to the idea of such special units. Because I hadn't heard a peep from Ponomarenko, I thought that now we might be able to quickly and easily form special units from the trainees of the OUTs and other partisan schools and from Spanish volunteers. And such trained and experienced troops would certainly receive all necessary support!

I dug out my photo albums from Spain and returned the next day to General Vorob'yev, who really dampened my enthusiasm. He stated that he personally had no objections to mining operations in the enemy rear, but that the Independent Motorized Special Rifle Brigade (OMSBON) had been given the task of demolitions in the enemy rear, and that he, as chief of engineer troops, could not recommend to the leadership the creation of engineer units for the same purposes. The general ordered me down from the clouds again and told me to get moving on the manpower and equipment tables for the special engineer brigades! I came down to earth and worked conscientiously with my colleagues on the manning tables, but I never stopped thinking of creating *spets* units: you see, no one had ever worked up a table of equipment necessary for engineer brigade operations behind enemy lines.

Then it dawned on me that the present deputy people's commissar for defense was the chief of artillery of the Red Army, Col. Gen. Nikolai Nikolayevich Voronov, my old senior adviser from Spain. He had given very flattering testimony about the work that my demolitions men had done in the enemy rear area. Maybe he still retained his former high regard for the miners.

I got an appointment with Voronov, asked him for his advice, repeated the substance of my conversations with Vorob'yev, and showed him my Spanish album. Voronov remarked that this was not an artillery problem, but suggested that I go to see the chief of airborne troops, Maj. Gen. Vasiliy Afanas'yevich Glazunov, and personally arranged an appointment for me with Glazunov on the spot. When I went to see Glazunov, he was not alone: Major General Spirin, chief of staff of airborne troops, was also there. The generals pointed out that their mission was to conduct surprise attacks to seize objectives or positions not far behind enemy lines and to hold them until the main forces arrived. Sabotage work behind the lines, particularly deep in the enemy rear, was definitely not their mission. Further, they were quite firm that they had no competence to discuss the creation of special units or brigades for such missions. Then Glazunov surprised me: he asked if we could help train his troops! I couldn't refuse, and I certainly did send a group of mine warfare instructors to the airborne troops, but would that really solve the problem?

I was very much involved in figuring out how to develop equipment that reflected the latest technology and would stand up to the rigors of prolonged operation in the enemy rear. I was so involved that I didn't accord much significance to the call from Balezin when he thanked me for the Taganrog notebook. In the interim, however, that call from Balezin has assumed great significance. I should have been most grateful to him for it, and I would have expressed my gratitude to him if only Stepan Afanas'yevich would have explained to me that what I'd thought to be chemical formulas in the notebook were, in fact, *diagrams of uranium processing*. But Balezin never uttered a word to me about that. Balezin and Kaftanov theorized that the German officer killed at Krivoi Spit had been sent to search for uranium. According to excerpts from Kaftanov's memoirs, published only in 1985 in the Soviet journal *Chemistry and Life*, the notebook—and conclusions about the disappearance of publications on atomic energy from the Western press—led Kaftanov and A. F. Ioffe, members of the Academy of Science, to write to the State Defense Committee, recommending establishment of a center for research on atomic weapons.[2] At the time, however, I wasn't even thinking of atomic energy: I was completely swallowed up by ideas about special units. Unfortunately, I had no time for anything more important in those days since I was ordered to the Kalinin Front to work on barrier operations in that area.

2. According to recently declassified information from KGB files, Soviet intelligence had learned of the atomic bomb project as early as September 1941 from Donald MacLean, member of the "Cambridge Five" spy ring, and the information was confirmed between September 1941 and July 1942, by "Perseus," an unidentified U.S. physicist working on the Manhattan Project. This individual, said to be still alive and living in New York, passed his information to the USSR through Morris Cohen (alias Peter Kroger), an American Communist sympathizer and Soviet agent who was later arrested and convicted of espionage in England.

A Company Isn't the Right Unit

Under the warm May sun, the roadside fields were sprouting, the surviving woods were ablaze with green fire, and the groves burned out by the war stood like widows, dressed in black.

The engineer staff of the Kalinin Front was located in one of the villages west of the town. We reached the village over country roads, which were drying out in the heat.

The chief of Front engineer troops, Col. V. V. Kosarev, was a powerfully built fellow, deliberate in both speech and movements. He immediately introduced Chepak, Il'yushenkov, Romanyuk, and me to the engineer troops political officer, Regimental Commissar A. K. Popov. Then he briefed us on the barriers that already had been erected, the work that was going on, and the needs of the Front. We agreed that our group would visit the armies and inspect the defensive lines, and that we would then come to joint decisions on the strengthening of the barriers, most importantly mine and explosives barriers.

The tour of the defensive lines took two days. When we returned to the Front staff, I dropped in at the village of Sheino, where the northwest operational group of the Central Committee of the Communist Party of Belorussia was located. The northwestern group leaders advised me that the partisans didn't have enough mines and explosives. I promised to talk about their needs with the commander of the Kalinin Front. When I had discussed the questions of construction and strengthening of mine and explosive barriers with Kosarev and his assistants, I also passed on the requests of the northwestern Party group, and raised the possibility of using the Front engineer troops for interrupting communications in the enemy rear. I described the work of the *spets* battalion on the northern shore of the Taganrog Gulf, and got Kosarev's agreement to support me in making a direct request to the Front commander. I seized the opportunity:

"Okay, so what are we waiting for? Let's go and see the Front commander right now!"

Kosarev smiled and shook his head, but he didn't refuse, and within half an hour, we were in the office of the Front com-

ander, Lt. Gen. Ivan Stepanovich Konev.[1] In 1942, Konev was
orty-five years old. He was of medium height, a powerfully built,
tout fellow with a weather-beaten, sunburned face and a strong
eck, which was tightly constrained by his tunic collar. He had a
haved head and a high forehead with three vertical folds, a big
ose, and bright, inquisitive, and very attentive eyes. He was calm
nd seemed to be very self-confident. He listened to our presen-
ation and asked for Kosarev's opinion. Kosarev cautiously sug-
ested that a company be detached for demolitions in the enemy
ear, but Konev differed sharply: "For this kind of work, a com-
any isn't the right unit, Comrade Colonel! We'll use a whole bat-
alion! And even a battalion may not be enough to have an
ffect." He rapped a carefully sharpened pencil on the desk. "If
e want our attacks on the enemy lines of communication to have
significant effect, the Front needs not less than a brigade. A spe-
ial brigade, and preferably airborne!"

He then had his duty officer place a call to Moscow, to the
hief of the general staff, Vasilevskiy. This thing was getting off
) a flying start!

Konev told me that he would discuss the need for special en-
ineering brigades with Vasilevskiy and ordered me to follow up
ith Vasilevskiy upon my return to the capital. I left the Front
eadquarters feeling like a kid who has just gotten a long-awaited
resent. When I returned to Moscow, I requested a meeting with
Vasilevskiy at the first opportunity and found that he had changed
is mind. Vasilevskiy said that special units would not be orga-
ized for operations behind enemy lines. Special engineer bri-
ades were to be organized for defensive barrier operations,
owever, and battalions of those brigades could be used for oper-
tions behind enemy lines. And to my great surprise, he offered
he command of the special engineer brigade on the Kalinin
ront! I didn't like the idea of the defensive barrier operations
nission, but I knew that commanding the brigade would give lots
f opportunity for operations in the enemy rear, and so I accepted
he assignment to command the Kalinin Front's independent spe-
ial engineer brigade. In my presence, Vasilevskiy called my boss,
Vorob'yev, and got his approval. While the discussion was going
n in Vasilevskiy's office, the recently appointed chief of the op-
rations directorate of the general staff, Lt. Gen. Pavel Ivanovich
Bodin, walked in. When he found out the subject of our discus-
ion, he asked me to work up an operations plan for strikes at the
nemy rear as soon as possible.

In approaching Konev, Starinov was "singing to the choir": Konev had trained special operations units
a Spain, and must certainly have heard of Starinov, if he did not know him personally.

When I got back to my office at the engineer directorate, General Vorob'yev shook his head. "Well, you got your own way, didn't you! You helped work out the tables for the brigade, so I guess that means that you're completely satisfied with them."

I pointed out that the tables had been developed without considering the fact that the brigade mission was also to include operations behind enemy lines. He said that I'd get a chance to fix that problem; and ordered me to write a draft letter to the Front Military Council concerning the potential of engineer assets for operations in the enemy rear area. In the draft, I spoke about the necessity of including the operations of engineer units behind enemy lines in the range of operational measures at the disposal of the Front and armies. For these purposes, I said, each Front should select and train an engineer battalion, and each army should select and train a sapper company.

Suddenly, Vorob'yev inquired as to just what I was still doing in Moscow. I looked at him, confused. Vorob'yev, pleased that he had caught me off guard, smiled. "The order has been signed designating you as brigade commander! So get over to Konev and get busy! Good luck!"

In the Brigade

Before my departure from Moscow, I dropped off my plan for operations in the enemy rear on the Western and Kalinin fronts, and took the opportunity to draw the attention of General Bodin to the fact that the tables of organization and equipment that had been drawn up for the unit were not based in assumptions of operations in the enemy rear. General Bodin thought it over and decided to use three battalions from the 5th Engineer Brigade, and the 110th Independent Motorized Engineer Battalion, for operations behind enemy lines.

General Vorob'yev gave a lot of attention to the brigade: he sent me a very experienced military engineer, Military Engineer 2d Class E. I. Pal'chik, as my technical deputy, and allowed me to pick volunteers from the Nakhabin school for operations behind enemy lines. He didn't even object to my plan to recruit young officers who had gotten combat experience at Kharkov and Rostov, as well as all the instructors and Spaniards who had worked with me.

At the staff of the Kalinin Front, good news awaited me: the group that I had left, consisting of Captains Chepak, Romanyuk, and Il'yushenkov, had been able to train the troops of the 110th Independent Motorized Engineer Battalion. They had dispatched the first units of well-trained saboteurs behind enemy lines in the sector opposite our Third Shock Army, and had sent several groups of instructors to partisan detachments and brigades, along with a large quantity of explosives. In addition, our comrades had organized partisan schools at the northwest operations group of the Belorussian Party, and at the staff of the Kalinin Front.

The first mines that blew up on the enemy lines of communication were those set by the groups led by Romanyuk, K. S. Sokolov, G. A. Kriyulin, and the familiar Spaniards: Canel', Francisco Gaspara, and Mariano Chico. Chepak's group was sent off separately, to operate on the important Smolensk-Vyazma highway.

It was gratifying to know that officers who had been trained during wartime could operate successfully and reliably in the enemy rear without supervision, but there was also bad news. It appeared that there weren't enough good mines at the Front. Further, the construction units from which we intended to form the brigade were understrength, and we could not count on replacements from Front reserves. In addition, in view of an anticipated worsening of the military situation, all Front engineer units, without exception, were to be used in defensive mining, and this included the 110th Independent Motorized Engineer Battalion!

My brigade political officer, Aleksey Ivanovich Bolotin, was a great help to me in those difficult days. Bolotin had formerly been senior lecturer in the fundamentals of Marxism-Leninism at Moscow State University and had fought at the battles of Moscow and Kalinin. With his assistance, we quickly started production of mines and to make arrangements with the Kalinin Regional Committees of the Party and Komsomol for sending to the brigade 250 young men and women who had expressed their desire to fight behind enemy lines. It was also possible to prove to the Front engineer staff that we would still have to send one or two battalions of miners behind enemy lines if we were to fulfill the plan that had been presented to the General Staff Operations Directorate.

German forces, tied down in the long pocket between Rzhev, Zubtsov, Sychevka, Gzhatsk, and Vyazma, could receive reinforcements and supplies only along the main rail line between Smolensk and Vyazma and the highway that ran parallel to it: the enemy didn't have a developed network of railroads and highways in that area. The transportation routes that the enemy did possess, he used without any particular precautions, and the destruction of rolling stock, personnel, and equipment moving to the front along these lines could have a significant impact on the enemy capability. We might have convinced the Front engineer chief, but we still had to convince the Military Council. The chief of staff of the Front engineer troops, Colonel Timofeyev, Bolotin, and I went to see Konev and the Front political officer, Corps Commissar D. S. Leonov. Konev had given us about five hundred submachine guns, but couldn't spare any radios: radios weren't even available for units that were required to have them according to approved tables of equipment. Nonetheless, Konev told us to commence operations, first with a battalion, and then, when we had gotten some experience and when additional equipment was available, he'd assign a second battalion to us. He gave his permission with one condition, however: the Front defensive barrier plans had to be completed! I assured him that the plan would be completed on schedule.

Leonov, the Front political officer, was interested in discussing the recruitment of brigade personnel and problems of supply. We also talked about the part that the Spanish volunteers would play in the brigade. The Military Council had already given permission to recruit the Spaniards for the brigade and to use them on sorties behind enemy lines. I was trying to promote the Spaniards who were already in the brigade to the ranks which they had formerly held in the Republican Army. I'd already sent some of the best Spanish volunteers in the brigade to partisan detachments, but I knew hundreds of other Spaniards in the USSR had also asked to enlist, and I wanted to recruit them as well.

Konev gave his permission to enlist all the Spaniards I could find, by any means, and he also gave me approval to promote the Spaniards in the brigade to their former ranks. These decisions raised the morale of the brigade, and the Spaniards were particularly happy. I remember carefully pinning a captain's red rectangles on the lapels of Francisco Guillon's tunic, and how the other Spaniards smiled with joy and some embarrassment the first time that they appeared before us in the uniforms of Red Army officers.

We had accelerated training of brigade personnel in methods of warfare in the enemy rear, but unfortunately, we could only send small groups of miners. Not a single battalion, either from our brigade or the 110th, could yet begin operation behind enemy lines. The Front staff steadfastly demanded that we give first priority to mining their defensive lines. This requirement was dictated by the steadily declining military situation. It became obvious that it would be impossible to develop any kind of powerful strikes on enemy communications lines if we were to rely on the personnel and equipment allocated to the typical Front engineer brigades. These brigades simply had too many things to do. For this reason, on 1 July 1942, Bolotin and I wrote a report to the operations directorate of the general staff, informing them that the plan for cutting the enemy's lines of communication on the Kalinin and Western fronts had failed and that the airborne brigade, which Front commander Konev had requested from the people's commissar for defense, had not been assigned.

A few lines of this report are included below:

About two to three months still remain that are quite favorable for massive destruction of enemy trains and vehicles. This will certainly tie down the enemy in a number of sectors of the front and hamper his operational and logistics mobility. For the present, we only need one airborne brigade. Later, we can form another brigade from the 110th Independent Motorized Engineer Brigade and two battalions of the 5th Engineer Brigade.

We sent off the report and had to await the response. In the meantime, there was plenty to do: defensive mining operations, taking care of our people, traveling all along the front, and even visiting the Northwest Front. On these travels, I never missed any opportunities to proselytize for operations in the enemy rear. On my trip to the Northwest Front, for example, I met Lt. Gen. P. A. Kurochkin, whom I had known since the beginning of the war when he commanded the Twentieth Army. Kurochkin recognized me and expressed an interest in the operations that my demolitions men carried out in the enemy rear. As a result, a school for demolitions men was created at Valday in the Northwest Front area. At Kurochkin's request, we sent several instructors there, and they performed quite well. On another occasion, I met the commander of the 6th Railroad Brigade, Col. D. A. Teryukhov. In 1924, we had graduated from the same railroad school together. I asked him if he couldn't loan me just one company from his brigade for operations behind enemy lines. After a little discussion, he agreed to detach a company for me, as long as no one else knew about it. As he pointed out, these were experienced men and needed little training: they knew what to do, and how and when to do it. We sent three instructors, under the command of Il'yushenkov, to the 6th Railroad Brigade. When they arrived, Teryukhov put together a student company of about one hundred volunteer enlisted men and young officers under the command of Capt. P. I. Okolo-Kulak. These men learned very rapidly, and by the end of July, some detachments from the company had successfully completed their first trips behind enemy lines under the supervision of their instructors. Then, the company began to operate independent of the instructors. Later, when Teryukhov's superiors had learned about the successful operations of Captain Okolo-Kulak's troops, they detached the company from the 6th Railroad Brigade, to Teryukhov's great disappointment and chagrin. It was only after the war that we found out that the captain's outstanding unit had conducted prolonged successful operations in the German rear without sustaining any losses.

Moscow Meetings

In the afternoon of 2 July, I returned to the Front staff from a trip to the First Shock Army. The first person I saw was Colonel Timofeyev, and he was most concerned. It seemed that the Thirty-ninth Army under Lt. Gen. Ivan Ivanovich Maslennikov, had been threatening the German-held railroad lines between Smolensk and Vyazma from the north, and the highways between Vyazma and Rzhev from the east.[1] The Thirty-ninth had penetrated deep into German defenses and seized an area of more than four thousand square kilometers. The corridor connecting the Thirty-ninth with the rest of our forces was quite narrow and remained the most vulnerable area of our front, causing a great deal of concern for the army command and the Military Council. It would be only natural for the enemy to attack this salient, to cut off the Thirty-ninth and surround it, and that was exactly what was happening. On the same day, he had given orders to gather the forces of the 5th Brigade to lay more mines along our defensive lines. In view of its strength, the attack on Maslennikov's army might be the beginning of a new *Wehrmacht* drive on Moscow.

Unfortunately, the Kalinin Front didn't have the forces required to reopen the corridor to Maslennikov's army, which had been cut by the Germans. The army commander himself had been wounded and evacuated early in the battle, and his absence just aggravated the already serious situation for the surrounded units and formations. They nevertheless valiantly fought their way out

1. The Thirty-ninth was one of two NKVD Special Purpose Armies operating under direct control of Beria. In addition to conducting combat operations against the Germans, these formations also were often deployed behind regular Soviet frontline units to prevent their retreat, and were frequently employed behind Soviet lines, during and after the war, to liquidate unreliable civilian populations and anti-Soviet partisans.

of the encirclement and returned to their own lines. None of the encircled army corps or division commanders ever gave a thought to going over to partisan operations in the enemy rear. Captain Chepak was commanding a group of miners attached to one of the corps: the corps commander even denied Chepak's request to remain behind to fight in the enemy rear, and ordered Chepak to break out with his men. During the course of the breakout, Chepak's men took unnecessary and unjustifiable casualties. Kosarev had to request the Front commander to order formation commanders that in the future, saboteurs would not be used as infantry, no matter how critical the situation.

In those tense, sultry days, while we were hastily mining the front lines, we learned about the creation of the Central Staff of the Partisan Movement and Front-level partisan-movement staffs. In spite of the numerous earlier requests made by regional and republic Party officials to the Central Committee and to Stalin himself, it was only on 30 May 1942 that the State Defense Committee had finally gotten around to establishing the Central Staff of the Partisan Movement and designating P. K. Ponomarenko as the chief of the staff. At the same time, staffs of the partisan movement were created on the Ukrainian, Bryansk, Western, Kalinin, Leningrad, and Karelian fronts and subordinated to the Central Staff. Later, additional subordinate staffs were created on the Southern or Krasnodar Front (3 August 1942), on the Belorussian Front (9 September 1942), in Estonia (4 November 1942), Lithuania (26 November 1942), Latvia (8 January 1943), in the Crimea (July 1943), and on the Voronezh Front (October 1942). In the Stavropol district the district party committee created a partisan staff on 30 December 1942. In the spring, the Central Staff was led by a collegium composed of the chiefs of the staff sections and two additional members: representatives from the NKVD and the GRU. The command party of the Central Staff also included Party, government and Komsomol workers, officers of the Red Army and NKVD border troops, and state security and intelligence officers. Many of these had experience in partisan operations in the first year of the war, but only two had experience in Spain. By decision of the State Defense Committee, chiefs of the various Front and republic partisan movement staffs and representatives of the Central Staff were approved as members of the Military Councils of the Leningrad, Northwestern, Kalinin, Western, Bryansk, Voronezh, Stalingrad, Northern Caucasus, Southwestern, and other fronts. Partisan staff operations groups were also created in the Military Councils at army level. The full range of possibilities of centralized command were never realized, however, because there was no designated commander in chief of partisan forces and because many special units playing major roles in the partisan struggle were not subordinated to the Central Staff. These included reconnaissance and sabotage units of the NKVD, the OMSBON,[2] the GRU, and the Party.

Around this time, the first really thorough training of partisan officers and specialists took place in the so-called Special Belorussian Muster, in the city of Murom in the Gorki region. Between April and October 1942, training was conducted for more than twenty-six hundred Belorussian military personnel from reserve units of the Moscow, Urals, and Volga Military Districts.

Fourteen partisan detachments and ninety-two organizing groups were formed from these well-trained cadres of officers and specialists and inserted into the enemy rear.[3]

At about this same time, the order came to hide small stores of mines and demolitions material near the front lines in those areas where the Germans were most likely to attack. It was assumed that in the event of our withdrawal, this material would be used by partisans. In order to give an idea of the scale of this activity, I will note that just the 166th Engineer Barrier Battalion alone constructed forty-six of these caches. At the Front staff, we also helped the partisan movement staff of the Kalinin Front, giving them explosives and mines.

In the first part of June, seventy-three groups of miners were sent behind enemy lines. When they had completed their missions, they returned to the brigade, sustaining hardly any losses at all. The successful operations of these independent groups, which were so poorly equipped from a technical viewpoint, was convincing! If we were to send regular units of special troops behind enemy lines, troops able to carry out massive, centrally controlled operations along enemy communications lines, the results might be far beyond those that we had already achieved. With their capabilities, such special troops, operating together with partisans, might be able to completely cut off the supply of replacements, equipment, ammunition, and fuel to the enemy armies. It was possible that the Germans would not have even been able to launch their attack on Maslennikov.

Bolotin and I talked a lot about this and came to the conclusion that it was time to write to Stalin again! No one else except the

2. A "special-purpose" NKVD brigade consisting of two regiments led by NKVD officers, OMSBON was employed on a wide variety of missions behind German lines including diversion, intelligence collection, and assassination.

3. The scale and thoroughness of this training program, conducted by the Belorussian Party, may have helped considerably to ensure Ponomarenko's appointment as chief of the Central Partisan Staff.

people's commissar for defense and the chairman of the State Defense Committee could make the decision to create special forces to strike the enemy rear areas. I cleared the letter through Colonel Kosarev, Commissar Popov, and Colonel Timofeyev. Kosarev warned me not to send the letter off without the approval of Konev, the Front commander. Konev was under extreme pressure at the time: he was preparing the Rzhev-Sychevka offensive operation, which was to be undertaken simultaneously by the troops of the left wing of the Kalinin Front and the right wing of the Western Front. They were to destroy the main forces of the German Ninth Army and liquidate the Rzhev salient.

Although Konev was carrying an enormous responsibility, he still found time to familiarize himself with my draft letter to Stalin. He said that he agreed with the basic propositions, and he shared our views concerning the creation of special units for destroying enemy lines of communication. He sent the letter off to Stalin, and then unexpectedly said to me: "And you follow the letter! Let the staff of the Red Army engineer troops get involved in this business!"

Bearing a copy of the letter to Stalin, we arrived at the office of the chief of staff of engineer troops, Gen. K. S. Nazarov. General Vorob'yev was off somewhere, on the Bryansk Front, if memory serves me correctly. Nazarov advised us to try to line up expert support for our position while we awaited the call from the Kremlin. He suggested going to the commander of airborne troops, General Glazunov, which we did, only to be met with disappointment. He agreed that airborne troops were the best qualified to carry out sabotage missions in the enemy rear, but unfortunately, all of the airborne units were fighting as regular "straight-leg" infantry on the Southern Front, including the troops who had been trained by our instructors. We left his office in a state of confusion: if airborne units were being employed as regular infantry, then the situation was really very serious and consideration of our letter could not be postponed: the only thing that would help Soviet forces now was an attack on enemy communications lines!

We traced the letter through the correspondence control section of the Central Committee to Voroshilov's office. I called several times for an appointment, but was fended off by various assistants. Bolotin and I were getting worried: my brigade was without both its commanding officer and its commissar; increasingly bitter battles were unfolding at the front; and here we sat, condemned to inactivity! I kept calling until Voroshilov himself picked up the phone. I asked him to give us an appointment, and he did!

We arrived at the Kremlin, reassured and excited. Voroshilov was not alone: sitting by the high window of the office, a bit slumped over in his chair, as if looking at his beard, was Mikhail Ivanovich Kalinin. The presence of Kalinin, the most senior member of the Party, member of the Politburo of the Central Committee, president of the Presidium of the Supreme Soviet of the USSR, could only mean one thing: he was involved! This was encouraging, but it also meant that we were committed to doing a lot!

Voroshilov and Kalinin accepted my recommendations for creating special units, particularly since, as Kalinin said, the appearance of regular Red Army units in the enemy rear would raise the morale of the civilian population. After an hour's discussion, they called the Central Committee and made an appointment for me with G. M. Malenkov, secretary of the Central Committee and a member of the State Defense Committee.[4] Forty minutes later, we were in Malenkov's office. He read through our letter, declared his agreement, and told us to return the next day with the chief of engineer troops, and to bring a draft decision on the creation of special brigades for operations on enemy communications lines. We returned with Nazarov since Vorob'yev was still absent.

Malenkov called General Vasilevskiy, chief of the general staff, simply informed him that some representatives of the engineer troops would be coming to see him, and ordered him to compose a directive for the signature of the people's commissar for defense, i.e., Stalin, to create special brigades to operate along enemy communications lines. Vasilevskiy said something inaudible. Malenkov told him that the decision had been made, and hung up.

"Off you go to the general staff, comrades! Good luck!"

Within the hour, Gen. Vasilevskiy received us. He received us all right, but he was very cold. Maybe it was an inopportune time for us to arrive, maybe the chief of the general staff was tired, or out of sorts: in any case, in the summer of 1942, there were plenty of reasons for our military leaders to be emotional! The meeting was brief and strictly official. When Vasilevskiy looked at the draft decision, he commented drily: "Tell Lieutenant General Konev that the general staff is preparing an order concerning the creation of special engineer troops. You may go."

The cold reception at the hands of the chief of the general staff could not chill our happiness.

* * *

4. Malenkov, a close associate of Stalin, was an extremely powerful and dangerous man who had played a key role in the Yezhov purges. He became a secretary of the Central Committee in 1939, and was a member of the State Defense Committee during World War II. Immediately after Stalin's death, Malenkov became chairman of the Council of Ministers and was the central figure of the "collective leadership" that succeeded Stalin. Forced to resign in 1955, he died in obscurity in Siberia.

Before returning to the Kalinin Front, Bolotin and I wanted to get one more problem resolved: the problem of enlisting in our brigade the former Spanish Republican Army veterans and other Spanish comrades. The majority of those people were members of the Communist party of Spain, and therefore, any questions about their participation in military operations had to be settled with the leadership of their party. The Spanish Communist party was not in Moscow at that time, however, so Bolotin and I had to turn to the Spanish section of the Comintern. There, we were received very politely, but we were told that the question of Spanish enlistments would ultimately have to be settled by the general secretary of the executive committee of the Comintern, Comrade Georgiy Mikhaylovich Dimitrov.[5] We were a bit concerned: was it proper to trouble such a highly placed leader of the international workers and Communists movement with such a simple question? They assured us it was not at all improper, and within twenty-five minutes we were entering Dimitrov's office. As we opened the massive door, a tall, athletic man with a great shock of silver hair and a moustache as black as tar came out from behind his desk to meet us. In 1942, Dimitrov was sixty-nine years old; sixty-nine years of a difficult life, filled with struggle. His sojourns in prisons had left their marks on his masculine face, the features of which seemed to be harsh and stern. Only his large dark eyes looked encouraging.

I informed him of the purpose of our visit, and we began a conversation that lasted about two hours. Dimitrov was not only interested in the question of enlisting the Spaniards in my brigade, but he asked me about my own experience in partisan warfare and inquired as to whether my experiences might be of use in resistance movements in Europe, with the French *maquis*, for example. I responded that our experience certainly couldn't hurt them, and I got into specific aspects of that experience that might be useful. Dimitrov asked many questions, about all sorts of things, e.g., methods of crossing enemy lines, moving around in occupied territory, and mining enemy communications lines. When we left, Dimitrov shook hands with us warmly, and thanked me for the information. Soon thereafter, the brigade got reinforcements: one hundred Spanish comrades! They quickly got started training for operations in the enemy rear.

5. Dimitrov was also head of the Bulgarian Communist party, and later became first Communist chief of state of Bulgaria.

A Sharp Turn

The results of our trip to Moscow satisfied Colonel General Konev, and the Front engineer staff congratulated us on our success. The officers and men of the 5th Engineer Brigade, confident that they would be the first to be included in the special brigade, carried on like kids at a birthday party. Bolotin and I also believed that in the near future the 5th Engineer Brigade would receive a new status, and with that new status would come new tables of organization, new weapons, and most important, the necessary radio gear!

In the meantime, everything was going on as before: the majority of the units were involved with mining the front lines, and only a few groups were sent behind enemy lines. When the Sovinformburo reported on 23 July that a unit commanded by Comrade Starinov had derailed ten enemy trains, we evaluated this not only as giving due recognition to the miners but as an indication that the creation of special troop units was near at hand!

I certainly don't want to give the reader the impression that somehow questions of interfering with the functioning of enemy communications lines, questions of demolitions operations in the enemy rear, and of creating specially trained units to perform these tasks, only arose on the Kalinin Front with me and my friends. The reader will certainly recall the names of General Nevskiy and Military Engineer 2d Class Yastrebov, organizers and participants in the massive Kharkov mining operation. In the summer of 1942, they were on the Karelian Front. In answer to my letter, Yastrebov reported that on the Karelian Front in an independent special engineer brigade of which he was deputy commander, they had begun training hundreds of miners for operations behind enemy lines. Only after the war, did I learn that in 1942 on the Western and Southern fronts, miners from several engineer brigades, miners from army sapper and engineer battalions, and miners from engineer battalions of infantry divisions frequently went into the enemy rear to blow up communications lines and highway facilities, to kill enemy troops, and to destroy their equipment. I must suppose that their combat activities spoke for themselves, but Nevskiy, Yastrebov, and other commanders of engineer troops, also turned to the high command with proposals to intensify the strikes on enemy communications lines. In a word, the idea of creating special troops for destroying enemy personnel and equipment in the enemy rear, before they could even reach the front, was certainly in the air. On the southern wing of the Soviet-German front, the Red Army was being forced to withdraw to Stalingrad, Rostov, and the Caucasus foothills after 17 July, in a series of bloody battles and counterattacks. The desperate nature of our situation only confirmed my belief that any further delay in striking the overextended enemy communications lines was absolutely impermissible.

Then, unexpectedly, I was recalled to Moscow, to the deputy people's commissar for defense and chief of the Main Directorate for Unit Activation, Col. Gen. E. I. Shchadenko.[1] I thought this would be about our special units, and so I took Bolotin along with me: we started this thing together, and we'd see it through to the end! When I checked in at the Engineer Directorate, no one, including both General Nazarov and General Vorob'yev, knew why I had been called. It was late at night, and since I considered it inappropriate to go to the deputy commissar at that hour, I hurried to see him in the morning.

Army Commissar 1st Rank Shchadenko was a man of medium height, thickset, and already a bit past his prime, with a puffy face. He listened to my presentation, motioned me to a chair, and asked if I knew why I had been summoned. I said that I had no idea, and then he broke the news: "The People's Commissariat is sending you to a new position: a position on the Central Staff of the Partisan Movement, Comrade Colonel."

Noticing my confusion, Shchadenko tried to encourage me:

"This is a demanding and important assignment. Today, you will receive signed orders and report to Comrade Ponomarenko."

He smiled, and I thought I understood what was happening.

"Understood, Comrade Army Commissar 1st Rank! Special troops will be raised by the Central Staff of the Partisan Movement!"

Shchadenko's broad brows contracted into a triangle. "What kind of special troops?"

"You know, for mining and blowing up enemy communications lines!"

We looked at each other; I was radiating smiles, and

1. Shchadenko was a veteran of the civil war, in which he fought with Yoroshilov and Budenny in the First Cavalry Army against Denikin. Like Malenkov, he was another sinister member of Stalin's inner circle. Professor Conquest considers that Shchadenko and Mekhlis were largely responsible for the purges in the army.

Shchadenko was chewing his lip and looking as if he had just noticed my presence. Finally, he shrugged: "I don't understand.
Ponomarenko isn't raising any kind of special troops now, and
he's not going to in the future, either. You have been misinformed,
Comrade Colonel. There's enough work on the Central Staff without even thinking about such things. You'll see!"

Shchadenko indicated that our interview was over, pushed aside
his notebook, and called in an assistant. I stood up, not asking his
permission to leave. I just couldn't find the right words: the special units that we had so diligently worked for were just about to
be created, our brigade had been reorganized, and now they were
going to remove me from the picture?

"Comrade Army Commissar 1st Rank! The brigade which I
command has just been reorganized and is just now beginning to
operate in the enemy rear. . . ." I heard my own fading voice.

Shchadenko raised his head. In his tired eyes, from which the
thin disguise of cordiality was fast fading, I could read perplexity.
"Well, dammit, let them run operations! You've got other work
now—what's so difficult to understand about that?"

I told him that I wouldn't give up the brigade, and asked if he
would let me stay in my present assignment. You could contradict
people who were senior in position and rank only if you were in
great distress, and I was desperate!

Shchadenko asked what I meant by the words: "remain" and
"not give up." I tried to explain, but he told me that people
worked where they were assigned, not where they wanted to be;
that the decision on my transfer had already been made; and that
there was no use in discussing it further. He called his assistant to
prepare my orders. When the assistant left to get them,
Shchadenko shook his head: "Give him an important Party assignment, and he's talking about staying where he is!" Shchadenko
said to himself. Then he turned to me: "You'd better think over
the matter of the Spanish comrades, too. There are other needs to
be met—you're way off the target on that score."

A half hour later, I descended to the vestibule, where Bolotin
was waiting. He guessed what had happened: I had no explanation
for him. That day, Bolotin and I took a long time saying good-
bye, but we never lost touch. We corresponded, sharing whatever
thoughts and news that we could entrust to the field postal service,
and conferring on the most diverse subjects, but the joys of joint
effort and daily association vanished. What more could you do?
Our paths didn't cross again until the end of the war.

I didn't return to the 5th Engineer Brigade, but I really can't leave the reader perplexed as to what events unfolded after my departure.

I will begin by saying that the idea of creating special units for hampering the operations of the enemy rear area services was only partially realized: on 17 August 1942, independent guards miners battalions were created in the Red Army, at Front level, by order of the people's commissar for defense. An independent guards miners brigade was also created, under control of the Stavka of the high command, "for the purposes of mining and blowing up communications in the enemy rear." This wouldn't solve any problems at all since there was still no unified command authority to ensure coordination of all the diverse Party, NKVD, and GRU assets at our disposal.

On the Kalinin Front, the 10th Independent Guards Miners Battalion was formed. The majority of officers and men of my 5th Brigade wound up in the guards battalions, but the 160th and 166th Battalions of the 5th continued to operate in the enemy rear. They were especially active during the period from April to August of 1943 when A. A. Vinskiy had been designated chief of staff of engineer troops on that front. This was the same Vinskiy with whom our engineer operations group evacuated Kharkov in the fall of 1941. At the end of May 1943, the Front commander visited the 160th Battalion, and drew the attention of the brigade command to the need for focusing all their resources on strikes in the enemy rear, and requested that they develop clear operations plans in coordination with the operations of the 10th Independent Guards Battalion. Colonel Vinskiy made arrangements with the command of the airborne army that had been assigned to the Front, organized parachute training for the miners, and in July 1943, companies of miners were inserted by parachute in the enemy rear opposite the Kalinin Front. The officers and enlisted men who had been trained in the 5th Brigade fought honorably, tenaciously, and successfully behind enemy lines, and seven of them were awarded the title of Hero of the Soviet Union.

And how about the young Lieutenants Goncharov and Andrianov, whom I had brought over from the Nakhabin school? Their combat records were brilliant. The group commanded by Goncharov made frequent jumps behind enemy lines and blew up enemy trains and vehicles. By the end of 1943, he had been promoted to captain and had received many decorations. Mikhail Goncharov finished the war as a major, studied at the A. A. Kuybyshev Engineer Academy, and spent many years teaching there in the mines and barriers department.

Petr Andrianov was renowned among the miners on the front

for mining enemy rail lines in broad daylight. His work was characterized by his striking composure, foresight, and creativity. With his own hands, he had been able to place mines right ahead of the wheels of moving enemy trains. He was also well known for guiding Soviet citizens out of the enemy rear. At the end of August 1943, he led out six hundred people, no more, no less, among them many women and children. In September 1943, Andrianov's detachment of twenty-five men overpowered and captured eighty-eight enemy saboteurs who were dressed in Red Army uniforms and armed to the teeth. At that time, Andrianov had already been decorated with combat orders, although he was just a captain.

On one of his missions, Andrianov froze his foot and was suffering severely. After his recovery, it was suggested that he take a staff job, but the young officer insisted on returning to his troops and continued to run combat missions. In 1944, Captain Andrianov's group was surrounded by a much larger German hunter-killer force. After an all day fight, Andrianov led his people in a breakout during the evening, clearing the way for his comrades with grenades; but he himself fell, struck by an enemy bullet.

If the readers of these lines ever visit the Volga River, they might see a beautiful steamer, on whose high side shines the name PETR ANDRIANOV, written in golden letters. The motherland has immortalized the memory of the young demolitions officer.

In a New Assignment

From the People's Commissariat for Defense to the Central Staff of the Partisan Movement (*Tsentralniy shtab partizanskogo dvizheniya* = TsShPD) was a short trip, but I had a lot to think about as I made it. I understood the significance of the Central Staff: the centralization of leadership of partisan operations was urgently needed and the creation of the Central Staff was an event of extraordinary importance! The only thing that I couldn't understand was why it was necessary to pull me out of the front lines and send me to the Central Staff! Of course I had written several times to Ponomarenko, now chief of the Staff, and perhaps the letters had been the cause of my transfer.

The Central Staff of the Partisan Movement was located in a spacious old building, with a mezzanine and false columns, in the courtyard of a mansion where the Marx and Engels Museum is presently located. The courtyard was surrounded by the former noble inhabitants' stables and sheds, which had been adapted to serve as garages and accommodations for the guard force.

Handing my credentials to the duty officer, I went up the carpeted stair to the second floor. Everything sparkled: the polished parquet, the copper of the well-polished door handles, the new paint on the plinths and walls. Ponomarenko's adjutant spent about five minutes in the chief of staff's office, announcing my arrival, but finally, I was asked to go in. Ponomarenko smiled, asked me to take a chair and pushed aside a file lying on the table. "Well, I've just been looking at your personal file here, to try to figure out what assignment to give you."

How are you supposed to react to a statement like that? If I had been taken from the front, they should have determined my assignment well in advance, but—maybe, at the last minute, they had reconsidered, or maybe someone on the staff had to take leave.

I tried to help Ponomarenko with his indecision, and made some suggestions: for example, I suggested creating a partisan staff in the enemy rear opposite the Western Strategic Direction, and sending in an operations group from the Central Partisan Staff at the earliest possible moment. No, Ponomarenko said, partisan activities in the enemy rear were the responsibility of the local Party organizations. I protested that I wasn't talking about political leadership, but operational leadership and training for partisans. Ponomarenko was firm: we didn't need that kind of thing! I then suggested forming sabotage brigades, and told him that I could train a brigade and take it behind enemy lines in two or three weeks, but he wouldn't hear of that, either. He asked me if I really thought he had gotten me transferred just to send me off behind enemy lines. Obviously, he'd already made up his mind: "I think that what we really need is to organize something like a partisan academy; for short, let's call it a 'higher partisan school.' Also, the staff needs a chief for the technical department, and I'm thinking that such a position would best suit you. So, why not combine these two responsibilities—chief of the technical department and chief of the higher partisan school—and why not assign you that responsibility?"

"It's not for me to decide, Panteleymon Kondrat'yevich."

Ponomarenko called in Lieutenant Colonel Timoshenko, head of the cadres department of the staff, informed him of my new assignments, and ordered him to take care of my paperwork. "Well, that's all for today, Comrade Starinov," he said, leaning on the desk. "Get busy."

When I appeared at the Central Staff, work was already underway on identifying and registering all the partisan detachments and on establishing radio communications with them. Efforts were being made to supply partisans with explosives, weapons, and medicines, and to organize medical treatment and evacuation to our rear area for the sick and seriously wounded.

General direction of the Central Staff came from the State Defense Committee, i.e., K. Ye. Voroshilov. Needless to say, when discussing the designation of the staff in the State Defense Committee, Voroshilov suggested giving it the title that it would have been given in Lenin's days, i.e., "Central Staff of Partisan Detachments, or Partisan Forces." However, other points of view prevailed.

My old combat comrade from Spain, Col. Khadzhi-Umar Dzhiorovich Mamsurov, otherwise known as Ksanti, told me about these discussions. I met him in the staff corridors, looking as slender, tanned, and handsome as ever. Colonel Mamsurov was chief of the central staff intelligence directorate. Mamsurov said that he thought that Voroshilov had been correct in his opinions about naming the staff. Mamsurov felt that a staff was an organization for planning and developing operations that were conceived by a command authority, and how could you have a staff of a "movement" without a command authority? Nevertheless, he felt that we had to simply go with the title we had been given for now—there was still time to change it.

Mamsurov had the enormous responsibility for ensuring the accuracy of intelligence data on the enemy disseminated by the Central Staff. We received intelligence from the partisans, but it was fragmentary and irregular. Any intelligence has to be checked and confirmed in a timely fashion, but given the state of our communications with the partisans at that time, that was an extremely difficult thing to do. It was no easier for other members of the staff to operate than it was for Mamsurov. For example, to supply partisan units with explosives and munitions, constant, secure radio communications had to be available. The radio communications department chief, Col. Ivan Nikolayevich Artem'yev, was an outstanding specialist in radio technology, but he was very limited in what he could do since only *one-sixth* of the partisan detachments and formations trained by the staff had radios!

Calm and restrained, Ivan Nikolayevich listened to the complaints of Mamsurov and the chief of the operations department, Col. Vasiliy Fedorovich Sokolov, without displaying his own feelings, and then he quietly advised his colleagues to address themselves to the State Defense Committee, or better still, to the supreme commander, in order to get the necessary quantity of radios, and at the same time get some aircraft for flights into the enemy rear.

At that time there was still much that had not been finally decided: the vacancies in the staff departments had just barely been filled, the official responsibilities of some staff members had not been specified, and the procedures for contacting the general staff and the staffs of each of the various forces (e.g., engineers, airborne, ground forces) had not yet been worked out. The Central Staff had only been created two months before, and no thought had been given to the potential uses of partisan forces, the methods of command and control of partisan detachments and formations, and the most effective means of carrying on partisan warfare.

I was appointed chief of the new Central Staff school on 1 August 1942. To create the new school, which was designated as the Higher Special Operations School (*Vyshaya operativnaya shkola osobogo naznacheniya* = VOShON), I requested former staff members of the OUTs and Spanish comrades from the 5th Brigade to be assigned as faculty. The chief of engineer troops on the Kalinin Front, Colonel Kosarev, got a bit uptight at first, but then came around to my side and met my request. It's also true that the veterans of partisan warfare weren't very pleased to be recalled to Moscow, either. Then I sent a letter to General Glazunov, chief of airborne troops, and requested that he send thirty paratroopers. They arrived soon thereafter; tall, physically tough youngsters. The Higher Military Pedagogical Institute also responded to our request for graduates. They were also young, in new uniform tunics, with new, squeaky briefcases; they frequently stared in fascination at the gold stars sewn on their sleeves and the red squares on their lapels. Many of these political workers had experience with Party and government work and had received good military training, but all that they knew about partisan warfare in the enemy rear they had read in Fadeyev's book.[1]

The mine and demolitions instructors who had worked at the OUTs school at Kharkov and Rostov and on the Kalinin Front belonged to a special category of school staff personnel. These included: Mariya Stepanovna Belova, Capt. Semen Petrovich Mineyev, Capt. Vladimir Pavlovich Chepig, and some others. Although they were teaching mines and demolitions in VOShON, they were also studying and mastering tactics to be used in the enemy rear. And as you might suppose, the veteran Spanish saboteurs—Campillo, Lorente, Conisares, Sanchez, Coronado, Viesca, Fusimanio, Francisco Guillon, Angel Alberca, Benito Ustares, and Joaquin Gomez—were improving their knowledge and sharing their experiences with the novices. I ordered that the administrative personnel be encouraged to take training in the school so that they would know who they were supporting, with what, and for what purpose. I forced my finance officer, Capt. A. S. Yegorov, to issue this order. Yegorov was a remarkable man and an outstanding worker, and for precisely this reason, he was not about to permit the school to deviate one iota from the innumerable paragraphs of the innumerable instructions that regulated finance. I secretly hoped that Yegorov would be drawn to mines and demolitions and would become a bit more flexible. Alas, my subversion wasn't successful: the finance chief thoroughly studied mines and demolitions and partisan tactics, and a year later became deputy for sabotage operations under Hero of the Soviet Union A. F. Fedorov, but he never once indulged me and my assistants while he was chief of finance.

Among the school personnel, we also found other comrades who became enthusiasts for mines and demolitions and carried out operations in the enemy rear. These included the chief of the medical department, B. N. Kazakov. The problems of translators for our Spanish students was easily solved: I called my wife and children back from their evacuation site! Anna had already gotten to know the Spaniards on operations at Jaen and Granada, knew mines and demolitions very well, and was still fluent in Spanish. Once again, she became my trusted assistant!

Changes

August 1942 was hot and stuffy. The voice of Levitan, the Radio Moscow announcer, was gloomy: there was heavy fighting on the Southwest and Southern Fronts, and our troops were evacuating city after city. But it was precisely during these threatening, tragic days that many emerging problems of partisan warfare were settled.

On 13 August, we began testing various means of sabotaging railroads. We were setting off our regular explosive charges as well as shape charges in which a cone-shaped inner cavity in the explosive focused the force of the explosion on a limited area. We produced derailments with the help of various kinds of mines, tested the effectiveness of igniters, shot at locomotives and tank cars with rifles, machine guns, and antitank weapons. We also searched for the most rational way to set antitrain mines in order to produce the best possible results with the expenditure of the smallest amount of explosives; for partisans, every TNT cartridge was worth its weight in gold!

After listening to my report on the test results, Ponomarenko asked if we shouldn't organize a demonstration of mines and demolitions for a group of partisans who would soon be coming to the staff. I responded that I would contact the chief of Red Army Military Communications, I. V. Kovalev, and ask him to select a railroad test track. He permitted us to use a test loop, and set a date: 18 August.

The "sabotage group" arrived on the site nearly at midnight. It was black as pitch! The careful steps of the "patrols" guarding the railroad were audible. The "patrols" included the partisans to whom the equipment was to be demonstrated. These were attentive, careful people, but the "saboteurs" could also take care of themselves. Morning arrived, and the "patrols" and the "saboteurs" gathered together. Ponomarenko and the other staff personnel arrived. We suggested that they examine the railroad with the partisans. The inspectors looked with uncertainty at the railroad bed, the diesel-oil-streaked ballast, the ties, the smooth rails, and then gingerly took their first steps. Three partisan trainees probed the ballast with rods before they set foot on it: they understood that someone might have prepared a surprise for them! Alas, soon there was a report and a puff of smoke: the first mine, set to destroy probers, went off, followed by a second and a third ...

No one was able to find and disarm a single mine. Then the train came down the test track, and things began to happen: flash-smoke; flash-smoke; flash-smoke! When the train began to back up, there were more explosions! These were the reports of delayed-action mines and *rapida* or wheel-switch mines.

In this fashion, we were able to convince partisan leaders of the advantages of some mines that were completely invisible to locomotive engineers and could be set up in ten to twenty seconds, as well as the advantages of the delayed-action mines that would work reliably even if set in the ballast, out of contact with the rails and the ties. Then we demonstrated how to make mines out of parts that the partisans might be able to get or to make themselves. As "dessert" we used the nonremovable mines, demonstrated by S. V. Gridnev. Unfortunately, we were unable to get these mines to partisan detachments very quickly.

Every evening, after we had finished training at the school or conducting tests on the proving ground, I returned to the Central Staff, where I stayed far into the night. I was working on documents, the most important of which was a draft order for the People's Commissariat for Defense, entitled: "On the Missions of the Partisan Movement."

The necessity for publishing such an order was dictated, in part, by the lack of a single unified opinion concerning the potential of partisan forces, the tactics of partisan forces, the methods of fighting the enemy in his rear area, and by the necessity for exercising operational control of partisan forces and resupply of those forces from the Soviet rear.

Some military leaders, e. g., Mekhlis, maintained that partisans had no special partisan strategy and tactics, and that partisan strategy and tactics couldn't exist: you simply fell on the enemy as the occasion arose, and then you hid! To people like Mekhlis, recommendations for supplying partisans with weapons and explosives were just silly. Further, it was felt that resupplying partisans would breed a feeling of dependency among them, which would cause them to avoid hostile contact with the enemy! The adherents of this point of view actually maintained that partisans would simply sit around in the woods and swamps if they were regularly resupplied! The feeling was that they should run their sorties, attack the Germans, and get their own supplies and weapons, and not come begging on the doorsteps of the Party and the Soviet government!

Experience is a good teacher, however, because partisan detachments grew most quickly in size and operated most energetically in those places where we were able to provide constant support from our side of the lines. The Vitebsk partisans in Belorussia, for example, got this kind of assistance. From March to September 1942, they were sent more than eleven thousand rifles; six thousand submachine guns; one thousand machine guns; five hundred antitank guns; and large quantities of ammunition, grenades, and explosives. And what was the result? At the beginning of 1943, the Vitebsk partisans made up almost half of the total number of partisans in Belorussia, although the operating area of the Vitebsk unit only covered one tenth of the Belorussian Republic!

Voroshilov stood firmly against the views of Mekhlis and the other people who were inexperienced in the problems of partisan warfare. For this reason, part of my draft order was devoted to clearly defining the basic strategic mission of partisan warfare: to destroy the enemy's personnel and equipment *while they were moving up to the front, on the railroads.*

At the end of August or beginning of September, the Central Staff of the Partisan Movement was commissioned by the Central Committee of the Party to hold a conference for the representatives of the Party underground organizations, and officers and commissars of large partisan formations in the Ukraine and Belorussia, and the Smolensk and Orel regions. Personnel of the Central Staff also participated in this conference. Many of us who had been involved in training partisans in the thirties expected that the creation of a central partisan staff would see the end of the amateurish and disjointed approach to partisan warfare that had been employed thus far. But this didn't happen: Ponomarenko gave a report in which he preached rank amateurism, denying the existence of any guiding principles or theoretical basis for partisan operations, and encouraging partisan leaders to follow a catch-as-catch-can approach, killing Germans wherever possible and with whatever they had at hand. He indicated that the Central Staff wouldn't get involved in operational control! Further, Ponomarenko didn't take the required steps to stop enemy traffic on the railroads and highways.

The officers and commissars of the partisan units nevertheless unanimously pointed to the need for operational control of partisan forces; suggested that the staff work out large-scale operations against the enemy, and posed some very sharp questions about the delivery of weapons, explosives, and radios to the partisans.

The partisans wondered why thousands of tons of explosives could be dropped on railroad junctions from the air, but they were getting only tens of kilos of the same explosives. The partisan officers confirmed that blowing up an enemy troop or supply train always produced a more profound effect than that produced by aerial bombardment. After the war, Hero of the Soviet Union M. I. Duka recalled that thousands of bombs dropped on the Bryansk railroad junction only produced a four-hour interruption of Nazi troop traffic; but with the same amount of explosives he could have paralyzed all traffic in the entire Bryansk area and put hundreds of engines, thousands of coaches, flat cars, and tank cars out of commission.

S. A. Kovpak, commander of the Ukrainian partisan raiding formation, requested improvements in partisan supply. He was convinced that he should first give his formation explosives alone, and not cartridges: if they had explosives, they would send out many small sabotage groups, in many directions, to attack enemy communications; they could inflict more casualties on the Germans, sow panic in the enemy camp, and completely disorient the Nazis. That way, there would be no problems if the partisans went out on a raid several days later.

Ponomarenko promised to keep track of partisan needs and requests (during the war, the partisans received from Soviet sources almost 100 percent of their radio gear, more than 95 percent of their fuses, 70 percent of the explosives, more than 90 percent of the antitank weapons, and about 80 percent of the submachine guns and the ammunition for them).

On the night of 1 September, the conference attendees went to a reception in the Kremlin given by Party and government leaders. Four days later, on 5 September, I. V. Stalin signed an order entitled "On the Missions of the Partisan Movement," and the next day, the position of supreme commander of partisan forces was introduced into the Red Army. K. Ye. Voroshilov was appointed to that post. Formulated on the basis of the results of the conference and the Kremlin reception, the order assigned great importance to partisan operations, emphasized the need to increase the depth and breadth of these operations and to get all Soviet nationalities involved. New units were to be founded, including partisan reserve or replacement units, which were to be established in all towns and cities. The mission of attacking railroads and bridges and cutting enemy supply lines was unfortunately buried among nine other partisan missions, and no attention was given to demoralizing units of enemy troops and Soviet collaborators.

Voroshilov's entry into this position was marked by the assignment to the Central Staff of experienced senior military officers: Lieutenant General of Artillery Sivkov and Lt. Gen. P. R. Khmelnitskiy. Sivkov was given the leadership of the operations directorate, and Khmelnitskiy got the logistics support directorate. As a military officer, Voroshilov could have actually become commander in chief of partisan forces, because he had the position and authority to direct and coordinate the operations of the Special NKVD and GRU troop units and guards miners units, which had not previously been subordinated to the Central Staff of the Partisan Movement.

Considering that, in mid-September, the enemy had only a very small number of guard units, ragged reserves, and rear area units to cover the 1.5 million square kilometers of occupied Soviet territory, Voroshilov thought it necessary to immediately prepare and carry out heavy strikes in the enemy rear and to paralyze enemy railroad operations.

Lieutenant General Sivkov and his subordinates began to work out a plan for a series of large-scale operations. The entire staff was involved in working up the future partisan requirements for explosives and weapons, ammunition, radios, mines, and other items.

Voroshilov, resolutely striving to get radios for partisan support, tirelessly repeated that that this was neither a military problem, nor a technical problem, but primarily *a political problem*! In accordance with the marshal's orders, we were constantly writing requests for aircraft to deliver supplies to the partisans in the enemy rear. They gave us aircraft, but never enough of them, and Voroshilov gave the order to create stocks of supplies and equipment. As a member of the State Defense Committee, he knew that in the spring of 1943 there would be increases in the production of tanks, aircraft, artillery pieces, and other forms of weapons; ammunition, mines and demolitions materials, and communications gear. He therefore had the idea to not only create reserve stocks of supplies and equipment for the partisans but to work out and then obtain official status for tables of equipment and supplies that had been requested by partisans. Naturally, questions arose about tables for mines. The marshall ordered us to put on a mine display so that the best models of mines could be selected. At the end of September, the technical department of the staff prepared an exhibit, and an order for a whole series of the mines that had been exhibited was sent off to the Military Engineer Directorate of the Red Army.

Voroshilov also supported General Sivkov's idea of creating a regular partisan army in the enemy rear. The chief of the operations directorate was basing his views on the fact that large numbers of Soviet military personnel had been encircled in 1941 and still remained in the enemy rear. Some of these units went over to partisan operations as entire formations, such as the 208th Motorized Rifle Division, commanded by Col. V. I. Nichiporovich. Some also joined local partisan units. I should add that 10 percent of the units trained by our staff were made up of military personnel who were forced to stay behind on occupied territory. In the partisan districts and zones in the fall of 1942, there were also millions of adult Soviet citizens who were capable of work.

Sivkov proposed that we rely on the capabilities and combat experience of Soviet military personnel who remained behind enemy lines, the enormous manpower reserves represented by the population, and the territory of the partisan regions and zones liberated from the enemy, and create a partisan army that would really threaten the enemy. Sivkov discussed this theme with Voroshilov in my presence. Voroshilov listened carefully, thought it over, and told Sivkov to write a proposal to Stalin. Sivkov asked that I participate in preparing the proposal, since I was a witness—albeit an involuntary witness—to the discussion.

The proposal was quickly written. When we had set forth the conditions that had arisen in the enemy rear, which were favorable for creating a partisan army, we indicated that units of the proposed regular partisan army were not conceived as typical army formations, but as special, highly maneuverable organizations capable of operating either as small detachments or in large division-size formations. They would be able to carry on massive mining of enemy communications lines, to mount attacks on enemy garrisons, and to carry out long-distance raids in the enemy rear. It was recommended that personnel manning tables be introduced in the units of the partisan army, and that military ranks be established, along with pay scales commensurate to those ranks.

It was further recommended that the army be supplied with automatic weapons/communications gear, antitank weapons, mines and demolitions, and medicine.

Voroshilov also supported our suggestions for creating special technical and sabotage services in the partisan staffs, formations, and detachments. The fact was that when in storage, control-detonated mines required regular, detailed readiness checks because of the peculiarities of their construction. Partisan detachments simply had too few technically qualified people to carry out such checks. Unfortunately regular supply personnel were entrusted with the storage of the mines, and the results were soon obvious: a portion of the best mines, delivered to the partisans with great difficulty and risk, was irreparably damaged.

I recall that when A. F. Fedorov, the secretary of the Chernigov Regional Committee, flew into Moscow, he asked Voroshilov to provide his partisan formation with nonremovable, delayed-action, antitrain mines. Voroshilov called me and asked how many mines of this type we had, and how long it would take to deliver them to the people in Chernigov. I told him, but reminded Fedorov of the necessity of storing the mines carefully and handling them with great care when they were set. Voroshilov then asked Fedorov what he thought about our idea to establish technical services in the partisan units. Fedorov emphatically agreed.

There are two more events from those times that are connected with Voroshilov's official activities—these involve the dispatch of two partisan units made up from instructors and students at the Higher School into the enemy rear. At the beginning of September, M. N. Nikitin, the chief of the Lenningrad partisan staff, who was in Moscow at the time, asked me if it was true that we had Spaniards in the Higher School. I told him that we had them indeed and that they were eager to go behind the lines of Franco's "Blue Division." This division was composed of volunteers from Franco's Spain, who were fighting alongside the Germans on the Leningrad Front. Nikitin wanted to know what we were waiting for, and I told him that we had to get permission of the commander in chief, Voroshilov. Nikitin went to Voroshilov, and together they went to the Higher School and met with some Spanish officers (Anna was the interpreter). Voroshilov then gave his permission for sending a mixed unit of Spanish and Soviet soldiers into the rear area of the Blue Division.

There were 124 men in this detachment, including the Spaniards who had experience on the Southern and Kalinin fronts, and our students, who were young officers from airborne and railroad troops. We designated Francisco Guillon as commander of the detachment, with Angel Alberca as his deputy: the same Angel whose boot had kicked Fritzy's ass across the entire Gulf of Taganrog. The chief of staff was the young but very energetic self-starter, Senior Lieutenant Tsarevskiy.

We sent the second detachment from the Higher School to the Caucasus, and here's the way that happened: on a gloomy October day, I happened to run into General Vorob'yev in the halls of the Main Military Engineer Directorate. The general asked me to drop by his office, where he asked me what I thought of the idea of having our partisan-saboteurs run joint operations with the guards miners' battalion in the Caucasus. The situation at the front was difficult, and there was no reason for any optimism, but Vorob'yev looked unusually cheerful and animated, and I got the feeling that he was holding something back. He obviously knew that the German forces at Stalingrad were about to be completely encircled, and that the troops of our Northern Group of Forces on the Transcaucasus Front were also ready to launch a powerful blow.

I responded that coordinated operations involving our group and the guards miners were possible, but that only Voroshilov could give permission to send students into the Caucasus. Vorob'yev said that he'd make all the arrangements and told me to start selecting the people.

Within a day, Voroshilov actually gave the order to form a unit for operations in the Caucasus from volunteers. We got a lot of volunteers, chose a group of 135, and this detachment, under the command of Chepak,[1] with subordinate groups commanded by

---

1. The chain of command of this detachment is interesting: Captain Chepak, an NKVD Border Guards officer, was commanding a detachment including groups led by Spaniards who were senior to him both in rank (a major and a lieutenant colonel) and in experience. Chepak's level of responsibility in this case may simply be due to the dominant role played by the NKVD in partisan operations. It may also be due to a lack of trust in the ability of the Spaniards on the part of the NKVD, and the Soviet military. Finally,

Ungria and Bascuniano, left for Tbilisi on 11 November. In Tbilisi they would report to the engineer staff for the Transcaucasus Front and conduct joint operations with the guards miners that were already there.

Then, precisely six days later on 17 November, the position of commander in chief of partisan forces was dissolved, by a decree of the State Defense Committee! The decree stated that this action was taken "in the interests of greater flexibility" in directing the partisan movement, and "to avoid overcentralized leadership!"

Voroshilov obviously had known that the State Defense Committee decree was being prepared: we noticed that the marshal was gloomy, taciturn, and lost in thoughts, which he shared with no one. Soon, Generals Sivkov and Khemelnitskiy left the school, as did Colonel Mamsurov. The question of creating a regular partisan army was never raised again. (In the works of the Military Scientific Directorate of the general staff, published in 1958, it was stated that the suggestion for creating regular partisan armies in the enemy rear was submitted with the approval of the commander in chief of the partisan movement, that the proper preconditions existed for such a development, but that a final decision was never made!)

Having abolished the position of commander in chief of partisan forces, ostensibly to limit overcentralization, Stalin nevertheless left the Central Staff of the Partisan Movement in existence and, in effect, made himself the commander in chief of partisan forces. This is shown by the fact that in all of his decrees from 1 May 1942 to 23 February 1944, he assigned general missions for the partisans along with missions for the Red Army. He gave no specific separate orders for partisan forces, although he did approve the seasonal (e. g. summer, winter) operations plans for republic and regional partisan movement staffs. None of these plans was ever supported, however, due to a shortage of aircraft for the required supply drops.

it may be a result of the fact that NKVD officers normally had prerogatives one rank higher than the rank they wore, in which case Chepak's rank would have been equivalent to a Red Army major. In any case, this particular incident indicates the degree of penetration and control exercised by the NKVD in partisan operations run by the military and the Party.

To Disrupt the Enemy's Plans

It was getting cold; a heavy, wet snow fell, and the surface winds swirled. The people of Moscow were standing in long bread lines, shivering in old winter coats and quilted jackets, warming themselves by little tin stoves, and sitting in the dark at night to conserve electric power. But the call signs of the *Comintern* radio, which was just beginning to be heard, told the people of the capital to forget about cold and hunger: the offensive, which began on 19 November on the Southwestern, Don, and Stalingrad fronts was continuing, and the enemy had suffered a defeat!

Letters came from the Caucasus: Domingo Ungria and Major Bascuniano reported on their friendly reception by the engineer troop staff of the Transcaucasus Front. They recommended transferring the Spaniards who were still at the school to the Caucasus, assuring me that the climatic conditions there were more suitable for them. A more restrained letter from Captain Chepak contained hints of preparations for large-scale operations. I was happy that our comrades were so well received, but also a bit worried. I hoped their command would not make the same blunders that were made at Leningrad. When he was operating in the Leningrad area, we learned from Francisco Guillon's radio messages that the groups of his detachment had been inserted at different times over a broad area and were only able to reunite after long and dangerous marches through the enemy's rear, with some skirmishes. When they finally got together, the formation was running out of food. Inexperienced aviators unsuccessfully dropped the supplies designated for the detachment, as a result of which, a significant portion of the supplies was lost. Skis were delivered to the detachment only after great delay. The half-starved troops, carrying three severely-wounded men on homemade stretchers, kept moving for a long time, stumbling through knee-deep snow. Guillon's men kept fighting, even under those conditions. They set mines, derailed trains, blew up vehicles, and killed search-and-destroy units. But at what a cost!

We didn't want the same story to be repeated in the Caucasus.

December arrived with frost and blizzards, but the ring around the group of German troops at Stalingrad was finally locked tight;

then, at Kotel'nikovskiy, our troops defeated the enemy relief force that was trying to break through our encirclement at Stalingrad, and the liberation of the Don Basin was begun.

On the very first day of 1943, the Nazi command, fearing that the impetuous offensive on the Southwestern Front would lead to the encirclement of their troops in the northern Caucasus, began their rapid withdrawal from the Mozdok area in a northwest direction. The armies of the Northern Group of Forces of the Transcaucasus Front pursued the enemy. But it was more important to disrupt the enemy's plans for an orderly withdrawal of troops and equipment, and it was also important to delay the Germans so that they could be surrounded and destroyed. For this reason, the Stavka decided to intensify the strikes on enemy communications lines in the northern Caucasus. By 8 January, Ponomarenko, still the chief of the Central Staff of the Partisan Movement, approved an operational plan entitled "The Task of Intensifying Sabotage Work on the Occupied Territory of the Northern Caucasus." The plan charged the operational training detachments of the Higher School with the task of conducting massive sabotage efforts to destroy enemy troop and supply trains, aided by partisan detachments of the northern Caucasus.

Ponomarenko told me that since a large amount of resources had been transferred to the Caucasus, I would also be sent there. He told me to coordinate my work with the Front engineer directorate. While my orders were being drawn up, I found time to see General Vorob'yev, at the Red Army engineer staff, and arranged with him for the Higher School group to operate jointly with detachments of the guards miners' battalion on the Transcaucasus Front. Anna asked if she could go too, but I told her to stay home with the kids. The majority of Spaniards spoke Russian reasonably well, and so there was no need for an interpreter.

January in Tbilisi—low, heavy clouds; rain; dampness; wet paving stones; the turbid waters of the Kura River. The first thing that caught my eye was the windows: they didn't have strips of paper glued on them to prevent blast waves from shattering them! And the faces of the passersby did not look as tired as those of the Muscovites. And kids were everywhere! The number of kids surprised me, but then it dawned on me: children hadn't been evacuated from Tbilisi!

Lt. Col. Nikolai Fedorovich Slyunin, chief of engineer troops of the Transcaucasus Front, met me in the staff offices. We had known each other since the fall of 1941. His troops had been involved in mining the distant approaches to Moscow and with mining the communications lines at Yel'na and Vyazma. They had carried out sorties behind enemy lines, blowing bridges and trains between Smolensk, Orsha, and Roslavl.

Slyunin didn't look so well, probably from lack of sleep. After we exchanged greetings, he got out a map and told me to familiarize myself with it. I noticed red ovals, like drops of blood, scattered along the white-and-black railroad lines on the map. By each oval, a small red parachute had been neatly drawn. It was quite clear: the parachutes were drop zones for sabotage groups, and the ovals were operating areas for those groups. Slyunin explained that sixteen sabotage groups had been given the mission of foiling the organized withdrawal of troops and equipment to Rostov-on-the-Don. Twelve groups of about eight men each were ordered to blow railroad bridges, and four groups with six men each were ordered to mine the railroads. Only just the previous evening, another group, under the command of Major Aleksandrov and Major Bascuniano, had been dropped. They had command of all the groups that had previously been inserted. Slyunin joked, somewhat ironically, that we had quite a variegated group: miners from the engineer staff, our Spaniards, and intelligence personnel and radio operators from the Front intelligence directorate. He told me that the first group had been dropped before New Year's Day and the last on 17 January. The long delay in completing all the drops was due to poor flying weather and the lack of aircraft. He also told me, however, that he had been assured by the Front parachute landing service that everyone had hit the designated drop zones precisely.

I asked if there was any communications with the groups. It turned out that Lieutenant Campillo, who had been dropped first, had already returned to our lines. Lieutenant Lorente's group had joined up with our attacking units after four days, and Lieutenant Conisares had come up in radio communications. In the course of nine days, Campillo had blown up two enemy tanks and three vehicles, and wounded twenty to thirty Germans in skirmishes. Lorente remained for three days behind enemy lines. According to Slyunin, his group had killed twenty soldiers and raised a lot of excitement in the enemy rear. Conisares reported that he had reached the area of Sal'sk and had derailed a train.

"A lot of excitement," skirmishes, a total of two tanks and a few vehicles? This certainly wasn't going to delay the enemy's retreat! Nothing had been heard from the other groups, and Aleksandrov and Bascuniano had disappeared without a trace! Slyunin began to get angry: it seemed that the first plan had not considered the possibility of operating with coordinated groups.

Ungria and Bascuniano had insisted on this, as had the Front intelligence men. Slyunin couldn't understand why they had insisted, since the distances between the group operating areas were large, and no thought had been given to concentrating them. Slyunin pointed out that there were severe problems in controlling such groups from a distance.

Then I found out that the Front engineer troop staff had formed an additional three detachments from the troops of the 15th and 16th Independent Guards Miners' Battalions and the Higher School personnel. They were concentrated in the area of the Black Sea group of forces at Tuapse and Adler. They had selected the drop zones for inserting the groups, but no aircraft were available.

I asked Slyunin if he didn't think that the lack of aircraft was a fortunate thing, given the fact that we had no word from the majority of groups that had already been inserted. The silence put me on the alert. I knew these steppes from civil war days. Winter on the steppes was no time for men to be out: you could see a cat for a kilometer! If the pilots had made an error . . .

Slyunin admitted that he was worried, too, but he didn't think that anyone would listen to our concerns. Moscow was screaming that we were letting the enemy break contact and get away, but it was hard to do anything else. The Germans had blown up all the railroads, and in this locale, with the lack of good roads, it was even difficult to get around on vehicles or on horseback. We were forced to move artillery and supplies with camels!

In the end, we made arrangements for the engineer staff to accommodate the Higher School students who were arriving in Tbilisi and other cities, to arm them and equip them from the stocks of the guards miners' units. We would delay in inserting any new groups behind enemy lines until we received information from our comrades who had already been dropped in the German rear.

On the same day, I had a meeting with Captain Chepak. He had been able to get together with Campillo and Lorente and knew some things that Slyunin didn't know. Campillo and his group had been dropped in the western area, but Lorente's group, which was to have flown off after them, was held on the airfield due to weather. The whole night, Campillo waited to give the signal to the aircraft carrying his comrades, but the planes never showed up! When Lorente's group was finally inserted, a week later, they were almost dropped right on an enemy-held settlement. The instructor had already given the "go" command and opened the hatch, when Pvt. Yakov Kut', shuffling up to the hatch, noticed a stream of lights beneath the aircraft wing: it looked like there'd be

trouble ahead! Nevertheless, after two or three minutes, the jump-
ers leaped into the night. They landed in open steppe, and had to
wait till morning to find one of their number who had jumped late
and hurt his leg on landing. Their cargo chute, with the mines and
explosives, was never found. It had obviously floated down right
on the heads of the enemy. As a result, at dawn, enemy observation planes began to circle over the steppe, and the observation
planes were followed by a truckload of enemy burp gunners,
which rolled up to the landing zone. Fortunately, Lorente was able
to extricate his group.

Lorente had told Chepak that we didn't need pilots who flung
supplies around freely the way they flung bombs! Unlike Slyunin,
Chepak was doubtful that the other groups had hit their landing
zones. He was optimistic, however, that everything would turn out
all right because the Germans were running away fast, and our
front lines would overtake the detachments that had been inserted
behind enemy lines.

I remained silent. Why gratify yourself with possibly vain
hopes? And what was the use if the groups got out all right but
hadn't fulfilled their missions?

On the third or fourth day of our stay in Tbilisi (we were there
meeting troop trains from Moscow carrying students from the
Higher School), we learned that the troops of the Northern Group
of Forces of the Transcaucasus Front had advanced 300 to 320
kilometers. They had liberated many cities, including Cherkessk,
Nevinnomyssk, Stavropol, and Armavir, and had linked up with
the attacking troops of the Southern Front in the vicinity of Sal'sk.
But only the Conisares sabotage group returned to our lines.

The situation with the troops in the Black Sea group of forces
was not better. The Fifty-sixth Army, successfully advancing to
the northwest after heavy fighting, had broken out of the mountains into the Kuban valley and was approaching Krasnodar, but
of all the sabotage groups that had been inserted into the Krasnodar area, only Jose Viesca's group rejoined our forces. Nothing
was heard of the others.

Hoping to get information on our people operating with the partisans, I set off on a trip to Sochi, to the Southern Staff of the Partisan Movement, to see the chief of staff, P. I. Seleznev. A year
ago, this guy had angrily told me that partisan training was being
overdone in his district, and now he was partisan chief of staff!

Unfortunately, Seleznev didn't know anything about the fate of
our groups. He explained that because of the difficult physical environmental conditions, i. e., the surrounding steppe, the partisans
were forced to either operate from mountain bases or in the under-

ground (among the local populace), and communications with them were most difficult. He told me not to worry, that he'd be in touch the first news he got! From Sochi, since it wasn't too far, I traveled to Adler and Tuapse and met the people from the detachments about which Slyunin had told me. With the exception of the Spaniards, these were all nineteen- and twenty- year-old fellows; cheerful and eager for a scrap, but terribly naive, and totally lacking any idea about operations behind enemy lines. They needed some really serious training.

In Tuapse, Chepak reached me by telephone. He said that the local Military Commissariat had sent Spanish youth to the Higher School detachments. These were youngsters who had been taken from Spain as children during the years of the Spanish civil war, had grown up, and now considered the USSR their homeland. The number of these young fellows already greatly exceeded the number specified in Red Army Rear Area Service documents. How were they supposed to get along? We had to feed, clothe, and arm these boys!

I went to the staff of the Black Sea Group of Troops. They received me cordially, listened to me attentively, sympathized with me, and then explained that they had no right to enroll "superfluous people" on their supply rolls:

"Limits are limits, Comrade Colonel!"

I shared my concerns with an old friend, Colonel Yegnarov, an intelligence officer. He referred me to the Military Council, where I had another acquaintance, Maj. Gen. S. A. Kolonin. This was a smart, energetic, decisive man: he'd be the man to help me! He took me to the commander of the Black Sea Group of Troops, Lt. Gen. I. E. Petrov. Virtually all of the senior officers of the Red Army had heard about Petrov at that time, about his courage and his leadership qualities. Commander of the defenses of Odessa and Sevastopol, he had already become a legendary personality, although he didn't have a heroic appearance, and he actually resembled either a doctor or a teacher. It was just the eyes that showed the real man: they were the eyes of a tough soldier!

When Petrov had listened to Kolonin and me, he gave the order that all Spanish youth who were being sent to the Higher School detachments should be carried on the rolls of the Black Sea Group of Forces, and should be issued all the necessary supplies and allowances. Then he began to ask about the older Spanish comrades and about the students from the Higher School. I expressed concern about the unsuccessful parachute drops, and told him that I had reason to believe that some of the aircrews didn't have the necessary experience for drops, particularly at night. Petrov replied that experience was something that could only be acquired with time, and suggested that we check out the possibilities for amphibious landings for our groups with the Black Sea Fleet intelligence directorate. First, however, he asked me to drop by his operations directorate to acquaint myself with the situation and to put together a plan for operations behind enemy lines.

I followed Petrov's directions immediately. I introduced myself to the chief of staff of the Black Sea Group of Forces, Major General Yermolayev and to the officers of the operations directorate. They acquainted me with the situation. It was arranged that I would present them with a recommendation for operations along the enemy communications lines when I returned from the Black Sea Fleet.

The fastest way to get to the naval staff at Poti was by torpedo boat; the one hundred–kilometer voyage from Sukhumi took a little over an hour. But what an hour that was! It seemed as though the pitching and rolling of the PT, even over small waves, was greater than you'd get in the back of a truck driven by a crazy driver over a corduroy road at eighty kilometers an hour! I spent the whole trip on my knees, convulsively clutching the handrail. Captain 1st Rank Namgeladze, chief of the intelligence department of the Black Sea Fleet staff, not only told me about the possibilities for amphibious operations, but also acquainted me with the most favorable landing beaches, beginning with Novorossiysk and ending with the Crimean Peninsula. He promised full support for our sabotage detachments. Taking into account the opinions of sailors and of the operations staff of the Black Sea Group of Forces, Chepak and I worked out and presented to Major General Yermolayev a plan for interrupting enemy communications lines in the area ahead of the Black Sea Group of Forces. This took place on the eve of the well-known battles for *Malaya Zemlya*.

Pasaremos! We'll Get Through!

At the end of January 1943, troops of the Southern Front reached the eastern approaches to Shakhty, Novocherkassk, and Rostov-on-the-Don. When they liberated Kropotkin and Tikhoretsk, on the southern approaches to Rostov-on-the-Don and Yeysk, troops of the Northern Caucasus Front liberated Maykop, put pressure on the enemy in the area northwest of Krasnodar, and were approaching the Kuban and Ust'-Labinsk.

At the beginning of the operation, the Stavka of the Supreme Command ordered the troops of the Black Sea Group of Forces to seize Novorossiysk and liberate the Taman Peninsula, to prevent the enemy's escaping across the Kerch Straits. To coordinate with operations of the main body of the Black Sea Group of Forces to seize Novorossiysk, which was considered to be the key to the whole Taman Peninsula, amphibious landings began on the night of 4 January in the area of Yuzhnaya Ozereyka and Stanichka, two suburbs of Novorossiysk. On 5 February, General Petrov, commander of the Black Sea Group of Forces, and General Kolonin, member of the Military Council, approved the plan for disrupting enemy communications lines ahead of the Black Sea Group of Forces. According to this plan, between 7 and 15 February, we were to send into the German rear, north of Novorossiysk, two detachments of saboteurs of thirty men each and four groups of saboteurs of six men each to mine the probable withdrawal routes of the German forces and to put the railroad connecting Novorossiysk and Krasnodar out of commission.

We had to put in three groups of twelve men each on the Kerch Peninsula. After the railroad hub at Rostov-on-the-Don was put out of commission, the main route over which supplies flowed to Nazi troops in the Krasnodar district was on the Dzhanka-Vladislavovka-Kerch railroad line. It was this main line that our saboteurs had to attack, coordinating their operations with those of the Crimean partisans.

Radio communications with the detachments inserted on the Taman Peninsula were to be maintained by the intelligence department of the Black Sea Group of Forces, while communications with the groups inserted into the Crimea were to be maintained by the Southern Staff of the Partisan Movement. When he approved the plan, General Petrov drew our attention to the overwhelming importance of blowing up enemy communications on the Kerch Peninsula, and indicated the targets that were his first priority for destruction. We planned to insert the groups overland as well as by sea and by air. We immediately began training the groups and detachments.

The saboteurs who were to be inserted into the Crimea were most concerned, and they had reason to be! After the withdrawal of our troops and the fall of Sevastopol, the Crimean partisans, with whom our troops were to cooperate, were left face-to-face with an army of occupation possessing the most modern weapons and equipment. The enemy was able to besiege the partisans in the heavily wooded mountains and capture many of the partisan supply bases, which had been set up ahead of time for such contingencies. The partisans lost a lot of their effectives and were actually starving, but they continued the struggle even under these frightful conditions, distracting a considerable number of German forces away from the front lines. But it seemed doubtful that they would be able to give much support to our sabotage groups. My doubts were confirmed in a conversation that I had with V. S. Bulatov, the secretary of the Crimean Regional Committee. Bulatov explained that the partisans were trapped in the mountains between the sea and the steppe and that the relatively good road net in the Crimean mountains permitted the Germans to harass the partisans continually. He also noted that they had received very few supply drops. Bulatov told me that he had often requested air drops but that he had been told that the partisans had to support themselves off captured material and that he just didn't know how to organize partisan warfare! They had told him to just overcome his difficulties on his own and not to rely on Allah!

I listened to Bulatov, but didn't believe for a single moment that there was nothing to be done about resupplying the Crimean partisans. I offered to visit Comrade Kaganovich, a member of the Military Council of the Transcaucasus Front, to discuss the airdrops for the Crimean partisans, and Bulatov rejoiced. I got the appointment with Kaganovich, but just as soon as the conversation turned to Crimean partisans, Kaganovich interrupted me rudely, announced that he didn't give alms, cursed, and tossed me out of the office![1] I reported the details of the brief meeting to Bulatov, and he was able to promise me only one thing: he'd try to organize reliable radio communications with our groups.

At the beginning of February, many of our sabotage groups started to come out of the enemy rear area and rejoin our troops. These included Major Bascuniano's group. Weather-beaten and hoarse, he expressed himself with typically Spanish emotion about the pilots who had dropped his troops near an enemy airfield. "They sent out a whole company against us," rasped the major, straining his vocal cords. "We were surrounded! What can you do? Only one thing—lead the soldiers in a breakout! I led; and we broke out, but Pozdnyakova, the female intelligence officer, and Junior Sergeant Bazilevich are missing. Maybe they were killed, I don't know. We couldn't find out, so we took off. Then seven

---

1. From the 1920s, Lazar Kaganovich occupied a series of high Party and government positions, particularly in the fields of industry, transportation, and natural resources. He chaired the Party Control Commission, which directed the 1937 purges, and is described by Prof. Robert Conquest as "totally lacking in the restraints of humanity." Ejected from the Party in 1957, he survived in obscurity as a pensioner until 1991.

people got frostbite, and one wandered off at night. If they had dropped us on the designated drop zone, would we have lost so many people? Would we have had to fight like that?"

Like Lorente, Bascuniano was unable to collect the entire cargo of explosives and mines that had been dumped over the enemy positions. He therefore began to move to join up with the attacking units of our Northern Group of Forces. Along the way, he ran into some isolated groups of enemy officers and men, and in one spot he was able to blow up a rail line.

Even more tragic was the fate of the groups led by Lieutenant Coronado and Sgt. S. M. Fesyuk. We learned about this immediately after the liberation of Shkurinsk and Kislyakovsk villages. The Coronado group had been dropped next to Shkurinsk. The Germans combed the area immediately. Surrounded in the open steppe, the parachutists took cover in a big haystack. Some were killed in the unequal fight, but the survivors as well as the wounded were burned alive in the haystack. Fesyuk's group was dropped right on Kislyakovsk. Only Aleksey Sidorovich Deliy, a guards miner, survived out of that one.

It wouldn't do any good to blame a few pilots and officers of the parachute landing service for what had happened, especially since they had performed brilliantly in the parachute drops of other groups. For example, Lieutenant Riokha's group, which was dropped a good distance west of the village of Varenikovskyaya, was able to assemble without any problems, found their cargo chutes, and moved out to their assigned operations area in good shape. There, they mined the bridges and roads, collected some valuable intelligence data, and established communications with the local partisans of the Blinov group. They helped the partisans with weapons and explosives and reentered our lines without a casualty. In addition, they brought with them a naval parachutist, V. A. Bovta, and the surviving radioman, K. S. Sergeyev, from one of our bombers, which had been shot down.

Lieutenant Sanchez's group, which had also been dropped on the assigned drop zone, performed equally well and suffered no casualties.

We were later able to establish that successful parachute drops were generally accomplished either by pilots who had earlier served in the civilian air fleet and had flown on difficult routes—frequently being forced to fly blind because of sudden changes in the weather—or by military pilots with lots of flight hours, who had done a lot of night flying in peacetime.

Reporting on this to General Petrov, the commander of the Black Sea Group of Forces, I asked for his permission to assign only experienced night fliers to parachute drops. I also reported that I was concerned about inserting our sabotage groups overland. According to our intelligence, the enemy was massing a large concentration of forces on the Taman Peninsula, had occupied all the settlements, and had not cut back on his movement along the roads. Given the absence of safe natural cover, our sabotage groups were in great danger if they attempted to move cross-country. Petrov promised to take measures to select the best-qualified crews for the aircraft; he remarked that while there was no such thing as war without casualties, casualties resulting from sheer stupidity were criminal.

Days passed, and 9 February was already behind us. A storm was blowing up on the sea, and the wind bent the poplars and the cypress, but it wasn't strong enough to accelerate the slow movement of the mountains of gray, blue-violet, and blue-black clouds, which were clinging together, scarcely creeping along. The air force was grounded, and the fleet was only operating off *Malaya Zemlya*, where fierce fighting was going on. On the night of 10 February, taking advantage of the foul weather, we tried to send two groups across the front lines, but they were spotted while approaching the forward enemy positions and had to withdraw.

On 12 February, another attempt to sortie these groups behind enemy lines, in another sector, also ended in failure. The Germans they ran into displayed maximum caution, and German defensive lines had been saturated with infantry units.

On 23 February, Red Army Day, we were finally able to land our first sabotage group behind enemy lines, from the sea. Then, over the next twelve days, we were able to insert six more groups, including the groups led by Juan Lorente, Jose Viesca, and Campillo. They operated on the Taman Peninsula and completed their missions. The Lorente and Viesca groups suffered no casualties, but Campillo's group underwent a terrible ordeal.

Campillo's group consisted of fifteen men. After ten days in the field, they were to be picked up by a torpedo boat at a predetermined place. The first failure occurred on landing: the group was observed by a German coastal surveillance unit. They managed to break contact with the pursuers, but Lieutenant Campillo was forced to take cover in the swamps of the river floodplain, far from the area where he was supposed to be carrying out his attacks. With great effort, the group completed their mission, but the area was filled with German troops, and the shoreline and the approaches to it were heavily guarded. The miners couldn't reach the rendezvous point to meet the torpedo boat at the appointed time, and the torpedo boat was taken under fire by enemy antiaircraft guns and machine guns when it attempted to approach the rendezvous.

Lying among the rocks on the shore, Campillo's troops watched how the sailors maneuvered to remain close to the shore but were finally forced to withdraw to the open sea. So there they were— left alone! There was no food, and there was no sense at all in hoping that the torpedo boat would return. All the more so, because the Germans realized that the torpedo boat hadn't been hanging around there by accident, and they began to comb the area. It was time to go!

Campillo got on the radio to Chepak, asked for food and explosives, and headed for the settlement of Grekomaisk where the Blinov partisan detachment, about which Lieutenant Riokha had reported, was operating. If the air force wouldn't help him, maybe the partisans would!

The people were exhausted: they had been wandering on the steppes and in the floodplain without ever being able to take a rest or make a fire for fear the rising smoke would attract the attention of the enemy soldiers or Russian traitors to their hiding places. They had been sleeping in wet clothes on the bare ground, and then getting up again to make long marches every day. It might have been about one hundred kilometers to the area where Blinov was operating, and the most dangerous part of the route lay in the mountainous areas, on rocky and often steep paths. The group moved slowly, from necessity, because they had decided to give the last food that they had—condensed milk—to the man who had to find and drag in the cargo chutes after the aircraft had made its supply drop!

The plane arrived only on the fourth day. The cargo bags containing food and explosives for the group were fortunately dropped only 200 to 250 meters from the thick brush where Campillo's troops had concealed themselves. When they had rested and regained some of their strength, the troops cheered up. But they still couldn't go very fast as some of them had worn-out shoes and foot injuries. At night they were able to travel only eight to ten kilometers. The supplies, which had been dropped to them, only lasted for two days. The final two nights they went without food. And they got out: smack into an ambush set by a German hunter-killer group. It turned out that Blinov's partisans had been discovered by the Germans not long before and were cut to pieces: the remnants of the unit had fled to the mountains.

The Germans didn't succeed in surrounding Campillo's group, or in cutting off their escape. But in the fierce firefight, the detachment radioman, Lieutenant Pichkayev, was killed, as was Bautista, an expert miner and a man of greatest bravery.

Campillo and the surviving troops were able to break contact with the pursuers. Living on water and the stalks of wild plants, they reached the front lines. Marshaling their last remaining strength, they crawled and sprinted, under enemy fire, and reached our trenches. Only about twenty to thirty paces from our trenches, an antipersonnel mine went off under Lieutenant Campillo's feet. The fallen officer was dragged in and bandaged up; fortunately, the medics appeared immediately, and everything went off like clockwork: he was hustled off to the regimental aid station, then to a medical battalion, and finally to the hospital.

When I heard that Campillo had been wounded, I visited him. He was more concerned about the welfare of his troops than he was about his own condition. Campillo was also visited by the commander of the Black Sea Group of Forces, Lt. Gen. I. E. Petrov. He gave the heroic miner his best wishes for full recovery and awarded him the Order of the Red Star. He also ordered that the lieutenant's rations be increased, and upon his departure, he told Campillo that the Soviet people would not forget the heroic deeds of their Spanish friends. The attention which the commander gave to the Spanish officer pleased all the Higher School students who were in the Caucasus.

There's still one more operation I want to tell about, involving Soviet and Spanish troops who performed an especially important mission for the commander of the Black Sea Group of Forces in March 1943.

I have already written that the main enemy communication line supplying the German-Fascist troops in the Krasnodar area at that time remained the line connecting Dzhanka, Vladislavovka, and Kerch. The command ordered the partisans and our troops to attack this line. Further, at the beginning of March, we needed to verify intelligence reports about the arrival of new enemy equipment in one of the enemy's testing grounds in the Crimea. For this mission, the staff of the Black Sea Group of Forces ordered us to assemble a small, well-trained group of demolitions and intelligence men. Among the demolitions and intelligence men there wasn't one who didn't know how difficult it was going to be for anyone who was dropped in the Crimea, but we still had no shortage of volunteers!

The size of the group was fixed at eleven men. The candidates were selected most carefully, consideration being given to physical fitness and morale factors; experience in operations behind enemy lines; the quality of special training; and character traits. We gave preference to people who were cheerful, resourceful, and easygoing, and had quick reactions. The selection was completed on 10 March. Thirty-three-year-old Maj. Miguel Boiso was designated group commander, and his deputy was thirty-five-year-old Maj. Fusimanio. The radio operator was Lt. Vadim Andreyevich Tarnovskiy. The group also included Yegor Kuzakin, Aleksey Kubashev, Juan Armenteros, Rodrigues Bara, Luis Jose, Pedro Penchalo, Jose Peral, and Juan Poiso. Hero of the Soviet Union Koshuba and his flight crew, all special operations experts attached to the 2d Special Aviation Group of the general staff, were picked to fly the group into the Crimea and put them on the drop zone. On the night of 14 March, the Boiso-Fusimanio group flew off, deep behind enemy lines, and descended by parachute, not far from the village of Shubin.

For several days and nights, the radio operators of the intelligence department of the Black Sea Group of Forces tensely scanned the air waves, hoping to pick out Tarnovskiy's call sign from the chaos of Morse code. He came up in communications on the evening of the fifth day. He gave very valuable information about the approaches to the secret enemy proving ground, and reported on the destruction of three enemy trains on the Dzhanka-Vladislavovka line. Then he hastily rapped out bad news: the group had been discovered and was trapped with their backs to the sea. Then, the transmission was interrupted!

Later we found out that the demolitions and intelligence men had fought a numerically far superior German force to their last grenade and cartridge, and when the last cartridge was gone, those still left alive went after the Germans with knives, and died in hand-to-hand combat.

The information that Tarnovskiy transmitted enabled another group of demolitions and intelligence men to get through to the German proving ground to observe the new tanks and self-propelled artillery that were concentrated there and to collect information on the new German fighter, the Focke-Wulf 190A.

The northern group of forces was ultimately unsuccessful in surrounding and destroying the German troops who were fleeing to Rostov-on-the-Don and Azov. The detachments that were dropped in the enemy rear didn't have enough time to do their sabotage work: three to five days after they landed, they already found themselves within the operational area of our attacking forces.

The troops of the Northern Caucasus Front were also unable to liberate Novorossiysk in the spring of 1943, or to clean out the Germans from the Taman, Kerch, and Crimean peninsulas. For this reason, we couldn't fulfill our plan to interrupt the enemy lines of communication ahead of the Black Sea Group of Forces. Operating in the enemy rear, groups of demolitions men and composite detachments of demolitions men and intelligence men sustained losses, and three groups were wiped out. But the enemy also sustained losses in their fights with our demolitions and intelligence men, mainly from the mines that went off beneath their trains. Their losses were far greater than ours, but then, enemy losses can't bring back your dead friends.

Number 18, Tver Boulevard

On the morning of 9 March, Kolonin invited me over and informed me about the 7 March decree of the State Defense Committee, which disbanded the Central Staff of the Partisan Movement. The decree announced a fait accompli: there was no opportunity for reconsideration.

I read the text over twice, and just couldn't understand the reason for the decision. The Central Staff had only been in operation nine months, and the Germans were still in control of our territory around Leningrad, in Belorussia, and a large part of the Ukraine.

Kolonin gently took the decree out of my hands.

"Don't rack your brains over this. The Kremlin knows best."

"But how about our detachments?"

"For the time being, just continue to fulfill your assignments for the Front. They'll decide everything in Moscow."

And things were indeed decided quickly. On 11 March, a radiogram arrived from Moscow for me:

Your school has been completely disbanded. We are placing you and your personnel at the disposal of the chief of staff of the Ukrainian Front, Comrade Strokach. You are offered the position of representative of the Ukrainian Staff of the Partisan Movement, and member of the Military Council of the Southern Front. You will assume the duties and responsibilities currently being performed by the acting representative of the Ukrainian Staff, Major Perekal'skiy, who is in Rostov. To acquaint you with the situation and with the duties of your new position, a representative of the Ukrainian Staff is traveling to Rostov. Telegraph your acceptance.

Timoshenko, Sokolov, Strokach
11.03.43. No. 800

I telegraphed my acceptance to Moscow and flew off, two days later, to my new duty station. I have many good memories about my sojourn on the Southern Front. It was good to know that the enemy did not approach Rostov through the minefields we had emplaced, and that they didn't even try to clear the mines. It was also good to meet my old assistant, Major Artem'yev, who was serving there in a special engineer brigade, and to meet Col. I. P. Koryavko, the commander of that brigade, who was a strong advocate of action against enemy communication lines. My meetings with the Southern Front commander, Gen. F. I. Tolbukhin, are firmly fixed in my memory. He was a thoughtful, attentive officer, who always asked both our saboteurs and the partisans to collect intelligence against the enemy. I was also glad that fate brought me into contact with such people as the remarkable intelligence officer, Colonel Mikhaylov; the commander of the famous partisan detachment, Mikhail Trifonov, who worked in the underground under the cover name Yugov, and with the deputy representative of the Ukrainian Staff attached to the Fifth Army, the young and daring Capt. D. B. Beliy, a born partisan, who became a journalist and scholar in the postwar years. My sojourn on the Southern Front was very short, however, not more than a month, because in mid-April I received a categorical telephonic order to return immediately to the capital by plane and to report to the Ukrainian Staff to assume the position of deputy chief of staff. They only gave me two hours to pack my gear, and then I was once more sitting in an Li-2, winging northeast.

The longer the flight lasted, the more often I looked out the window, trying to guess how close we were to the Moscow area. The almost greasy blackness of the steppes gave way to snow-traced ravines and reddish fields set with bristly glades. Dark green pine waves of forests rolled up on these fields, and scattered patches of pale snow were still lying in the fields and meadows, while the roads, the villages, and the hamlets seemed to cluster closer together as if to warm each other from the cold. We'd be there soon, very soon!

My impatience is easily explained. The spring and summer battles were at hand, and no one doubted that the Germans would try an attack to avenge the defeat at Stalingrad and regain the strategic initiative. We could either launch a preemptive strike, or stand

fast in our planned defensive positions until the enemy had worn
himself out, and then launch a counterattack. This was generally
the opinion of Tolbukhin and the Military Council of the Southern
Front. There was no difference of opinion among them about
where the German attack was going to fall, either. They all felt
that the decisive events would take place in the center of the
Soviet-German front, most likely in the area of the Kursk salient,
where the German-Fascist troops held favorable positions. This
was only a hunch, of course, but nevertheless, everyone was living and working with forebodings of threatening events, just
around the corner. I related my call to Moscow and my assignment to the position of deputy chief of staff of the Ukrainian Partisan Staff with the preparations for these developments, and I
supposed that for the partisans, this would initially mean preparations for strikes at enemy rail lines. As a matter of fact, many
German communications lines crossed the Ukraine, and much in
the course of our spring and summer campaign of 1943, if not the
entire campaign, would depend on whether the enemy could make
full use of those lines, and whether we could cut the *Wehrmacht*'s
strategic railroad supply lines. And we could cut the enemy transportation lines!

This was the way I looked at it: we had significant partisan forces on Ukrainian territory that was still occupied by the enemy.
The Ukrainian Staff maintained continual, reliable communications with them, and our industry had already started production
of some remarkable engineer mines, including a delayed-action
mine. The Ukrainian partisans had already acquired experience in
operations behind German lines: if we were able to supply those
partisans with mines and explosives at the beginning of conventional combat operations, then hundreds of enemy locomotives
would be derailed, along with thousands of cars, flatcars, and tank
cars; then hundreds of German tanks and artillery pieces, and hundreds of thousands of artillery rounds would not reach the front;
and thousands of German soldiers would be missing from ranks
and not see the front lines. The railroad junctions occupied by the
Germans would, in effect, be besieged. The result of all that
wasn't too difficult to imagine!

The Ukrainian Staff of the Partisan Movement was located in
one of the wings of the building at 18 Tver Boulevard, where
many of the leaders of the Communist party and government of
the Ukraine were working.

I went straight to Tver Boulevard from the airfield, not wishing
to delay my meeting with the chief of staff, Maj. Gen. Timofey
Ambrosyevich Strokach, whom I had known since 1941. Strokach

greeted me warmly, and invited in his deputy for cadres, L. P. Drozhzhin, and his deputy for operations, Col. V. F. Sokolov, whom I already knew as well. Drozhzhin gave me an order to read and sign, which designated me as deputy chief of staff for sabotage. I learned that the partisan operations plan for spring and summer had been completed, and Strokach asked me to go over it with Sokolov and to report to him the next morning if I had any comments on it.

Strokach was interested in knowing how I planned to organize my work. I suggested that it was necessary to establish a sabotage department on the staff. There were lots of people available to work in such a department. In the future, we'd probably be able to acquire additional engineers and instructors in the field of mines and demolitions. We had to improve sabotage equipment, summarize and disseminate combat experience, and establish close contact with industry and scholars. The questions of creating a new "technical" department, and of taking onto the staff of that department Boris Fedorovich Kosov, Sergey Vasilyevich Gridnev, Fedor Ivanovich Pavlov who had flown up from the south with me, and the former Rostov students as well were all resolved on the spot by the highly competent departmental secretary, Nina Vladimirovna Mala.

Sokolov showed me to my office, only three doors down from the chief of staff, and next to Sokolov's own office. He asked me if I'd heard the news: the Central Staff of the Partisan Movement had been resurrected! I remarked that this meant that the dissolution of the staff had obviously been premature, and he agreed. I was concerned that the Ukrainian Staff would therefore be dissolved, but he assured me otherwise. The Ukrainian Staff of the Partisan Movement (with its Moldavian department) was not subordinated to the Central Staff, but only to the Central Committee of the Communist party of the Ukraine and to the Stavka of the Supreme Command! Two pieces of news at one time, but what news!

A third piece of news awaited me at home. At first, I didn't notice anything when I was greeting Anna and the children, pulling out of my knapsack the canned goods that I had saved for them, washing my face and hands, and exchanging the usual phrases that one employs after a long separation. It was only after dinner that I noticed that Anna was rather quiet. I looked at her intently but it seemed as if she didn't notice my stare. This was obviously something serious. I waited until the kids had been put to bed, and I asked her what was going on. I saw hesitation in the eyes of this normally decisive woman. She placed her hand on mine: "Guillon has been wounded."

When? Where was he hit?

"In the stomach. A bullet. While he was crossing the front lines."

"Did they come out long ago?"

"In March."

Anna went to the window, and stared into the darkness of our courtyard.

"Why don't you say something, Anna?"

She turned abruptly, her eyes filled with unshed tears, held back by the simple force of her will.

"Brace yourself . . . people will tell you anyway . . ." and then she told me that during the winter, our good Spanish friends Padillo, Lorente, and Justo had been killed on a mission, and that Angel Alberca, Joaquin Gomez, and Benito Ustarros had been killed crossing the front lines. I sat, with bowed head. These were brave, just people; experienced, tough soldiers who never asked for anything for themselves. Anna said that Alberca and Ustarros had been posthumously awarded the Order of the Great Patriotic War, First Degree, but that she didn't know if any of the others had received posthumous decorations.

My first evening at home after such a long absence thus turned out to be rather bleak. It would have been even more bleak if we had known that Francisco Guillon would soon die from the wounds he had received.

On the next day, I took up my new duties. I began by reading the bulky "Operational Plan for Combat Operations of Ukrainian Partisans in the Spring and Summer of 1943," which Sokolov gave me. In various orders and plans of the partisan movement leadership, particularly during the first phases of the partisan movement, appeals to strike at enemy communications lines were often buried under more numerous calls to destroy enemy staffs, garrisons, independent enemy units, and to burn warehouses, cut telephone lines, etc. Inexperienced commanders of partisan detachments and formations wasted their resources trying to accomplish two- and three-step operations. The situation changed for the better after the order of the people's commissar for defense of 5 September 1942, which gave the partisans the principal mission of closing the roads on which the enemy was moving reinforcements, equipment, ammunition, and fuel up to the front.

The operational plan that I was reading took into consideration the 5 September order. It ordered the strongest Ukrainian partisan formations to go into the western and southwestern regions of the

Ukraine and carry out attacks on twenty-six of the most important rail junctions. The plan contemplated inserting about three hundred political officers into the partisan detachments and formations, and not less than thirty-nine tons of various kinds of supplies. The transport aircraft of the 101st Air Regiment, commanded by V. S. Grizodubova, and transport aircraft of the 1st and 61st Air Transport Divisions were to make a minimum of 350 flights into the enemy rear to deliver these personnel and materials.[1]

The focus and scale of the plan were impressive, but I knew that the meaning of the phrase: "attack railroad junctions" included direct attacks on the junctions, and their capture; the destruction of switches, water towers, semaphores, warehouses, and station facilities. A warning signal flashed on in my mind at that point. This signal was especially strong after the previous evening's discussions with Anna concerning unjustifiable losses and unnecessary victims.

Immediately after failure of the blitzkrieg, the Nazi command began to pay very serious attention to the security of their railroads. As early as 16 October 1941, Goering had given an order to shoot or hang any Russian caught within one kilometer of a rail line! Later, similar directives flowed from other Nazis of all ranks, as if out of a horn of plenty. The enemy increased the strength of the railroad guard forces in direct proportion to the number of sabotage incidents. In many locales, it was very difficult for the partisans to even approach a railroad roadbed. The enemy gave even more attention to the security of railroad junctions! Furthermore, these junctions were at large cities, where the Germans had strong garrisons and in a number of cases, had positioned artillery and even tanks. In times of crisis, the commanders of such garrisons could call in air support. For partisans to attack large railroad junctions, armed only with rifles, two or three mortars, and, in rare cases, maybe a couple of cannon, without being able to count on reinforcements meant taking enormous risks and sustaining great losses without any hope of complete success. My entire being rebelled against this kind of thinking!

I went to Sokolov. When he had heard my opinion that we had to go over the plan again, and make some serious corrections to it, he threw up his hands. They had already worked on the plan for two months: spring was almost finished! I explained to Sokolov why, in my opinion, the present plan would not be accomplished by throwing in detachments and formations to try to

---

1. Grizodubova, a pioneer in long-range endurance flying in the thirties, is listed by Soviet official sources as having commanded a bomber regiment in WWII, but the 101st seems to be a long-range special operations transport regiment.

capture and destroy enemy railroad junctions. He asked sarcastically if I thought we ought to leave the junctions alone, but I responded that we had to orient the partisans on putting the railroad junctions out of action by means of massive derailments of enemy trains. I pointed out that we had stocks of good antitrain mines and wheel switches for just such purposes.

I then drew Sokolov's attention to a rather significant detail: the numbers of casualties sustained by the Ukrainian partisans were inversely correlated with the frequency of attacks on the enemy rail lines! The partisans took their heaviest casualties in 1941, when a total of thirty trains had been derailed. In 1942, personnel losses fell, but the number of sabotage incidents had risen to 220. Just in February and March of 1943 alone, our losses were insignificant, but during only those two months, we had already sent 121 enemy trains sky-high!

I convinced Sokolov, but he still protested that we couldn't delay getting final approval for the plan, not to mention rewriting it. He pointed out that every day the plan was delayed meant a decrease in the number of aircraft flights that would be available for dropping personnel and supplies to the partisans. The nights were getting shorter as summer approached, thus reducing the range of long-range aircraft operations during hours of darkness. He also assured me that the partisan leaders were very well trained and that they wouldn't go rushing off to directly attack German-held rail junctions for anything. He cited the operation of Kovpak's partisans at Sarny during the previous fall, where they blew the bridges around the city, but did not attack the city itself, and Saburov's partisans, who sent out small detachments to set mines along the tracks. He said that the other partisan leaders were beginning to operate like that, as well. Sokolov said that the first thing was to get the plan approved as it stood and that we could refine it later, using normal working procedures.

I hesitated, and said that I still felt compelled to report my concerns to Strokach, and he also agreed that I should, but warned me not to expect that we'd rework the plan: there simply wasn't any time left!

Strokach gave close attention, but was hesitant about accepting my recommendation to completely avoid attacks on rail junctions and concentrate on blowing up enemy trains. First, he remarked that the partisans were totally unfamiliar with many of our newer types of mines. These included the chemical capsule mines, and the delayed-action antitrain mines with vibration switches. He pointed out that he had only heard about the capsule mines from me, and that the graduates of the special school at Saratov didn't even know about the delayed-action mines. How could the average partisan know about them?

I couldn't pass up the opportunity! I told him that we could establish training for the partisans right in their own operating areas, in the enemy rear, using the instructors and graduates from the Higher School, who would soon be returning to Moscow from the Caucasus: I'd even go in with them! He wanted to know what would happen if the partisan units went off on raids, and I told him that we'd go off with them: we could even train the partisans while they were on raids!

Strokach suggested that I write a letter, setting forth my views, and that he would present it to the Central Committee of the Ukrainian Communist party. Based on his knowledge of the operations carried out by the Kovpak and Saburov partisan formations, he agreed with my position, but he still wanted to see what the higher-ups thought about the idea.

The Ukrainian Central Committee approved of my idea of blockading the railroad junctions with mines. They didn't ask us for a revised plan for spring and summer partisan operations, and they didn't completely abandon the idea of attacking railroad junctions. They recommended, in addition, that we immediately develop and duplicate instructions on the use of the newest mines and sent them to the partisans in the Ukraine; and that we also send mining and demolitions instructors to partisan detachments and formations, and plan for the delivery of new mines along with the delivery of explosives.

"You see," Sokolov said. "Little by little, everything works out."

To Wage War on Rails

On 23 April, General Strokach summoned Colonel Sokolov and me to his office. He looked worried. He told us that he had just had a serious conversation with the chief of the Central Staff of the Partisan Movement, P. K. Ponomarenko. In the Central Staff they felt, with good reason, that the disorganization of railroad transportation would not attain the scale necessary to have a significant influence on the support of German troops. This was mainly because the sabotage operations would not be carried out simultaneously, but piecemeal, and the Germans would be able to repair the damage from the individual incidents without much difficulty.

In Ponomarenko's opinion, blowing up enemy trains and bridges wouldn't give the desired effect even if we were to increase the number of the incidents two- or threefold. In his view, what was called for was a well-planned, massive strike on the enemy communications lines. We couldn't delay launching this strike, he felt, in view of the anticipated bitterness of the fighting in the summer. The Central Staff had therefore developed an operations plan under the code name RAIL WAR. In the course of this operation, all partisan efforts were to be devoted to blowing up railroad *rails*. According to preliminary calculations of the Central Staff, we could blow up three hundred thousand lengths of rail in a month. In the view of the Central Staff, this would completely paralyze all military transport on occupied Soviet territory. The Ukrainian partisans were to blow up eighty-five thousand to ninety thousand lengths of rails. I was taken aback by this: there was no question about the need for simultaneous strikes—but specifically on *rails*?

Strokach told us that the matter was not open for discussion. Ponomarenko had told him that the idea of "rail war" had been accepted in principal by Comrade Stalin. I pointed out that destroying the required number of rails would take a lot more explosives than we currently had, and Sokolov noted that we would need many more aircraft to deliver the explosives. Strokach responded that Ponomarenko had told him that both explosives and aircraft would be available. Strokach told us to get cracking: Sokolov was to correct the plan, and I was to calculate how many rails there were to destroy in the German-held parts of the Ukraine, and to generally assess the conditions of the railroads in those areas. There was no time to waste!

The next day, I went to the Central Directorate of Military Communications and submitted our request for information on the conditions of the railroads on presently German-occupied territory of the Ukraine. A colonel whom I knew took our request:

"So you're getting ready to blow up rails in the Ukraine, too? Isn't it enough that the Germans are bending the rails when they withdraw?"

That brief conversation aroused a strong feeling of resentment in me. We ourselves would actually have to replace the rails that we blew up. But more importantly, by Ponomarenko's narrow focus on just rails alone, much of the work accomplished by my technical department was going to be wasted!

We had gotten people to improve their knowledge of special

equipment and methods of sabotage; we were summarizing and disseminating experience of the best partisan demolitions men! The department had already prepared and submitted for printing a booklet describing the construction of some delayed-action mines and recommendations for their use, as well as directives on organizing sabotage services in partisan detachments and formations. We had inspected mine stores and had determined the suitability of electrochemical switches for use in summer; we had established contact with some institutes of the Academy of Sciences of the USSR and with a number of special institutes and design bureaus that were involved in the preparation of new explosives and the development of new mining and demolitions equipment. Did we really do all of this for nothing?

I took my doubts about this to Strokach. He advised me to continue working as in the past, and assured me that no one was going to do away with mines or mine warfare. He emphasized that the plan provided for mine warfare. His words, and the firm tone in which he uttered them, cheered me up considerably. While I awaited the response to our request to the Main Military Communications Directorate, my normal workload was driving me out of my mind, anyway.

Despite the fact that Stalin had approved the rail war plan, it never received the proper logistics support, and for this reason, the Ukrainian partisans didn't participate in it. Khrushchev and Strokach both knew that you shouldn't waste scarce explosives on breaking up rails, but on derailing trains. As a result, the Ukrainian partisans destroyed 3,143 trains in the second half of 1943, twice the number destroyed in the two years that had elapsed between June 1941 and June 1943. The rail war, on the other hand, really missed the target. The enemy didn't suffer any significant damage, and the massive destruction of rails on secondary track sections led to a reduction in the numbers of trains destroyed. In any case, one hundred to two hundred gram TNT charges didn't destroy the rails, but just blew out pieces twenty-five to thirty-five centimeters long. The Germans either cut the damaged sections and welded in new pieces with thermite, or used "rail bridges," eighty centimeters long and weighing about twenty kilograms each, to span the damaged sections. It was a paradoxical situation: during the rail war, the retreating Germans blew up rails on the main lines and ripped up and carried off rails from nonoperational lines. At the same time, some partisan formations were breaking up rails on secondary lines, which should have been maintained intact for our own troops to use!

On the eve of May Day, I had to give priority attention to the detachments of the now-dissolved Higher School, which were finally returning from the Caucasus. Captain Chepak, who had commanded the detachments, appeared in my office at the beginning of the work day. He reported that the troop trains with the detachments were moving very slowly. They frequently had to be sidetracked so that trains that were moving troops and equipment to the front could pass, and they had also been bombed. I presented Chepak to General Strokach. It was decided that the captain would head up the Special Purpose School of the Ukrainian Staff of the Partisan Movement and that the personnel of the former Higher School would be sent off—some to new schools, and others to partisan detachments and formations, to serve as instructors and to strengthen their sabotage services. The problem of what to do with our Spanish comrades who were still in school could not be solved without a visit to the Comintern, and so Drozhzhin and I went off again to see Comintern Secretary Georgiy Dimitrov. We found a friendly reception: Dimitrov wanted to know about our operations in the Caucasus and the Ukraine, and he talked about the problems facing the Bulgarian partisans. When we got around to discussing the Spaniards' further employment, Dimitrov reported that the Spanish Party asked that they either be used in their actual conventional military specialties in regular Red Army units or trained for the anticipated future struggle in Spain. Dimitrov was correct, of course, but it was going to be difficult to separate from the comrades with whom I had gone through so much! Soon, all of the Spaniards were enrolled in the ranks of the Red Army: only one—Ramiles—was able to argue with the Spanish Communist party that he was a specialist in mines and demolitions, and came back to me. Not long after, he flew off into the enemy rear, to the partisan unit commanded by Nikolai Nikitovich Popudrenko, where he became the deputy for sabotage.

Shortly after the meeting with Dimitrov, Starinov was sent off on a mission to the Voronezh and Central Fronts, where preparations were being made for launching an offensive after the enemy had been worn down in the Kursk salient. It was necessary that partisans and engineer troops coordinate their attacks on enemy communications lines between Belgorod and Kharkov and Belgorod and Sumy. Starinov worked with engineer staffs and personnel of the guards miners' battalions, instructing them in the use of delayed-action mines and new mining tactics for small groups of demolitions men operating behind enemy lines. These tactics included the use of mines as offensive

weapons, a matter which Starinov had long considered. Return-
ing to Moscow, Starinov was also called upon to give refresher
courses for partisans and Party officials who had been evacu-
ated from the German rear to recuperate from wounds and
were about to be returned to organize new partisan groups. Al-
though some were quite certain that they knew all there was to
know about blowing up trains, the new delayed-action mines
developed under Starinov's direction were a pleasant surprise
to them. Many volunteered for partisan and sabotage work in
this period, so many that it was impossible to honor all re-
quests, but during spring of 1943 alone, the Ukrainian staff
sent 120 well-trained demolitions personnel, including 67 in-
structors and 53 officers and staff personnel, on missions
behind enemy lines.

Before 10 May, the Central Directorate of Military Communications responded to our request for information on the railroads in
the Ukraine, informing us that on the occupied territory of the
Ukraine there were more than four million pieces of rail, that there
was no shortage of rails, and that the Germans were actually having some rails melted down. The enemy *did* have a serious shortage of locomotives, however; on the entire occupied area of the
USSR, at that time, there were less than five thousand fit for use.

These numbers puzzled Strokach. He was finally convinced of
the correctness of the position of our technical department: *the*
rails that the Ukrainian partisans were planning to destroy made
up only 2 percent of the total number of rails on the occupied ter-
ritory of the USSR, and in order to destroy this 2 percent, we were
going to have to use all the explosives that we would be able to
deliver to the partisans. Even then, it was uncertain if we would
be able to deliver such a quantity of explosives to the partisans:
for May, we had not yet been given the promised number of aircraft, and in July we had to anticipate a reduction of flying time
because of the shortened summer nights! Strokach asked me to
call the Central Staff and see if I could get more aircraft assigned:
I did, and the result was *one* additional aircraft for May!

Across the Front Lines

The situation in the enemy rear was becoming serious: the Germans were mounting large search-and-destroy missions against partisans, had driven the partisans away from the railroads in several places, and had managed to capture all but one of the partisan-held airfields that were close enough to the front to be reached on a one-way night flight from Soviet lines. This airfield was in the Lel'chitsy district of the Poles'ye region, and was held by A. N. Saburov's partisan formation. All Ukrainian partisan groups depended on this airfield for resupply. As a result of the logistics situation, all partisan operations were cut back considerably: the Ukrainian Staff issued a directive telling the partisan forces to concentrate their efforts on derailing trains with modern delayed-action mines, as opposed to simply destroyed rails. Destruction of rails was only to be carried out for the purpose of distracting enemy attention from the emplacement of the new delayed-action mines. Strokach felt that the Ukrainian partisans should not participate in the rail war ordered by the Central Staff, but instead should participate in a railroad war, i.e., a campaign to destroy rolling stock with mines. Strokach ordered Starinov and others to prepare for a trip behind enemy lines to the Saburov partisan formation, to personally inform Saburov and his subordinate partisan leaders of the required changes in operational plans.

Strokach was late. The sunset had faded, but—no general! It was completely dark, the stars were beginning to appear, and only far to the west, over the dark jagged shadows of the distant woods, the white-green afterglow of day was still visible between the clouds—but still no general!

A duty officer approached with a message from V. S. Grizodubova, the commander of the air regiment: "Comrade Colonel, the flight has been changed! You'll never make it to the partisans by dawn!"

Strokach's adjutant, his communications officers, and the instructors in mines and demolitions who were flying with us awaited my decision.

"Let's wait for Timofey Ambrosyevich," I said.

The duty officer went off shrugging his shoulders. I wondered whether to follow him, when I heard the sound of a speeding auto. The sound drew nearer, reached a peak, and then died: brakes screeched, doors slammed abruptly, and out of the darkness Strokach appeared, striding rapidly.

"You aren't in the plane yet?"

"The flight has been changed, Comrade General. It's too late."

"What's this 'changed' stuff? What the hell does 'too late' mean? Where's Grizodubova? Let's go see her, Ilya Grigor'yevich!"

Col. Valentina Stepanovna Grizodubova, Hero of the Soviet Union, listened to the general sympathetically: "Yes, yes, certainly we can fly," she said. "We just have to change the flight route. You'll fly via Lipetsk, Comrade General. There the night is about forty minutes longer, and the route to the enemy rear is shorter from there."

But Strokach protested. "For pity's sake, Valentina Stepanovna! Don't you see that it's at least five hundred kilometers to Lipetsk, if not more?"

"Five hundred," agreed Grizodubova. "That's nothing. I'm telling you, you'll make it to the enemy rear."

"But then you'll still have to fly from Lipetsk tomorrow!"

"Obviously."

"No!" interrupted the general. "I won't hear of any 'tomorrow'! The weather might turn bad, or some damn thing or other might happen, and every day counts. We have to fly today! Immediately!"

Grizodubova wavered, and finally backed down. "By your command."

The transport plane climbed, engines roaring and whining. We left darkness behind. The round rivet heads on the plane's gray wings became visible. So here I was, after a long break, going behind enemy lines once again!

The feeling of excitement that came over me was different from the excitement that was felt by the general's young adjutant and the staff communications officers. They might be upset by the unfamiliar situation, the feeling of danger, and the need to test and prove themselves. I once had similar feelings, long before, at Villanueva de Cordoba in Spain. Right now, however, I was totally preoccupied, going over our plan in my mind to see whether we had made any mistakes, no matter how small. I couldn't find any mistakes: we had enough of the most modern mines, and they would be given to the population that had risen against the occupation forces. The Germans weren't going to be able to avoid disaster!

We approached the front lines at a high altitude. Extra gas tanks installed in the fuselage of the aircraft seemed to be bubbling, giving off a reek of aviation gas. And down below, on the dark-shrouded earth, raged a soundless storm of dots and dashes of light: rosy, red, and yellowish streaks and points of light. Unfortunately, we knew that these were actually the flashes of heavy guns and exploding shells.

Suddenly off to the left of the plane, a string of lights burst into flame and hung suspended: these were "headlights," German illuminating rockets.[1]

Almost simultaneously, expanding columns of trembling light reared up and began to wander through the night sky: these were the beams of enemy searchlights. They were approaching, groping, aiming for us . . .

I was hoping that we'd slip through, and afterward Strokach admitted that he had hoped so, too, but we didn't quite make it. The interior of the fuselage suddenly became as bright as if we'd lit a chandelier with five hundred candles. The metal ribs of the airframe, the faces and the figures of the passengers huddled together on the benches along the sides of the plane suddenly emerged clearly from the darkness. Some squinted, and others covered their eyes with their hands. In the windows, you could see the flak bursting near by. In moments of mortal danger, there is absolutely nothing worse than enforced passivity. But there was nothing else that we passengers could do but sit and wait! We could only rely on the pilots, and not on ourselves!

The aircraft commander, Captain Slepov, abruptly threw the plane into a dive. The benches slid out from beneath us, and we had to hang onto structural members of the plane, and onto each other. Not everyone was able to hang on to something, and some slid right into the cockpit. Roaring, the plane accelerated its dive, and the pain in our ears was unbearable.

It became dark in the fuselage again, there were no more flashes in the windows; the plane was no longer falling; the engines were purring evenly. It was time for me to try to grab the bench. And I was successful! Slepov returned to horizontal flight, and there was darkness beneath us once more. The deadly dots and dashes of light had disappeared, which showed that the front lines were already far behind us.

Strokach grabbed me by the shoulder and told me to look out

1. These lights were known as "flaming onions" to British and American aviators in Western Europe.

the window. What was this, anyway? Flickering red and yellow lights appeared, arranged in squares, rectangles crossed by intersecting diagonals, and even in the forms of letters. Some of these figures were extinguished as we approached, others changed configuration, and still others were illuminated to replace those that had gone out. From the plane, these looked like partisan campfire signals. It was also possible of course, that some fires had been set by German hunter-killer missions, who were attempting to lure in inexperienced pilots. Well, the SS weren't going to play that trick on us; not by a long shot! After what we'd been through, all of us passengers on the plane trusted Captain Slepov and his assistants. Further, the endless partisan campfires cheered us: these showed that the German rear was really in fragile condition, while the scale of the popular struggle against the occupation forces was enormous!

But our jokes and laughter didn't last long. The short June night was fast coming to an end, and here we were, still flying toward Poles'ye. Strokach looked at his watch. According to calculations, we should have long since reached Saburov's airfield. All alone, in broad daylight, a defenseless Li-2 was a great find for German fighter planes. In an emergency, we were supposed to land, but where?

It became completely light, and the sun actually appeared. No one was talking or even smiling. Everyone was looking intently at the terrain drifting by beneath our plane. Then, someone noticed the traditional indications that we were going to land. I don't know who noticed them first: all I know is that I felt fatigue, mixed with relief.

There was a shock, then another, and the plane shook slightly and rocked. The bright foliage, flowing tailward past the plane window, slowed down, and came to a complete stop. There was a subsiding whirr of the propellers. The copilot ran down the cabin between us, in a crouch, opened the hatch, and fastened a metal ladder to the fuselage.

"You can get out, Comrade General!"

Light flooded in through the opening, along with the fresh early morning smell of earth, and the gentle rustling of leaves. Before us stretched a large clearing, at the edge of which were birch groves and huts with smoking chimneys. There were also grazing goats, fenced in with palings and tied to pegs, totally indifferent to the airplane. Partisans came running out of the woods. Some wore Soviet tunics, others wore captured German uniform coats, some wore padded jackets. A tall red-haired fellow in a Kuban cap presented himself smartly to Strokach:

"Company Commander Smirnov! Sent to meet and escort you!"

We heard the command: "Cover the plane!" and the partisans swarming around the Li-2 began to move the heavy machine. It slowly crawled to the opposite side of the field from the huts, where it was placed under a canopy of great branching oaks. The grass that had been pressed down by the plane wheels was straightened up, and then there was no plane, and not even a sign of an airfield: only a big clearing with a few woodsmen's huts, and some goats.

They gave us horses for the one-and-a-half-hour trip to Saburov's headquarters. The trail led us through woods and fields. The young leaves of the trees whispered serenely, and from afar, as if from the innocent days of my boyhood, I heard the magical call of a cuckoo. Between the copper-colored trunks of the pine trees, the Ubort' River flowed in blue and silver. The thick, waving, unmown grass threw rainbow reflections in our eyes, weeds poked up in the fields, and here and there, stands of tall corn caught the eye, among the turnips and other vegetables.

We came to a burned-out village. Along the overgrown street, there were only maples and fireplace chimneys. The mantels of the few surviving fireplaces yawned like shrieking black mouths.

"Hunter-killer mission," the leader of the party explained laconically. "Not many got out alive."

We stopped at an old well and took turns drinking from an ironbound wooden bucket. When I had taken my turn, I noticed a young boy about ten years old. He was barefoot and dressed in an old frayed shirt. He stood looking at me, a long stick in his hand, thrusting out his swollen stomach. In his bony face, beneath a tangle of uncombed hair, were unforgettable blue eyes. I almost felt guilty in front of him.

"Mister Soldier,"[2] he suddenly said in a cheerful voice, "Mister Soldier, give me a star."

I hastily found a spare shoulder-board star and handed it to the boy. He took it and skipped off.

We were stopped several times by partisan patrols, but finally approached the place where the Saburov staff was located. Between the trees, you could see the tops of bunkers jutting up, and clothes lines with wash hung out to dry; you could smell the smoke, and hear human voices.

In the midst of the trees, a clearing was lit by the morning sun, and in the clearing was a large log house. Before the house, stood a group of people. From far away, I was able to recognize

2. The exact term used was *dyaden'ka* "uncle," a quasi-honorific term used by Russian children to address unknown males, roughly equivalent in usage to mister.

Dem'yan Sergeyevich Korotchenko, Aleksey Fedorovich Fedorov, Sidor Artem'yevich Kovpak, and Stepan Antonovich Oleksenko. A man in a general's uniform, with distinct military bearing, separated from the group as we approached and came out to meet us. This was obviously Major General Saburov,[3] whom I had not previously met.

When we dismounted, Saburov gave his report, and when it was finished, he and Strokach embraced. Then, the whole group clustered around us, and it seemed as if the hugging and the handshaking would never end. I looked around and noticed the happy faces, the confident movements and voices of the men in officers' and generals' uniforms and shoulder boards. These were were not exhausted people who had been harried into the woods and outlands: these were powerful lords of their own domains. In order to present that kind of appearance, you had to have triumphed over every kind of grief and failure.

Meeting in Poles'ye

At tables set in the open clearing, they were waiting breakfast for us. Strokach looked at the spread and threw up his hands:

"I see that you do not live by potatoes alone!"

"We requisition this stuff from the enemy and exchange it in the villages for salt and kerosene," Saburov said. "Please Comrades, this way!"

Occasionally, I glanced across the table at the tanned, black-moustached commissar of Kovpak's formation, Semen Vasilyevich Rudnev. Although I had no friends or acquaintances with such a family name or patronymic, I couldn't get over the feeling that I had frequently dealt with him before.

Rudnev also seemed to be staring at me as if he were trying to recall something, as well. I seized an opportunity and leaned forward to the commissar: "Semen Vasilyevich, excuse me, but haven't we met before?"

Rudnev stroked his moustache and said: "You know, I once studied with an instructor named Ilya Grigor'yev . . ."

Suddenly, everything finally fell into place! It was Kiev, in

3. Saburov was a career NKVD officer who received the title of Hero of the Soviet Union for his partisan work in 1942.

1933, at the partisan school! I was teaching there under the name of Grigor'yev, one of my cover names at the time!

"And what family name were *you* working under, ten years ago, in Kiev?" I smiled. "Grigor'yev never had a student named Rudnev!"

"Is that you, Ilya Grigor'yev?" Rudnev suddenly stood up. "It certainly looked like you, but then they were calling you 'Starinov,' and I really wasn't sure whether I had made a mistake or whether you were operating under deep cover again!"

We grabbed each other's hands.

"What's this? Old friends?" Strokach asked.

"*Really* old friends, Timofey Ambrosyevich," Rudnev said.

It's awkward to indulge in personal reminiscences in front of people whom you don't know very well.

"When you visit our formation, then we'll talk," suggested Rudnev.

The tablecloth was taken away, the smokers lit up, and the aroma of tobacco smoke encircled the table. Saburov yielded his place at the head of the table to Dem'yan Sergeyevich Korotchenko. "Let's start the meeting, comrades!"

Korotchenko stated that our nation and our people stood on the brink of momentous events at the front, and then explained that Soviet forces stood ready to wear down the enemy and then go over to the offensive in the area of the Kursk salient. The Stavka of the Supreme Command, and Comrade Stalin personally, demanded that the partisans become more active. The Ukrainian partisans were assigned to attack railroads in the rear of the German Army Group South. The carrying capacity of the roads was to be reduced to "zero." This would facilitate the tasks that the regular Red Army were to accomplish. Korotchenko said that the summer operations plan had been reviewed by the Ukrainian Party and the Ukrainian Partisan Staff in light of the urgent needs of the moment. As a result, the plan had been revised, and greater detail had been introduced in some areas. He then turned the meeting over to General Strokach who was to take up the changes in detail. The changes were, in fact, quite serious: for example, Kovpak's formation was relieved of the responsibility for destroying the rail junctions at Zhmerinka, Kazatin, and Fastov. Instead, the formation was to operate in the Chernovtsy region, to attack communications lines, and organize partisan warfare in the Carpathian section of the Ukraine. Saburov's formation was not to transfer to the Stanislav region, but to take up the tasks of attacking Zhmerinka, Kazatin, and Fastov, as well as Korosten,

Shepetovka, and Kiev. Malikov's formation was to concentrate its efforts on the Berdichev-Zhitomir rail line, etc.

They listened to Strokach, occasionally throwing quick glances at him and at each other. Kovpak's eyes narrowed, as usual; he was squinting now at Vershigora, now at Rudnev; Saburov, his arms folded across his chest, was focusing on some point or other on the tabletop; Mel'nik had almost closed his eyes . . .

Something was obviously going on here, something expressed more clearly in body language than in words: the changes in the plan had clearly aroused some kind of resistance. Saburov, for example, immediately drew the attention of Strokach and Korotchenko to the fact that the changes in the plan required that the formations be broken up into small detachments. It was going to be difficult to operate and supply these detachments, far from each other, and small detachments would be unable to directly engage the enemy.

It appeared to me that Strokach had expected this kind of resistance. He firmly told them that the plan was to be viewed as a direct order, and said that he'd discuss with the commander of each formation the precise details of how to best fulfill the assigned missions. When he asked for questions, they had plenty: about the amount of explosives and weapons that they could count on, the precise timing of the operations, whether they'd be getting any radiomen, etc. Strokach answered some of the questions, and promised to answer the other questions when he visited the individual formations. The meeting broke up on that note. It's true that the partisan commanders and officers hung around talking for a while, but I didn't have the opportunity to listen to their unofficial remarks: I had been invited to conduct a training session with Saburov's mine specialists.

My new students included many elderly people: it seemed as if not only the youngsters wanted to get involved in sabotage! Because these were older people, and peasants as well, and because their formal education amounted to little more than what they had received in the mass illiteracy programs of the twenties and thirties, I shortened the theoretical portion of the training and increased the practical emphasis. After they had gotten the mines in their hands, had been taught to vary the time-delay, and had repeated the methods of application that we taught them, I was sure that they would be able to operate perfectly well, even without knowledge of the laws of physics and chemistry. I held no illusions about how well my novices ultimately mastered the material. For that, I had to completely rely on Saburov's instructors, who had much more time than I for checking student proficiency.

I was able to rely even more on these instructors since they were
S. P. Mineyev and his wife, Klavdia Mineyeva, the very same
Klavochka from the match factory, who had been so eager to get
into partisan work in 1941! We finished training when it got dark
and no one could see anything.

The next day we visited Kovpak's formation, which was three
to four kilometers from Saburov's camp. Strokach passed out
medals and orders[1] to three hundred or so troops of the first battalion, otherwise known as the Putivl' detachment. After Strokach
and Korotchenko went into a meeting with Kovpak, Rudnev, and
Vershigora, and commanders and commissars of the partisan detachments, I had the chance to check on how the mines and demolitions equipment was stored in the unit, how the instructors were
working, and how well many new miners knew their jobs. I also
conducted training for the instructors, showing them several new
developments in demolitions equipment. At dinner, Kovpak asked
whether I was pleased with the demolitions personnel, and I answered that I certainly was. At that point Kovpak turned to Strokach and complained that he wasn't getting enough explosives.

It was only after midnight that Rudnev and I had a chance to
be alone. We sat in the dark woods, on the trunk of a fallen tree,
and talked about prewar Kiev, our old friends, and how we were
training for partisan war, way back then. Rudnev told me that he
was fighting side by side with his son, who was called Radi. The
boy was brave, actually a bit too brave: possibly because he didn't
wish to reflect adversely on his father's position of authority. The
voice of Semen Vasilyevich broke: during the previous summer,
enemy fragments had penetrated the boy's throat, cutting his vocal
cords. "I'm worried that we won't have enough mines and explosives for our raids," admitted Rudnev. "You know, we're out of
range of supply aircraft."

"That's only if the front doesn't advance further westward, Semen Vasilyevich, but it's certainly going to advance!"

Suddenly Strokach called me: "Ilya Grigor'yevich, I need you!
There's work to do!"

"Okay, I'm coming"

Rudnev and I shook hands and bid each other good-night.
Later, lying on a heap of fragrant hay, beneath the parachute canopy that served as a tent, I realized with regret that we had not
even mentioned the names of some of our acquaintances who had
been "repressed" in the purges of the midthirties. This thought
kept me awake for a long time, and I lay there listening to the

1. In Soviet military terminology, "orders" are decorations awarded for special merit in building or defending socialism.

quiet murmurings of the woods, the sentries on their rounds, and the rustlings of something around my own tent, maybe a mouse, or a night beetle.

Early the next morning, Korotchenko, Strokach, their adjutants and their communications officers set out for the base camp of the formation commanded by Aleksey Fedorovich Fedorov. I was delayed in my own departure by the need to check some defective chemical fuses, which had been delivered by the last plane, and so I only arrived at 1:00 P.M. at the staff of the Fedorov formation, located in the village of Borovoye, which stretched along the banks of the Ubort'. After feeding us and permitting us to recover from our trip, Fedorov suggested that we go into the woods with him to visit his training grounds. I smiled inwardly. The nearest railroad line was thirty-five kilometers away from Borovoye: how could he have a "training ground" here? I knew, however, that the formation commander loved to play practical jokes on people, and got annoyed if they didn't fall for the jokes, so I decided to go along with him.

We didn't go far: there, in a long woodland clearing, a railroad embankment appeared before my eyes! It was incredible!! A railroad embankment with ties, rails, and ballast! The track led nowhere: it began and ended in the clearing. It was also not very big; twenty-five to thirty meters at most, but it actually existed! Partisan demolitions men were clustered over the shining rails and the oil-blackened ties, and I saw the tall, thin, and well-known figure of my old finance officer, Capt. Aleksey Semenovich Yegorov, who was now Fedorov's deputy for sabotage!

I was astounded. They'd had to obtain gravel and dump it there, carry ties and rails across dozens of kilometers, and put it all together in such a short time.

Behind me, Fedorov's voice rang out with his familiar sly intonation: "Well you know, it's not the Moscow test track, but nonetheless, it is something . . ."

I had to admit that he'd won again, and that I thought he was going to play a practical joke on me. The thought struck me that we could use his mock-up to train partisans from other units, and Fedorov declared that he wasn't against that idea, particularly in view of the fact that his men would be leaving the area in two days. We stayed at the training for about three hours: I asked Yegorov about the details of building the track section, and convinced myself that all the demolitions men, without exception, had completely mastered the tactical-technical details of the new mines. I also had the opportunity to observe the work of the captain's students for myself. They worked rapidly and expertly, and there was no need to check out any mines that they had set. Yegorov had trained 320 students so far! When I got back to Borovoye, I immediately told Strokach that we needed to send other demolitions men to train at Fedorov's training area. He agreed that it was a good idea, but for later: other developments had assumed first priority. He told me that he had received information that the German-Fascist command was massing a significant group of regular and antipartisan hunter-killer forces in the areas of Mozyr', Yel'sk, Ovruch, Olevsk, and Petrikov. According to Strokach, the enemy's total strength was about sixty thousand men. All indications were that they were preparing to launch a major sweep against the partisan units that had concentrated here. We had to send these units off on raids as soon as possible: we could not let the enemy entice the partisans into defensive combat. This changed things completely: I was just sorry that this unique partisan training ground in the enemy rear was not going to be fully utilized. A day later, the Fedorov and Kovpak formations went off in raids. The whole village of Borovoye saw off Fedorov. I was excited by Rudnev's parting words: "We didn't get to talk about the things we wanted to discuss. I've thought about so much, suffered so much. But what can we do about it now? I guess we'll have to talk about it after the war is over." And he stretched out his arms: "Let's embrace, Ilya Grigor'yevich!"

And we embraced. An hour later, the Kovpak formation moved out. I never saw Rudnev again.

According to a communication received by the editor from a source of the highest reliability, Rudnev was executed as an enemy of the people while participating in this operation behind German lines. The execution was carried out under orders of NKVD Gen. Pavel Sudoplatov who ran partisan operations for the Fourth Directorate (Partisans) of the NKGB. The source states that the unusual execution of Rudnev, an old Bolshevik political officer, who had participated in the storming of the Winter Palace in 1917, was carried out by Rudnev's female radio operator who was operating under NKVD control, as were all partisan radio operators at the time. NKVD control of communications was apparently deemed necessary by Stalin to guarantee security against possible anti-Soviet activities by partisans. In typically cynical Soviet fashion, Rudnev was posthumously awarded the title of Hero of the Soviet Union in 1944. Starinov was surely aware of Rudnev's fate. After paying tribute to his friend and former student, Starinov's use of the phrase: "I never saw him again," appears to be an attempt to indicate to the Soviet reader that Rudnev's demise was not due to enemy action, but to more sinister causes. Maj. Gen. Vasiliy Andreyevich Begma[2] states that prior to departing on the raid, Kovpak and Rudnev had been warned by the Central Committee of the Communist party of the Ukraine about the relationships that they had developed—or were developing—with Ukrainian nationalist (i.e., anti-Stalinist) partisans who were also operating in the area. As described below, Kovpak's Carpathian raid, on which Rudnev died, was a failure. Kovpak was relieved of command shortly afterward and replaced by Vershigora. Rudnev's death is almost certainly linked to the relationships established with the nationalist "enemies of the people." These relationships may also have provided some justification for Kovpak's replacement. This is not merely "ancient history," however, for according to the source, an attempt is at present being made in the Central Intelligence Service to bring Sudoplatov to trial for his role in the death of Rudnev.

After we spent the night in Kovpak's now-empty camp, our operations group traveled to the Rovno partisan formation, commanded by V. A. Begma. It was evening before we completed the thirty-kilometer trip over forest roads. The partisans had finished dinner, and music was resounding through the whole camp: here an accordion, there a fiddle, there a harmonica.

Strokach joked: "This isn't a formation—it's an orchestra! You're living well, Vasiliy Andreyevich!"

"Can't complain, we can't complain," Begma answered in the same tone. "The people need cultural recreation."

The next day was similar to the previous ones: presentation of medals to the partisans, meetings with detachment commanding officers and commissars, visiting Begma's detachments, inspecting the mines and demolitions stocks, checking the work of the instructors and training the demolitions men.

Several days later, I left the partisan area, by Strokach's order, to return to Moscow business and concerns. I was not able to wait until all the formations and detachments had gone off on their raids, but I flew away in a calm, optimistic mood. The partisans had received about thirty tons of TNT, more than five thousand mines of the latest models, and the necessary amount of igniters, fuses, switches, Bickford cord, and detonator cord. Further, every detachment included *hundreds* of demolitions men!

2. Begma, V. A. "Stranichki tekh let" (Pages from those years), in: *Geroi podpol'ya*, Moscow, 1972. Politizdat.

After Starinov's departure, it took several more days for the partisan formations of the Ukrainian Staff of the Partisan Movement to reach their respective operational areas. The first to report was Fedorov, whose detachments were to set thirty delayed-action mines on every railroad section that had been assigned to them. Any attempt to remove or disarm these mines would detonate them. The delayed-action mines were protected by yet other mines, designed to detonate upon the first touch of enemy sappers' probes. To divert enemy attention from the delayed-action mines, instantaneous mines were used to blow up trains on other stretches of track.

The gigantic battle of Kursk began on 5 July, and despite great losses inflicted by Soviet defenders, the enemy slowly advanced in the Kursk salient. Bitter fighting was also going on on the Central and Voronezh fronts, and Soviet losses were also great. Deep in the German rear area, however, partisan operations of an unprecedented scale were launched by Ukrainian partisans, according to the plan developed by the Ukrainian Staff. On 7 July, the first of Fedorov's delayed-action mines went off under a train carrying tanks and munitions. Then, the commanders of the other Ukrainian detachments—Kovpak, Naumov, Mel'nik, Malikov, I. F. Fedorov, etc.—began to report concerning their sabotage operations against enemy communications lines. After 10–11 July, reports of derailments of enemy trains, and blown bridges came in almost daily. To a large extent, the success of Soviet regular forces on the fronts depended on unseen rank-and-file demolitions men operating far behind German lines. During the most critical days of the Kursk battle, the Ukrainian Staff received word that the Central Staff of the Partisan Movement had also launched its rail war, employing around one hundred thousand partisans from Belorussia, and from the Leningrad, Smolensk, and Orel districts. It seemed that these operations were launched without any clear plan, however.

On 12 July, Soviet troops on the Bryansk and Western fronts went over to the offensive and broke through to Orel. Troops of the Central Front also took the offensive: Hitler's Operation ZITADELLE had failed. At this time, the Central Committee of the Ukrainian Communist party adopted a very important resolution entitled: "Concerning the Present Status and Further Development of the Partisan Struggle in the Ukraine." This resolution stated categorically that the most important task of the Ukrainian partisans was the destruction of the enemy railroad transportation capability by destruction of enemy rolling stock that carried personnel, equipment, fuel and lubricants, munitions, and supplies to the front. The resolution was broadcast to all partisan units.

These large-scale partisan operations were extremely successful. By early August, Fedorov's formation, operating with some Belorussian units, completely paralyzed the Kovel'-Sarny, Kovel'-Brest, and Kobrin-Pinsk rail lines, forcing the Germans to use the most indirect and time-consuming routes for their logistics and replacement transport. A single detachment of Fedorov's formation had destroyed more trains in July and early August than had all the Ukrainian detachments put together during the months of May and June. The Ukrainian Staff studied the Fedorov reports and ordered that additional detachments be sent to specified sections of the railroads to set more delayed-action mines. The Saburov and Malikov formations started their operations a bit more slowly than Fedorov, but also managed to achieve significant results, e.g., destruction of forty-one trains on the Sarny-Korosten' line during August.

A captured 26 August document on the rear area services of German Army Group South told the Ukrainian Staff what they already knew: ". . . the constantly increasing number of acts of sabotage committed on rail lines, has brought about an emergency situation in our overall transportation capability and a catastrophic situation in terms of our ability to supply the troops . . ."

The Truth About the Legend

A decision was made to transfer the government of the Ukraine from Moscow to newly liberated Kharkov in the last days of August. Since Starinov had been responsible for mining Kharkov before the Soviet retreat, he was now given the task of leading a Ukrainian Staff operations group to that city, to clear German and remaining Soviet mines, prior to the government's move. On the way to Kharkov, Starinov's truck column passed through Orel, where he was stunned by the damage inflicted on that city. He was nevertheless happy to learn from the surviving inhabitants that the "Orel firemen," i.e., the partisans and underground workers he had covertly trained in the first weeks of the war, had conducted acts of arson, sniping, ambushes, demolitions, and propaganda against the German occupation forces from the very first days of the occupation. The operations group then passed through the Kursk battlefield, crisscrossed with trenches and littered with the hulks of burned out "Tigers," "Panthers," "Ferdinands," and T-34s. The city of Kharkov was not the same as when he last saw it: cratered streets blocked by downed light and power poles and tangled wires, torn-up sidewalks; public gardens trampled down with charred or pulled down trees—all spoke of recent heavy fighting. Starinov went immediately to the city Party committee to inform them of his mission and enlist their help. From there, however, he dropped in at 17 Dzerzhinskiy Street, to verify with his own eyes the impact of his radio-controlled mine.

Dzerzhinskiy Street in general had not suffered severely, but in place of the villa that I recalled from 1941, a huge, oblong, water-filled crater yawned. Around the crater, white and pink remnants of the foundation stuck up, as well as piles of brick, vehicles flattened by falling brick, and charred and splintered chestnut trees.

In the next house (the number 15 was still visible on the enameled tin sign) I found some witnesses of the events of the night of 14 November 1941.

These were a mother and daughter—Anna Grigor'yevna, and Valentina Fedoseyevna Berenda. They told me that after the October holidays, a Nazi general, some kind of very important officer, had moved into the house at number 17. A week later, Anna Grigor'yevna and Valentina Fedoseyevna were awakened by a frightful shock and roar. Outside the window, there were flames; rocks seemed to be falling out of the sky, crashing down on their house, and the crockery flew in pieces from the shattered cupboard. The women hurried into the courtyard. It seemed as though number 17 had disappeared from the face of the earth. Above the place where number 17 had been, and over its garden, hung a huge dust cloud, illuminated by the weak light of the fires which were beginning to break out. There was a sour burning smell. On the boards of the fence and on the roof next door, dark objects were visible. Later, they saw that the roof next door was strewn with the remains of a grand piano, and scraps of uniforms were plastered on the fence boards. Sirens wailed, and German motorcyclists sped to the scene; trucks loaded with troops rattled up, and the Germans surrounded the former villa, trying to extinguish the fire. They did extinguish it, but it seems that they never found a single one of their men who were in the building at the time of the explosion, even though they dug for two days in the ruins.

This was the first information that I got on the results of the explosion of the radio-controlled mine under number 17.

From Dzerzhinskiy Street, I returned to the city committee offices, talked it all over with them, and then went to the staff of the Steppe Front. The Central Committee of the Ukrainian Communist party had charged me with finding an enemy sapper among the prisoners who might have taken part in the mining of the city during the German retreat. The Steppe Front SMERSH (military counterintelligence) directorate held many interesting documents, captured when the Germans were evacuating Kharkov. At SMERSH, I also got a promise of help in finding a prisoner. Three or four days passed. The operations group settled into two houses and began its work, inspecting buildings that were designated for use by the Ukrainian government, as well as other facilities. We found no mines. At first, this made us prick up our ears, but soon we ceased to be concerned: the enemy simply didn't expend the effort to respond to the attacks that Soviet demolitions men had made on them in 1941! The "supermen" didn't worry about mine warfare: they only thought about saving their skins!

On the third or fourth day, a comrade sent by the city committee came searching me out: the Front staff had called and invited me over, saying that they had a "surprise" for me! The surprise was German Capt. Karl Heiden who had been serving in sapper units and had arrived in Kharkov with the 68th Infantry Division, commanded by Maj. Gen. Georg von Braun. Heiden had been directly responsible for clearing the mines at 17 Dzerzhinskiy Street.

A lanky, lean prisoner was led into the room where I was waiting. He was dressed in a ragged officer's tunic, without officer's shoulder boards, but with enlisted stripes sewn on the sleeves. His crushed boots had wide tops. He had a tired face, reddish brown hair streaked with gray, and reddish brown bristles on his sunken cheeks.

I invited the prisoner to take a seat. He sat down on the stool, which I had indicated, shot a glance at me, and then looked down at his folded hands. He certainly had no idea of who he was talking to, and maybe it really didn't matter. I looked over the enemy officer who, two years before, had been chosen by fate to become my rival in mine warfare. Two years ago, my professional reputation—and even my life itself—had depended to a large degree upon this man. He was downcast now, but two years ago, Karl Heiden would not have lowered his eyes before a Russian!

Maj. Gen. Georg von Braun had also arrived in Kharkov as a victor, assigned to command the garrison of the "second capital" of the Ukraine. It had been a while since Lady Luck had smiled on the fifty-four-year-old von Braun. He had not made much progress in the First World War, and by 1934 had only reached the rank of major. But after the Nazis took power, his career began to gain momentum. He fought in Spain as a colonel, and now the Fuehrer had promoted him to lieutenant general and made him lord of a whole Soviet city!

Although Georg von Braun was not an especially talented leader of troops, he had other talents that were especially valuable to the members of the Nazi clique: he was an executioner. General von Reitenau's order, issued on 10 October 1941, called for summary execution of all Soviet citizens involved in partisan activities and for the application of capital punishment against the male population in order to avert planned partisan activities. None of the commanders in the German Sixth Army went as far in carrying out the letter and the spirit of this order as did von Braun. He celebrated the capture of Kharkov by hanging from the balconies on the main street of Kharkov men and women accused of membership in the Communist party.

On 28 October, a delayed-action mine killed the German artillerist, Lieutenant General Vernecker, and mines began to go off around Kharkov: on the roads, in the railroad station, at the airfield, and in buildings. General von Braun was apparently afraid to move into the city at first, but then requested that a suitable house be selected and cleared of mines so that he could take up residence.

The German sappers bent over backward to find something appropriate—and safe—for the general. Unfortunately, wherever they looked, they found evidence of the work of Soviet demolitions men, even in the house where G. I. Petrovskiy[1] had once lived, and in other attractive buildings, but the problem was that no mines were found in these places! That really worried the Germans: what if you report that the villa is cleared of mines and von Braun moves in, and then you find that the "Ivans" have played a dirty trick on you?

At first, the Germans didn't find a mine in 17 Dzerzhinskiy Street. Even though they knew that members of the Ukrainian Communist party lived and worked in this house right up to the last days of the defense of Kharkov, and even though they understood that it would have been practically impossible for sappers to emplace and camouflage a powerful mine in the short time between the departure of the Party officials and the arrival of the German troops, they still were hesitant to take over the house.

Captain Heiden got lucky. He found a traitor who told him that just before the evacuation of Kharkov, military personnel had gone into number 17 and done something. Heiden ordered his subordinates to methodically inspect the house and search for a possible mine. The sappers finally got down to the half-basement, to the boiler room with the coal pile in the corner. And . . . they saw a scarcely visible, mysterious wire! Heiden was well experienced and cautious. He knew well that if a mine and been set in the coal pile, it might be detonated by an insignificant vibration of the floor, by cutting the wire, or by the slightest pull on the wire. In a word, one false move and it could all be over.

Initially, the captain ordered that the coal pile be examined with mine detecting equipment. Negative results! Then he found a daredevil who offered to trace the wire. Heiden accepted the offer: to help the volunteer, he detailed two soldiers and the same informer who had led him to the house in the first place. The captain then moved all the other soldiers away from the house and set sentries around the gate. The German sappers worked slowly: the daredevil had obviously given some thought to the way in which this adventure might turn out! In any case, the Germans didn't find anything on the first day. Heiden decided to suspend work until the morning because the soldiers were tired. In the morning, they went back to the boiler room, and three hours later, they had

---

1. Petrovskiy was an old Bolshevik who was nominal head of the Ukraine for twenty years. He survived the purges, but was "kicked downstairs" to a museum post in 1939 and never regained prominence.

actually found a mine! A mine with complicated, interconnected, backup fuses and switches! They successfully removed it.

The captain triumphantly reported the results of his work to von Braun, who was staying in a house in the Kharkov suburbs. The next day, the general moved into the house on Dzerzhinskiy Street with the senior staff officers of the 68th Division. At last they could move into a house that was appropriate to their status in the Reich and their combat services.

On the night of 13 November, Captain Heiden again reported to General von Braun about the functioning of an electrochemcial switch from a Russian mine, which they had been observing. The general knew that delayed-action mines were going off all over town, but he didn't realize that he was sitting on one!

The residents of Dzerzhinskiy Street said the General von Braun normally went for a walk in the garden of his house in the evening. He would then return to the villa, and soon the light in his second-floor bedroom would go out. That was how it happened on the evening of 13 November, too. But the general wasn't going to wake up.

"The mine in the coal pile really misled us," Captain Heiden admitted. "Who would have thought that there was a second, even more dangerous, mine right underneath it?"

"And would you really have guessed that the bigger, more dangerous, second mine would be detonated by radio control?"

"No, Colonel! The German Army has no such mines!"

"Well, are you still as firmly convinced that the German Army is equipped exactly the same way as the Soviet Army?" I smiled.

Heiden apparently concluded that it would be a mistake to use strong language, so he replied in a flat tone: "Excuse me, Colonel, it's a habit . . ."

I recalled Order No. 98/41 of 8 November 1941 issued by the 516th Infantry Regiment of the 68th Infantry Division, and asked Heiden if it was such a habit that guided the German command in lying to their own soldiers and to the inhabitants of Kharkov.

"Is it really possible that you and your commanders didn't know that the mines that you could easily remove were nothing more than mine casings with inert filler? Is it possible that you didn't know that delayed-action mines, as a rule, remained undetected, and that if you detected them and tried to remove them, you'd be destroyed?"

"No, certainly, we very soon found out that the mines that we were finding were not real mines, but wooden blocks and booby-trapped casings," the captain reluctantly admitted. "But we found it 'more convenient,' as one might say, to circulate the lie that the Soviet mining effort was slipshod."

"And what did you personally get out of this 'more convenient' option?"

Heiden threw me a sullen look: "For me, Colonel, sir? I got reduced in rank, sent to the front lines, and—here I am!" And he ran his fingers through his prematurely gray hair.

Stories about who was responsible for the mysterious assassination of von Braun had been circulating for a long time among the people of Kharkov. Some said it was the underground, some said it was the partisans. These stories didn't spring up in a vacuum: the underground and the partisans had operated in the city from the first to the last day of the occupation, and they operated heroically. The Ukrainian Staff of the Partisan Movement had maintained close contact with them.

But truth is truth, and only truth deserves to become legend: the legend of the Soviet scholars and mine warfare experts who invented the first radio-controlled mine. The enemy only discovered about 10 percent of the 315 delayed-action mines that were emplaced in Kharkov and the vicinity, and was able to disarm less than half of those; the other 23 had to be detonated in place, thus producing the desired destructive effect. The undiscovered delayed-action mines exploded beneath troop and supply trains, causing numerous casualties, the loss of much rolling stock, and the destruction of bridges and track sections. Mines also made it impossible for the Germans to use the Chuguyev-Kharkov highway and forced them to bulldoze a completely new road, parallel to the original. The Kharkov airfields were rendered useless to the Germans until late spring 1942 by mines emplaced in the hardstands, on the runways, and in the hangars.

Recognizing the results that were achieved, I should like to express my sincere thanks to the inventors of the remarkable radio-controlled mine—engineers V. I. Bekauri and Mitkevich, General Nevskiy, Military Engineer Yastrebov, Military Technician Leonov, the young Kharkov lieutenants, railroad brigade commanders Kabanov, Pavlov, and Stepanov; Sergeants Lyadov and Shedov, Lebedev, and Sergeyev, and Miners (Pvts.) Sakhnevich and Kuznetsov—to all who prepared the terrible mine weapons, and who worked in Kharkov during the difficult fall of 1941, turning the city into a pitfall for their sworn enemy. Their feats of arms were not in vain!

In September, Soviet troops were advancing toward the Dnepr and the Molocha rivers after defeating thirty elite German di-

visions at Kursk. The operations plans of the Ukrainian Staff had to be revised once more—this time, the partisans were to render direct support to Soviet troops who would be forcing the Desna, Dnepr, and Pripyat rivers. The revised plan called for partisans to seize and hold two crossings each on the Desna and Dnepr, and all the ferry crossings on those rivers and on the Pripyat. The operations plan called for seventeen thousand men initially, with an additional twenty-five thousand reinforcements within ten to fifteen days. Plans were made to deliver 286 tons of weapons and munitions to the partisans, as well as 20 artillery pieces and their crews, totaling 100 men. For this purpose, 125 C-47 flights were to be allocated between 17 and 30 September. The plan was approved by the Military Council of the Voronezh Front on 15 September, and the operation began. Soviet regulars forced the Desna on 17 September with partisan assistance, while other partisan formations were moving into position for subsequent phases of the operation. Some encountered heavy enemy opposition, however, and were forced to break contact, so that the anticipated early successes of the operation could not be successfully developed. Acting on a direct personal appeal from Lt. Gen. I. I. Zatevakhin, chief of airborne troops, Starinov was able to mobilize Ukrainian partisans in an emergency operation to rescue troops of regular Soviet airborne units who had landed in a botched mass parachute drop in the Cherkassk region of the Ukraine on 25 September. Many paratroopers fell directly on German units: many had been killed, and the survivors were either engaged in fierce fighting or had been dispersed. Starinov was able to immediately insert the Istrebitel' *(Exterminator) special partisan detachment, commanded by D. A. Kurshikov, directly into the area where the paratroopers were trapped, and to arrange for support from other partisan units already operating in that area. The rescued paratroopers remained with the partisan units, conducting operations behind enemy lines well into November. Partisans were also able to help out other regular Red Army units that had been cut off and surrounded by the Germans after crossing the Dnepr. In these cases, the Red Army men didn't retreat to their own lines, but advanced into German-held territory and joined up with partisan formations that were operating there.*

"Explosives!"

Although Stalin and his henchmen destroyed the partisan cadres that had been so well trained during the thirties, our partisan detachments and formations represented a formidable force by the summer of 1943 and were able to carry out very significant strikes against the enemy. With clever and carefully planned partisan operations, the Red Army was able to cut off the enemy from his supply sources and put him in a critical situation. Even with the shortage of mines and explosives, Ukrainian partisans alone blew up 3,143 enemy trains during the second half of 1943, almost twice the number that had been blown up in the previous two years of the war! Unfortunately, a single unified plan for partisan warfare still didn't exist, and no one was going to work one out, and the quantities of mines and demolitions materials delivered to the partisans were totally inadequate.

This was especially true for Fedorov—every radio message from him was a cry from the heart: "More TNT and mines!" The number of trains that he destroyed declined rapidly from August to September, but only because the explosives were not delivered. It certainly wasn't because we hadn't been bothering the people "upstairs" every day—and even every hour—on his behalf! The same shortage was experienced by Kovpak, Begma, Grabchak, Mel'nik, and Naumov.

The partisans themselves did all that they could to make up for the deficit in the mines and explosives: they cut down on the size of explosive charges, experimented with mechanical devices for derailment, and melted TNT out of enemy bombs and artillery shells. Their creativity was really surprising! But the most surprising of all were the partisans led by NKVD Maj. A. M. Grabchak, who were able to take the enemy completely by surprise and blow the bridge over the Ubort' River without any losses. It happened this way: several attempts by the partisans to approach the bridge had been unsuccessful. The bridge was guarded by a garrison with four pillboxes, machine gunners, teams with three regimental-size mortars, and a battery of flak guns. The open area and the high railroad embankment on which the guard force was encamped gave them good all-around visibility. The Ubort' riverbank was heavily mined by the enemy, the minefields were surrounded by four rows of concertina wire, and the railroad at both ends of the bridge was closed by metal gates. As the saying goes, a mouse couldn't get past—but the partisans did!

Grabchak's intelligence established that twice a week, the local German commandant arrived at the bridge on a section car to check on his subordinates' performance of their duties. This fact suggested to them a very original idea for sabotage. The work took two weeks. The partisans mounted the bed of a section car on two sets of wheels, fitted it with a motor, and loaded the section car with five unexploded aerial bombs. Between the bombs, they fastened a long pole. The lower end of the pole was connected by a wire to a safety pin in the fuse of an initiating charge. When the upper end of the pole struck the cross bracings of the bridge span, the pole would be pushed back, and the wire would pull out the safety pin. Then, on top of the aerial bombs, the partisans sat the "commandant" and his "driver," made out of German uniforms stuffed with straw and branches.

At 4:00 P. M. on 31 October, Grabchak's people put the section-car torpedo on the track rails near the village of Tepenitsa, about a kilometer from the bridge, started up the engine, and gave it a push. The bridge guard didn't fire a single shot at the approaching section car, and didn't even close the bridge gate. There was a mighty blast! Some of the struts and upper wind bracings of the nearby girders, as well as the entire upper and lower chords of the bridge, were crumpled or completely severed.

The dumbfounded German garrison began firing furiously—ten minutes after the explosion—either to clear their consciences or out of simple fear. It took four full days for them to repair the bridge and to slide a regular train over it, taking extraordinary precautions.

The humiliated occupation forces concocted a legend about some kind of extremely complex torpedo that had supposedly been delivered to the Ubort' "right straight from Moscow" and was driven by "Red kamikazes"—Soviet suicide officers—who supposedly died, detonating the torpedo on the bridge.

Grabchak's success was not ignored in the Ukrainian Staff. A conference was immediately held on the subject of portable "torpedoes," to be used in destroying heavily guarded enemy facilities. A design team was assembled, and prototypes were built and tested. Production was begun, and the first units reached the partisans in late November. This conference also addressed ways of improving fuses of delayed-action mines to ensure their reliability under any weather conditions.

In October, the task of preserving and controlling the most experienced partisan formations in the deep enemy rear became quite stressful and complicated. The Red Army was advancing, and many partisan units were suddenly finding themselves behind Soviet lines. At the same time the Ukrainian Staff and the Ukrainian Party Central Committee wanted to increase rather than decrease the number of well-trained partisan units in the enemy rear, and to keep them available for further action. Representatives from the staff were sent on personal visits to partisan units to encourage them to withdraw to the west after they had finished their missions in support of the Red Army, and to collect intelligence there, deep in the enemy rear. Partisans whose units were overtaken by the army were either returned behind enemy lines, or sent for more advanced training. Some partisan units were also dissolved and their personnel either sent into the army or to Party or government work in the liberated areas.

October also saw the completion of Kovpak's famous Carpathian raid. The staff received a report from P. P. Vershigora, who had commanded a group of detachments on that raid, and seemed to have survived it in better fashion than most. Vershigora—a Red Army officer soon to rise to the rank of major general and receive the title of Hero of the Soviet Union—was a cool, calculating leader who had mastered the fine points of partisan war. According to him, they had a really rough time on the Carpathian raid. When they arrived in the Carpathians, the partisans ran into a numerically superior enemy force and had to accept combat on unequal terms, with neither experience in mountain warfare nor the equipment appropriate for that kind of combat. The formation was forced to destroy and abandon its heavy equipment, to break contact, and to return to their home base area in separate groups and detachments. Vershigora didn't dramatize things but did not conceal the truth, and frankly summarized the reasons for the failure of the operation. His conclusion, however, was unexpected at first glance but completely correct: long-range partisan operations should be continued without letup, and raids should be conducted not only within but outside of the borders of the USSR in coordination with the partisans of Poland, Czechoslovakia, Bulgaria, Romania, and Yugoslavia. He even recommended conducting raids into Germany itself, given the proper conditions! Soon after this, we learned that Sidor Artem'yevich Kovpak was relieved of his command due to advanced age and health problems and that he went to work for the Soviet government. The unit that he had commanded was designated as the Hero of the Soviet Union

S. A. Kovpak Partisan Formation. The new commander was P. P. Vershigora, and he was preparing for a new raid!

Starinov's account of Vershigora's dissatisfaction with Kovpak, and Kovpak's subsequent replacement, appear to be indications of major problems in the Ukrainian partisan movement. These problems may have involved far more than relationships with anti-Stalin Ukrainian nationalists. They may be simply reflections of more serious differences between the Party, the military, and the NKVD over control of partisan forces and partisan tactics, strategy, and ultimate objectives. It is quite likely that the strictly personal animosities of Stalin, Beria, and those of senior members of the NKVD hierarchy, also played a role.

Three Missions

When Soviet troops crossed the Dnepr, they arrived at the edge of the partisan district, which stretched from the river all the way to the western border of the USSR. Partisan detachments and formations in the "right bank" section of the Ukraine carried out uninterrupted operations with the Red Army. On 17 November, Saburov's Zhitomir formation and troops of the Thirteenth Army liberated the railroad junction city of Ovruch, cutting the communications between the central and northern groups of German forces. A break was thus formed in the enemy lines, eighty kilometers wide and over two hundred kilometers deep. This was the famous "Ovruch corridor." Day and night, partisan units, supply trains with explosives and mines, weapons and ammunition, passed through this corridor heading west, while convoys with wounded, intelligence personnel and couriers passed eastward.

In November, the Germans concentrated their forces in the Korosten' area and tried to launch a counterattack, but their plans were foiled by troops of Lieutenant General Chernyakovskiy's Sixtieth Army and partisans of the detachments commanded by Saburov, M. G. Salai, S. F. Malikov, and M. I. Naumov. The 1st Ukrainian Front was preparing for the big Zhitomir-Berdichevsk operation in which the Ukrainian partisan forces, as always, were destined to play a major role.

On 14 December, Strokach called his deputies together for a conference in which the decision was made to send out staff representatives to check on the readiness of the partisan formations for new raids into the deep enemy rear and to examine the conditions of the Ovruch-Slovechno-Sobychin-Snovidovichi road to see if it could handle heavy tanks. Starinov was given these tasks, and told to get a staff together and get started immediately. After an auto journey through the Ovruch corridor, he reached the bustling town of Ovruch, where he got a rather cool welcome from Saburov, whose partisans were defending the northern edge of the corridor. Saburov, as an NKVD officer, would probably have been aware of Rudnev's execution and of Starinov's association with Rudnev in the partisan training of the thirties. It would have been logical for Saburov to avoid anyone so closely associated with a recently deceased "enemy of the people." Starinov didn't linger long with Saburov, however, but went off to Malikov's formation where the reception was better. Malikov was ready to depart on a raid: he believed that a partisan's place was behind enemy lines, and he asked Starinov to request Strokach to relieve his unit from the duty of defending the southern border of the corridor and turn him loose on a mission behind enemy lines. Starinov then set out for Vershigora's formation, traveling along the partisan highway leading to Slovechno and Perga, through a vast region that had long been under partisan control. The Soviet government organization in this area had continued to function throughout the war, the schools had never stopped, and the farmers in the collective farms sowed and harvested their crops without the Germans getting a single grain of wheat. The inhabitants of this region were busy repairing and improving the damaged roads and bridges when Starinov and his party passed through. He had the opportunity to stay overnight with some collective farmers who were living in dugouts in the Perga area, talk with them about the conduct of the war, give them current newspapers, which he had brought along with him. The inhabitants of the Perga area, well known to the Ukrainian Staff, had conducted successful operations against the enemy since the very beginning of the war, ultimately confining the German troops to fortified strongpoints from which they seldom ventured. After their overnight stay with the collective farmers, Starinov and his party returned to the banks of the Ubort', where they found Vershigora's deputy for sabotage, Eng. Maj. Sergey Vladimirovich Kal'nitskiy, waiting for them. He had decided to meet them halfway so as not to waste time. An operational test of an im-

proved model of one of Starinov's delayed-action mines was to be conducted by Vershigora's men on the railroad between Olevsk and Belokorovichi. The sabotage group that would conduct the test was waiting for Starinov and his party at Zamyslovichi. They traveled along roads strewn with wrecked German vehicles left from the summer's fighting, and arrived at Zamyslovichi. There, Starinov warned the sabotage team members about the peculiarities of the improved electromechanical fuse mechanism, and impressed them with the importance of the test that they were to conduct. From Zamyslovichi, the entire party traveled on sleds, reaching the operational area at the edge of an old forest at about 10:00 P.M.

The distance from the edge of the woods to the railroad was negligible, only about a kilometer and a half. The enemy himself was marking the railroad location very clearly with flares and signal rockets. Off to the left flank, the dull rattle of a machine gun abruptly broke the silence. Kal'nitskiy and I stayed at the edge of the woods. The partisans split into two groups and moved out across the field. Soon, their camouflaged capes blended with the snow and darkness. One group was supposed to attract the enemy's attention while the other group emplaced the delayed-action mines. Twenty minutes passed: suddenly, on the railroad directly in front of us, signal rockets began to soar skyward, one after the other, and dogs began to bark, but they were drowned out by machine-gun fire.

I looked at Kal'nitskiy. The engineer major remained calm, and the partisans didn't return the enemy fire, even though rockets were going up left and right, and machine guns opened up for over a kilometer on both sides. Was it really possible that the Germans hadn't seen our people? I wanted to talk to Kal'nitskiy, but then the machine-gun fire began to subside, the illuminating pyrotechnics faded out, and total quiet reigned once more.

Ten or twelve suspense-filled, exhausting minutes passed, and suddenly, right from the spot where the fire flare was launched and the first enemy machine guns had barked into the darkness, there was a flash, like a flicker of distant lightning, and after a second or two, there was the sound of an explosion. We knew that the first delayed-action grenade had gone off! And the enemy immediately panicked! Rockets shot up, one after the other; machine guns opened up as if competing with each other. Two more explosions rang out on the railroad: the rockets chased each other, and there was an uninterrupted drumroll of machine-gun fire as the enemy tried without success to find the partisans.

"Okay—the first group completed their mission," Kal'nitskiy said with satisfaction.

As if to confirm his words, there was another flash over the railroad, and another explosion was heard, provoking yet another wave of rocket madness and machine-gun rattles. Then there was another flash and explosion, in the same place.

The explosions of the delayed-action grenades continued at various intervals for another thirty to forty minutes. Each explosion was answered by a salvo of rockets and torrents of machine-gun slugs. The diversionary group returned. The group commander, a short demolitions man, reported that the mission had been accomplished, and that he had thrown thirteen delayed-action grenades. Up to that point we had only counted nine explosions, but just then, the tenth went off. Now there was quiet: even the dogs were still. The frosty stillness was broken only now and then by a machine-gun burst, fired by the Germans to keep up their own spirits.

The second group returned after an hour and twenty minutes. They had set both delayed-action mines and had done everything that was required. When we were taking our seats in the sleigh, we heard the report of the eleventh grenade. There were just two left. The Germans would probably have to deal with them later. At Zamyslovichi, they led us to a spacious dugout.

When they awoke us, it was still dark; we had some tea, and it had just become light when we set out for the woods again. In daylight, the forest didn't appear as thick and as broad as it did at night, and the railroad with its bunkers and machine-gun nests was quite close at hand. The morning breezes were blowing, swaying the odd dark shrub here and there and covering the partisan's tracks. At Kal'nitskiy's suggestion, I took the powerful binoculars and looked: the lenses brought the high railway embankment up quite close, with its cinder-dusted snow, the dark entrance of the bunker, and three German soldiers, washing their faces in the snow.

Finally the sun came up. The day began dull and cheerless. At least it wasn't raining and snowing. From the direction of Olevsk, we heard the whistle of an approaching train. We didn't have to wait long. Eight German soldiers appeared with mine-hunting dogs, and rolling downgrade, after the soldiers came two flatcars loaded with road ballast. At first I was a bit surprised: if the flatcars picked up speed, then what? But then; into my field of vision came a steel cable, stretching out behind the flatcars, and then an armored train appeared, holding back the flatcars with the cable. Well, that's something! It looked like they sent the dogs in first to

sniff out TNT, and if the dogs didn't sound the alarm, then they
let the flatcars pass over the area. (The flatcars were very heavy:
contact-detonated mines might not be triggered by the weight of
the soldiers, but under the weight of the flatcars they would certainly go off!) The armored train would move ahead only if the
area was completely secure.

The dogs and the soldiers suddenly stopped, as did the flatcars,
held back by the armored train. The sound of barking reached our
ears: the dogs thought they had found a mine. Actually, it was just
a few crumbs of TNT which had been left in the gravel. Invisible
to the eye, they were obvious to a dog's nose. The Germans hesitated, then began to set an explosive charge. Their approach was
simple: blow up the charge and destroy the perfidious Russian
mine. The charge was set, the soldiers scattered and flung themselves down in the snow. Twenty, thirty, forty seconds and—
boom! Pieces of rail went flying, but it appeared that there was no
mine there. The soldiers ran back to the embankment, climbed up
on it, and continued on their way. The mine dogs gave the danger
signal three more times, and three more times the Germans blew
up rails to destroy our mines, and were subsequently convinced
that there were no mines there. The enemy sappers then clearly
decided that this section of track was not dangerous. They took
rail "bridges" from the flatcars that trailed them, placed these
"bridges" over the damaged sections of track, and waved the "all
clear" to the armored train engineer.

The armored train slowly crept over our delayed-action mines
toward Korosten' where intense fighting was going on . . .

The first undetected mine was set to go off in the vicinity of
2:00 P.M., and the first enemy train from Korosten' appeared at
11:40. It was dragging flatcars with damaged tanks and artillery
pieces. The train barely crawled over the rail bridges. Behind it,
twenty minutes later, came a train of passenger cars and heated
vans. This was undoubtedly carrying wounded. Behind the train
with the wounded came a work car: the Germans brought in new
rail sections, removed the rail bridges and patched the damaged
roadbed. At about 1:00 P.M., trains were running merrily from
Olevsk to Korosten', one after the other. Then, just as confidently,
and at a good speed as well, three more trains came along: two
from Korosten' and one from Olevsk. The enemy was becoming
more courageous, but the appointed time was approaching! Then
it was 2:00 P.M. The mine fuses became active. Frost didn't
bother them. At least that was what we thought in the technical
department, and that was what I thought. Finally, the decisive moment had arrived.

A routine enemy train approached from the direction of Korosten', moving at a speed of not less than fifty kilometers per hour, pushing two flatcars loaded with ballast ahead of the engine. They were hurrying to get to Sarny before sundown. And all the cars in the train were passenger cars: that meant officers!

Now!

A powerful explosion blew snow, gravel, sand, rails, and ties in all directions. Both flatcars and the locomotive were derailed, and crashed down the embankment, dragging the coaches behind them. There was a grinding of shattered iron, splintering wood, and flames. Germans began leaping from the cars that had not yet fallen over. They were jumping out on our side: on the other side, the railroad ran closer to the woods, and they were afraid that they'd be fired upon if they went that way.

"Everything's in order. Shall we go, Comrade Colonel?" Kal'nitskiy asked.

"Okay, Comrade Engineer Major, let's go!"

We heard sporadic firing from the vicinity of the train derailment for a long while afterward: the Germans were carrying on a desperate battle with the empty forest.

After the mine test, Kal'nitskiy had to leave for other business at Yurlov and Belokorovichi, and Starinov and his party set out for Sobychin where Vershigora's staff was located. On the way, they met two young partisans who told them of the exploits of an NKVD border guard group commanded by Buiniy (the Wild Man), which had been conducting partisan activities in the area for sometime. This group was extremely daring: they operated like a regular border guard detachment, and stayed in one place. The group encouraged the populace to tell the Germans exactly who they were and where they were located. They advised the locals that anyone with any questions, including collaborators in the uniforms of German field police, be sent directly to them, and promised that the partisans would straighten out their problems for them. Farther along the road, Starinov and his group heard what appeared to be a fierce firefight going on, involving artillery, mortars, and machine guns. It turned out that this was only the partisans of the Kovpak formation, checking their weapons in preparation for a raid. Although only twelve kilometers from a strong enemy garrison, Kovpak had so completely managed to turn the stables on the Germans as a result of his attacks on rail junctions and his sabotage operations that the Germans had gone on the de-

fensive and didn't dare attack. It was they who felt surrounded by the partisans, and not the other way around.

Starinov arrived in time to see the final stages of preparation for Vershigora's long-range raid westward. The mission was to take control of enemy communications in the region of Stanislav, L'vov, Ternopol', Chernovtsy, Rovno, and Drogobych. Other formations were to follow him. The Vershigora formation had been working hard to recruit and actually train conscripts for the Red Army in the areas that they had liberated. Starinov saw off Vershigora and his troops on their raid and followed their progress through official reports. When he had finished investigating the partisan operations on the Korosten'-Sarny road, Starinov received word that the Central Staff of the Partisan Movement had finally been dissolved. The Ukrainian Staff was still in operation, with plenty to do, however, and Strokach ordered Starinov to the city of Gorodnitsa to check on the combat readiness of the Grabchak formation and to develop some recommendations concerning their further employment.

"Halt! Password!" a loud shout rang out. The driver reigned in the horse. I threw back the heavy collar of my sheepskin coat. On the left of the sleigh was an untouched field of sparkling winter whiteness; on the right, a motionless spruce forest, its snow-burdened green branches drooping to the tops of the drifts. Not a sign of a human being. Then, two figures in white camouflage capes, armed with submachine guns, came out of the spruces. Under the cape hoods, I could see the brims of winter fur caps. Grabchak's people were supposed to wear hats like that. I gave the password, heard the countersign, and told them that I was looking for the staff. One of the partisans sat on the side of the sleigh next to the driver.

"Here, on the other side of that spruce, head into the woods!"

On the other side of the spruce, we found a road that wasn't really a road, but a sufficiently level cut through the trees, and the sleigh crawled slowly along that cut into the depths of the woods. The escort delivered us directly to the large dugout of the formation commander. Five or six men were in the dugout, all in uniforms with fur vests, and I couldn't really tell which one was Grabchak. Noticing that I was standing there, looking from one officer to the other, a lean fellow of medium height, with deep wrinkles around his lips, guardedly introduced himself as Major Grabchak. He said that Kiev had informed him that I was coming.

* * *

On 17 January 1942, two transport aircraft from Grizodubova's regiment took off from a Moscow airfield on course for Lake Chervono in the Belorussian woods. Aboard the aircraft were parachutists, mainly former NKVD border guards, who had been well trained for behind-the-lines operations. The group commander, deputy commander, and commissar were also border guards. The group jumped on the campfires set by Kovpak's people on the ice of the lake. This was the beginning of the history of the partisan formation commanded by Andrey Mikhaylovich Grabchak, known to the local population as the Wild Man (*Buiniy*). This was the pseudonym used when he signed leaflets that were distributed and posted in enemy-occupied cities and villages. The first group of reinforcements that the group received came from the lakeside village of Lyakhovichi: the residents carried out a voluntary mobilization and brought a group of seventeen- and eighteen-year-olds to the parachutists. Grabchak's men taught the recruits how to cut foot-cloths out of parachute canopy, how to wrap their feet with the cloths, and then gave them submachine guns. Foot-cloths were used routinely under boots, in place of socks.

Then, a group of saboteurs commanded by Sr. Sgt. Vyacheslav Antonovich Kvitinskiy arrived to strengthen the detachment. Kvitinskiy was an artillery man: he and others had been surrounded at the beginning of the war and had fled into the Belorussian woods. On their own, they had set ambushes, then joined up with one of the partisan detachments, and when that was cut to pieces in combat, he took command of the survivors and operated independently.

At the beginning of March 1942, the Grabchak detachment had derailed two trains. In retaliation, the Germans had descended on the village of Yurlov, burned it to the ground, killed some of the residents, and rounded up the rest to take them to Germany. When the peasants told Grabchak, his partisans set up an ambush, killed some of the hunter-killer group, put some of them to flight, and distributed the captured weapons to the liberated people of Yurlov, advising them to set up their own partisan detachment. They did.

The echoes of explosions and bursts of partisan machine-gun fire spread far and wide through the woods, drawing more and more people to Grabchak.

At the moment of our arrival, the formation consisted of five independent detachments, organized along the lines of border guard posts, and a cavalry squadron mounted on captured German horses. Serving in the detachments and the squadron were not only Russians but Uzbeks, Belorussians, Turkmen, and Kazakhs.

The formation had 106 troop- and armored-train derailments to its
credit, as well as many vehicles with troops and freight, and many
bridges blown, including the memorable bridge near Olevsk,
which was destroyed with the torpedo I described above. I remembered the young partisans that I had met on the road at Perga
and what they had told me about the Wild Man.

"Tell me, is it true that you've advised the villagers not to conceal the strength of your detachment or your escape route?" I
asked Grabchak, and his commissar, N. M. Podkorytov.

The commander and the commissar looked at each other:
"Yeah, that's the way it was," Podkorytov said gaily. "You know,
it's really important to show the people that we've come to stay
and that we're the bosses. We called ourselves a border guard
post, not a detachment."

"It wasn't by accident, either," added Grabchak. "These people
have a tradition of helping out the border guards in every way."

"That's right!" the commissar continued. "We wanted to resur-
rect that tradition! And we wanted to show that we could tie down
the enemy to his lines of communication and that we weren't
afraid of him! If he tries to track us, it'll just be worse for him:
he'll fall into an ambush!"

"But you nevertheless risked . . ."

"Didn't risk a thing, Comrade Colonel!" Grabchak interrupted
excitedly. "The enemy was so busy guarding the road and removing wrecked locomotives, he wasn't able to throw any large formations into action against the partisans. And it wasn't hard to
wipe out small units. We just sat around and waited, and when
they caught us, we took the appropriate steps: we're professionals
above all!"

"What do you mean?"

"I mean that you hit the Germans where they least expect it.
The enemy runs into mines, and ambushes, and he quickly breaks
himself of the habit of sniffing along our trail. But we do have
some problems we'd like to take up with the Ukrainian Staff,
Comrade Colonel!"

"What are they?"

"You've given us an inadequate amount of TNT and mines. We
have to spend far too much time and energy to procure explosives—more time than we spend in using them! And the bigger
the mines that we plant and the more trains we blow up, the less
time the Krauts have to organize hunter-killer missions. They'll be
sitting over there along the railroad, day and night, guarding the
approaches to it, and pulling apart pileups of flatcars and passen-

ger cars. On the other hand, if we cut back on sabotage activities, they get arrogant and start making sweeps!"

Nikolai Mikhaylovich Podkrytov supported his commander:

"Without mines and explosives—there'll be trouble! Don't you see, we could use them more extensively!" Smiling, he told me how they had used mine and demolitions equipment to build various kinds of booby traps: sometimes they had mined strongboxes, sometimes sent package bombs, other times, knowing the strong proclivities of the occupation troops for chicken, they sacrificed a whole chicken house . . .

Starinov also visited other partisan formations in the Kamenets-Podolsk region, including those commanded by S. A. Oleksenko, A. Z. Odykh, and F. S. Kot. These formations were operating in the enemy's tactical defensive zone, providing constant support to advancing units of the Red Army. In the previous summer they had also operated along the Shepetovka-Tarnopol' rail line, blowing bridges, and preventing through traffic. When the Germans began to withdraw, the partisans prevented them from destroying the rails and many of the bridges and stations. The Germans were also forced to leave mountains of grain, dried sugar beets, and other foodstuffs. All of this was done with minimum partisan casualties. Partisan formations still could not take on German line units in open combat, however, and Starinov was an unhappy witness to one unfortunate attempt. At the town of Izyaslavl, Oleksenko's partisans, some two thousand strong, supported by a Red Army regiment, drove a German force out of the city and beat back three strong counterattacks, but suffered great losses. Starinov returned to the Ukrainian Staff at Kiev and reported to Strokach that the units that he had inspected were combat ready but that they should never be employed in open combat. He further recommended that these units should be supplied with additional weapons and enough mines and explosives, then sent immediately to the enemy rear. His recommendations were accepted.

Shortly after his return to Kiev, Starinov was sent off by Strokach to command a group charged with assessing the effectiveness of partisan operations, with a view to identifying the best equipment and methods for conducting further partisan operations, particularly those conducted against railroads. This trip covered 15,800 kilometers of track, interviewing railway personnel who had remained in the enemy rear during the occupation and people who lived near railroads. He also studied captured German documents. All that he saw testified to the effectiveness of partisan operations. Despite enemy security, partisans were generally able to get through and attack railroads and highways. Strokach was satisfied with the results of his report and viewed it as a vindication of the Staff's position on the subject of attacking the enemy lines of communication. Things were going well at the front: Soviet troops were at the borders of Romania, Czechoslovakia, and Poland—victory was in the air!

Victory Spring

It was after 20 April—I can't recall the exact date—that I was called into Strokach's office on an urgent matter. Strokach wasn't alone: at his desk sat a man in the uniform of a major general of the Polish Army.

"Let me introduce you," said Strokach. "Colonel Starinov, this is the deputy commander of the Polish First Army, Major General Zavadski."

We shook hands. Zavadski had a pleasant face, with fine features, blue eyes, and neatly combed hair in elegant waves.

"A Polish Partisan Staff is being created," Strokach said. "We have to decide how we can assist the Polish comrades."

To begin with, that assistance would be in the form of instructors and equipment, and that's what we talked about. Strictly speaking, the Ukrainian Staff of the Partisan Movement, and the Ukrainian and Belorussian partisans had been helping their Polish comrades for a long time. Acting on his own, without any direction from above, Khrushchev had also given a direct order to the Ukrainian Staff and local Party leaders that they should help raise partisan units from native Poles who lived in the Ukraine. These units were armed well and later inserted into Polish territory. In the spring of 1943, Polish volunteers were already training alongside volunteers from the other nations of Eastern Europe in the Special School of the Ukrainian Staff of the Partisan Movement commanded by Pavel Aleksandrovich Vykhodets. By spring of 1944, there were 507 foreigners training in Vykhodets's school, along with 967 Soviet citizens. In September 1943, A. F. Fedorov's formation had made contact with the Gvardiya Lyudova in the Lyublin region and had given them significant amounts of weapons and ammunition. In Polish territory, composite Polish-Russian partisan detachments had arisen independently, enjoying the support of Belorussian as well as Ukrainian partisans. And later, in February 1944, the Twice Hero of the Soviet Union S. A. Kovpak 1st Ukrainian Partisan Division,[1] commanded by Vershigora, had completed a raid across four Polish provinces. Then, the partisan formation of NKVD Maj. Gen. M. I. Naumov reached Sandomir in a forced march, helped the residents of the Polish villages and towns to organize their own partisan detachments, shared weapons and explosives with them, and taught them how to blow up enemy trains.

During our meeting, I noticed that Zavadski seemed familiar with mines and demolitions, and I asked him if he had fought in Spain.

"No, I didn't have the chance to," he replied, in lightly accented Russian. "And now I've got to learn this mines and demolitions business, and the teacher isn't too bad, either. It's just a shame that he doesn't want to recognize his former students!"

I stared at our visitor in embarrassment. His blue eyes were smiling. But as God is my judge, nothing rang any bells, nothing!

"*Pan kapitan* (Polish for "Captain, sir"), give it to me ..." Zavadski uttered these words in a cheerful tone, extending his palm up, as if to receive something. And suddenly, suddenly and painfully, came total recall: the scent of June leaves in the Moscow woods; through an open classroom window, the creaking sounds of the dray carts on the cobblestone street descending to the Skhodna River; a sea of students' faces, and among them the very young face of the senior student, with its fine features. The senior student loved to do everything with his own hands!

"Thirty-three! Swierczewski's school!" the words burst forth.

"You finally remembered!!" Zavadski said, with a broad grin. "Yes, it was ten years ago, just like the story of Alexander Dumas!"

Strokach turned his attention from me to Zavadski, and then from Zavadski back to me, tore a sheet of paper from his notebook, and handed it to me.

"Here, Ilya Grigor'yevich!"

"What do you want me to do with this, Timofey Ambrosyevich?"

"Just write down the names of the people that you *didn't*

1. Kovpak got his second Hero award in early 1944, hence the slight alteration in the unit designation.

actually train. Then list the names of those who *don't* pass themselves off as having been your students!"

And he and Zavadski broke out laughing.

Instructors were selected for the Polish Partisan Staff. These included the former finance officer at the Higher School, Aleksey Semenovich Yegorov; the commander of the "Red Fougasse" partisan detachment, Vyacheslav Antonovich Kvitinskiy, and Aleksandr Romanovich Kuznetsov. Zavadski also asked for Starinov, on behalf of the Polish Communist party and the Polish Army. The request was granted by the Central Committee of the Ukrainian Party. Starinov reported to Moscow for his new assignment. After working with the Polish partisans, he was sent to Yugoslavia in the summer of 1944 as a member of the Soviet Military Mission led by Lt. Gen. N. V. Korneyev, and visited Romania with the same mission. While in Yugoslavia, he had a happy reunion with his old comrade from Spain, Ivan Kharish, the Thunderer, who ultimately rose to the rank of major general as a result of his brilliant record in partisan operations against the occupation forces in Yugoslavia. Later in the winter of 1944, Starinov was assigned to the Main Highway Directorate of the Red Army to organize mine-clearing operations along highways in Germany. Col. Ilya Grigor'yevich Starinov's active military career did not end there, however, but that is all the information available at this time.

Afterword

In the war years, Stalin, as the supreme commander, called the people to conduct partisan warfare in the enemy rear, but he displayed incompetence and indecision in directing that war.

Stalin referred to the partisan forces as our "second front," but throughout the war, that "second front" was left without a commander! Five times, Stalin decided to create a unified military command structure for the partisan movement. He changed his mind twice. Three times, he actually established a central partisan staff: the first time, the process was interrupted while the staff was being formed; the second time, the staff was established, but existed for only nine months. It was dissolved, and then reinstated with only partial responsibility: the important Ukranian Staff was not subordinated to it! The Central Staff was liquidated, for good, on 13 January 1944, at a time when the largest number of partisan forces were operating in the enemy rear, maintaining good communications with Soviet territory.

The partisan war in the *Wehrmacht* rear lasted more than forty-six months, but a single centralized command structure for partisan warfare in the enemy rear actually existed for only two and one-half months of that period, i.e., the time when Voroshilov was the commander in chief of partisan forces. As a senior military officer and, more importantly, a member of the State Defense Committee and the Politburo, Voroshilov could have exerted an influence on the support and employment of GRU, NKVD, and guards miners' units in the enemy rear, and ensured coordination of their operations with those of the partisans. The chief of the Central Staff, Ponomarenko, had no such options because of his relatively far less significant position and his lack of military training and experience.

Stalin's insistence on using the underground Party structure, and often incompetent Party leaders, to direct partisan operations, his lack of attention to the need to train partisan officers and special troops, his demand that partisans rely on captured matériel for their support, and his underestimation of the great potential of large-scale, planned operations with modern mines and explosives in the enemy rear, all worked together to cause major operational problems and heavy casualties for the partisans. And there's another question: just how much did Stalin's order to burn the forests—his scorched earth policy—cost us? No *sane* person would take a position that was so injurious to partisans! *Stalin's incompetent leadership of the partisan war cost our people dearly: his criminal repressions in 1937–38 (and thereafter!), coupled with his mistakes in directing the war in the German rear, helped the enemy kill millions of Soviet citizens on the occupied territory of the USSR.*

Appendix A

Commanding Officers of Sabotage and Partisan Schools Where Col. I. G. Starinov Taught

Place/Date	Sponsoring Agency	Commander
Kiev: Fall 1929	OGPU/DTO	M. K. Kochegarov
Kiev: Fall 1929	OGPU	I. Ya. Lisitsyn
Kharkov: Fall 1929	OGPU	?
Kupyansk: Fall 1929	OGPU	?
Kiev: 1930–1933	GRU/Ukrainian Mil. Dist.	M. P. Mel'nikov
Odessa: 1930–33	GRU/Ukrainian Mil. Dist.	?
Moscow: 1933–1934	GRU	Karol Swierczewski

Appendix B

Literature Used in Partisan Training Schools, 1929–1934

Classical Marxist-Leninist literature

Lenin, V. I.
"Partisan warfare" and "On Partisan warfare." *Collected Works*, Vols. 14 and 20.
Frunze, M. V.
"A unified military doctrine and the Red Army." (Essay) June 1921.

Military Historical Literature

Davydov, D.
A test of the theory of partisan operations. St. Petersburg, 1848
Engel'gard, Lt. Gen. A. E.
A brief outline of small war for all types of weapons. (3 parts). St. Petersburg, 1850.
Vuich, Col.
Small War. St. Petersburg, 1850.
Golitsyn, Maj. Gen. of the General Staff, Prince N. S.

Concerning partisan operations on large scales, reduced to a system of rules. St. Petersburg, 1858.

Novitskiy, N. D.

Lectures. Tactics for small war. Odessa, 1865.

Greshel'man, F.

Partisan war. St. Petersburg, 1885.

Klembovskiy, P. N.

Partisan Operations. St. Petersburg, 1894.

Anonymous

Collection: the practice of small war in occupied Serbia. Moscow, 1927.

Karatygin, P.

Partisan operations. (Thirty-page pamphlet dealing with Russian civil war partisan operations) No date.

Classified publications produced by partisan training schools, 1920s–30s:

"Techniques and tactics of sabotage," 12 pp.

"Ambushes on lines of communication," 10 pp.

"Movement of partisans into the enemy rear," 2 pp.

"Fundamentals of security for urban partisans," 3 pp.

"Bases for partisan mobilization in wooded and steppe locales," 3 pp.

"Reconnaissance activities of partisans," 3 pp.

The following instructional documents were also produced in limited editions of thirty copies each:

"Storage of weapons and ammunition in caches,"

"Mines and demolitions work for partisans and saboteurs,"

"Fundamentals of communication in partisan mobilization,"

"Outfitting and guarding partisan bases in wooded and swampy regions."